A.E. Housman: Classical Scholar

A.E. Housman around the age of 40, as photographed by
Hermann Lea, presumably when Housman travelled to
Dorset to meet Thomas Hardy in 1899 and 1900
(with thanks to Mr G. Stevens Cox).

A.E. Housman

Classical Scholar

Edited by

D.J. Butterfield and C.A. Stray

B L O O M S B U R Y

LONDON • NEW DELHI • NEW YORK • SYDNEY

Bloomsbury Academic
An imprint of Bloomsbury Publishing Plc

50 Bedford Square	1385 Broadway
London	New York
WC1B 3DP	NY 10018
UK	USA

www.bloomsbury.com

Bloomsbury is a registered trade mark of Bloomsbury Publishing Plc

First published in 2009 by Gerald Duckworth & Co. Ltd.
Paperback Edition first published by Bloomsbury Academic 2013

British Library Cataloguing-in-Publication Data
A catalogue record for this book is available from the British Library.

ISBN: HB: 978-0-7156-3808-8
PB: 978-1-4725-3360-9

Library of Congress Cataloging-in-Publication Data
A catalog record for this book is available from the Library of Congress.

Typeset by Ray Davies

Contents

Preface

One hundred and fifty years after the birth of A.E. Housman the study of Latin literature finds itself in a considerably more confused state than he, even in his most pessimistic reflections, could have imagined. Although the twentieth century saw clear and concrete progress in several important fields of the classics, the elucidation and criticism of ancient literature seem to stand in greater disharmony at the beginning of the twenty-first. Textual criticism continues to be distinguished artificially and arbitrarily from literary criticism and is, along with close linguistic and stylistic analysis, in dire need of general rehabilitation among Latin scholars. It therefore seems a particularly apposite time to publish an assessment of Housman's contribution to classical studies now that the dust which he threw up has largely settled. For few can doubt that this provocative scholar, whose primary sphere of excellence was the textual criticism of classical Latin poetry, deserves a place on the all-time podium for British practitioners in the field. Closer analysis of Housman's scholarship should depict his overall contribution in clearer colours, thus providing a more accessible introduction than his austere editions can for those justifiably curious about the man *qua* scholar.

The present volume contains fifteen essays concerning Housman's classical work divided among scholars whose primary interests lie in the study of ancient literature, the history of classical scholarship, or both. The first (and much the largest) section, 'Housman the Scholar', attempts to summarise and evaluate, so far as is possible, Housman's contribution to classical studies. Much, of course, yet remains unsaid; nevertheless, these essays should serve to open up a potentially fruitful debate against which to judge the present-day focuses of Latin scholarship. The second section, 'Housman's Scholarly Environment', attempts to position Housman in relation to other significant figures in classical scholarship during his lifetime and provides important context for his *prima facie* wholly independent lines of study. The final section, 'Housman's Legacy', contains three shorter pieces in which the wake of Housman, in both its intellectual and material forms, is more briefly considered; naturally, Housman's scholarly *Nachleben* is a matter that will allow more productive analysis farther into the future.

The editors are pleased to include in the book much unpublished material by or relating to Housman (correspondence, lecture notes, marginalia). For permission to publish this, we are grateful to The Society of Authors, as we are to the Librarians of Trinity College, Cambridge, and St John's College, Oxford, for their kind assistance throughout the project. We also thank the editors of *ICS* for permission to reprint a revised version of the third chapter. Yet greater gratitude is owed to Paul Naiditch, the leading expert in Housmannian studies, who has read through all of the following chapters and offered many an acute correction or instructive lead. Finally, the book is dedicated to the memory of five Latin professors, all of whom wrote about Housman at some stage in their formidable careers. Deeply influenced by the inspiring example of the man's work, each made notable advances in classical studies through their unmitigated passion for scholarship. If Housman would never admit to reading a book of this sort, it is hoped that they might.

David Butterfield, Cambridge   23 March 2009
Christopher Stray, Swansea

Contributors

David Butterfield, W.H.D. Rouse Research Fellow, Christ's College, University of Cambridge.

Edward Courtney, Emeritus Gildersleeve Professor of Classics, University of Virginia.

James Diggle, Professor of Greek and Latin, Fellow of Queens' College, University of Cambridge.

Stephen Heyworth, Maurice Bowra Fellow, Wadham College, University of Oxford.

Neil Hopkinson, Fellow of Trinity College, University of Cambridge.

Edward Kenney, Emeritus Kennedy Professor of Latin, Fellow of Peterhouse, University of Cambridge.

Colin Leach, Former Fellow of Pembroke College, University of Oxford.

Luigi Lehnus, Professore ordinario di Filologia classica, University of Milan.

Georg Luck, Emeritus Professor of Classics, The Johns Hopkins University.

Robin Nisbet, Emeritus Corpus Professor of Latin, Fellow of Corpus Christi College, University of Oxford.

Stephen Oakley, Kennedy Professor of Latin, Fellow of Emmanuel College, University of Cambridge.

Michael Reeve, Emeritus Kennedy Professor of Latin, Fellow of Pembroke College, University of Cambridge.

Christopher Stray, Honorary Research Fellow, Department of History and Classics, Swansea University.

Gareth Williams, Violin Family Professor of Classics, Columbia University.

Abbreviations

Burnett = A. Burnett (ed.), *The Letters of A.E. Housman* (2 vols, Oxford, 2007)

CP = F.R.D. Goodyear and J. Diggle (edd.), *The Classical Papers of A.E. Housman* (3 vols, Cambridge, 1972)

Juvenal = A.E. Housman (ed.), *D. Iunii Iuuenalis Satirae* (London, 1905)

Juvenal ² = A.E. Housman (ed.), *D. Iunii Iuuenalis Satirae* (Cambridge, 1931²)

Lucan = A.E. Housman (ed.), *M. Annaei Lucani Belli Ciuilis Libri Decem* (Oxford, 1926)

Man. I = A.E. Housman (ed.), *M. Manilii Astronomicon Liber Primus* (London, 1903)

Man. II = A.E. Housman (ed.), *M. Manilii Astronomicon Liber Secundus* (London, 1912)

Man. III = A.E. Housman (ed.), *M. Manilii Astronomicon Liber Tertius* (London, 1916)

Man. IV = A.E. Housman (ed.), *M. Manilii Astronomicon Liber Quartus* (London, 1920)

Man. V = A.E. Housman (ed.), *M. Manilii Astronomicon Liber Quintus* (London, 1930)

Man. ed. min. = A.E. Housman (ed.), *M. Manilii Astronomica* (Cambridge, 1932)

Abbreviations for ancient authors are drawn from *OLD* and *LSJ*, abbreviations for classical journals from *L'Année Philologique*.

Introduction

C.A. Stray

Housman's lifetime (1859-1936) spans a period of significant change in classical scholarship in Britain. In the year of his birth, the *Journal of Classical and Sacred Philology* ceased publication after twelve issues. Like other classical journals before and after it, it sought to attract multiple constituencies in order to survive.[1] Based in Cambridge, it benefited from the support of Greek scholars in the university whose interests encompassed both sacred and secular texts; not only its moving spirit, the missionary's son J.E.B. Mayor, but also J.B. Lightfoot, later Bishop of Durham.[2] In 1864, when Housman was five years old, Munro's commentary on Lucretius appeared – the edition which, as Housman hinted in the preface to his edition of the first book of Manilius, re-established British claims to scholarship after a period of forty years after the removal of Blomfield, Dobree and Monk by death or preferment in 1824-5 (*Man.* I, xlii). In the next forty years, classical scholarship gradually detached itself from the embrace of Anglicanism. Munro was ordained (a precondition for the long-term retention of a college fellowship), though one does not think of Munro as a parson, and indeed he never preached. The reference by Richard Jebb, descendant of bishops, at the end of his Glasgow inaugural lecture in 1875 to a higher source of knowledge than Greek may have been a diplomatic utterance: though in the 1890s, as an MP, he spent considerable time on church-related legislation. His successor in the Glasgow Greek chair, Gilbert Murray, managed to get away with reading but not signing the Westminster Confession in 1889.

Housman, on the other hand, though he lost his Christian faith at 13 and faith in a deity at 20, retained throughout his life an emotional as well as intellectual familiarity with the King James Bible and the *Book of Common Prayer* (Jocelyn 1988, 31). After the repeal of the Test Acts in 1871, almost all university posts in Oxford and Cambridge had been open to non-Anglicans – as long as they were male. Housman's young manhood was thus spent in the first years of a new regime, in which religion was slackening its grip on academic life but remained a looming presence. Benjamin Jowett, the man whose scholarship Housman scorned as an undergraduate, had heralded such changes from within the Anglican church. Elected to the Oxford Greek chair in 1855, he had alarmed conservative churchmen with his contribution to *Essays and Reviews* (London, 1860). Kept from the mastership of Balliol in 1854 by the supporters of Robert Scott, he was admitted to the post in 1870 after Scott was removed to the deanery of Rochester to make way for him. Jowett's vision of liberal education and imperial rule, conveyed through the inspirational context of the tutorial, contrasted sharply with Mark Pattison's ideal of professorial rule and (to use a contemporary phrase) the endowment of research. Pattison's supporters included not only the 'Museum vote' (the campaigners for science and archaeology, including Arthur Evans and Percy Gardner) but also textual scholars like Henry Nettleship who had been inspired by German achievements. Nettleship brought back from Germany a serious scholarship which was based on comparative philology; but Housman's model, Hugh Munro, was relatively uninterested in such things, being concerned mostly with the elucidation of texts.

Housman can be described, simply but not entirely inaccurately, as a Cambridge man who happened to go to Oxford (cf. the opening remarks in Kenney's chapter). His eventual arrival in Cambridge in 1911 was thus in a sense a homecoming. The characterisation of the contrasting scholarly styles of the two universities he offered in his inaugural lecture belonged to a ceremonial and diplomatic text. But Housman's notion of 'scholarship with no nonsense about it' (Cambridge) vs Oxford scholarship, which embodied an erroneous tendency toward literary appreciation (Housman 1969, 15-16), in fact accurately depicts his perception of the opposition between a critical analysis of language and the ambition to go beyond that to the appreciation of literature.[3] Like Kant, Housman was keen on boundaries: and his categorical distinction between critical scholarship and literary appreciation was as sharp as that between Professor Housman the scholar and Mr Housman the poet. He could be abrupt and aloof in defending this boundary; yet his letters reveal a gentle, amiable, sociable and generous man (cf. Burnett 1.xxii). Compare Dawe's verdict on Richard Jebb: 'a restrained and dignified figure, his warm and boyish humour kept for his family and friends' (Dawe, 'R.C. Jebb' in Briggs and Calder 1990, 239-47, at 245).[4] This should remind us that famous individuals tend to be stereotyped, and that hauteur provokes anecdotal myth-making. In Housman's case his homosexuality has acted as a reinforcing factor, heightening the tendency to stereotyping.

The division between scholar and poet has operated to retard our understanding of Housman in several ways. The biographies or semi-biographies have all been presented with the problem of assessment. How can a classical scholar assess Housman's poetry? How can a literary biographer assess his scholarship? Housman's friend and protégé Andrew Gow, who was well qualified to assess his scholarship, offered an essay accompanied by a bibliography (Gow 1936a). Norman Page, an experienced literary biographer, provided an account of his life (Page 1983) which included a chapter on his scholarship largely taken from Gow. The middle way was taken by Richard Graves, whose biography (Graves 1979) is hardly satisfactory on either front. The obvious alternative is to provide a collaborative study of the man and his work. This was attempted in *A.E. Housman: A Reassessment* (Holden and Birch 2000), which however hardly touched on his work as a classical scholar.

The present volume contrasts interestingly with an earlier assessment of Housman's friend Gilbert Murray, *Gilbert Murray Reassessed* (Stray 2007), which includes a discussion of the two men by Malcolm Davies (*ibid.*, 167-80). Murray presents different problems because of his wide range, of which the book's subtitle 'Hellenism, theatre, and international politics' offers only a condensed summary. In addition, many of the facets of his life and work formed an integrated whole, in stark contrast to the separation between private and public, scholar and poet, which is evident in Housman.[5] In a way Murray could be seen as the Jowett of his time – a liberal post-Anglican rather than a liberal Anglican, an assimilated ex-colonial rather than an ideologist of colonialism, his vision linking Hellenism with an international community rather than an empire – and fond of actresses rather than of Florence Nightingale.

Housman arouses strong responses of different kinds. A scholar whose university holds books annotated by Housman thought of investigating them; but on reading them, she found his comments so unpleasant that she decided not to pursue the project. One of the contributors to the present volume hesitated to write, feeling that it was not for him to criticise a scholar of Housman's magnitude. Quite apart from the question of gendered responses to Housman's life and work that is raised by the first of these examples, there is a more general problem of just how scholarship – and life – is to be assessed. In this introduction I have been trying to locate Housman in a series of historical contexts. Do these in fact locate and identify, or do they tie the subject down to a Procrustean bed? Here we have to beware the romantic ideology of the undefinable self which constitutionally resists classification. Housman was unique, but so are we all. The challenge is to describe in what his uniqueness consisted.

The chapters which follow rise to this challenge, in bringing into focus the nature of Housman's scholarship: his preferences, his intellectual style, his strengths and his weaknesses. One form of assessment is through comparison with other scholars; here the candidates are Robinson Ellis (Williams), Eduard Fraenkel (Oakley), Richard Jebb (Stray), W.M. Lindsay (Butterfield) and J.P. Postgate

(Hopkinson). Ellis, the butt of one of Housman's cruellest remarks (that he possessed 'the intellect of an idiot child'), is revealed as an aesthetic antiquarian, the possessor of large but unfocused learning, while Housman in contrast is organised, sure-footed and decisive in judgement. Lindsay and Housman were both committed to 'scientific' scholarship, but for Lindsay this was constituted almost entirely by palaeography and the history of transmission, and the conjectural emendation at which Housman excelled was barred. Fraenkel, Housman's preferred successor to himself, was characterised by Shackleton Bailey (quoted by Oakley) as 'a great scholar who was not a great critic' ('textual' being understood before 'critic'). Housman's skill as a textual diviner and emender far outstripped Fraenkel's, but the latter's depth of scholarship on a far wider front, from Roman law to Attic vases, brought the ancient world to life in ways that Housman could not (cf. West 2008).

If we home in on the kind of scholarship Housman practised, we find clear evidence of his preferences and dislikes. A notable dislike was for *Überlieferungsgeschichte*, which he once equated to 'fudge' (Reeve; Butterfield on Lindsay). Housman's strengths and weaknesses are also thrown into relief. Among his weaknesses, we might mention his indifference to direct inspection or collation of mss (Heyworth) and his occasional willingness to accept metrical anomalies (see Butterfield's chapter on metrics). Housman was also curiously inconsistent at times, and cases are discussed in this volume where he erred in ways which would have brought down his sarcastic invective had the error been that of another scholar. It is useful to be reminded that he could err, as the cult of Housman tends to veil this possibility. Williams is prepared to describe some of Housman's procedures as 'foolish', and Oakley denounces his notorious phrase 'editorum in usum' as 'silly'.[6] But as Oakley points out, the occasional weaknesses do not outweigh the strength of Housman's overall achievement. And as both he and Reeve suggest, having identified a weakness, one needs to ask, what difference does it really make? (As the American pragmatists used to ask, is it a difference that makes a difference?)

Did Housman cast light or shadow? It has been suggested that his example has been a negative one, emphasising destructive criticism and encouraging a fear of correction which discouraged the public offering of ideas. To this it might be added that a cultic obsession with any scholar, however gifted he or she might be, carries its own dangers; and that while textual criticism and emendation doubtless has its mysteries, it would be a general benefit for a demystifying process to be incorporated into undergraduate courses. They might well begin with Housman's own comments on the phrase 'rustling hedge' in a newspaper printing of Walter de la Mare's poem 'Fare well' (*Man.* V, xxxv-xxxvi).[7] Then perhaps conjectural emendation might become the sport, if not of kings, at least of those who enjoy the intellectual and linguistic challenges of literary texts. In the past, textual criticism has at times been employed as an exclusionary device to separate out those who talk of 'Classics' from the minority who remain true to 'philology'. Here Oakley's comparison of Housman and Fraenkel offers a salutary perspective. It is worth remembering that German scholarship incorporated the intensive study of texts within a wider, indeed from F.A. Wolf onwards enyclopaedic, study of ancient culture. It is true that text-based and culture-based emphases were early identifiable and in tension, as with the *Methodenstreit* between Hermann and Boeckh (Most 1997); but one might hope that these could now be replaced by mutual respect, and indeed collaboration. When the American-trained exile Moses Finley established himself at Cambridge in the 1950s, some of his colleagues claimed that he was unable to write a Greek prose. It is probably true that he had never been asked to do so; but also that he was very skilled at reading Greek texts (including inscriptions) and extracting meaning from them. The curricular specialisation promoted by the Cambridge Classical Tripos since 1881 has served to encourage such tensions. The tendency was deplored a century ago by Richard Jebb, who on being asked in 1902 to choose which British Academy committee he wished to be attached to as a Fellow, wrote in reply:

I have decided to ask that I may be placed on the committee for the Section for History and Archaeology, as well as that for Philology. My reason is that, all my life, I have been much interested in history, especially that which touches my special work at so many points; & that for many years I have taken an interest in classical archaeology, though I am not a specialist in it ... In Cambridge I have long felt that the extremely rigorous specialisation fostered by part II of the Classical Tripos has had the effect of narrowing our scholarship & partitioning the field in a <u>rigid</u> manner which has scarcely a parallel in any other University. I do not want to see this view of literary studies, whether historical or philological, reproduced in the Academy.'[8]

To return to Housman, it is worth noting that though his own schooling was embedded in the Victorian English tradition which prized classical composition above almost all other skills, he himself showed little interest in it (see Butterfield's chapter on metrics) – though the few verses he is known to have written have attracted much admiration.

Housman's presentation of himself in his published work deserves attention. His habit of berating other scholars was a well-known scandal, and even worried staunch supporters like Henry Jackson. A focus on his invective (see Naiditch 2005, 52-69) has overshadowed less obvious matters, such as his choice of language in introducing and commenting on texts. A man who insisted that we should attend more to dead than to living scholars might be expected to use Latin: why then did he use English for the introduction to his Manilius? Courtney plausibly attributes this to the example of Housman's hero Munro in his edition of Lucretius (1864). The matter is however complicated by the general shift from Latin to English in nineteenth-century English classical editions, and by the variety of markets and readers at which they were aimed. The shift from Latin to English was most fiercely resisted for the apparatus criticus, where Latinate concision was widely believed to be essential (Stray 1998, 96-102), and this helps to explain the choices Housman made for his Manilius.[9] His use of Latin for the commentary is perhaps less surprising than the choice of English for his introduction.

So much for Housman's scholarship and for his relations with his contemporaries. But though he had formally only one pupil (W.H. Semple (1900-81)), many scholars of later generations have been in effect his pupils, and in Part III of the book two of them, E.J. Kenney and Georg Luck, tell just what they have learned. In addition, the co-editor of Housman's classical papers, James Diggle, offers a glimpse into the perpetuation of Housman's memory via two personal effects: his cap and his pen. Such memorabilia play an important part in preserving the memory of a great scholar within the institution with which he was particularly associated.[10]

Notes

1. The short-lived Oxford journal *Terminalia* (1851-2) had sought to attract contributors and subscribers outside Oxford in a vain attempt to survive. The Cambridge-based *Journal of Philology* (1868-1920) added an Oxford scholar to its editorial committee to strengthen its subscription base. The *Classical Review* (1887-) similarly recruited an American editor and built up a readership in the USA.

2. On Mayor, see Henderson 1998; on Lightfoot, Treloar 1998.

3. It should be remembered that Housman prefixed his remarks by saying that '[b]y the fourth quarter of the century the distinction was fading away, and it cannot be said to exist at present' (Housman 1969, 25).

4. Dawe goes on to liken Jebb to Fritz Kreisler, in contrast with Jascha Heifetz, though he does not take the further step of likening Housman to Heifetz, the austere autocrat of the violin. Some of Jebb's letters were printed in his widow's memoir (Jebb 1907); a larger selection of about 270 letters will appear in Stray 2010.

5. Not all – Murray's detailed work on the texts of Euripides and Aeschylus, and his work as a telepath, for example. The judgment of Oswyn Murray (no relation) that the contributions to the book were 'technical' discussions which failed to recognise the organic unity of Murray's life ('Greek for peace', *TLS* 21/28 Dec. 2007, 31) took no account of this, nor of the memoirs contributed by two of his grandchildren (Stray 2007, 17-32).

6. Cf. Diggle 2007, who is scathing about some of Housman's earliest conjectures.

7. Characteristically, he avoided giving the correct reading ('rusting'), just as in criticising Jebb's notes on Bacchylides twenty years earlier he had referred to 'three or four supplementary violations of metre are proposed in the notes by Professor Jebb', without specifying what they were (see Stray's chapter). In the de la Mare poem Housman missed, or chose not to discuss, another misprint, 'these' for 'those'.

8. Jebb to Israel Gollancz, 15 Dec. 1902. The letter will be published in Stray 2010.

9. He must have noticed (though he may not have cared) that Jebb's edition of Sophocles (1883-96), introduced in English, began with textual notes in Latin but changed to English.

10. The editors are glad to be able to include contributions from three subsequent holders of Housman's chair (in chronological order, Kenney, Reeve and Oakley).

R.E. Mortimer Wheeler's caricature of Housman on his delivery of the Foundation Oration at University College, London, on 23 March 1911. The Scottish poet Thomas Campbell was one of the founders of the University of London, which in 1836 became University College, London.

Part I

HOUSMAN THE SCHOLAR

1

Housman and Propertius

S.J. Heyworth

Emendationes Propertianae

The *Journal of Philology* of 1887[1] opened with an extraordinary 35-page piece entitled *Emendationes Propertianae*. The first half consists of textual suggestions on some 240 passages of the poet, presented essentially without comment. Besides verbal changes, the author postulates *lacunae*, transpositions and deletions, in a briskly efficient manner. This is an impressively creative and informed contribution to the textual criticism of a famously troubled text, but it is perhaps less impressive than what follows, a detailed examination of the first elegy of the first book. Here are displayed the learning, the sharpness of insight, and the power of argument that were to mark the author's career as a critic of Latin poetry. It was the first public demonstration of Housman's involvement with the text of Propertius, which had begun, disastrously,[2] in his undergraduate years, would dominate the first third of his career,[3] and would still be manifest in his late review[4] of the commentary by H.E. Butler and E.A. Barber (Oxford, 1933). A critical history of his dealings with Propertius may be found in the account by G.P. Goold.[5] Fixed points are provided by Housman's letter to Macmillan offering the edition (11 December 1885 = Burnett 1.58-9: 'The collection and arrangement of materials for the commentary will naturally demand further time and labour; and I therefore judge it best that the text with its apparatus criticus should be issued separately'), and by the publication in the *Journal of Philology* in 1892-3 of the three papers laying out his view of 'The Manuscripts of Propertius', for this effectively marked the end of his efforts to get an edition published (Cambridge University Press having followed Oxford and Macmillan in declining to publish a book: cf. University Library, Cambridge, Pr.B.13.9.59). Yet Housman's manuscript survived the scholar himself, and Professor Sandbach told more than once the story of visiting A.S.F. Gow, Housman's colleague at Trinity, in his rooms in 1936, and finding him stoking the fire in which he was burning the famously unpublished edition.

The examination of Prop. 1.1 displays the range of critical analysis and argument that typifies Housman's scholarship. He begins with a defence of the manuscript reading in verse 3 and verse 5; he postulates a lacuna after verse 11; he commends recent conjectures (a bold one in the case of Palmer's *comminus ille* for *ille uidere* in 12, less radical with Hertzberg's *Cytinaeis*, 23, and Otto's *torum*, 36). He supports German editors against English ones in their preference for the conjecture *aut* over *et* in 25. In 13 he explains, as plausibly as anyone has done, the strange corruption of *Hylaei* to *psilli* (already emended in the fifteenth century) and argues for Baehrens' *uerbere* as mediating between the manuscript variants *uulnere* and *arbore*. A concern for what happens in manuscripts is visible also in the discussion arguing for Fontein's *fides* for *preces* (16), *fata* for *sacra* (20), and the *pellacia* (for *fallacia*, 19) attributed to Fruterius and Palmerius. His own conjectures feature transposition (of words and letters, when he suggests *et manes et sidera uobis* for the transmitted *uobis et sidera et amnes* in 23) and an unusual use of familiar vocabulary (*non nostra* = *non secunda* in 33). The article was not of course the first Housman published, but, given his concentration on Propertius and the rejection of his edition in 1885, the psychological importance is obvious: he puts on display both the quantity and the quality of what he has to offer the hitherto ungrateful world.

The discussion also sparkles with Housman's judgements on scholars, mainly in this case favourable. Thus Baehrens is castigated for reading *cunctas* in 5, but we are left in no doubt about the positive implication of the reference to 'a scholar of Mr Baehrens' acumen' (*CP* 42). In acknowledging that the problem he points up in verse 16 has not been recognised except by Fontein, he finds an opportunity for rehearsing the names of the great: 'this flagrant discrepancy has run the gauntlet of Scaliger, Heinsius, Hemsterhuys, Markland, Schrader and Lachmann, half a dozen of the greatest names in criticism' (*CP* 46), before going on to say of Fontein's conjectures: 'many of them of course are the mere guesses which we all jot down in our margins simply to help us take up the thread of thought to-morrow where we drop it today...;[6] but the residue betoken one of the most acute intellects that have ever been bent on the study of Propertius.' As so often when Housman writes on those he admires, one feels he is partly talking about himself: the generalised element of self-description ('we all') carries over and becomes more focused as we enter the climactic clause.

As a young graduate student, I mentioned to Sandbach my delight at acquiring a copy of Housman's *Classical Papers*, the first volume of which I regarded as vital to my research on Propertius. He expressed caution: he was not convinced that *any* of the early conjectures were necessary (it should be remembered that he had lectured on the text of Propertius in Cambridge, and produced a number of fine conjectures of his own).[7] Whether or not it was literally true, this was clever rhetoric, a salutary warning to a student who was liable to be caught up in enthusiasm for Housman's genius. But it was not in the end effective. When I eventually brought out an edition, the text contained 39 conjectures, lacunae, transpositions published by Housman, rather more than anyone else working in the nineteenth century,[8] and another 81 published suggestions appeared in the apparatus. Even without the lost edition the work he published on Propertius thus continues to have a major effect. But there was an aftermath also, and to that I now turn.

Housman's Propertii

In his catalogue of surviving books owned by Housman, P.G. Naiditch lists sixteen texts of Propertius,[9] plus others combined with Catullus and Tibullus. One of these (item **10** below, preserved at Housman's Cambridge college, Trinity) is very rich in marginalia, and was exploited in the 2007 Oxford Classical Text. I have now inspected the nine annotated editions preserved in Housman's undergraduate college, St John's in Oxford.[10] The annotations reveal much about his ways of working as a scholar and a reviewer, and it may be useful to give a more detailed account than the brief 'annotated' or similar that were all Naiditch had room to offer.

These are the St John's editions:

1. L. Müller (Cat. Tib. Prop.; Teubner, Leipzig, 1870)

Little annotation; there is some sidelining of the *Praefatio*; the conjecture *incudere*, attributed to Dilthey at 2.34.43, is said to be 'as old as Bentley's time' (xxxv). However, there is a line through the note, so Housman perhaps decided he was mistaken.[11] Bentley does not cite the line with *incudere* when he discusses the passage in his commentary on Hor. *ars* 441 (as David Butterfield reminds me): he there uses Gellius 9.8.3 to defend *includere* against the attack of Scaliger; but Scaliger had chosen the *componere* of F and its descendants.

There is minimal annotation in the Catullus (some underlinings in the preface, and on p. LXXI a list of opening spondees in glyconics)[12] and the *Priapea*; none at all that I have spotted in the Tibullus.

2. F.A. Paley (London, 1872[2])

Sparsely annotated, with sidelining, correction of slips, and deletion of nonsense. Occasionally attention is drawn to details of grammatical interest, e.g. *an* introducing a direct question at 1.6.13, 2.25.23; and the short second syllable of *caue* at 1.10.21 and elsewhere.

3. M. Haupt (Cat. Tib. Prop.; Leipzig, 1879)

A very small edition, without notes or apparatus; Housman's copy is interleaved with larger pages that allowed him room for copious notes. This has far more additions by Housman than any of the other St John's volumes, including a number of unpublished conjectures; but its main function for the scholar was as a repository for parallels and material to support textual argument. See below for illustration and further discussion.

The Catullian portion has no annotation, as far as I have noticed. Tibullus, on the other hand, is adorned with underlinings, and (though not to the extent of the Propertius) accompanied by parallels, notes,[13] alternative readings and a few conjectures: 1.2.58 *ille*] '*ipse* MSS: *iste* A.E.H.?' (hardly compatible with *ille* in 57); 1.5.42 *pudet*] '?*rubet* ?*spuit* A.E.H.' (useful as offering an alternative approach to *a pudet* [Müller] or *heu pudet* [Wunderlich]); 1.5.61 '*pauper semper erit praesto tibi* A.E.H.' (unappealing to open with a spondaic word); 1.7.36 *incultis*] '*infultis* A.E.H. cf. Prop. 3.17.18 [*pressantes inquinet uua pedes*]' (*incultis* is awkward in this praise of civilisation, but this is not an attractive alternative); 2.3.36 *operata*] '? *reparata* A.E.H.' (cf. Cic. *Ver.* 2.5.186 *praedam improbissimam comparauit*; Sil. 15.199; but both the prefix and the tense are awkward; *onerata* would be an easy alternative – 'booty is burdened with much bad baggage'); 3.6.13 *dites*] '? *mites* A.E.H.' [iam recc.]

4. A. Palmer (Dublin, 1880)

The textual notes in the *Praefatio* have quite a lot of sidelining; in particular a double line is used to mark notions of particular attraction, e.g. 1.1.12* [in the postscript] *comminus ille*; 1.8.25* *Artaciis*; 1.13.17 *ueris*; 1.20.52* *ni uis perdere rursus Hylan*; 2.26.39 *montis duo*; 2.33.12* *mandisti, arbuta*; 2.34.29* *plectri*; 3.6.22* *nolo*; 3.9.7 *neruis*; 3.9.38* the transmitted *semper* retained; 3.12.18 *cui sis*; 3.22.3* *Dindymis* (iam Unger); 4.4.47 *cessabitur*; 4.7.57 *uehit*] *ratis*; 4.9.70 (*haec lex aeternum*). Of these, some were supported by Housman in published work (marked with an asterisk), others were not: they deserve careful attention from future editors. There are also more critical comments: 'my dear sir, don't you see that *cineri* and *emerito* are virtually the same thing?' (on 2.14.16).

The text opens with a large number of underlinings, most of those in 1.1 relating to the notes at *CP* 41-54; after 1.4, however, they are mainly limited to drawing attention to polysyllabic pentameter endings, which are marked consistently. A paragraphus in the margin marks the end of every 26th line in the text: Housman was presumably aiming at a reconstruction on the lines of Lachmann's for Lucretius (where the archetype can be deduced to have had 26-verse pages); if so, nothing came of the attempt (it never gets related to transpositions in this volume, e.g.), and it was foolish to make no allowance for titles and omissions.

There are a few marginal notes and conjectures, including the following that were never published: 2.32.61 *tuque es... Latina*] *turpes ... Latina's*; 2.34.8 *nonne*] *pone* [the superior *nempe* appears in item **10**]; 3.5.11 *maris*] *miseri*.

However, most of the annotation in this edition without an apparatus is concerned with transposition and deletion: couplets and longer sequences are marked off with square brackets, and often accompanied by phrasing such as 'to follow 4' (on 2.4.17-22); elsewhere reordering is suggested by marginal numerals or letters.[14]

5a. J.P. Postgate (Cambridge, 1894: *ad tempus recognouit* on the title page; no reference to the publisher, and no preface)

This is inscribed as a gift from the editor. Most openings have one or two queries and corrections to text and apparatus; there is one conjecture Housman did not publish: 1.9.32 'fort. *ille*' (Smyth attributes this to Postgate, without a date, perhaps mistakenly, as the note in the *Select Elegies* suggests: 'It is better then to suppose *iste* = *ille*.'). There is almost no correlation between the corrections, mainly of slips, and the review, which is to be found at *CP* 369-77 = *CR* 9 (1895), 350-5.

5b. J.P. Postgate (London & Cambridge, 1894: publishers given as G. Bell & Sons in London, Deighton Bell in Cambridge; contains a 5-page preface; text same as 5a)

The annotations are almost entirely corrections of slips or omissions. However, at 3.15.8, there is a *caret* after *uix memini*, and in the margin: 'you should insert *ut* / Ov. her. 18.25-6 / or read *ut* for *uix*'. Again, there is no connection between the annotation and the review. However, this volume holds several loose sheets, among them some that contain lists in Housman's hand of conjectures and transpositions made by Postgate (in one case grouped into 'good', 'bad', 'unnecessary', 'perhaps right'); and these were obviously made in preparation for the review.

6. J.S. Phillimore (OCT, Oxford, 1901)

There are only occasional marginalia, mostly in the form of exclamation mark, question mark or 'x', for example '!' beside *uisura, dolebat / illa tamen,...* at 1.15.13-14 (Housman's underlinings). On the title-page Housman wrote the following couplet:

> Quae, Philomore, fui carmen iuuenile Properti,
> Cynthia, nunc crimen sum iuuenile tuum.

7. H.E. Butler (London, 1905)

This still contains a card from J.P. Postgate, offering it to Housman for review ('You can take your own time'; if he did, it cannot have cost him much labour), and there is a clear correlation between the (mainly minimal) marginalia and Housman's trenchant comments on this humdrum edition (*CP* 630-6 = *CR* 19 (1905), 317-20). In the commentary at 1.8.27 the words 'She was here all the time' are underlined, and an exclamation mark in the margin leads to the response (*CP* 633): 'Of course she was, or not a word of lines 1-26 could have been written ... the only people who say such things are live madmen and dead classics.' Elsewhere we find 'x' or 'no'[15] appended, with similar effect. '>' marks places where a note is needed (see *CP* 634).[16]

8. C. Hosius (Teubner, Leipzig, 1911)

This is the first edition, not the second, which was reviewed by Housman at *CR* 37 (1923), 120-1 = *CP* 1088-9. The book does not contain much annotation, though there are several deletions of improbable conjectures in the apparatus, and the occasional '!'. A repeated concern is with (i) orthography, especially of Greek words, and (ii) the correct attribution of conjectures. (i) Underlined in the text are, e.g., the final letter of *Alcidem* at 4.9.38 (read *-en*) and the *eio* of *Theiodamanteo* at 1.20.6 (read *Thio-*).[17] The interest in orthography, and in the arguments that one could properly deploy in an area where medieval MSS are notoriously unreliable, had led Housman to publish his 'Greek nouns in Latin poetry from Lucretius to Juvenal' in the *Journal of Philology* in 1910 (*CP* 817-39). (ii) At 2.12.6 'haut uano Housman' is corrected to 'Nodell', for example; and when Hosius attributes Bergk's excellent *Craugidos* at 4.3.55 to Buecheler, this provokes 'liar' in the margin: cf. *CP* 1089 (and n. 1 there) for details on this. On the other hand, *haec non sum* at 1.13.13 is claimed for 'A.E.H.' despite its having been published by Rossberg in 1877.[18]

Hosius accepts N's reading *Famae* at 3.1.23, rather than the *omnia* of the later manuscripts. This elicits a 'bravo' from Housman. Though the text with *omnia* is not without awkwardness,[19] *Famae* cannot itself be correct without further change, and it would be clear (even without the note at *CP* 272-3, already published) that this is Housman's typically sarcastic appreciation of an editor following the supposed *codex optimus* into inappropriate places.

9. O.L. Richmond (Cambridge, 1928)[20]

Again the annotation is sparse, especially after the first book, and largely negative: repeatedly we find 'no', 'ha', '!' and 'ugh' (twice on p. 50). Housman picks up too on the false attribution to him of Palmer's *gaza Midae* at 2.26.23 (underlining and exclamation mark), and writes 'no' in the margin at 1.1.31 (33 in Richmond's numeration), where the apparatus claims 'aura *Puccius laudat, Housmannus*'.[21] An exclamation mark accompanies 2.10.1, printed by Richmond as the first line of his book 4, even though it reads *Sed tempus lustrare aliis Helicona choreis*. Apparently positive is the sidelining at 2.32.5 where *correxi*, referring to the conjecture *cur ita te* (accepted by a number of subsequent editors, such as Barber and Goold), has been underlined. Burnett 2.96-7 gives Housman's response to the gift of the 'stately tome'; he apologetically refers to Tennyson's acknowledging merely the arrival of Rossetti's poems, 'to avoid giving an opinion', but does go as far as to cast doubt on the credentials of the C family, on which Richmond had founded his lacunose and much re-ordered text.

One note of historical interest comes on p. 11, where the phrase 'the common exemplar of AF' elicits '? see Ullman' in the margin: this is a reference to B.L. Ullman, 'The manuscripts of Propertius', *CPh* 6 (1911), 282-301, which had showed decisively that F is a descendant of A. Though Housman never published on the manuscript tradition later in his career, this reveals that he did revise his views in the light of later research.

Finally the Trinity volume,[22] which has the richest store of marginalia:

10. E. Baehrens (Leipzig, 1880; shelfmark adv.c.20.41).

Marginalia were added at various times and consist largely of conjectures (many afterwards deleted) and citations of parallels, both for Latinity and the habits of scribes. The vast majority of the tolerable conjectures were published in Housman's early Propertian articles; others (e.g. 1.17.3 *sontem*, 3.19.19 *eius furias*) found their way into the Manilius and other later work. But a proportion remained unknown to the world until they were published in Goold's 1990 Loeb edition or the Oxford Text I brought out in 2007. For more detail see *Cynthia* pp. xi-xii; and for further material the pages listed under 'Housman, unpublished notes' in the General Index (add '304'); p. 357 has a complete transcription of a sequence of notes on 3.13.61-2.

Some unpublished annotations

Three of these volumes are particularly important: items **3**, **4**, and **10**. Each was produced by an editor that Housman respected: see e.g. *CP* 234-5 for all three, 29 for Baehrens and Palmer; 42-4, 305-9 for Baehrens; 471-2 on Palmer; 1065 for Haupt. Palmer's edition (**4**), which is without a proper apparatus criticus, served as a repository for transpositions, as has been said. Most of those marked were published, and even in this capacity it was superseded by the other two, as is illustrated by a note in the upper margin before the start of the manifestly disordered 3.7: 'The arrangement proposed below is largely wrong: see in my Baehrens.' The order suggested here runs 1-8, 17-20, 9-16, 43-50, 29-38, 21-4, 39-42, 51-70, 27-8, 71-2. Item **10** has the order published in '*Emendationes Propertianae*'.

Baehrens (**10**) provided a good apparatus, and so it is here that Housman works on his conjectures, though not without transpositions (as has been seen) and parallels (for which item **4** was preferred). The annotations on 1.13 (pp. 21-2), though a small amount compared with some portions of the text, illustrate the range (material in square brackets is my addition):

1.13.12 text   *nec, noua quaerendo semper, Adonis eris*   commas deleted
        a.c. left mg.:   *inicus* A.E.H. 2.7.8 [*in ore* ç: *more* NF: *amore* Δ]
1.13.17 right mg.:   Pers. 1.107 [*uero*] *uerbo* PR]
                    Ov. *met.* 10.559 [*uerbis* uel *labris* codd.]
        a.c. right mg.:   ~~rebus~~ A.E.H. ?
                    ueris Palmer 2.28.43 [*pro quibus optatis*]
1.13.25 a.c. <u>*amantes*</u>:²³ Cat. 68.129 [*horum magnos uicisti sola furores*]
1.13.29 left. mg.:   [Eur.] *I.A.* 49-57
                    [Leda's three daughters, Phoebe, Clytemestra and Helen]
1.13.35 a.c. left mg.:   *qui tibi* Palmer

The interleaving of the Haupt edition (**3**) is a clear indication of an intention to make use of the extra space; this is employed for the accumulation of parallels, not just for the text printed by Haupt,²⁴ but also for corruptions, Latinity and conjectures that Housman notes as enticing elsewhere. So, for example, at 1.20.4 the note 'Stat. *silu.* 5.4.5 [*trucibus fluuiis*], Luc. 3.250 *duces*] *truces* Bentley' provides support for Housman's own conjecture *trux erat* (for *dixerat*), and at 3.1.1 'Sen. epigr. 20.9 *mea fata = me mortuum*' relates to Baehrens' *fata*, not anything printed by Haupt. The volume continued to be used throughout Housman's career: there are references to Birt's *Kritik und Hermeneutik* (Munich, 1913), his own Lucan (published 1926), and Löfstedt's *Syntactica* vol. 2 (Lund, 1933).²⁵ Here are the notes on 1.13 (pp. 216-18):

1.13.6:   6. *certus* is part of what is negatived?
1.13.12:   12. Cic. *pro Clu.* 23.64 emend. A.E.H. [*iniquus*] *inimicus* codd.
              aliquot]
1.13.13:   13. *ego* om. NF. *haec non* <*sum*> *rumore* A.E.H. *augere* Luc. 7.203
1.13.14-15:   14 sq. 'uidi ego (me ... potes?) | uidi ego te' etc. A.E.H.
1.13.17:   Petron. 79.[8.]3-4 [*transfudimus hinc et hinc labellis* | *errantes*
              animas] Ciris 496 [*multis optata labella*]
1.13.24:   Ou. *met.* 1.313 MSS [*Oetaeis*] *actaeis*]
1.13.25:   C.F.W. Mueller ap. Friedlaender Juv. 6.520
1.13.29:   *Ioue dignus* Ov. *her.* 9.22, 14.99

The edition contains the following unpublished conjectures[26] (I suspect that among the many parallels others may lie hidden that I have missed):

1.1.20   ? *picare* (cf. Verg. *ecl.* 8.82 *incende bitumine laurus*) ? *parare* ? *patrare*,
          but see first what Haupt says
              ? *sacsa* [i.e. *saxa*] *liquare* (cf. 4.4.10, 4.5.12)
1.4.14   *sub Tacita dicere teste* [*sed Tacita ... teste* Palmer[27]]
1.15.29   <*in cap*>*ut alta prius labentur* [*ad caput alta p- l-* T. Korsch, *Nordisk
          Tidsskrift for Filologi* 5 (1880-2), 259]
1.16.38   *figere tela* [*figere theta* iam Müller] cf. 2.13.2 [*spicula fixit*], Ou. *ex P.*
          4.6.36 [*linguae tela*]
2.1.41   *conueniat* ? [so subsequently Giardina[28]] cf. *thes.* IV, p. 835.28-77
2.3.7   *haut ego sic*
2.3.27-8 post 25-6
2.15.28   *certum* ? Auien. *Arat.* 133 [*cardine toto*?], Plin. *n.h.* 10.104 [*neutri nota
          adulteria. coniugii fidem non uiolant*]. [*solum* suggested in item **10**]
2.22.7-8 post 4 uel ante 5
2.25.45   *cultaque* cf. Plin. *n.h.* 16.251 *sacerdos candida ueste cultus.* Suet. *Ner.*
          32 *matronam in spectaculis uetita purpura cultam.* Juv. 3.95 [*Dorida nullo* |
          cultam palliolo]. Petron. 32[.4 *lacertum aurea armilla cultum*], 47[.8]
          capistris et tintinnabulis [*culti*]
2.29.36   *uolutantis incubuisse* [also in item **10**, along with the published
          concaluisse: both are deleted there]
2.32.7-8 post 2
2.32.24   *furit* [so subsequently Barber[29]]. Sil. 7.504 *fama furit uersos hostes
          Poenumque salutem* | *inuenisse fuga.* Verg. *Aen.* 4.666 *concussam bacchatur
          fama per urbem.* The same corruption occurs at 4.6.56 and perhaps 3.22.28
2.33.41-4 post 24
3.6.6   *timens*] *tamen*
3.7.22   *Mimantiadae*
3.11.7   Surely his *iuuenta* was not past. ? *praecipiti*
3.15.3   *pudor*] ? *pauor*

19

3.18.19 *omnia granis* | ... *Indis*. Cf. Tertull. [*de resurrectione carnis* 7.30] *rubentis maris grana candentia*

3.21.6 *posset* [so Richards, *CR* 13 (1899), 16]

3.21.7 *bis tantum* A.E.H. or can *tamen* be kept? or perhaps *tandem*? [*bis* Cornelissen[30] in 1879]

4.1.8 '? *finis. anth. Lat.* 423 *ultima cingebat Thybris tua, Romule, regna:* | *hic tibi finis erat, religiose Numa*
cum bubus nostris aduena Hiberus erat?' (citing Mart. 9.91.10, Verg. *A.* 7.663)

4.1.33 *minus*] ?*metus*. Or = *urbs magis suburbana Bouillis* [*metus* iam Willymott]

4.1.88 *regna subacta* or *sepulta* or rather *superba*. Or *saecula longa*. [*regna superba* published]

4.2.41-2 post 12

4.2.43-6 post 18

4.3.51 ? *Poenis bis purpura fulgeat*. cf. Mart. 1.26.2 *totiens*.

If I had known of them before producing the OCT, I would have mentioned 2.25.45 *culta*, 2.32.24 *furit*, 3.18.19 *granis*, 3.21.7 *tantum*, 4.1.8 *finis* in the apparatus criticus, and I now see that the *metus* of the ed. Etonensis deserves to be cited at 4.1.33. There are gleanings still to be had in this field, I suspect; and what is true for Propertius is likely to be true for other authors too.[31] Anyone editing or writing a commentary on a text for which a Housman volume can be identified is strongly encouraged to investigate further.

The manuscripts of Propertius

There is an extraordinary contrast between Housman's work on the manuscript tradition of Propertius and the contemporaneous research of Postgate.[32] Housman's articles have great value for the textual criticism of individual passages, and individual notes serve as useful illustrations of method in stemmatic argument; but the complexity of the structure he argues for, and the lack of attention to historical data mean that the stemma he argues for is implausible as well as wrong. Postgate on the other hand puts most of his effort into presenting a simple picture of some MSS that his researches have uncovered. In particular he brings to light L and µ (M in the OCT), and judges their positions in the stemma almost correctly:[33] L derives from the same lost exemplar as F (through one remove, it now appears[34]), and it gives a more accurate picture of the branch, for 'F is a bad copy of its exemplar' (*TCPhS* 4 (1899), 26); M derives from a lost sibling (perhaps cousin, rather) of N. Postgate also usefully points to the possibility of accidental correction in a carelessly written MS such as F (27-8), and shows that Naples 268 is a descendant of F and thus to be eliminated. The penultimate section, on 'O and N' (61-75) is what provoked Housman's ire. Again there are wise things said here: when Postgate asks (66), 'For what if Δ arose from a codex not differing very much from AF to start with, into which readings had been copied from N or some cognate manuscript and also from some other source, say W, whence come the characteristic DV readings?', his hypothesis is close to one that is now regarded as true: D and V have inherited some archetypal readings from the group the OCT denotes with the siglum Λ and their own peculiarities are a mix of fifteenth-century error and fifteenth-century conjecture.[35] He was right too on Housman's indifference to the date of N: though dates may theoretically be unimportant, in fact they can be decisive in getting stemmata to hang from the right points. Given their dates and what those dates imply about the milieu in which they were written, it is hardly surprising that 'Δ is much more deeply interpolated than N' (71).

Housman's response (*CP* 351-68 = *CR* 9 (1895), 19-29) displays much logic in its argumentation, rightly claiming that what Postgate 'presents as proofs' 'are not proofs at all' (*CP* 353), but the judgement is on Postgate's side in all the large issues, Housman again led astray by his notion that a manuscript (this time L) is a hybrid. We find assertions here that subsequent scholarship has found reason to doubt, e.g. 'the legitimate glory of a MS is not correctness but integrity'. It is true that we need to look cautiously at MSS that scatter specious readings amidst errors of the later tradition, but if a MS has both attractive (that it to say plausibly true) readings and regular reflections of archetypal error, that MS deserves the greatest attention: correctness is a strong pledge of integrity. Both N and L seem to a modern editor of the text to be comparatively 'sincere' in taking their readings only from the text in their respective exemplars.

However, the qualities of Housman's papers must be appreciated too. Read through §2 and 3 'N better than O: continued' (*CP* 241-57) and you find a sequence of notes that as a group confirm N's independence and individually establish either the true reading[36] or a correct analysis[37] of problems in the transmitted versions. Often of course the truth has been seen by an earlier scholar, but a clear statement of the correct reasoning can still be important. Thus at 3.14.27-8 (*CP* 274) and 3.9.35 (*CP* 276) Ovidian imitations confirm a widely accepted conjecture and the reading of half the tradition respectively. In the latter case too, Housman makes a subtle point in favour of the transmitted *findo*, 'the earliest example in Latin poetry of a spondee transformed into a trochee by the shortening of a final *o*.' He continues 'every change must have a beginning', and shows how likely it is that Propertius would have started what Ovid then continues. In between he simply reads the context with more care than others in arguing that at 3.23.11, the indicative *fuerant* (or rather *fuerunt*) is more likely to be right than the subjunctive *fuerint*, on the grounds that whatever he uses with *forsitan* elsewhere, in this case *aut dixit* follows in verse 15. Such a scholar is always required reading, and an editor deviates from his view with reluctance.

Yet it is striking that someone with such concern for accuracy and evidence should have been willing to base his textual arguments, even in his editions, largely on the reading of others. In *Juvenal*, for example, we find these sentences:[38]

> I began to gather from the printed sources the recorded variants; and I soon discovered that Juvenal's modern editors were ignorant or regardless of even the printed sources. I consulted the oldest MSS in the British Museum, but there was little to be learnt from these; so returning to the published records I chose out seven authorities which seemed to emerge above the crowd and to possess some value of their own. Two of these, thanks to Mr Hosius, were collated already; two were in England, so I examined them myself; three were abroad, but of these I procured enough knowledge for my purpose.

However, the Juvenal was explicitly 'not meant for a model', but 'an enterprise undertaken in haste' (*Juvenal*[2], xxxvi). Moreover, when we review Housman's work on the MS tradition of Propertius, we should remember that he was an amateur in this period. Both in Oxford and London he had access to the books that mattered, but none of the MSS thought important was within easy reach. He had a living to earn in the Patent Office; already his obsession had cost him his degree at Oxford. His classical reading was done in his leisure time, and it should not surprise us that he did not choose to use up that time collating. If he had been able to prepare his own collations he might well have seen how unreliable even those produced by careful scholars can be. But he was not, and, having established his way of working for the unpublished Propertian edition, he persisted with his dependence on others in later years when he had the professional status and time that would have made collation an easier matter.[39] Of course, he was not alone in this period in working so; but his has been a peculiarly influential example, even among those who celebrate Housman's exacting scholarship; so we find D.R. Shackleton Bailey in his centenary talk on 'A.E. Housman as a Classical Scholar'[40] showing foolish disdain: 'Collation is a job for clerks[41] or electronic machines, and a scholar who happens to possess a brain capable of more delicate operations is right to let others do it for him whenever he fairly can.' For all his greatness as a textual critic, Shackleton Bailey was not seldom led astray by his indifference to manuscripts,[42] and we would be better advised to follow not Housman's example, but the moral of his scholarship, that we should build our textual arguments on the firmest foundation possible.

Housman's Propertius and the literary aftermath

One very striking aspect of Housman's dealings with Propertius is how little effect they seem to have had on his poetry. *A Shropshire Lad*, published in 1896, was mostly written, as Housman told Sydney Cockerell, 'in the first five months of 1895 at a time of ill-health, and partly perhaps as a reaction from a learned controversy in which he was then engaged'. Naiditch,[43] surely rightly, takes this to be the polemical exchange with Postgate about the MSS of Propertius: Housman's response to the Cambridge Philological pamphlet was published in the first fascicle of *Classical Review* of that year, Postgate's reply in the third (dated April; already announced in the second). By this time Housman had been studying Propertius intently for fifteen years or so and his mind must have been thoroughly imbued with the poems, yet allusions are very hard to find, even though the poems owe much in tone to the pastoral and epigrammatic[44] traditions of antiquity, both of them important to Propertius' manner of composition. For example, Burnett's commentary[45] cites Prop. 3.7.12 on *Last Poems* XX.9-12;[46] 2.9.1 (*Iste quod est, ego saepe fui*) on XXXIV.25-6 ('Ay, yonder lads are yet / The fools that we were then'), and 1.12.13-14 *longas solus cognoscere noctes / cogor* on *More Poems* XIX.11 ('I, / Who only spend the night alone');[47] to *A Shropshire Lad* Burnett's only references are Prop. 2.13.35-6 on XI.10-14 and 3.18.21-2 on XIX.5. Although it is true that the first stanza of *Last Poems* XI has a number of motifs in common with Prop. 1.16.17-44, it equally does with a number of other ancient *paraclausithyra*. Poems XXV and XXVI both begin with reference to 'a year ago'; but they share nothing significant with 1.1 (7: *iam toto furor hic non deficit anno*).

Of course, the two poets share major themes: in particular love and death. Ghosts speak in Propertius 1.21, 4.7, 4.11; and in *ASL* XXI, XXVII, XLII. But it is perhaps willingness to make poetry of the physical effects of death that is the most important shared characteristic: thus Housman emphasises the skeleton in *ASL* XLIII 'The Immortal Part' as Propertius in (e.g.) 4.8.94 *mixtis ossibus ossa teram*, and thus he ends XXIV (5-12):

> Send me now, and I shall go;
>   Call me, I shall hear your call;
> Use me ere they lay me low
>   Where a man's no use at all;
>
> Ere the wholesome flesh decay,
>   And the willing nerve be numb,
> And the lips lack breath to say,
>   'No, my lad, I cannot come.'

apparently in imitation of Prop. 2.13, which envisages the poet's funeral and then ends as follows (51-2):

> sed frustra mutos reuocabis, Cynthia, manes:
> nam mea quid poterunt ossa minuta loqui?

Moreover, we might wonder about the influence of Propertius 3.4 on *ASL* I '1887' (Queen Victoria's Golden Jubilee): both combine celebration of an empire[48] and its sovereign with awareness at home, in peace, of the lives lost.[49] It is hard to give much weight to the echo in Housman's 'God save the Queen' (I.25) of Propertius' *ipsa tuam serua prolem, Venus* (3.4.19). But there is similarity as well as difference in the antitheses:

> We pledge in peace by farm and town
>   The Queen they served in war,
> And fire the beacons up and down
>   The land they perished for.   *ASL* I.21-4

> praeda sit haec illis quorum meruere labores:
>   mi sat erit Sacra plaudere posse Via.   Prop. 3.4.21-2

Most interesting, however, is this quatrain:

> It dawns in Asia, tombstones show
>   And Shropshire names are read;
> And the Nile spills his overflow
>   Beside the Severn's dead.   *ASL* I.17-20

The use of foreign rivers is a detail shared with the Propertian poem (as well as, e.g., Verg. *A*. 8.711-28). As transmitted, 3.4.3-4 run:

> magna, uiri, merces: parat ultima terra triumphos;
>   Tigris et Euphrates sub tua iura fluent.

But in trying to remove the apparent use of *tua* to refer to the plural *uiri*, Housman had suggested a change that would make an Italian river flow beside the Asian one, and shown how such oppositions recur (*CP* 247):

> magna, uiri, merces: parat ultima terra triumphos,
>   *Thybris*, et Euphrates sub tua iura *fluet*.

Though it may be pleasing to find a case where the textual critic impinges on the poet, this remains a small haul, and we should wonder why. Partly I think it is simply the difference between Latin and English poetic style: the metonymical specificity of the one lends itself to allusion, and this in turn creates expectations in poet and reader; Housman's language is more metaphorical; the specifics typically belong to Shropshire and the closest that comes to Propertius is in the line 'Wenlock Edge was umbered' (*Last Poems* XLI.25). Moreover, their attitudes towards love are very different: Propertius speaks nearly always in his own voice and concentrates from his first word on Cynthia. He cannot travel away from her; their love should last beyond the grave. Housman, on the other hand, is a poet of separation, whether through death or distance, and he varies his voice persistently: any sense of identification between poet and the 'I' is as fleeting as love and life themselves (he is not, of course, a Shropshire lad). Love is an emotion the poet knows, but he uses his knowledge for general reflection rather than to reveal his pain. The tone is thus far more like the experienced Horace of the *Odes* than an elegist.

*

If Housman's Propertius had been published, it would probably have made no difference to his reputation as a classical scholar, and little to the editing of Propertius – the conjectures and the most acute arguments appeared anyway; but it would have removed one poignant strand from the Housman myth, the myth of a brilliant youth so caught up in love and in building himself a monument that he ruined his early career *and then* made himself a great name as a poet and a scholar, though his first attempt at a monument was never finished:

Pollard:	I know what you want.
Housman:	What do I want?
Pollard:	A monument, Housman was here.
Housman:	Oh, you've guessed my secret.
Pollard:	A mud pie against the incoming tide.
Housman:	A fine way to speak of my edition of Propertius.

Tom Stoppard, *The Invention of Love*, Act II

With carefully designed irony, the monument was destroyed by his death, and thus became central to his immortal myth:

Housman:	I'm sorry, they're calling me. Did you finish your Propertius?
AEH:	No.
Housman:	Have you still got it?
AEH:	Oh, yes. It's in a box of papers I've arranged to be burned when I'm dead.

Ibid., Act I

Notes

1. Like other numbers, this has a discrepancy between the date on the cover (1887) and the date given inside (1888): that publication was in 1887 is clear from the Bodleian copy, however, as it bears the accession stamp '28SEP87'.

2. Whatever other causes there were for his failure in Greats, it seems certain that one was his engagement with textual criticism and consequent inattention to Ancient History and Philosophy.

3. 'Propertius had been Housman's first love' according to Gow 1936a, 12; but note that the love was at least partly of the corruption of the text: 'these three scholars [Paley, Postgate, Palmer] award the poetry of Propertius commendation which I think too high' (*CP* 52). The elegist is the concern of 161 pages of the 421 in the first volume of the *Classical Papers*: 29-54, 232-304, 314-47, 351-77.

4. *CR* 48 (1934), 136-9 = *CP* 1234-8.

5. 'On editing Propertius' in Horsfall 1988, 27-38, at 27-30.

6. This explication of marginalia must of course be taken into account when assessing the unpublished material I reveal later in this paper: what matters is the excellence of the best insight, not any moments of weakness.

7. Cf. the similar observation of Patrick Wilkinson mentioned by Luck in his contribution in this volume (his n. 6). On Sandbach and Propertius see Heyworth 2007b, xii, 177-9, 423-6 (e.g.). The major paper is 'Some problems in Propertius', *CQ* 12 (1962), 263-76.

8. The only others in double figures are Palmer (28), Lachmann (20), Baehrens (19), Postgate (18), Rossberg (14).

9. Naiditch 2003, 108-51 (at 140-2).

10. They are kept in two inscribed cupboards, one with classical volumes, the other with primarily English poetry. I am most grateful to Catherine Hilliard and her staff for their hospitality in making the books available for my repeated inspection, and to David Butterfield for passing on his notes about these volumes and for encouraging me to explore them. I also leafed through the few pamphlets on Propertius there (all registered in Naiditch 2003, at 140-2). Nothing of scholarly importance, I believe, but regular expressions of exasperation, and one or two funny moments: A. Hänel asks why a scribe was not consistent, and Housman answers in the margin 'because he was a scribe' (*De Propertii codice Neapolitano 268* (Greifswald, 1902), 42); and when Postgate writes (*AJPh* 17 (1897), 31) 'on a foreigner falls the ungrateful task of instructing two German scholars in the researches of their countryman', in place of 'ungrateful' the margin offers 'voluptuous'.

11. Smyth 1970 ad loc. attributes the conjecture to Dilthey.

12. More interesting is the conjecture (apparently unpublished, and certainly unmentioned in recent editions) *Indis* for *ludens* in the appended Cinna fr. 4 Bl. = 5 Courtney = 17 Hollis *atque imitata niues ludens legitur crystallus*. Editors print the *lucens* of Rutgers, but it is not clear that an epithet is wanted for *crystallus* in addition to *imitata niues*. Though the conjecture looks palaeographical in origin, it is appealing in that it integrates *legitur* more fully with its sentence, and it fits the concentration on geography that we now find in the *Lithica* of the Posidippus collection (1-20: epigram 16 is on crystal from Arabia). On the other hand, *Indis* does nothing to ally the verse to Juvenal 6.155, the line it is used to illustrate (see Hollis 2007, 47).

13. Sometimes rather elementary: *Caryste* at 3.3.14 is glossed 'a town in Euboea'.

14. Given that I found myself puzzled once or twice, it may be worth pointing out that the annotation was mostly done with a soft pencil, and where it stands in the inner margin this has occasionally left a mirror image on the opposite page. The same thing has happened occasionally in other volumes.

15. Also 'ugh' at 2.15.35, beside '*dolores.* the sorrows which love brings with it', though Housman seems to have been unable to find the words to convey this in his review.

16. At times, it should be said, Housman's judgement is questionable: to a modern reader it seems absurd to deny that *pede* at 3.1.6 is an 'allusion' to the metre of Callimachus and Philitas (Butler has chosen his phrasing carefully); but there are also classic demonstrations of Latinity (e.g. that pluperfect is not used for perfect (*CP* 631)), and sense (the impossibility of *persuadent* at 1.2.13 (*CP* 632)).

17. This reminds me that I mis-spelled the word in the OCT, seduced by *OLD* and the preponderant evidence for *Therod-* in the manuscript tradition into forgetting the convention that Greek ει becomes Latin *i*.

18. So Smyth 1970; I have not seen the publication either.

19. See my discussion ad loc. in Heyworth 2007b.

20. Not listed by Naiditch 2003.

21. Naiditch 1988, 31, suggests that Richmond's note may point to a contribution by Housman to the edition. Housman's denial on this point of detail may stand as counter-evidence, alongside the letter to S.C. Roberts expressing his unwillingness to referee the book (Burnett 1.630).

22. David Butterfield reports that Housman's copy of Butler & Barber, also at Trinity (adv.c.20.66), has annotations from perhaps a single read-through for his review (see n. 4), including two characteristic notes: at 3.14.19 (on 'the loss of *capere*'), 'Do you desire to have readers who can be so deceived? When the mind can deceive itself by so transparent a trick as this, it is in no fit state to conduct enquiry' (cf. *CP* 1237-8); and at 4.3.49 (on 'The greatest love is wedded love for a man who is openly acknowledged as one's husband') 'false and irrelevant'.

23. This word is underlined in the text.

24. As Haupt's reputation might suggest, the text is rather good, and admits a number of fine conjectures that later editors forget.

25. On dating, see Naiditch 1988, 198 n. 61-10, adding arguments from handwriting and abbreviations for texts such as the *Eclogues*.

26. Some published conjectures appear here too, e.g. the transposition of 2.15.31-6 after 2.1.56, and *marcori Ossaeis* at 2.2.11.

27. A. Palmer, *Hermathena* 9 (1883), 71.

28. G. Giardina, *Properzio, Elegie: edizione critica e traduzione* (Rome, 2005).

29. E.A. Barber, *Sexti Properti Carmina* (OCT, Oxford, 1953).

30. J.J. Cornelissen, *Mnem.* 7 (1879), 98-110.

31. Thus from **3** itself I can offer the following conjectures: at 1.4.13 Housman quotes Lucil. 1257-8 M. (= Gell. 9.14.22) and suggests that *sanguis* be read for *tantis* in the transmitted *facie quod honestae / tantis accedit*; and at 2.13.45 he suggests *homines* or *animae* for *enim* at Sen. *Suas.* 4.3 *incertae sortis uiuimus enim*.

32. See also Butrica 1984, 6-8, and the fuller account of relations between the two scholars in Hopkinson's contribution to this volume.

33. 'Almost', for it does not appear that L (or its exemplar) does exploit another branch: Butrica 1984, 48-9; Heyworth 2007a, xxiv-xxviii.

34. Butrica 1984, 52-3; Heyworth 2007a, xvi-xvii.

35. See Butrica 1984, 125-9, especially the final paragraph, which enumerates a large number of sources for the group. Housman thought N the hybrid.

36. E.g. 4.8.37, 3.6.21-2, 3.8.19, 2.22.33; 2.33.37, 3.1.27, 2.7.3, 3.24.6, 4.3.51-2, 2.26.15, 2.28.9, 3.4.19, 4.1.28, 4.7.41.

37. 2.25.2, 2.32.5-6, 3.22.3, 4.2.2, 4.5.21.

38. *Juvenal*[2], v.

39. Thus in the preface to his *Lucan* (xxxv) he announces '[m]y reports of the manuscripts are selected from the apparatus criticus of Mr Hosius' third edition', though on p. xxxiii he had acknowledged '[t]he manuscripts collated in his first edition were indeed too few, and the collations in his second were often inexact.' He did acquire photographs for the Manilius. See further the contribution of Reeve in this volume.

40. *Listener* 61 (1959), 795-6 = Shackleton Bailey 1997, 317-23; the quotation is from p. 321.

41. Given Housman's early career, this is a spectacular misjudgement.

42. See, e.g., M.D. Reeve's review of Shackleton Bailey's Teubner edition of *Anthologia Latina* I.1 (Stuttgart, 1982) at *Phoenix* 39 (1985), 174-80, or (on a small scale) n. 5 to my 'Horace, *Sermones* 2.3.62-3', *Mnem.* 48 (1995), 574-6.

43. Naiditch 1988, 82-3.

44. This is a general point about the rural settings (e.g.) and the use of the voice of the dead, but can be seen in specific cases, such as when *ASL* XXXIV draws on Theocritus, *Idyll* 14, LXII on *Idyll* 10, or XLVIII on *AP* 7.472 (Leonidas). The most obvious debt, that of XV to the Narcissus episode of Ovid, *Met.* 3, has affinities to both traditions.

45. Burnett 1997.

46. *AP* 7.285.2 and 374.1 are equally relevant.

47. I should add that *MP* XXXI.9-16 uses a strikingly Propertian structure to end the poem: cf. 1.6.31-6, and especially (given the similarity of sentiment, though not of addressee) 2.1.75-8.

48. *ASL* III also marks a soldier's departure and pictures the return of 'The conquering hero'.

49. *Crassos clademque* (3.4.9), and in the implications of 19-20. Death comes to the fore in the closely related 3.5.

2

Housman's Manilius[1]

E. Courtney

After his appointment as Professor of Latin in University College, London in 1892, Housman, whose scholarly production until then had consisted entirely of articles and two reviews, must have been anxious to establish his position firmly by publishing a major work, and until 1894-5 anyone would have said that this would be the edition of Propertius which he had been contemplating for ten years or more (Burnett 1.58, Gow 1936a, 12). This avenue seemed closed by the publication of Postgate's 1894 treatise 'On Certain Manuscripts of Propertius', the conclusions of which ran counter to Housman's previous work and were not well received by him, and his recension of the poet in his *Corpus Poetarum Latinorum*, which won a broadly appreciative review from Housman. For the ensuing ten years, until his review of Butler's commentary in 1905, Propertius is not the subject of any of Housman's publications. This situation must have been galling to a man who later, in his preface to Arthur Platt's collected essays, penned the phrase 'a scholar who means to build himself a monument' (*CP* 1272), a phrase with deep roots in his own aspirations and one which is tellingly compared with *More Poems* 45 by Graves 1979, 212-13, as before him by Nisbet 1969, 238.

What then was to be the stuff of such a monument? Laurence Housman (22) describes a childhood astronomical game invented by his brother Alfred, and in a letter to Maurice Pollet (Burnett 2.328) Alfred attributes his interest in astronomy to 'a little book we had in the house' in his childhood. Manilius probably caught his attention when Robinson Ellis published his 'so-called' collation of the Madrid manuscript in 1893-4; in V, xviii n. he records that when he first sat down to read Manilius through he had this by him. In the next few years it became apparent that Manilius, unlike Propertius, did not seem likely to attract a serious competitor. The aged Breiter, whose first publication on Manilius predated Housman's birth by five years, showed no sign of producing an edition. Postgate did not appear to intend continuation of work on this poet after his *Silva Maniliana* (1897), which was provoked by the edition which Bechert was preparing for his *Corpus Poetarum* (the relevant fascicle was published in 1900), and while Housman must have known about this commission, Bechert's previous work would not have been judged by Housman to offer serious competition (see his review, *CP* 525-7). It is worth noting that Postgate was in fact Housman's colleague at University College, London, where he was Professor of Comparative Philology[2] from 1880 until 1909; I do not know how much he would have physically appeared in the corridors of UCL.[3] A sign of Housman's early studies of Manilius was his first reference in print to the poet in 1897 (*CP* 409), where he makes a suggestion suppressed in his edition of 1903. His first publication specifically on Manilius (Book 1) followed in 1898 (*CP* 492; the date of 1899 given by the editors and Gow 1969, 19 is that of the whole volume of *Journal of Philology*, not the first fascicle), and then came a paper on Book 5 in 1900 (not 1901, for the same reason); discussion of problems in the technical astrological Books 2-4 had to wait until publication of the edition of Book 1 in 1903 (this section was omitted in the 1937 reprint as it had been superseded by the intervening publication of Books 2-4).

When the edition of the purely astronomical Book 1 appeared, various references show that he had already formed the project of editing the whole poem; see e.g. the note on 1.44 'cum ad 4.602 peruenero' and Goold 2000, 145. However, his attention was diverted to Juvenal by Postgate's invitation to edit this poet for his *Corpus Poetarum*; both the *Corpus* text and Housman's independent edition came out in 1905. A multitude of other topics claiming his attention also intervened, and so did the need to study up astrology for the technical books of the poem (Goold 2000, 146). There seems to be no evidence that this subject had attracted serious attention from him earlier, but in 1908 and 1910 he produced papers on authors other than Manilius concerning astrological matters. So his edition of Book 2 did not come out until 1912, by which time he had procured photographs of the Madrid and Leipzig manuscripts. Before this Breiter's edition of the whole poem had been published in 1907-8 and Garrod's of Book 2 in 1911. Garrod had evidently failed to notice the indications in Housman's edition of Book 1 that he intended to edit the whole work, and he disclosed (1913) some consternation at the competition; indeed in October 1911 he had clearly written to Housman, who replied in courteous and encouraging tones (Burnett 1.277), very unlike those in which he spoke of the book in V, xxv-vi; apart from Garrod's deficiencies Housman may have been soured by his attempt to claim precedence for a conjecture (see addenda on 2.935b). To say the least it is ungenerous for Housman here to pen the sentence 'His conjectures were singularly cheap and shallow' when, to confine myself to Book 2, in his later addenda, published simultaneously with the introduction to V, he referred to that on 252 as 'not bad' and that on 326 as 'just as good' as that adopted from Bonincontrius, though it is true that neither required great perspicacity. He also on 5.217 praises a conjecture made by Garrod on 2.226. He declares that Garrod was not the first to understand 681ff., though Garrod had anticipated himself, but his notes do not specify any predecessor in comprehension. Worst of all, on 2.872 Housman declares that nobody had adopted a reading which stands in Garrod's text; if anyone else had committed this oversight, we would find the word 'lie' being bandied about (see below).

The other three volumes of the edition appeared at intervals until 1930, and the work was crowned with the *editio minor* in 1932, published by the Cambridge University Press, whereas the individual volumes had been entrusted to the rascally publisher of 'A Shropshire Lad', Grant Richards. In V, v Housman records that the 400 copies printed of each book had been sold out only in the case of Book 1 (in 1926).

This much for necessary factual background. To turn to specific features of the edition, one will note first the format of the work, introductory matter in the vernacular language (English in this case) and commentary in Latin. None of the great nineteenth-century editions of Latin authors admired by Housman, such as those by Madvig, Lachmann, Munro, had adopted such a format; all were written entirely in one language or the other. I surmise that the decision to put the prefatory matter in English was dictated largely by the example of Munro's edition of Lucretius (and to a lesser extent his *Aetna*). Munro's introductions to his volumes of text and commentary cover the following topics among others: the manuscripts, the history of the editing of Lucretius (what he says about Gifanius, Havercamp, Wakefield much resembles some of Housman's comments on editors of Manilius; Havercamp's 'scissors and paste' echo in the 'paste and scissors' of van Wageningen, V, xxvi), Lucretius' life and relations with contemporaries, and the question of the state of the poem, finished or unfinished. All of these are matters covered also by Housman, who adds discussions of issues on which many contemporary Latin scholars had gone astray: impartial evaluation of manuscript evidence and of dubious readings, and application of two methods of emendation underused at the time. It will be recalled that Housman respected the scholarship of his great predecessor in the Kennedy Chair (not then so called) at Cambridge (see e.g. Graves 1979, 166) and as an undergraduate had had some correspondence with him (ibid., 47, Gow 1936a, 4, Naiditch 1995, 14). Why Housman did not follow Munro's example and write the commentary in English remains obscure to me.[4]

In 1893 Housman had reproved Baehrens for his 'foolish scurrility' (*CP* 235) in referring to Leo as 'asinus sub leonina pelle latens', which is not much worse than some of the things which Housman later said of other scholars, e.g. when on Manilius 2.940 he compared Bechert's recourse to unacceptable readings to a sow wallowing in the mud. Until the previous year he had had no stable position in the hierarchy of classical scholars, and his disagreements had been expressed in reasonably restrained and impartial terms. But one year later, when, as it seems, he now felt securely established, the deficiencies of K.P. Schulze's revision of Baehrens' edition of Catullus provoked for the first time a torrent of (justified) invective. But, however justified, the terms in which Housman wrote certainly impeded recognition of the quality of his work, and when one reads what he has to say about the miserable Stoeber (I, xix-xx and *passim*), one cannot but feel that this whipping-boy was too easy a target to be worth the attention. One observes too that criticism sometimes seems selective in its victims. Thus on 4.687 a silly error is adduced from *TLL*, and an equally silly one is adduced, or rather dragged in with no relevance whatsoever to Manilius, from the excellent C.F.W. Müller, apparently for the sole purpose of granting a pardon seldom granted by Housman to the lexicographers of *TLL*. It is hard to deny that Housman took artistic pleasure in wielding his rapier, even going to the lengths of composing a Latin epigram based on 4.794 against Jacob (I, xxi). As for the famous notebook, I shall not get into that argument (see Graves 1979, 206, Page 1983, 145-6 and n. on 226, Naiditch 2005, 56-9).

There is one particularly objectionable feature in the criticisms, however justified, of other scholars, namely that it is allowed to take on moral overtones where moral judgments have no place. Jocelyn in his review of C.O. Brink's book on *English Classical Scholarship* remarks of Housman (*LCM* 12 (1986) 112), 'noteworthy is the prominence of religious imagery in the castigation of philological delinquents', this imagery being accentuated by Housman's masterly use of the language of the King James Bible, of which specimens can be seen in I xxxii-iii, xli; it looks as if designed deliberately to give the impression of a prophet crying in the wilderness to a largely indifferent mob. One sees this tendency particularly in the characterisation of errors as 'lies', of which I have noticed nine examples, Jacob being the victim more often than anyone else; he is followed by Breiter and van Wageningen, though even Scaliger comes under the lash at 5.207. It is true that there have been classical scholars who have been liars (think, for instance, of Caspar Barth), but the word is quite out of scale for these lapses. The converse of such language is the exaltation of 'truth' as a scholarly aim, of which more below.

At the end of his preface to I Housman states (lxii):

> This commentary is designed to treat of two matters only: what Manilius wrote and what he meant. From the illustration of his phraseology and vocabulary, as distinct from the elucidation of his language, I have purposely abstained; not that I despise this industry ...

This criterion sometimes seems applied with excessive severity in I (e.g. most editors would have written a note on 783, or at least have given a cross-reference to 417, about the relationship between Apollo and the raven), but as the work progressed he seems to have relaxed his austerity somewhat; in V, for example, purely verbal parallels are quoted in places where neither text nor interpretation is in doubt (on 280, 473, 545 etc.). If one asks what side of his work was dominant in his mind, it unsurprisingly emerges with sufficient clarity from V, xxxiv-vi that it was emendation, especially when this passage is compared with the statistical reckoning under authors (V, xvii-viii) of the corrections adopted in the text or approved in the commentary, in which Scaliger's score is 220 and Bentley's 238. In reviewing *Man. ed. min.* Hosius uttered this verdict (1933, 1190):

> Scaliger und Bentley, die uns jeder mit weit mehr als zweihundert Textänderungen... entgegentreten und in dieser Zahl nur von H[ousman] selbst übertroffen werden.

In view of Housman's frosty remarks about Hosius in his Lucan, I hesitate to guess how he felt when he read these words. In fact I have made a calculation, using criteria as similar to Housman's as I could guess, on the basis of *Man. ed. min.*, and Housman's score in his own eyes I reckon to be 339 (in this total I include alterations of punctuation); Shackleton Bailey in *CPh* 74 (1979) 161 reaches a total of 236 (not counting repunctuations), so one should probably conclude that one or other of us is a bad arithmetician, even allowing for differences in criteria.

Housman expresses (V, xxxiv) particular pride in three emendations. Hast thou appealed unto Caesar? Unto Caesar shalt thou go. One of these emendations (*eguit Ioue* for M's *esurcione* at 1.423 = 377) is indeed both certain and brilliant. The second is 4.800-1

> Piscibus Euphrates datus est, ubi <ab> his ope sumpta,
> cum fugeret Typhona, Venus subsedit in undis,

referring to the legend that when chased by Typhon Venus saved herself and Cupid by jumping into the Euphrates and either riding to safety on the backs of fish or metamorphosing into fish. Here the manuscripts read *ubi pisces* (or *piscis*) *uruptor*. In this emendation the line ends with two disyllables. Manilius does this twelve times (I do not count 1.707, deleted by Bentley) on the pattern of e.g. 4.852 *non uidet astris* or 1.422 (= 376) *di quoque magnos*, and according to the manuscript tradition varies from this pattern only at 1.521 *semper fuit idem*. Housman's text also presents *duplicare erit a te* at 4.248, where the manuscripts read the certainly corrupt *duplicari et arte*. That is not all; elision at the point of the verse where Housman introduces it in

4.800 is found only five times, one of them conjectural, in Manilius; they are listed in Housman's note on 2.430, and on 5.87 he remarks, not mentioning his emendation here, that of them only 2.184 involves a pyrrhic word.[5] One observes that Housman here makes no attempt to defend the metrical configuration, though he does at 4.248. And there is more. Manilius at 2.33 and 4.597 refers to the second variation of the myth, that of metamorphosis, whereas here Housman's emendation presupposes the first, though *subsedit in undis* looks like the second. And finally the emendation is justified by a piece of that palaeographical juggling of which he was overfond, the assumption being that *his ope sumpta* was corrupted to *iscpesuruptor* and then the scribes, indifferent to this nonsense, became solicitous of the metre and deleted *ab* (or, even more unlikely, this was omitted in a second independent corruption because of its resemblance to *ubi*). An emendation which incorporates four improbabilities (I do not say impossibilities) would seem to stand little chance of being right. I think that we would do better to resort to the obelus (on which see below), but will venture a tentative guess that we might read *pisce suborto* 'when a fish sprang up in her place'. For a somewhat similar use of the verb Lewis and Short supply me with Arnobius 3.9 (do the gods have genital organs) *ut ... noua quaque suboriente fetura quicquid prior aetas abstulisset recidiua substitutio subrogaret?*

The third emendation on which Housman prided himself is at 5.461

> uix una trium memorare sepulchra
> ructantemque patrem natos,

where the manuscripts for the first three words read *atri* (or *auri*) *luxum*, and some of them a plainly interpolated variant *sepulchri*, and the reference is to Thyestes' consumption of his three sons. This is translated by Goold, 'to tell of scarce one burial accorded three', where 'scarce' refers to the fact that the sons were not completely eaten because Atreus had cut off their extremities, which would have betrayed his crime. I find this very hard to swallow, if I may put it that way, and I also find it very unlikely that, despite Housman's 'parallels' for the poetic plural *una*, Manilius would have used this in a context where Housman's emendation makes him draw a contrast between the three corpses and the one tomb, Thyestes' stomach; all instances of this which I can find, such as Var. *Men.* 184 *uel decem messis ubi una saepiant granaria*, have some special justification, such as accompanying nouns which are either *pluralia tantum* or may be treated as such. Again the emendation has to be justified by palaeographical sleight of hand. Between us David Butterfield and I arrived at this suggested solution, *a<lui> triplex memorare sepulchrum*, *triplex sepulchrum* (the initial step) being due to him and *alui* to me;

the *-um* at the end of *luxum* would then be a misplaced correction of the termination of *sepulchra*.

These emendations are quoted in a defiant tone; 'two of [these emendations], I can well believe, will make the hair stand up on many uninstructed heads'. One wonders whether the bluster was an attempt to conceal inner uncertainty, but one must also note the implication that only a select few are fit to judge the emendations of A.E. Housman. As an example of a daring but seemingly correct conjecture I would rather quote 3.294 *excipiunt uicibus* (*eius in exemplum* codd.) *se signa sequentia uersis* (this was too strong for Garrod's (1917, 108 n.1) digestion, but Goold accepts it though he had declared (1959, 110) that all Housman's introductions of the word *uices* into Manilius were unsuccessful). As other examples, selected out of many, of fine emendations I will instance 1.145 *pugna ingeniis* and the interchange of words between 2.488 and 498. On the other hand see 4.568-70 (the last part of Capricorn)

> militiam in ponto dictat puppisque colendae
> dura ministeria et uitae discrimen inertis.

This is plainly corrupt, and Housman alters the last three words to *tenui discrimine mortis* very appropriately but at the cost of supposing at least two independent errors. I suggest that it may be sufficient to change the last word to *inermis*. In 560-7 Sagittarius is said to create warriors; Manilius then represents the sons of Capricorn as also engaged in warfare with the sea, and with my emendation he would carry on this metaphor, with a near oxymoron explaining that the perils there encountered involve no weapons. At 5.541ff. the manuscripts present the following (with 514 transferred to this place by Jacob):

541		totis cum finibus omnis
542	incubuit pontus, timuit naufragia tellus
514	et quod erat regnum pelagus fuit.

After the loss of something *naufragia* was presumably stretched from *naufraga* by someone who could count syllables even if his grasp of prosody was feeble. Housman raised a pedantic cavil against *timuit* to arrive at the emendation *fluitauit naufraga* (still mentioned in *Man. ed. min.*), with no attempt to explain the corruption. I would rather suggest *timuit <mare> naufraga*, supposing that the supplied word was omitted because of homoeoarchon. We would then have a threefold antithesis between land (*finibus*, *tellus*, *regnum* of Cepheus) and sea (*pontus*, *<mare>*, *pelagus*), with varied designations for each in each clause. Such verbal ingenuity would be very much in the style of Manilius.

These discussions imply that there are places in Manilius where an obelus might be thought appropriate, and indeed this mark is freely applied in *Man. ed. min.* (though not in the above places), with the justification that the reader no longer has the commentary to alert him. But what is more interesting is that it is now applied in eight places (2.860; 4.280, 314, 417, 424, 467, 788; 5.207) with no suggestion for correction, though in the commentated edition Housman had, with various degrees of tentativeness, proposed solutions to the problems. Goold adopts readings mentioned by Housman in all these places except for his own conjecture at 4.467. The reader needs to be aware that it was on principle that Goold refused to employ the obelus in all the texts which he edited. In at least some of such places it is hard to avoid the suspicion that Housman was primarily concerned to show his fertility in conjecture; on 5.87 for instance he puts forward two conjectures, neither thought worthy of mention just two years later in *Man. ed. min.* The same suspicion arises at 2.365, where a trivial error in M invites Housman to warn the reader against making a conjecture which would occur to nobody but himself, and 2.943, where again a trivial error in L and omission of the line's last word by M make him state that 'you would almost suspect' the true reading to be one with no superiority over that of GL2 (see just below). Again neither of these ideas survives in *Man. ed. min.*

On this subject one must of course bear in mind that in the normal course of human events subsequent emendators have sometimes produced solutions preferable to Housman's; I think, for instance, of Hübner's (1987, 28) elegant proposal at 5.440-41 *delatus et ille / hunc iacit.*

In II-V, when adequate information about the manuscripts had become available, the text is immediately preceded by a stemma of the manuscripts, again presented with one detail subtracted and others added in *Man. ed. min.* ix. The detail subtracted concerns some readings offered by GL2, sources which present readings unquestionably derived from an earlier stage of the tradition, but also others which are 'false and obviously conjectures' (V, xiii), which is the sum total of what Housman says about these readings in V, though on the stemma he labels them as produced by an 'interpolator'. This indication has disappeared from the stemma in *Man. ed. min.*, and the accompanying account simply mentions 'many interpolations of the 11th century', to which one must react by wondering how he knows their date, though it is quite possible that such an interpolator could have introduced his ideas into both manuscripts, since G appears to be only a little younger than L and both were assigned by Traube to the same neighbourhood (Goold 1998, vii), as Housman (see addenda to I p. 82, V, viii n.) must have known but, presumably because of his aversion to *Überlieferungsgeschichte*, chose not to mention. The suspicion arises that Housman was uncomfortable with his postulate of two separate sources for GL2 readings, a postulate imposed by his justified intent to bolster the credibility of many readings offered by GL2. Goold's stemma (1985, xi; see also 1959, 97-9) is much more convincing in following up Housman's suggestion of marginal variants in the tradition and tracing all GL2 readings, both transmitted and (though Goold is not quite explicit about these) innovated, to the same source.

One other complaint about the stemmata in II-V is that for no obvious reason they ignore the now lost Venice manuscript, though it appears on that in *Man. ed. min.*; on V, xlvii it is actually listed among derived manuscripts.

And now the meat of the edition, the commentary. The astrological portion of this (and of the introductions) will unfortunately have to be passed over here because of the lack of expertise of the present writer; to his untutored eye it certainly looks impressive, involving as it does consultation of very rare books, some of them texts not edited since the sixteenth century (Goold 2000, 146) and in one case (on 4.105) still unedited, and it even overcomes his ignorance by making the subject-matter intelligible. Housman is warmly thanked by Stuart Jones in the preface (vii) to the ninth edition of the lexicon of Liddell and Scott for his help with Greek astrological vocabulary.

When we turn to the purely explanatory notes, it is impossible to overpraise the profound and exact familiarity with the author which they show, and not only with Manilius but also with the usage of Latin writers (particularly poets) in general; I will instance the discussion of quasi-adverbial uses and enallage of adjectives in the note on 1.226. The parenthesis in the last sentence implies a mild criticism, namely that one occasionally misses a wider perspective. Thus on 3.328 he comments on *conscendes ... scandensque* 'ita solent poetae' and quotes three instances from Ovid, giving the reader no idea that the idiom is widely found, in prose as well as in verse, and has ancient, indeed Indo-European, roots; see my *Archaic Latin Prose* (Atlanta, 1999) 2, 22, *Musa Lapidaria* (Oxford, 1995) 319 etc. Likewise on 5.292 quotation of a very few examples of change of ictus in repeated words, of which many instances are adduced e.g. by N. Herescu, *La poésie Latine* (Paris, 1960) 197, and some by Lachmann on Prop. 2.3.43-4, can only mislead. To the exclusively poetic instances of the idiom remarked on 3.68 one might add Cic. *Ver.* 5.145 *quaecumque nauis ex Asia, quae ex Syria, quae Tyro, quae Alexandria uenerat.* On similar lines at 5.615, where Manilius speaks of a wedding-present (namely life itself) given by Perseus to, or perhaps for, Andromeda and called a *dos*, for a parallel he goes to German custom as described by Tacitus *Germ.* 18.2 (modern numeration), though he quotes two passages in which Nonnus in the context of Perseus and Andromeda mentions a ἕδνον. Manilius in this mythological context is correctly referring to the institution of a bride-price which he knew from Homer; for the sake of brevity Tacitus calls this *dos*. *dotalis* is similarly applied to mythological figures (Claud.

Rapt. Pros. 1.28, Ov. *Fast.* 5.209, the latter place referred to by Lactant. *Inst.* 1.20.8 as *quasi dotis loco*) and foreigners like the Germans (Man. 1.915, where see Housman's note and addenda, Sidon. *Carm.* 5.458, Sil. 17.75; some of these passages are adduced by Drakenborch on Silius loc. cit. after Barth, who also refers to Manilius).

One is also occasionally surprised to see things overlooked. Thus at 4.439 *ostendisse deum nimis est* he takes objection to *nimis*, which Goold quite acceptably understands as a rhetorical exaggeration and translates 'more than enough'; but at Lucan 2.276, where Housman does not comment, *nimium* occurs precisely so used and by Duff, who regularly consulted Housman, is again translated 'more than enough'.[6] At 3.92 he is perplexed by the reference of the pronoun in *illius negoti*, where in his addenda he translates 'of such and such a business'; it means rather 'the business in question', a rare use (briefly discussed in Hofmann-Szantyr 182) but found at Juv. 3.274-5 *illa nocte* (which I have seen 'emended'), 264 *ille*. κείνην is similarly used at Hdt. 2.40.2. In the addenda to 1.385 (= 427) he objects to *uno ... in astro ... quod sidus* on the grounds that, where the designation of the antecedent is varied between relative and main clause, the relative clause should precede; yet examples to the contrary are quoted by Kühner-Stegmann 2.284, to which others could be added (e.g. Cat. 64.73). On 4.422 *cadit post paulum gratia ponti*, where for the last word GL offer *christi*, he draws attention to the well-known phenomenon of 'Christian interpolation', which would have made scribes at some level of consciousness think of *Paulum*, the apostle Paul, and of the technical theological term 'grace' (*gratia*) but does not seem to realise that they will then also have thought of *Ponti*, Pontius Pilate, whom they would certainly not have regarded as a vehicle of grace (for they would not have known or cared about his canonisation as a saint by the Ethiopian church!); on 5.168 he notes that recollection of this man has caused G to corrupt *pilarum* to *pilatum*. On 5.534 *silicem riuo saliente liquabit* he remarks *silicem igne liquefaciet, ut riuus fiat saliens*, but says nothing about the 'resultative Ablativ', as it is called by Hofmann-Szantyr 123. This name certainly conveys the effective sense, but I am not sure that this should be isolated as a syntactical category (it was not widely recognised as such in Housman's day); anyway many ablatives which might be so classified are collected, e.g. by Bömer on Ov. *Met.* 5.673 and 10.494, Knox on *Her.* 2.3 etc., but could do with careful sifting. One may note that *silicem* in the parallels quoted by Housman means limestone, whereas here the reference is to the smelting of silver ore; but perhaps he intended purely verbal illustration. In any case cross-references between this passage and 4.247 with the addenda would have been welcome, and there are other places too where cross-references would have been helpful, e.g. between 2.617 (where the occurrence of the same phrase in different senses might have invited a reference to Madvig on Cic. *Fin.* 2.64) and

3.114, 1.774 and 5.106, 2.20 and 4.250. On 4.534 *se quisque et uiuit et effert*, after providing a useful list of this type of word-order, which the Greeks would have included under the name of διὰ μέσου, he gives one Greek example of the double conjunction in this idiom and states that he knows no Latin instance, but in Greek he might have added Theocr.(?) 25.71-2, and in Latin there is Liv. 3.15.9 *se Volscos et Aequos et omnia extrema temptaturum et concitaturum*. On 1.245, where he understands *somnosque in membra locamus* to mean *membra in somnos locamus*, he claims support in *Culex* 205 *in fessos requiem dare comparat artus*, which, on the rationalistic argument that men give their bodies to sleep but it is nature that gives sleep to bodies, he interprets to mean *dare fessos artus in requiem* (why then would the author not have written *in requiem fessos*?), but he has forgotten Verg. *A.* 8.30 *Aeneas... dedit per membra quietem*, so that the passage of the *Culex* is actually against him. Housman loved to detect hyperbata, not quite always successfully; he understands 1.780 *maiorque uiris et Cloelia uirgo*, to mean 'and the young girl Cloelia greater than even men', but to me it seems to mean 'and Cloelia, greater than men even though a young girl' (in the addenda to this passage he needlessly lists Stat. *Theb.* 9.512 as a hyperbaton).

On the negative side one must also suspect that some things are not mentioned because they are inconvenient; this has been remarked above on the discussion of 4.800-1, and in *ANRW* 2.33.1.845 I noted two similar instances in Juvenal, where mention of relevant facts would have obstructed two emendations. His own emendations sometimes pass tests which they would fail if they came from others; I remarked (2005, 118) that at 5.83 his parallel for a use of the local ablative is relevant only in contexts referring to rivers, and at 2.898, a passage which I shall be discussing in a forthcoming article, he himself admits that his parallel for his emendation is not exact. At 3.285 he quotes a parallel for the corruption of *quinta* to *quarta* from 2.335 'in some manuscripts', but these manuscripts are of such late date and little credibility that he does not mention them there. At 3.172, on nit-picking grounds, he alters *quae primum pars est numerosis dicta sub athlis* to *q. primum e. aerumnosis pars d. s. a.*, and still mentions this conjecture in *Man. ed. min.*, but fails to note that this rhythm has its parallel only at 5.126 *et fidum Laertiadae genuere syboten* with a proper name. In exegesis the same attitude appears in the note on 4.724, where the passage quoted from Strabo is actually quoted by him from Posidonius (*fr.* 49.327-30 Edelstein-Kidd, with Kidd's commentary pp. 268, 274); but see how Housman at I, lxxiii (with addenda ad loc.) and on 2.93 dismisses source-hunting which lights on Posidonius.

Outside Manilius himself one must not overlook the numerous passages of other poets (seldom prose writers) emended or elucidated in the notes; I myself certainly derived great profit from these discussions when I was editing Valerius Flaccus, and to the best of my recollection found myself convinced in every case. But it has to be admitted that the rate of success is not quite so high with all authors. On 2.303, for instance, he advocates the alteration of Verg. *A.* 7.598 *omnisque in limine portus*, where *omnisque* (whatever the editors say or do not say) certainly seems corrupt, to *somnique in limine postus*, thereby eliminating Latinus' reference to the proverbial *naufragium in portu*. Yet more remarkably, on 5.451 he tries to smooth out the construction of Catullus 10.29-30, where Catullus had brilliantly conveyed stammering embarrassment by disjointed phraseology; it is strange that one who was himself a creative writer should so allow literary sensitivity to lose out to pedantry.

On the other side one must admire the wide learning, not confined to the astronomical and astrological subject-matter nor to Manilian and general Latin usage, exhibited throughout the commentary. I will select just one illustration of this in a passage (5.165-7, the last line perhaps out of place) still not satisfactorily explained[7] and not beyond doubt emended; here the note assembles potentially relevant material from Galen, Horace, Isidore, Oribasius and Aristotle. Numerous too are the passages misunderstood or mistakenly altered by others which Housman vindicates; take for instance 4.540, 629. See too 1.613, where he candidly admits that his previous alteration (*CP* 493) was erroneous.

I commented above on Housman's use of the word 'lies'; he also uses its opposite 'truth' to exalt his own approach to classical scholarship. See I, xliii 'the faintest of all human passions is the love of truth' (not of course that the writer is thus defective); I, xviii 'Bentley's faculty for discovering truth'; *CP* 126, 1060-1. As well as truth, morality enters the picture; see Lucan, xxvii: 'moral integrity and intellectual vigilance are for [emendators] not merely duties but necessities'; *CP* 547 'this practice of concocting fictions ... is naturally attended with a certain amount of moral and intellectual damage'. He managed to impose the view of himself as a pillar of scholarly morality on his contemporaries, particularly in Cambridge, and it can be seen e.g. in Gow's memoir; thus he states (28) 'the love of truth ... with Housman was the strongest [of the passions]', phrasing which echoes verbally one of the above quotations and, more tellingly, the sentiments of Housman's University College address at the opening of the academic year in 1892, which he himself later characterised as 'rhetorical and not wholly sincere'. See too Shackleton Bailey 1982, 112 'that quasi-emotional dedication to truth' and 1997, 322 'a bad reading in Manilius and a world war can spring from the same moral and intellectual roots'(!), though he admits (321) that Housman tended to put things too dogmatically and that his presentation of a case was often rhetorical and one-sided. And here is J. Enoch Powell as quoted by T.E.B. Howarth, *Cambridge Between Two*

Wars (London, 1978) 89; after mention of Housman's 'passion for truthfulness' comes this: 'For Housman textual criticism was the exercise of moral self-discipline ... No-one, I believe, ever heard Housman on Horace, *Epistles* 1.7.29 ... without receiving the moral enlargement of a great sermon'(!). It is a relief to turn from this nonsense to Goold's (2000, 141) more balanced judgment which sees not 'desire for truth' but something more modest, 'an insistence on accuracy and a hatred of inaccuracy' and concludes by separating two qualities united in two of the above quotations (united too by Housman himself, *CP* 1145 'evidence only for the intellectually or morally deficient') and stating that 'Housman's strength was intellectual not moral'. I would only modify this by suggesting that 'accuracy' is too reductive a word, and we should at least include 'unbiased judgment' and the like.

The reader by now may be convinced that I set out to do a hatchet job on the edition of Manilius. In fact the reservations which I have expressed represent *egregio inspersos corpore naeuos*. Of the great classic editions of Latin texts the one which in my view most nearly approaches flawlessness is Madvig's *De Finibus*. Housman's Manilius falls behind this in dispassionate analysis of problems, for it is for ever looking to convey the editor's superiority to the generality of scholars, but in compensation we are stimulated by a wide-ranging richness of content. Overall evaluation of Housman's work runs into a nuisance perceptible in some comments quoted above, what Sullivan (1962, 105 = Ricks 1968, 146) called 'the intensely English cult of A.E. Housman'. The purport of is repeated by Hübner (1984, 130 'Housmans ... Ausgabe ..., die dem Engländer als Muster editorischer Kunst gilt', with references in n. 12;[8] this impact was not just scholarly, but also sprang from the striking union in one person of austere scholar and romantically gloomy poet. I should like to stress the word 'English' in the above quotations, since it does not mean 'British'. Though Sullivan was born in England, he had strong Irish roots which gave him a certain detachment despite his Cambridge education. The present writer too, Irish by birth and upbringing, may take the opportunity to say something about his own interaction with Housman. I first encountered his work at school when we read a book of Lucan and some satires of Juvenal. The late John Cowser, an outstanding teacher and a devotee of Housman, introduced us to his scholarship and lent me his editions of these writers, as well as Manilius I. As my studies advanced, I came to see how much I could learn from these editions for the type of work which I felt that I might be suited to do and able to do in classical scholarship, and there is only one other scholar to whom I feel a comparable debt. However, as time passed I became more aware of the reservations aroused by a certain proportion of his pronouncements. It will be obvious from what I have written above that I think it does less honour to Housman to accept his conclusions uncritically than to exercise the best of one's judgment on them, aware that a few will be flawed, as our common humanity, and in this case psychological factors which I do not feel inclined to go into, dictate; contrast Gow 1936a, 46: 'At the Philological Society ... one commonly came away from the meeting with the feeling that so would the recording angel on the Judgment Day read his scroll, and so would faults be amended beyond appeal or dispute ... the paper left nothing to debate.' It would be a pity if nothing had been found to debate in the Manilius.

Notes

1. In this chapter large Roman figures, e.g. IV, indicate the five volumes of Housman's commentary, so that e.g. V, ix will mean the ninth page of the introduction to vol. V, and references such as 4.22 refer to book and line of the Latin text; where the *editio minor* offers as an alternative a substantially different numeration, this is added in parenthesis.

2. I.e. what we would nowadays call Linguistics. Not 'Comparative Literature', as Page 1983, 65 absurdly has it; this is a modern industry with which Postgate would have had no truck. For further discussion of the relationship of Housman and Postgate, see Hopkinson's chapter.

3. Not very often, according to Naiditch 1988, 77-8, 86, 112.

4. At this point I may deal with one matter touched on just now, namely the chronology of Manilius. There has recently been considerable discussion of this, and the items for 1950-99 are listed by Bajoni 1999, 146-50, and also 157 on an article by M. Neuburg in *MD* 31 (1993), 243-57, which for ignorance and futility represents the nadir of this debate (see e.g. on 246 n. 6 his criticism of Goold for not noting a non-existent variant in M). In my own opinion nothing has seriously shaken Housman's conclusion that Books 1-2 were written under Augustus and 4-5 under Tiberius, but I want to draw attention to a discussion, with which I disagree, overlooked by Bajoni, that by Bowersock 1990, 385-7. He suggests that when Suetonius *Aug.* 94.12 says that Augustus was born (*natus*) under Capricorn, he means that Augustus was conceived under that sign, and that the reference in Man. 4.773-7 to a Caesar *genitus* (i.e. born; cf. Suet. *Aug.* 100.3) under Libra is really to Augustus and his birth sign, the inference being that the whole poem was written under Augustus. So, in his view, either Suetonius' *natus* refers to conception or he misunderstood an earlier source which used the word *ortus* (with which he compares Man. 2.509 *Augusti ... ortum* in relation to Capricorn) in that sense. The first of these ideas is impossible (see *Man.* I, lxx(-xxi) n. 1), the second presupposes that Suetonius based himself for this important fact on a poetic source (who?), for no prose writer could so employ the word *ortus*, and that he neglected to check his information on this critical matter. All this is in the interest of maximising the implications of the famous (and, to say the least, controversial) sundial in the Campus Martius, and shows the misfortunes which can befall historians when they attempt to force literary texts into a predetermined historical mould; one may turn back Bowersock's own words to state that he understands the Augustan world better than the text of Manilius.

5. It is noteworthy that at Juv. 3.109 Housman introduced an identical elision with no parallel in that author; see Nisbet's chapter, p. 52.

6. This observation is due to Bühler 1959, 477-8.

7. No help is to be gained from E. Wegner, *Das Ballspiel der Römer* (diss. Rostock, 1937-8) 20-1, since he regards the quite unsuitable Renaissance conjecture *saltu* as a transmitted reading. H.A. Harris, *Sport in Greece and Rome* (Cornell, 1972) 107-11, with some inaccuracy, does his best.

8. One must note that Hübner found it possible to write the entry on Manilius in *Der Neue Pauly* without mentioning the name of Housman (or for that matter of Bentley), and to end the article with the statement that 'die philol[ogische Erforschung des Gedichts begann] erst in den 1970er Jahren, bes[onders] in It[alien]'! The reader will have noted that I have found no occasion requiring mention of recent editions of the poem.

3

Housman's Juvenal

R.G.M. Nisbet

This is a shorter version of my article in *ICS* 14 (1989), 285-302 (reprinted in Nisbet 1995, 272-92). Since then I have recorded many further disagreements with Housman in my contributions to Willis' Teubner edition (1997). I discuss ten further passages at *AantHung*. 39 (1999), 225-30; these are cited with a few further suggestions in J.F. Miller et al. 2002, 61-6 (note especially 6.296 *Sagaris* for *Sybaris*).

At 2.150 I now support Heinsius' *Porthmeaque* for *et pontum* (*P*) or *et contum* (Ψ = Φ), which Housman must have known but does not record; *cocitum* comes from the interpolated branch of Liutprand's tradition (J.F. Miller et al. 2002, 61-2), and must be regarded as only a conjecture. At 5.105 *pinguis torrente cloaca* I now accept *torpente* (Rutgers), which suits *pinguis* better. At 6.011 I see no escape from Lee's *pulsatoremque tridentem*, which was later supported by an inscription (Courtney) that Leo did not know; see J.F. Miller et al. 2002, 63. At 8.6-9, where Housman did not recognise interpolation, I should now read *quis fructus generis tabula iactare capaci / fumosos equitum cum dictatore magistros / si coram Lepidis male uiuitur?*, i.e. I follow the vulgate tradition (Ψ = Φ) in omitting only line 7 (which is found in *P*) but accepting 6 and 8; it is surely significant that M. Lepidus was *magister equitum* in Caesar's dictatorship. At 15.133 Housman's explanation is very hard to believe, and I am now inclined to accept Courtney's *amictum* (line 134).

Housman's edition made a notable contribution to the textual criticism of Juvenal, but I should have been more critical of its shortcomings, particularly in its reluctance to look for interpolations and its disregard for the contributions of other scholars. The cult of Housman was so pervasive that for a long time it was difficult to resist, especially as his aggressive style of argument inhibited rational discussion, but the time is now due for a more balanced reassessment.

*

The assessment of famous editions is more difficult than is sometimes supposed. Snap judgements can be made about other works of scholarship in a library or a bookshop, but to criticise a textual critic it is desirable to have wrestled with the problems oneself, as well as to know the state of opinion before he came on the scene. That is a tall order with Housman's Manilius, so that with a few distinguished exceptions eulogies derive from Housman himself, but Juvenal at least is relatively familiar and intelligible. The present sketch is the sequel to my article in the Skutsch *Festschrift* (Horsfall 1988, 86-110), where a number of proposals are made on the text of Juvenal. Apart from Housman himself, I have used particularly the texts of Jahn, Knoche, Clausen, and J.R.C. Martyn (Amsterdam 1987), as well as the commentary by Courtney (1980; note also his text of 1984).

Housman's first text of Juvenal appeared in 1905 in the second volume of Postgate's *Corpus Poetarum Latinorum*; it had a greatly abbreviated apparatus but was otherwise virtually identical with the separate edition. This was published in the same year 'editorum in usum' by Housman's friend Grant Richards; the second edition (Cambridge, 1931) has some 20 additional pages of introduction but only minimal changes elsewhere. For Housman's articles and reviews on Juvenal, I refer to the index of his *Classical Papers*. One may note especially his expositions of the Oxford fragment (481ff., 539ff., 621f.), which presumably led to the invitation from Postgate, and his mauling of S.G. Owen (602ff., 617f., 964ff.), whose rival Oxford Classical Text of 1903 he ignores in his own editions.

Housman's first service to Juvenal was his clear-headed and clearly expressed account of the manuscript position. On the one hand there was *P*, the ninth-century Pithoeanus, with a few congeners, on the other hand the vulgate tradition, from which with uncanny flair he singled out seven witnesses (his Ψ, roughly equivalent to Clausen's Φ). Jahn and Buecheler, against whom he was reacting, had followed *P* except where it offered manifest nonsense, and sometimes even then. In a typically forceful passage (xi) Housman points out that if Ψ were derived from *P* it should never be used, but seeing that it is independent, its readings must be considered on their merits; and he listed 26 places where *P* had been wrongly preferred (xviii). Some of his expressions might seem to undervalue manuscript authority, as when he recommends an open mind about the relative merits of P and Ψ (xiv); after all, when an editor is about to issue his edition, he has gone beyond that preliminary agnosticism. But in practice he recognised the superiority of *P*, and was ready to prefer it when there was little to choose (xv).

When Housman mocked *Überlieferungsgeschichte* (xxviii) as 'a longer and nobler name than fudge' (*Lucan*, xiii), he was thinking of attempts to conjure up ancient editors ('Nicaeus and his merry men') from the bald assertions of *subscriptiones*; and here at least his scepticism was justified.[1] But though he could analyse acutely the relationships of manuscripts from given data, he was not much interested in looking at them within their historical context: hence some of the deficiencies of his stemma of Propertius, where it is now realised that he was wrong against Postgate.[2] On the other hand the tradition of Juvenal suited him well: he understood the essential set-up, which was quite straightforward, and what was needed was not stemmatological refinement but the discrimination of the critic. Yet even with Juvenal a little more might have been said about the history of the tradition.[3] W.M. Lindsay in his cool review asserts that only one ancient MS survived the dark ages (*CR* 19 (1905), 463); when Housman talks of two ancient editions, he was surely right against the manuscript expert, but he does not really argue the matter. Something more is needed about the character and date of the interpolations, which are already imitated in poets like Dracontius. And when the reader is invited to consider corruption, it is never made clear enough what letter-forms and abbreviations are envisaged.

'No amount ... of palaeography will teach a man one scrap of textual criticism';[4] and a textual critic need not be and seldom is an expert palaeographer. Housman used palaeographic arguments, sometimes to excess, to support solutions that he had reached by reason, but he never believed in altering a letter or two to see what happens.[5] Like Porson, he seems to have derived little enjoyment from collating; his gastronomic tours of France did not lead him to the Pithoeanus at Montpellier, and he did not himself exhaust even the famous Oxoniensis, in which E.O. Winstedt as an undergraduate had discovered 36 unique lines. He relied for his reports of readings on printed sources or inspection by acquaintances; he acknowledges particular indebtedness to the collations of Mr. Hosius, though he is ready enough to insult him elsewhere. When his Ψ group speaks with divided voices, one is left without a clear view of the preponderance of the tradition, but too much information may be more misleading than too little. As Housman retorted to an early work by Knoche: '[h]e complains that Leo and I use too few MSS and despise most of those which Mr. Hosius collated and which Jahn professed to collate. We despise them because we find them despicable' (*CP* 1106).

However superficial Housman's recension may seem, later industry has made remarkably little difference. In 1909 C.E. Stuart called attention to Parisinus 8072 (*R* in later editions), a further congener of *P*, and Housman in his second preface records interesting readings in three places (1.70, 2.34, 2.45); the most striking of these is the first, where he had printed *quae molle Calenum / porrectura uiro miscet sitiente rubetam*. Here Plathner's *rubeta*, which he had not recorded, is now supported not only by *R* but by the first hand of *P* itself; it is certainly right (Housman in his second edition simply says 'perhaps'), for *uiro* must be dative after *porrectura*. In the same year A. Ratti, the future Pope Pius XI, discovered in the Ambrosian Library a palimpsest containing scraps of the fourteenth satire;[6] Housman in his second preface mentions a few notable readings (lv), none of which was both new and true. In 1935 C.H. Roberts published a papyrus from Antinoopolis, which showed errors going back to antiquity (*JEA* 21 (1935), 199ff.). Its most interesting novelty was a mark indicating doubt at 7.192 *adpositam nigrae lunam subtexit alutae*, which had been deleted by Prinz and Jahn (1868) without a word from Housman; in fact the best solution is that of M.D. Reeve, *felix et [sapiens et nobilis et generosus / adpositam] nigrae lunam subtexit alutae* (*CR* 21 (1971), 328).

The scrutiny of minor manuscripts since Housman has produced still less of consequence, and even the better new readings are so thinly supported that they are likely to be conjectures or accidents (for details see Knoche and Martyn). 2.38 *ad quem subridens* (against *atque ita subridens*) may simply be derived from Verg. *A*. 10.742. 5.105 *pinguis torpente cloaca* (of a fish in the sewers) had been proposed by Rutgers, and is worth considering against *torrente*; yet the Elder Pliny talks of torrents in the *cloacae* (36.105). At 8.38 *sic* had been proposed by Junius and endorsed by Housman; at 8.229 *seu personam* is questionable (see Courtney). A more interesting case is 8.240ff., a passage that has been plagued by bad conjectures:

> tantum igitur muros intra toga contulit illi   240
> nominis ac tituli quantum †in Leucade, quantum
> Thessaliae campis Octauius abstulit udo
> caedibus adsiduis gladio.

Here a stray manuscript plausibly reads *sub Leucade*, a phrase that already appears in the scholiast's note; see also Walter of Châtillon, *Alexandreis* 5.493f. *cum fuso sub Leucade Caesar / Antonio* (cited by P.G. McC. Brown, *Hermes* 114 (1986), 498ff.).

In his apparatus criticus Housman helpfully signalled his own conjectures with an asterisk; there are some 30 such asterisks. We may begin with 6.157f. (on a precious ring):

> hunc dedit olim
> barbarus incestae, dedit hunc Agrippa sorori.

For the inanely repeated *dedit hunc*, which disassociates *incestae* from *sorori*, Housman printed *gestare* (lost after -*cestae*), citing Verg. *A*. 12.211 *patribusque dedit gestare Latinis*. This was the kind of proposal that makes 'the hair stand up on many uninstructed heads' (*Man.* V, xxxiv), but it was characteristic of its author (posit the loss of an easily lost word followed by interpolation to restore the metre); Housman rightly insists that the plausibility of a conjecture does not depend on the number of letters changed. I have described *gestare* as the best emendation that has ever been made in Juvenal (*JRS* 52 (1962), 233), and this view has been endorsed by Professor Courtney in his commentary.

Others of Housman's conjectures are almost as brilliant; like Bentley, he was at his best when things were difficult. See 3.216ff. on the presents given to a rich man who has lost his possessions in a fire:

> hic nuda et candida signa
> hic aliquid praeclarum Euphranoris et Polycliti,
> haec Asianorum uetera ornamenta deorum,
> hic libros dabit et forulos mediamque Mineruam,
> hic modium argenti.   220

Here *haec* disrupts the series of *hic ... hic*, and the demonstratives seem one too many for the flow of the passage. Theoretically one might consider a long word in place of *haec Asianorum*, such as *phaecasiatorum* (derived by C. Valesius from the widely attested *phaecasianorum*); but 'slippered gods' has no obvious meaning, and plural *ornamenta* is unattractive in opposition to *aliquid praeclarum*. Housman proposed *hic aliquid praedarum, Euphranoris et Polycliti / aera, Asianorum uetera ornamenta deorum.*[7] The enjambment produced by *aera* is persuasive, and *ornamenta* now fits well. If this is accepted, *praedarum* must follow (since cited by Knoche from a minor manuscript without authority); Courtney reads *hic aliquid praeclarum Euphranoris et Polycliti / aera*; but that compromise impairs the balance.

Juvenal tells us that the young, unlike the old, do not all look the same (10.196f.):

> plurima sunt iuuenum discrimina, pulchrior ille
> hoc atque ille alio, multum hic robustior illo.

The second *ille* is omitted by *P* and a few other MSS; it clearly gets in the way. Housman proposed *ore alio*, 'with another face' (see *Juvenal*[2], liii = *CP* 878f.); but he comments in his apparatus 'alia conici possunt uelut *uoltuque alio*; minus bonum uidetur *aliusque alio*'. The decisive argument is provided by the scholiast's comment *quidam pulcher est, alter eloquens* (cited not by Housman but by Courtney); this looks like a misguided explanation of *ore alio*, and is hard to explain any other way. Martyn's *eloquio*, 'stronger in eloquence than him', produces an impossible confusion of ablatives.

At 10.311ff. we are told of the fate that awaits a good-looking young man:

> fiet adulter
> publicus et poenas metuet quascumque mariti
> exigere irati debent, nec erit felicior astro
> Martis ...

49

Line 313 appears thus in Ψ (with a variant *exire*), which is a foot too long; *P* reads the metrical but meaningless *mariti / irati debet*. Housman proposed *lex irae debet*, pointing to 314ff. *exigit autem / interdum ille dolor plus quam lex ulla dolori / concessit*. Nothing else that has been suggested fits in so well with the following context.

Others of Housman's conjectures are plausible even if less striking. At 4.128 *erectas in terga sudes*, the turbot's fins are described as an omen of war; Housman comments '*in terga erigi non possunt, cum sint in tergo*', and proposes *per terga*. E.W. Bower, followed by Courtney, interprets 'spines running up the back', comparing *erigere aciem in collem* (*CR* 8 (1958), 9); but when *erectas* is applied to stakes, it ought to have a more literal meaning. At 9.60 *meliusne hic* Housman's difficulty about *hic* has not been met, nor his *melius nunc* clearly bettered (though note Castiglioni's *dic*).

It is not the purpose of this paper to analyse the Oxford fragment of the sixth satire, where Housman hoisted his asterisk five times. At 2 *obscenum, et tremula promittit omnia dextra* he restored the metre by transposing *et* to precede *omnia*; but von Winterfeld's *promittens* gives a more natural word-order. At 8f. *longe migrare iubetur / psillus ab eupholio* he ingeniously conjectured *psellus* and *euphono*. At 11 *munimenta umeri pulsatamque arma tridentem* he proposed in the apparatus *pulsata hastamque tridentem*, but one might prefer a long word agreeing with *tridentem*. At 12f. *pars ultima ludi / accipit as animas aliosque in carcere neruos*, his *has* and *aliusque* are obviously right. He sorted out the punctuation of 27 *quem rides? allis hunc mimum! sponsio fiat*. Beyond this he elucidated indecencies that were unintelligible to everybody else.

Housman had no hesitations about the authenticity of the passage: he notes at the end with the braggadocio of an earlier age 'Buechelero ... et Friedlaendero ... Iuuenalis editoribus huius aetatis celeberrimis eisdemque interpolationum patientissimis, hi XXXIV uersus, quia ipsi eos non expediebant, subditiui uisi sunt; quod ne ex hominum memoria excidat, quantum potero, perficiam.' One may agree that once allowance is made for the obscurity of the subject and the uncertainty of the transmission, some of the passage sounds splendidly Juvenalian: note especially 15f. *cum quibus Albanum Surrentinumque recuset / flaua ruinosi lupa degustare sepulchri*, 21f. *oculos fuligine pascit / distinctus croceis et reticulatus adulter* (a passage imitated by Tert., *Cult. Fem.* 2.5.2 *oculos fuligine porrigunt*, like other lines that are certainly by Juvenal). But Housman has not satisfied everybody that the situation described makes sense and is relevant to the context. In particular Axelson[8] has pointed to the difficulty of the closing lines: *noui / consilia et ueteres quaecumque monetis amici* (O29f.) is clumsy compared with the alternative *audio quid ueteres olim moneatis amici* (346).

Housman improved the text of Manilius and Lucan by many

repunctuations, and it is well known how by moving a comma he made sense of Catullus 64.324 *Emathiae tutamen opis, carissime nato.* Similarly at Juv. 2.37 everybody accepts his *ubi nunc, lex Iulia, dormis?*, where previous editors had swallowed *ubi nunc lex Julia? dormis?* At 5.32 he joins *cardiaco numquam cyathum missurus amico* to the following sentence (*cras bibet Albanis aliquid de montibus*), thus sustaining the contrast between the menu of the host and the guests. At 6.454ff. he points to the absurdity of *ignotosque mihi tenet antiquaria uersus, / nec curanda uiris opicae castigat amicae / uerba: soloecismum liceat fecisse marito*; here he punctuates after *uiris* and reads *castiget* with a stray manuscript, but admits merit in the minor variant *haec curanda uiris?* In the fourteenth satire he rightly placed 23-4 between 14 and 15 (I say nothing of his rearrangement of 6.116-21, where no proposal seems entirely satisfactory).

Some of Housman's repunctuations were less plausible: the involuted hyperbata that he delighted to detect in other Roman poets do not suit Juvenal. At 4.117f. he punctuates *caecus adulator dirusque, a ponte, satelles, / dignus Aricinos qui mendicaret ad axes* (that is to say, he takes *a ponte* with *mendicaret*); but he puts forward this fantastic notion with unaccustomed diffidence. Perhaps Juvenal means that Catullus has come from a beggar's mat by the Tiber, and is sinister enough to ply his trade even at Aricia (where the virtuoso performers may have congregated). At 8.142f. Housman punctuates *quo mihi te, solitum falsas signare tabellas, / in templis quae fecit auus*, but his comma after *tabellas* is undesirable (see Courtney); legal documents could be signed in temples, and this provides a better parallel to what follows (*quo si nocturnus adulter / tempora Santonico uelas adoperta cucullo?*). At 13.150ff. Housman reads:

haec ibi si non sunt, minor exstat sacrilegus qui   150
radat inaurati femur Herculis et faciem ipsam
Neptuni, qui bratteolam de Castore ducat;
an dubitet, solitus, totum conflare Tonantem?

But he rightly doubts his own commas round *solitus*, and considers deleting the line as an interpolation (without noticing that J.D. Lewis had said that the line would be better away); other proposals are *solitum est* (Munro), *solus* (codd. dett., Leo), and *solidum* (D.R. Shackleton Bailey, *CR* 9 (1959), 201). There is a further difficulty at 15.131ff.:

                    mollissima corda
humano generi dare se natura fatetur,
quae lacrimas dedit; haec nostri pars optima sensus.
plorare ergo iubet causam dicentis amici
squaloremque rei.   135

Housman pointed out the unnaturalness of taking *squalorem* with *amici* as well as with *rei*; he therefore joined *sensus* to the following sentence as the first object of *plorare* (interpreting 'emotions'). A strong pause occurs in this place elsewhere in the satire (72, 147, 159), and *ergo* can come third word in the sentence (Housman cites 15.171); but this may be less natural when it is second word in the line. As an alternative, Housman suggested genitive *census* ('endowment'); for other proposals see Courtney.

Housman made some suggestions for lacunae that he did not signal with his asterisk. At 1.155ff. his insertion must be on the right lines:

> pone Tigellinum, taeda lucebis in illa   155
> qua stantes ardent qui fixo gutture fumant,
> <quorum informe unco trahitur post fata cadauer>
> et latum media sulcum deducit harena.

Here it is often said that the subject of *deducit* is *taeda*, derived as Latin allows from the ablative of 155; but the burning of a single individual would not produce a trail of light, and a furrow in the sand must be more literal. Housman is less convincing when he proposes a lacuna after 1.131. From 95 to 126 Juvenal has dealt with the *sportula*; then from 127 to 131 he gives a meagre and irrelevant summary of the client's day; then at 132 we are told *uestibulis abeunt ueteres lassique clientes*. Rather than assume a lacuna, it seems best to delete the five irrelevant lines with Jahn (as reported by Knoche); as they are lively in themselves, they presumably originate from a genuine satiric source. Housman's suggestion of a lost line after 2.169 is much more plausible. A less convincing case is 8.159ff.:

> obuius adsiduo Syrophoenix udus amomo
> currit, Idymaeae Syrophoenix incola portae   160
> hospitis adfectu dominum regemque salutat.

Housman admits that after the subject has been repeated by epanalepsis, the verb *salutat* is not wanted; he suggests that a line may have fallen out after 160. Leo's *salutans* had independently occurred to him (*Juvenal*[2], li), but this plausible idea is not recorded in the apparatus.

Something has fallen out at 3.109, where *P* reads *praeterea sanctum nihil ab inguine tutum*, and various stop-gaps have been tried by manuscripts and editors. Housman himself printed *nihil aut tibi ab inguine*, but Juvenal does not elide at the trochaic caesura of the fourth foot. He made a more interesting supplement at 3.203ff. (describing the poor man's modest furniture):

lectus erat Codro Procula minor, urceoli sex
ornamentum abaci, nec non et paruulus infra
cantharus et recubans sub eodem marmore Chiron.   205

Here the scholiast refers to marble statuettes; on the other hand marble is too grand for the sideboard, and in any case now irrelevant. C. Valesius proposed *sub eo de marmore* (which gives a weak demonstrative), Housman much more convincingly *sub eodem e marmore*. As an alternative I have toyed with *rupto de marmore*, to underline the tawdry appearance of the man's ornaments.

Housman's text brackets 17 lines as interpolations, but he was responsible for none of these deletions himself: see 3.113, 3.281, 5.66, 6.188, 8.124, 8.258, 9.119, 11.99, 11.161, 11.165-6, 12.50-1, 13.90, 13.166, 14.208-9 (as well as 6.126, which is poorly attested, and 6.346-8, which have to go if the Oxford fragment is accepted). At 7.50ff. he considers:

nam si discedas, [laqueo tenet ambitiosi   50
consuetudo mali,] tenet insanabile multos
scribendi cacoethes et aegro in corde senescit;

but to say no more, after the general *discedas* there is an anticlimax at *multos* (at Horsfall 1988, 99f. I argue that something has been displaced by line 51). He rightly suspects 8.134 *de quocumque uoles proauum tibi sumito libro*, but does not notice that Ribbeck had questioned the line. He plausibly casts doubt on 8.223 ('facetiarum lepori officere mihi uidetur'), 13.153 (see above), and 14.119 (which had already been questioned by Duff).

Housman often makes conjectures where it would be better to posit an interpolation. There is a striking instance at 6.63ff. (on the reactions of women to the dancer Bathyllus):

chironomon Ledam molli saltante Bathyllo
Tuccia uesicae non imperat, Apula gannit,   65
sicut in amplexu, subito et miserabile longum;
attendit Thymele: Thymele tunc rustica discit.

Here Housman transposed *gannit* and *longum*, awarding himself two asterisks, but Guyet's deletion of 65 seems certain; the conjecture was not known to me when I made it independently in *JRS* 52 (1962), 235. The impossible *miserabile longum* is removed more economically than by Housman; the proper names are put in a pointed relationship (add this to the instances collected at Horsfall 1988, 45); and *sicut in amplexu* gives the plodding explanation of *gannit* that is characteristic of a gloss.

Juvenal says that famous ancestors are of no avail if you behave disgracefully in front of their statues (8.1ff.):

> stemmata quid faciunt, quid prodest, Pontice, longo
> sanguine censeri, pictos ostendere uultus
> maiorum et stantis in curribus Aemilianos
> et Curios iam dimidios umerosque minorem
> Coruinum et Galbam auriculis nasoque carentem,   5
> quis fructus generis tabula iactare capaci
> Coruinum, posthac multa contingere uirga
> fumosos equitum cum dictatore magistros
> si coram Lepidis male uiuitur?

In 7 Housman proposed *pontifices* for *Coruinum* (ineptly repeated from 5) and accepted Withof's *posse ac* for the meaningless *posthac*; but it is simpler to omit 7 with Ψ, and better still to delete 6-8 with Guyet and Jachmann (for the arguments see Courtney). It may seem inconsequential to say 'what avails it to boast of the Curii when you live badly in front of the Aemilii'? (cf. Courtney 1980, 384); but for such a distribution of examples see Nisbet and Hubbard on Hor. *Carm.* 1.7.10.

At 8.108ff. Juvenal describes how extortionate governors loot even the most trifling possessions:

> nunc sociis iuga pauca boum, grex paruus equarum,
> et pater armenti capto eripietur agello,
> ipsi deinde Lares, si quod spectabile signum,   110
> si quis in aedicula deus unicus; haec etenim sunt
> pro summis, nam sunt haec maxima. despicias tu
> forsitan imbellis Rhodios unctamque Corinthon:
> despicias merito.

Housman rightly objected to the *inanis strepitus uerborum* at *haec etenim sunt / pro summis, nam sunt haec maxima*; he proposed *quis sunt haec maxima, despicias tu / forsitan. imbellis Rhodios unctamque Corinthon / despicias merito*. That disrupts the natural sequence *despicias ... Corinthon: despicias merito* (as does Manso's deletion of 111 *si quis ... 112 despicias tu*). It seems best to delete *haec etenim ... haec maxima* and to restore the metre by something like *deus unus* (thus Heinecke and Heinrich).

At 8.199ff. the degenerate nobleman becomes a *retiarius*, who is worse than other kinds of gladiator:

>   et illic
> dedecus urbis habes, nec murmillonis in armis   200
> nec clipeo Gracchum pugnantem aut falce supina;
> damnat enim tales habitus, sed damnat et odit,
> nec galea faciem abscondit: mouet ecce tridentem.

Line 202 is absurdly repetitive (while *sed* is meaningless); if it is deleted (thus Ruperti), the pieces of equipment are set against each other in Juvenal's usual manner. But Housman incredibly transposes *sed damnat et odit* and *mouet ecce tridentem*, thereby destroying the climax.

At 11.167f. Housman proposed *nerui* in the apparatus for *Veneris*, and *ramitis* in the text for *diuitis* (p. xxx 'the conjecture of which I expect to hear most evil'); but it may be enough to delete with Jachmann the irrelevant 168f. *maior tamen ista uoluptas / alterius sexus* (*NGG* (1943), 216ff.). At 15.97f. *huius enim quod nunc agitur miserabile debet / exemplum esse cibi sicut modo dicta mihi gens* Housman proposed *si cui* for *sicut* (accepting the poorly attested *tibi* for *cibi*); but the lines are nonsense (see Courtney), and should be deleted with Guyet. Consider again 16.17f. (on the alleged advantages of military justice) *iustissima centurionum / cognitio est igitur de milite, nec mihi derit / ultio, si iustae defertur causa querellae.* Here Housman proposed *inquit* for the meaningless *igitur*; I believe that the simplest solution is to delete 18, assigning the thought to a centurion (Horsfall 1988, 109).

Sometimes where a difficulty had been solved by deletion, Housman turns a blind eye to the problem. There is an interesting case at 1.81ff. where Juvenal is saying that wickedness is now worse than ever before:

> ex quo Deucalion nimbis tollentibus aequor
> nauigio montem ascendit sortesque poposcit
> paulatimque anima caluerunt mollia saxa
> et maribus nudas ostendit Pyrrha puellas,
> quidquid agunt homines, uotum timor ira uoluptas   85
> gaudia discursus nostri farrago libelli est.
> et quando uberior uitiorum copia?

Lines 85-6 are untrue, disruptive, and produce a top-heavy sentence; they were rightly deleted by the neglected Scholte (with the familiar change to *ecquando* at 87). E. Harrison independently made the same proposal at the Cambridge Philological Society in 1920, but though his colleague Housman was present he did not express dissent either then or later (*CR* 51 (1937), 55).

Housman disregarded many other proposals for deletion, or mentioned them in the apparatus when he might have marked them in the text. I select some notable cases in a list that in no way aims at completeness:[9] 1.14 (Dobree), 1.137-8 (Ribbeck), 3.104 (Jahn), 3.242 (Pinzger), 4.17 (Ribbeck), 4.78 (Heinrich), 5.63 (Ribbeck), 6.138, 359, 395 (Scholte), 6.530 (Paldamus), 7.15 (Pinzger), 7.93 (Markland), 7.135 (cod. U), 9.5 (Guyet), 10.146 (Pinzger), 10.323 (Heinrich), 10.365-6 (Guyet), 13.236 (Jahn), 15.107 *nec enim...* 108 *putant* (Francke). Since Housman's edition deletions have been made by G. Jachmann (*NGG* (1943), 187ff.), U. Knoche (who usually expelled the wrong lines), and M.D. Reeve (note especially *CR* 20 (1970), 135f. for the excision of

10.356 *orandum est ut sit mens sana in corpore sano*). I have made some further suggestions at *JRS* 52 (1962), 233ff.; here I revive two points about Hannibal that have not attracted much attention. 10.148ff. *hic est quem non capit Africa Mauro / percussa Oceano Niloque admota tepenti, / rursus ad Aethiopum populos aliosque elephantos.* Line 150 gives an unconvincing asyndeton (not solved by Astbury's *rursum et ad*), a false suggestion that Hannibal's empire extended far south, and a cryptic reference to 'other elephants'; a concurrence of oddities should always arouse suspicion. 10.159ff. *uincitur idem / nempe et in exilium praeceps fugit atque ibi magnus / mirandusque cliens sedet ad praetoria regis, / donec Bithyno libeat uigilare tyranno.* Line 160 prosaically fills up a gap in the story, *nempe* is used elsewhere by the interpolator (3.95, 13.166), and *magnus* shows a misunderstanding of *mirandus*: Hannibal was an object of astonishment not because he was a great man but because he was a client.

Housman argues forcibly in his introduction for the recognition of interpolations (xxxiff.), and he may have thought himself radical compared with Buecheler, who deleted one line, and Friedlaender, who deleted none at all (whereas Jahn had expelled 70). In practice he was untypically conservative, largely because of the prevailing state of opinion; and perhaps he preferred to show his ingenuity by verbal conjecture. In fact in an author like Juvenal, where there is a significant number of interpolations, nothing should be taken for granted; unsatisfactory lines can be deleted with much more confidence than in a text that has not been tampered with. Many of the interpolations tend to follow recurring patterns;[10] usually they are metrical explanations rather than glosses turned into verse. There are a fair number of marginal cases that may legitimately be questioned even where proof is impossible; it is absurd to think that doubts cannot be raised unless guilt can be proved. Textual critics are not simply concerned with grammatical absurdities, and in the great classical authors they look for something more felicitous than what satisfied a fourth-century schoolmaster. 'Improving the author' it is called by a curious *petitio principii*, but Housman at least should have been free from that misconception.

Housman did well to use the scholia as a guide to the ancient text (xxviii 'our purest source of knowledge'), but sometimes he may attach too much significance to imprecise or ambiguous comments.[11] At 4.5ff. Juvenal says that Crispinus' riches do not matter:

> quid refert igitur quantis iumenta fatiget   5
> porticibus, quanta nemorum uectetur in umbra
> iugera quot uicina foro, quas emerit aedes?
> nemo malus felix, minime corruptor et idem
> incestus, cum quo nuper uittata iacebat
> sanguine adhuc uiuo terram subitura sacerdos.   10

For 8 *minime* Housman read *qum sit* on the basis of the scholia (joining the two sentences together); but there is no need to pursue his reasoning, as he virtually recanted in the second edition (xv). The simplest solution is to delete 8 with Jahn; the point is not the unhappiness of the wicked but the general contempt in which they are held. The interpolator failed to appreciate that *incestus* was the postponed subject of *fatiget, uectetur, emerit*, and so introduced a new line; for similar misunderstandings on his part see Horsfall 1988, 97.

At 9.133f., after mentioning the homosexuals who flock to Rome, Juvenal proceeds:

> altera maior
> spes superest: tu tantum erucis inprime dentem.
> gratus eris, tu tantum erucis inprime dentem.   135

Thus the Pithoeanus, but the repetition is intolerable; the vulgate tradition omitted the last line. In 1889 (*CP* 107f.) Housman confidently proposed *derit amator* for *altera maior* (omitting the last line and making metrical adjustments before *derit*); he supplied one of his unconvincing palaeographical justifications (*derit* turns into *diter*, and 'the difference between *diteramator* and *alteramaior* is not worth considering'). In his edition he takes seriously the scholiast's comment *multos inberbes habes tibi crescentes* (which previously he had waved aside); he now supplies *spes superest: turbae properat quae crescere molli / gratus eris*. But great obscurities will remain (see Courtney), notably the need to provide a transition to 135 *haec exempla para felicibus.*

Juvenal's slave, unlike the rich man's, will be home-born, so that you order your drink in Latin (11.147f.):

> non Phryx aut Lycius, non a mangone petitus
> quisquam erit et magno; cum posces, posce Latine.

For *a magno* (Ψ) P reads *in magno* (which would have to mean 'when you ask for a pint'); neither reading is convincing. Housman proposed and printed *qui steterit magno*, a conjecture that goes back at least to 1891 (cf. *Man.* I, xxxvii); he cites the scholium *quales uendunt care manciparii*, but that may simply be an attempt to interpret the vulgate reading ('sought at a great price'). In fact the emphasis should not be on the price of the rich man's slaves but on their alien origin. G. Giangrande proposed *Inachio* (*Eranos* 63 (1965), 3ff.); that does not seem a natural word for 'Greek' in so prosaic a context (E. Courtney, *BICS* 13 (1966), 41), but there are attractions in some epithet that balances *Phryx, Lycius, Latine.*

At 14.267ff. Juvenal addresses the merchant who suffers at sea while conveying saffron from Cilicia:

Corycia semper qui puppe moraris
atque habitas, coro semper tollendus et austro,
perditus †ac uilis† sacci mercator olentis.

Housman saw that *P*'s *ac uilis* does not go well with *perditus* (while Ψ's *a siculis* is obvious nonsense). He conjectured and printed *ac similis*, i.e. the merchant turns as yellow as his cargo; he cited the scholiast's *tu foetide*, but that may simply be a muddled gloss on *sacci olentis*. In fact sea-sickness seems too temporary an affliction to characterise the man (especially in view of the repeated *semper*); Housman says that he is called *perditus* because he cries *perii* in a storm (*Man.* I, xxxvi), but again one looks for a more permanent attribute. At *JRS* 52 (1962), 237, I proposed *perditus articulis* (he is arthritic from living in a damp ancient ship); cf. Pers. 1.23 *articulis quibus et dicas cute perditus 'ohe'* (where *articulis* is Madvig's necessary conjecture for *auriculis*).

Some other asterisked proposals fail to convince, though they usually contribute to the argument. 6.50f. *paucae adeo Cereris uittas contingere dignae / quarum non timeat pater oscula.* Here Housman's *teretis uittas* is too mild to balance the following clause, and Giangrande's *Cereris uictus* seems to give the required point (*Eranos* 13 (1965), 26ff.); Housman himself had suggested something like *Cereris contingere munera dignae* (*Juvenal*[2], xlvi). 6.194ff. *quotiens lasciuum interuenit illud / ζωὴ καὶ ψυχή, modo sub lodice relictis / uteris in turba*: Housman saw that the endearments of octogenarian women cannot be described as 'recently left under the blanket'. He regarded as certain (xxx) his own *ferendis*, 'only to be endured', and it is undoubtedly on the right lines (see Courtney); but I prefer my own *loquendis*, which may combine better with *uteris* (Horsfall 1988, 96f.). At 9.118 Housman rejects *cum ... tunc* as a solecism, only to produce the questionable elision *tum est his.* 12.12ff. *(taurus) nec finitima nutritus in herba, / laeta sed ostendens Clitumni pascua sanguis / iret et a grandi ceruix ferienda ministro* (*iret et grandi P*). Housman pointed to the ambiguity of *sanguis iret* of the walking bull, and proposed *et grandi ceruix iret ferienda ministro*; but the origin of the bull was shown by his colour rather than his blood. Castiglioni proposed *grandis* for *sanguis*, and I have considered *tergus*; that leaves Housman's problem about *a* with the gerundive (not elsewhere in Juvenal), especially as the scholiast glosses by dative *sacerdoti.* 13.47ff. (on the small number of gods in Saturn's day) *contentaque sidera paucis / numinibus miserum urguebant Atlanta minori / pondere; nondum †aliquis sortitus triste profundi / imperium Sicula toruus cum coniuge Pluton.* Here the meaningless *aliquis* is omitted by *P* and is presumably an interpolation. Housman supplied *imi*, but a proper name would be more forceful; I have suggested *Erebi* (Horsfall 1988, 108). I refrain from discussing 14.71, where Housman ingeniously proposed *si facis ut ciuis sit idoneus;*

I once doubted this (*JRS* 52 (1962), 237), as Courtney does for different reasons, but am now unable to make up my mind.

I turn now to those of Housman's conjectures that are confined to the apparatus. He points to the faulty tense at 2.167f. *nam si mora longior urbem / †indulsit pueris, non umquam derit amator* (the problem is not solved by Clausen's *indulget*, as the verb has jumped from 165 *indulsisse*); he suggests *praebuerit*, and I have tried *induerit* (Horsfall 1988, 91). 8.47ff. *tamen ima plebe Quiritem / facundum inuenies, solet hic defendere causas / nobilis indocti; ueniet de plebe togata / qui iuris nodos et legum aenigmata soluat*; here Housman suggests *pube togata* (to avoid a pointless contrast with *ima plebe*), but he does not mention *togatus* (Scriverius), which elegantly balances *Quiritem*.[12] At 10.184 *huic quisquam uellet seruire deorum*? he reasonably suggested *nollet* to sustain the irony. A more intractable place is 10.326f. *†erubuit nempe haec ceu fastidita repulso (repulsa Ψ) / nec Stheneboea minus quam Cressa excanduit*; here Housman proposed *coepto* for *nempe haec*, but a line has probably fallen out (Markland, Courtney). At 12.78f. *non sic †igitur mirabere portus / quos natura dedit* (on the harbour at Ostia), Housman saw, unlike some editors, that *igitur* is meaningless in the context; his *similes* is too restrictive and his *ullos* too dull, and I have tentatively considered *ueteres*.

Housman does not cite nearly enough conjectures by others; here I record a few cases of particular interest. Jahn placed 3.12-16 (on Egeria's grove) to follow 3.20; this is a necessary transposition, but either something has been lost after 11 (Ribbeck), or 11 should be marked as a parenthesis (my own solution, Horsfall 1988, 92f.). At 3.260f. *obtritum uulgi perit omne cadauer / more animae* Eremita proposed the adverb *uulgo*, 'indiscriminately'; *uulgus* would refer to the common people in general, not like *turba* to a particular crowd. 6.44 *quem totiens texit perituri cista Latini*. In this bedroom farce Latinus, who owns the chest, should be the injured husband rather than the concealed lover; Palmer's *reditturi* (cited by Owen) is worth reviving (cf. Hor. *S.* 1.2.127 *uir rure recurrat*, etc.). 8.219ff. (the matricide Orestes is favourably contrasted with Nero) *nullis aconita propinquis / miscuit, in scaena numquam cantauit Orestes, / Troica non scripsit*. Weidner's witty *Oresten* was ignored by Housman, and the conjecture had to be made again by C.P. Jones, *CR* 22 (1972), 313. At 10.90f. *uisne salutari sicut Seianus, habere / tantundem* Lachmann proposed *auere* (cited by Jahn), which balances *salutari* much better. The verb is normally confined to the imperative, but for the infinitive cf. Mart. 9.6.4 *non uis, Afer, hauere: uale*. 11.96f. *sed nudo latere et paruis frons aerea lectis / uile coronati caput ostendebat aselli*. Henninius proposed *uite*, a certain emendation that has been ignored; he cited the paraphrase at Hyg. *Fab.* 274 *antiqui autem nostri in lectis tricliniaribus in fulcris capita asellorum uite alligata habuerunt*. 13.43ff. (the simple life of the gods in

Saturn's time) *nec puer Iliacus formonsa nec Herculis uxor / ad cyathos, et iam siccato nectare tergens / bracchia Vulcanus Liparaea nigra taberna.* Housman records and ought to have accepted Schurtzfleisch's *saccato* (the nectar's sediment is strained as with wine); he mentions the scholiast's note *exsiccato faeculento aut liquefacto*, where the second word gives the clue.[13] I have recorded some other neglected conjectures, and put forward some new ones, at *JRS* 52 (1962), 233ff. and Horsfall 1988, 86ff.

Where it is a question of weighing one reading against another, Housman's decisions are usually difficult to refute. But at 1.2 he reads *rauci Theseide Cordi* (thus *P*), where Ψ offers *Codri*; *Codrus* is not only a type-name for a bad poet (from Verg. *Ecl.* 7.22), but combines pointedly with *Theseide* to suggest the kings of early Athens. At 1.125f. a client receives the *sportula* on behalf of his wife, who is alleged to be resting in a closed litter: '*Galla mea est*', inquit, '*citius dimitte. moraris? / profer, Galla, caput. noli uexare, quiescet.*' The scholiast assigns *profer, Galla, caput* to the cashier (cf. p. xliv), and this leads better to *noli uexare*; it also seems best to accept Ψ's *quiescit* rather than to derive an idiomatic future from *P*'s *quiescaet* ('don't disturb her because she is resting now' is more to the point than 'if you disturb her, you'll find that she is resting'). At 7.114 Housman follows *P* in calling the charioteer *russati ... Lacernae,* but the cloak used in country drives (1.62) was perhaps too cumbrous for a race; Ψ's Lacertae ('Lizard'), is an excellent name for a quick mover (Courtney cites *ILS* 5293), and as lizards are usually green there is a pointed combination with *russati*. At 8.4f. (on a nobleman's battered statues) Housman reads *et Curios iam dimidios umeroque minorem / Coruinum.* Here 'impaired as to the shoulders' (*umeros P*) is better than 'diminished by a shoulder' (*umero* cod. det.): a statue does not lose a shoulder without losing an arm as well.

Even when he does not debate the text, Housman sometimes gives explanations that are open to challenge. I do not believe that 1.28 *aestiuum ... aurum* refers to light-weight rings for summer wear (for the use of the adjective cf. 4.108, also on Crispinus); or that 1.144 *intestata senectus* means that old age among patrons is unattested (I delete 144 *subitae ... 145 et*); or that 3.4f. *gratum litus amoeni / secessus* illustrates a genitive of quality[14] (I propose *limen*): for all these points I refer to the discussion at Horsfall 1988, 86ff. At 1.47 *omne in praecipiti uitium stetit* Housman interprets 'vice has come to its extreme limit' (*CP* 613f.); that does not convey the precarious position of vice, a thought that leads to the following *utere uelis*, 'use all your energies to attack it.'[15] 7.61f. *aeris inops, quo nocte dieque / corpus eget.* Housman comments that the body needs food night and day rather than money, and mentions sympathetically Ribbeck's *quom*; but this spoils the paradox that we are using up resources even while we sleep.

No critique of Housman's Juvenal can ignore his extraordinary style of debate. His admirers sometimes imply that his opponents deserved all they got, but his gibes are scattered too widely for that defence to be tenable. He could be generous to the schoolmaster S.T. Collins, who at 16.25 *quis tam procul absit ab urbe?* (of a defending pleader), irrefutably proposed *adsit* (lvii 'we ought all to be ashamed that the correction was not made before'). He was indulgent to J.D. Duff's 'unpretending school-edition' (xxix) and to the commentary of H.L. Wilson, who quoted his own work respectfully and made no claims of his own (*CP* 611ff.). But to professional rivals he was persistently offensive, and not just to Owen but to Buecheler and Leo (even Jahn among the dead); and the effect on rising scholars was inhibiting. He rebukes non-critics who at Prop. 3.15.14 read *molliaque immittens* (v.l. *immites*) *fixit in ora manus* (xii); that must be a reprisal against Phillimore, who in his 1901 edition had criticised Housman's boldness in conjecture. He denounces the author of the *TLL* article who by relying on Buecheler's text had failed to pick up *aeluros* at Juv. 15.7 (lvf., repeating his Cambridge inaugural of 20 years before); his solemn rodomontade was absurdly disproportionate to its object[16] ('this is the felicity of the house of bondage' etc.), and caused lasting offence. This reversion to the manners of previous centuries was due not just to a love of truth, 'the faintest of the passions', as he called it, though error grated on him more than on most; the explanation must surely lie in an underlying unhappiness[17] that found a more creditable outlet in his poetry. All this makes one sceptical of the claim that Housman was uniquely objective; less original scholars may find it easier 'to suppress self-will', to use his own phrase (*Man.* V, xxxv).

None of this dislodges Housman from his position: he continues to impress alike by his subtle and original poetry, now more justly valued,[18] the energy of his prose style (especially by academic standards), and his formidable intellectual and rhetorical powers. The *Juvenal* remains the most stimulating introduction to textual criticism that there is, and a classic demonstration of a particularly English mode of scholarship, impatient of theory, sparing of words, displaying no more learning than necessary, going for the vital spot, empirical, commonsensical, concrete, sardonic. Housman himself said that 'a textual critic engaged upon his business is not at all like Newton investigating the motion of the planets: he is much more like a dog hunting for fleas';[19] but the irony should not mislead. Though he himself had felicity of instinct (as every good editor must), he probably showed it less persistently than some other great critics.[20] It is his lucidity of mind and argumentative power that place him next to Bentley, and one can never disagree without being conscious that something may have been missed.

Housman's dominance is so great[21] that it is difficult to avoid the cult of personality, but eulogies concentrate on the most brilliant feats without looking at an edition as a whole. In textual criticism there are horses for courses, and Housman found Juvenal well-suited to his talents: the style was vigorous and incisive, but it did not strain normal Latin usage. Even so, his solutions were often unconvincing, and not just because the edition was undertaken in haste, 'for the relief of a people sitting in darkness' (xxxvi); he had 25 years to change his mind before the second edition, though his manner of argument may not have made retraction easy. It is not that he was too acute for his author, the criticism that used to be orthodox; as he emphasised himself in his London 'Introductory Lecture',[22] the great classical writers had a standard of finish that is lacking in more recent literature. The truth of the matter is that in textual criticism, as in other scholarly activities, you win some and you lose some: new evidence is noticed, fresh arguments are devised, and no edition is sacrosanct. We should not surrender to Housman's authority, and assume that nothing remains to be done: there is no greater incentive for finding corruptions in a text than the fact that corruptions have already been found.

Notes

1. Zetzel 1981, 211ff.
2. Butrica 1984, 6ff.; G.P. Goold in Horsfall 1988, 28ff. (who cites Housman's offensive criticisms of Postgate). See also the chapters of Heyworth and Reeve in the present volume.
3. See now E. Courtney, *BICS* 13 (1966), 38ff., R.J. Tarrant in Reynolds 1983, 200ff.
4. Cited from Housman's 'The application of thought to textual criticism', *PCA* 18 (1922), 68 = Carter 1961, 131 = Ricks 1988, 325 = *CP* 1058.
5. Ibid., Carter 1961, 142 = Ricks 1988, 333 = *CP* 1064-5. See also *Man.* V, xxivf., Kenney 1974, 122f.
6. *CP* 815 'It was a fine August morning which placed in Monsignore Ratti's hand the envelope containing this fragment, and he gives us leave to imagine the trepidation with which he opened it and the joy with which he discovered that the parchment was in two pieces instead of one. When a scholar is so literary as all this, it would be strange if he were quite accurate ....'
7. Housman's proposal is commended by Willis 1972, 66.
8. Axelson 1939, 41ff. = Axelson 1987, 173ff.
9. See also the interesting study of E. Courtney, *BICS* 22 (1975), 147ff. He considers 40 lines 'pretty certainly spurious' (160), but does not include a fair number of interpolations that I should regard as likely or at least possible.
10. I give some instances at *JRS* 52 (1962), 233f.; see also Courtney (as prev. n.), 161. For a more general treatment of the typology of interpolations see R.J. Tarrant, *TAPA* 117 (1987), 281ff.
11. Courtney (as n. 3), 41ff.
12. In the same passage P.G. McC. Brown plausibly deletes *solet hic defendere causas / nobilis indocti* (*CQ* 22 (1972), 374).
13. Martyn attributes *exsaccato* to Schurtzfleisch and *saccato* to myself, an honour I never claimed; the proposal was already known to J. Jessen, *Phil.* 47 (1888), 320, to whom it is assigned in Housman's edition of 1905.

14. Housman cannot have found the passage straightforward: in 1900 he had actually considered taking *amoeni secessus* as a nominative plural (*CP* 518).

15. F.O. Copley, *AJP* 62 (1941), 219ff., D.A. Kidd, *CQ* 14 (1964), 103ff.

16. See especially Wilson 1938, 83ff. = Ricks 1968,14ff.

17. For a realistic view see Graves 1979.

18. See Ricks 1968, 1ff. (with other contributions to this collection), and 1988, 7ff.

19. Carter 1961, 132 = Ricks 1988, 326.

20. This point is made by Goold in Horsfall 1988, 28.

21. For two notable more recent assessments of Housman as a scholar see Brink 1986, 168ff., and Jocelyn 1988, 22ff.

22. Carter 1961, 9ff. = Ricks 1988, 265f.

4

Housman, Lucan, and Fraenkel[1]

S.P. Oakley

[A]nyone who knows enough Latin and wishes to appreciate the difference between a great critic and a great scholar who was not a great critic cannot do better than compare Housman's *Lucan* with Fraenkel's review.[2]

I

'Had Bentley never edited Manilius, Nicolaus Heinsius would be the foremost critic of Latin poetry.'[3] Had Housman never edited Manilius, his edition of Lucan would secure his reputation as one of the foremost editors of classical Latin texts in the twentieth century. Had Housman never edited Lucan, literary critics of Lucan, who recently have done much to further our understanding of the broader themes of his text, would struggle far more with the detailed understanding of their author. Housman professed to have no admiration for Lucan as a poet: 'Lucan would do you no good. He has rhetoric and epigram but no true poetry,' he wrote to J.G. Leippert in 1928.[4] Yet, in Lucan's dense brachylogies, in his hyperbata, predictable only in being surprising, in the fertile imagination displayed by his magnificent quest for point, and in his sheer difficulty, the mature Housman found a poet more than worthy of his attention; conversely, Lucan found in Housman the ideal modern interpreter of his style. Since Housman's death there have been many fine editions of, and commentaries on, classical authors, but in most the advances have been of the kind that many hard-working and learned scholars could have made; to take Lucan as Hosius (1913) bequeathed him and to transform our understanding of the text required an ability granted only to a very select few.

II

Housman published on Lucan first in 1900, in a review of the third fascicle of Postgate's *Corpus Poetarum Latinorum*, for which W.E. Heitland, later a friend in Cambridge, had edited Lucan.[5] By Housman's standards the strictures on the Lucan were quite mild, but they still drew forth from Heitland a reply,[6] to which Housman in turn responded.[7]

Taken together, these pieces foreshadow several aspects of the edition that would appear a quarter of a century later: the observation that Lucan's style was less well understood in Housman's own time than in earlier centuries, the evaluation of Francken's many faults and fewer virtues, the careful choice between ms readings (esp. on 3.276), the careful scrutiny of Bentley's conjectures (esp. on 1.463), and the habitual precision of thought (esp. on 1.531). The retort to Heitland contains also a trenchant expression of his views on how contemporary Germans practised textual criticism, and very well-phrased advice on how far one's opinion of a ms's authority should influence one's assessment of its readings. Probably from this phase of work on Lucan comes the splendid conjecture in 1.234 published in the note on Man. 1.657.[8] That a new edition was needed Housman must have seen; whether he already planned to produce one, there is no knowing, since in this period Manilius dominated.

III

Housman's translation to Cambridge in 1911 effected a great change in his style of teaching, no elementary instruction but many more lectures now being required of him. On no author did he lecture more often than Lucan, the whole of whose poem was discussed between 1912 and 1921: Book 1 in the Lent Term (= L) 1912, Book 2 in the Michaelmas Term (= M) 1912, Book 3 in L 1914, Book 4 in L 1915, Book 5 in L 1916, Book 6 in M 1916, Book 7 in L 1918, Book 8 in L 1919, Book 9 in L 1920, and 9.839-10.546 in L 1921. Before the publication of his edition he lectured again on Book 1 in the Easter Term (= E) 1925; after its publication he lectured in E 1931 and 1935 and on Book 2 in M 1928.[9]

The exercise books in which Housman wrote his lectures remain in Cambridge (see Appendix below). His comments are polished in style and must have been written up from other notes; that these took the form of post-card sized scraps of paper is suggested by some loose leaves in both the lecture-books and Trinity College, Cambridge, adv.c.20.25, Housman's own interleaved copy of his Lucan, in which some correspondence connected with the book survives. Housman includes much more elementary and unoriginal matter than he was to include in his edition.[10]

The work involved in the preparation of these lectures was fundamental to the edition of 1926, and many notes in the edition find a close precursor in the lectures. However, there are differences, since in the lectures Housman's thoughts on Lucan are seen in less developed form: he had not yet made much use of Cortius' edition (which later he was often to cite with approval), and he had not yet divined all the

66

conjectures of his own that he was later to print in text or apparatus. Comments from Housman's lectures that correspond to some of the passages discussed below have been transcribed in an appendix to this essay. A double asterisk (**) beside a passage of Lucan indicates that one should consult this appendix.[11]

IV

Housman had almost certainly decided to edit Lucan by the time he published a short discussion of the text of 7.460-5 in 1920.[12] The edition was published in January 1926 between his editions of *Man.* IV (1920) and *Man.* V (1930). References to his work on it may be found sporadically throughout his correspondence of the 1920s. Of these the most interesting is to be found at Burnett 1.576, addressed to Messrs Macmillan & Co. Housman wished, as usual, to have the book printed and published at his own expense, but Grant Richards, who was publishing his Manilius, was in financial trouble and owed Housman money.[13] When Charles Whibley had suggested that Macmillan might be willing to undertake this task, Housman wrote on 16 October 1924 (Burnet 1.576) to see whether this was indeed the case. However, his enquiry contained the astonishingly provocative sentence '[a]s in 1895 you refused to publish another book of mine, *A Shropshire Lad*, under similar conditions, I did not think this likely; but he assures me that you are now less haughty', and the request was declined. Two years later Macmillan changed their mind, but too late.[14] On 27 December 1926 Housman wrote thus to Sir Frederick Macmillan: 'I am much obliged by your amiable letter. The Lucan however was published last January, and is now nearly sold out, which testifies to such efficiency in the publisher as even you could hardly surpass.'[15] The publisher was Basil Blackwell. Sadly, the reorganisation of the Blackwell archive has not to date produced any correspondence pertaining to the publication of the book, but a few notes from Sir Basil Blackwell to Housman, which do indeed bear witness to the speed at which stock was exhausted, may be found at Trinity College, Cambridge, adv.c.20.25. This volume contains also Housman's instructions for the Addenda and Corrigenda as they appear in the 1927 and subsequent impressions.

V

Eduard Fraenkel, 29 years Housman's junior, was born on 17 March 1888 in Berlin. A pupil of Wilamowitz and Leo, he had made his name with the publication in 1922 of his first and most celebrated book, *Plautinisches im Plautus*. Its success allowed him to move from Professor Extraordinarius in Berlin to Professor Ordinarius in Kiel. At the same time the scope of his writings, which previously had been dominated by Greco-Roman drama and Latin lexicography, expanded. In 1924 he published 'Lucan als Mittler des antiken Pathos',[16] a general lecture that offered a very sympathetic portrait of Lucan, unusual for its time. Having made Lucan the subject of study in seminars in both Berlin and Kiel, it was natural that he should wish to review Housman's edition in the new journal *Gnomon*, of which he was a founder editor.

VI

On the influence and importance of Housman's edition Shackleton Bailey (1987, 74) wrote:

> After sixty years Housman's text, with its apparatus stretching half way into a commentary, remains paramount ... Housman's textual contribution lay not so much in his emendations, of which he was very sparing, as in his choices among existing readings, concisely and for the most part conclusively defended in his notes.

Indeed, given the complexity of Lucan's thought and style, the number of occasions on which reputable recent scholars agree that Housman printed the wrong reading is remarkably small.[17] To write a full review of such a book 85 years after its publication would be pointless: it was fully and properly reviewed on publication,[18] and any assessment of how subsequent scholarship has dissented from Housman's judgement would largely repeat the work of Shackleton Bailey's Teubner editions (1988; 1997[2]).[19] Rather, I shall illustrate the characteristics (mostly virtuous) of the edition with examples, and shall note in passing how far these characteristics were appreciated by Fraenkel, and how far Fraenkel himself made an additional contribution to the study of Lucan.

The manuscripts

The treatment of the evidence provided by the mss is fundamental to the success or failure of any critical edition of a Greek or Latin text. For the readings of the mss that he cited Housman derived his evidence almost entirely from Hosius. For this he should not be criticised: duplication of scholarly labour is pointless; the gains from collation would hardly have repaid the labour involved; and Housman's own special genius was for explication and emendation of Latin texts – not for tasks that a Hosius could accomplish.[20]

He selected ruthlessly from Hosius' apparatus, shedding many *lectiones singulares*. For the student of Lucan's text (as opposed to his transmission) little is lost.[21] However, Fraenkel (1926, 499-502 = 1964, II 270-3) was right to observe that by failing to report corrections to most of the mss that he used, Housman obscured the strength with which some readings were attested in the ninth and tenth centuries. This is particularly important for corrections to the ms Z, in which many interesting readings are first attested.

Housman's remark about *Überlieferungsgeschichte* and fudge – as silly as the 'editorum in usum edidit' on the title-page – was occasioned by the views of Hermann Usener, Hosius' teacher, on the identity of the Paul of Constantinople who corrected an ancestor of P.[22] Housman (*Lucan*, xiii-xviii) explodes much fantasy and shows that the identity and activities of Paul have virtually no practical bearing on the constitution of Lucan's text. But these pages are a rhetorical diversion, of little real importance, even though Fraenkel (1926, 503 = 1964, II 274) thought Housman's thunderbolts 'sehr nötig'.

By far the greatest virtue of Housman's treatment of the mss of Lucan is that he saw more clearly than any earlier scholar that truth inherited from antiquity could lurk in any of his primary witnesses. In a memorable paragraph he explained why this is so (*Lucan*, vi-vii):

> The five manuscripts on which we chiefly depend, **ZPGUV**, cannot be divided and united into families or even classes. The circumstances in which Lucan's text was transmitted from his own time to the scholars of the Carolingian renascence did not afford the requisite privacy and isolation. There were no sequestered valleys through which streams of tradition might flow unmixed, and the picture to be set before the mind's eye is rather the Egyptian Delta, a network of watercourses and canals. Lucan was popular; variant readings were present not only in the margin of books but in the memory of transcribers; and the true line of division is between the variants themselves, not between the manuscripts that offer them. The manuscripts group themselves not in families but in factions; their dissidences and agreements are temporary and transient, like the splits and coalitions of political party; and the utmost which can be done to classify them is to note the comparative frequency of their shifting allegiances.

There is no more elegant statement of the historical and geographical circumstances that make the rigid application of stemmatic method inappropriate for the editing of some classical Latin texts; and for ZPGUV what Housman says is almost entirely true.

However, it is not true, or demonstrably true, for the wider transmission of Lucan in the Middle Ages. Housman's remark 'the true line of division is between the variants themselves, not between the manuscripts that offer them' was aimed at Hosius, who had championed Montpellier H 113 (M) as the best ms of Lucan and who had often and unwisely adopted its peculiar readings. As a rhetorical ploy Housman had deliberately banished M from pp. vi-x of his preface. For much of Lucan it is in fact closely related to Z, and the two witnesses plainly derive in this portion from a shared ancestor; it could easily be included among the mss on which 'we chiefly depend'.[23] Furthermore, Housman had (quite reasonably) ignored the ninth-century mss ABR, which derive from Z: taken as a group ZABRM do constitute a family susceptible to genealogical analysis; the derivation of ABR from Z dates the corrections in Z already mentioned to the ninth century; and ABR, too, contain (admittedly sometimes by contamination – or so one may suspect – but sometimes perhaps by their own innovation) readings attested also in later mss that Hosius and Housman did use.[24]

When some 500 mss of an author survive and when editors use fewer than a dozen, it is natural to wonder whether lost gems lurk in those unexplored; and Housman's 'Delta' and 'factions' may encourage the notion that mss of the later Middle Ages may contain evidence for the constitution of the text independent of that which he and Hosius employed. Fraenkel certainly thought that this could be the case; he enthusiastically collated Laur. 35.10 (s.xii) and regularly cited it and other Laurentiani.[25] Therefore it is worth making these three observations. First, for a ms to make a really notable contribution to the constitution of the text of Lucan, with readings both new and true, it would have to have an ancestry at least partly independent of all other mss and reaching back to a good copy of the text made in the years immediately after Lucan's death; that such a ms exists is conceivable but scarcely likely. Second, just because the tenth-century mss used by Hosius and Housman are not susceptible to genealogical analysis and just because a stemma cannot be used mechanically to edit the text, it does not follow that a stemma cannot be drawn for many of the mss written between 1000 and 1500; indeed, it is very probable that proper investigation of another 450 mss of Lucan would show that very many derive from extant witnesses. Therefore without this proper investigation it is extremely dangerous to claim that any ms in the Laurenziana or elsewhere provides support for any reading. What if the ms in question derived ultimately from one of ZMPGUV?[26] Fraenkel's use of the Laurentiani is like the fumblings of those playing blind man's buff. Third, this criticism applies also to those allergic to genealogical and historical investigation who practise the gospel of 'untrammelled eclecticism'[27] in their work on other traditions; one fears that the Englishmen among them have been encouraged more by Housman's remarks than by Pasquali.

Gotoff (1971) fires many salvoes at Housman's Lucan as it sails its imperious course, and he scores several undeniable hits. Yet how much does it matter? That he had provided a very poor model for the aspiring student of *Überlieferungsgeschichte* would not have bothered Housman; he would have been more pleased that Tarrant's survey (Reynolds 1983, 215-18) shows that the judgements in the paragraph quoted still stand.[28]

Explanation of the text

Fraenkel (1926, 530-1 = 1964 II 307) drew attention to the numerous emendations, many certain, that Housman proposed in both the scholia to Bern 370 edited by Usener in 1869 and the *adnotationes* edited by Endt in 1909.[29] However, he did not do justice to one of the most striking features of Housman's edition: the employment of the scholia on Lucan for elucidation of the author's meaning. On these scholia Housman comments thus (vi): '[t]he scholiasts were not well equipped in the matter of brains for understanding him, but they possessed another organ: they understood him with the marrow of their bones, which was the same stuff as his'. As the years went by Housman perhaps became increasingly aware of the importance of these scholia; he makes rather less use of them in his lectures. The apparatus to 2.591 *noti ... erepto uellere Colchi* provides a good and very brief illustration of Housman's employment of them: '*noti erepto uellere*, ante Iasonem ignoti: recte **a**'.[30]

Fraenkel (1926, 529-30 = 1964, II 305-6) justly remarked that one may learn a great deal about Latin idiom and poetic style from Housman's notes. Often Housman explains crisply phrases, idioms, lexical items, and metrical practice, regularly adducing material for the first time.[31] Unravelling hyperbaton was a particular speciality. For example, at 2.174-6** Hosius had printed

cum uictima tristis
inferias Marius forsan nolentibus umbris   175
pendit, inexpleto non fanda piacula busto.

Housman removed the comma, and explained the order as *cum uictima Marius, umbris* (abl.) *forsan tristes inferias nolentibus, pendit piacula*.[32]

Some of the longer notes contain large and important stores of information, and Fraenkel drew attention to some of the best. Two are selected here for more extended discussion.

In the famous passage at the beginning of the poem in which Pompey and Caesar are contrasted, Lucan writes (1.143-5): *sed non in Caesare tantum / nomen erat nec fama ducis, sed nescia uirtus / stare loco, solusque pudor non uincere bello*. This is Housman's comment:

> **145** *non uincere bello*, 'sine bello uincere' c, 'ut erubesceret, si sine proelio quod cupiebat implesset, id est uel deditione uel foedere' a. V 814 *n o n superi t a m laeta parabant*, VII 393 *puluere u i x tectae p o t e r u n t monstrare*, Varr. Atac. fr. 20 Baehr. *Indica n o n magna m i n o r arbore crescit harundo*, Gell. III 16 21 *negotio n o n rei tunc p a r u a e postulante*. Luc. II 439-46, III 51 sq. *nec uincere tanti, | ut bellum differret, erat*, 360-6, VII 96 *metuunt ne non cum sanguine uincant*.

That the scholiasts and Housman are right is at once obvious: if *non* be taken with *uincere*, the sense is impossibly flat. The virtues of

Housman's note are also immediately apparent: he cites six parallel or analogous passages in which *non* or *uix* is thrust forward and away from the word it modifies (all, it seems, gleaned from his own personal reading), and three passages from elsewhere in the poem that confirm his interpretation. In the marginalia in his own copy he adds references to Gratt. 42-3, Val. Fl. 1.284, and Löfstedt 1928-33, II 397-8.

On 1.333** *quem tamen inueniet tam longa potentia finem?* Housman's note begins thus:

> **333** *tamen*, quamuis *tam longa*. hoc Cortius intellexit, se non intellegere ostenderunt Hortensius Oudendorpius Bentleius Franckenius, ceteri non ostenderunt [i.e. they offered no explanation]. omittitur *quamuis* ut I 378 et III 251, sed praeterea anteponitur *tamen*, quod fit Verg. *Aen.* III 341 *ecqua t a m e n puero est a m i s s a e cura parentis* (quamuis amissae)

He then goes on to cite eighteen more passages. The note remains an excellent starting-point for anyone interested in concessive sentences in which *quamquam/quamuis* is omitted and *tamen* is brought illogically forward, and nowhere are more examples cited.[33] Whether Housman had consulted Kühner-Stegmann II 98 it is hard to say, since he cited grammars and lexica only when they erred; but there only three of Housman's passages are cited, together with the irrelevant Cic. *Fam.* 12.10.4. *tamen* was something of a speciality of Housman's: on Man. 4.413 he discussed the related idiom, in which *quamuis* is omitted but *tamen* more naturally comes after the word or phrase bearing the concessive notion (as at e.g. Verg. *Ecl.* 1.27 *libertas, quae sera tamen respexit inertem*).[34]

Repunctuation

Housman's punctuation of the text was as great as any of his services to Lucan; it illustrates supremely well his feeling for sense and style and the power of his concentration. Knowing that punctuation often reveals whether or not an editor had correctly understood a passage, he took great pains to point out who first had punctuated a passage correctly, and he regularly criticises editors for faulty punctuation. Often he was the first to punctuate correctly. Here are three examples of his improvements.

5.104-10. Only what has been fixed by fate is uttered at the Delphic oracle, which makes no allowance for human prayers. This is Hosius' text:

> haud illic tacito mala uota susurro
> concipiunt. nam fixa canens mutandaque nulli   105
> mortales optare uetat iustisque benignus
> saepe dedit sedem totas mutantibus urbes,
> ut Tyriis ... | dedit ... | sustulit ... | resoluit.

And this is Housman's:

> haud illic tacito mala uota susurro
> concipiunt, nam fixa canens mutandaque nulli   105
> mortales optare uetat; iustisque benignus
> saepe dedit sedem totas mutantibus urbes,
> ut Tyriis ... | dedit ... | sustulit ... | resoluit.

Housman saw that the clause introduced by *nam* goes closely with what precedes, and that the clause containing *dedit* is part of the sequence that follows.

5.310-13. Caesar faces his mutinous troops, and the poet laments that they have tired of war before their commander. This is Hosius' text:

> Non pudet, heu! Caesar, soli tibi bella placere   310
> iam manibus damnata suis? hos ante pigebit
> sanguinis? his ferri graue ius erit? ipse per omne
> fasque nefasque rues?

And this is Housman's:

> Non pudet, heu, Caesar, soli tibi bella placere   310
> iam manibus damnata suis? hos ante pigebit
> sanguinis? his ferri graue ius erit, ipse per omne
> fasque nefasque rues?

As Housman observed, the poet does not ask whether the *ius ferri* will be burdensome to the troops: he shows that it is burdensome. Rather, he laments that, though it is burdensome to the troops (*his* = τούτοις μέν), Caesar will still (*ipse* = αυτὸς δέ) rush to pervert all morality.

7.419-23. The poet laments that Rome has fallen from the height of prosperous empire into the abyss of civil war. This is Hosius' text:

> quo (*with* Z) latius orbem
> possedit, citius per prospera fata cucurrit.   420
> omne tibi bellum gentis dedit omnibus annis:
> te geminum Titan procedere uidit in axem;
> haud multum terrae spatium restabat eoae.

And this is Housman's:

> quae (*with most witnesses*) latius orbem
> possedit, citius per prospera fata cucurrit?   420
> omne tibi bellum gentis dedit, omnibus annis
> te geminum Titan procedere uidit in axem;
> haud multum terrae spatium restabat Eoae.

With Hosius' text the statement in 419-20 is intolerable when surrounded by questions including a second person. However, the scholia on Bern 370 explain 419 *quae* (agreeing with *urbs* understood from *Roma* in 418) as introducing a question, and Housman saw that this is right. He showed that the ellipse of *urbs* can be paralleled, and that *citius per prospera fata cucurrit* means not 'more swiftly came to the end of felicity' but 'more swiftly joined one success to another'. In punctuating 420-1 Housman followed the anaphora *omne ... omnibus*; as he observed, Hosius' text makes the first clause too long, the second too short.[35]

Fraenkel (1926, 530 = 1964, II 306) rightly drew attention to this aspect of Housman's edition.[36] Interestingly, the only stricture of his that Housman accepted concerned repunctuation – at 9.490-2, where Lucan describes the manner in which the wind destroyed city walls.[37] Housman had printed this:

saxa tulit penitus discussis proruta muris   490
effuditque procul miranda sorte malorum:
qui nullas uidere domos uidere ruinas.

Fraenkel (1926, 525-6 = 1964, II 300-1) removed the colon and placed a semi-colon before *miranda*. Even though the authenticity of the verses is very suspect,[38] he was probably right to take *miranda sorte malorum* as referring to the circumstances attendant upon the people and not to the manner in which the storm operates.

Choice of reading

In general, the text of Lucan is well preserved, and editors are better able to show their mettle in choosing between readings than by choosing between conjectures. Housman's note on 4.252-3** *ac, uelut occultum pereat scelus, omnia monstra / in facie posuere ducum: iuuat esse nocentis*, where Hosius and most editors had printed *faciem*, provides a good illustration of the sureness of his touch:

253 facie (Z)ς, -em W: *in facie* ut vi 158 sq. *peterem felicior umbras | Caesaris in uoltu* et passim *in ore, in oculis. in conspectu ponere* septiens in thes. ling. Lat. adfertur, nusquam accusatiuus.

Fraenkel's touch (1926, 512-14, 516-17 = 1964, II 285-7, 289-91) in discussing passages of this kind was less sure. Sometimes he was plainly right against Housman (e.g. on 2.59-61, 4.427, 6.24), sometimes plainly wrong (3.149, 408-11, 6.708-9).

Very occasionally, Housman makes a gaffe that gives heart to lesser mortals. At 2.289-92**, Cato tells Brutus that no one could sit idly by as the cosmos comes to ruin:

> sidera quis mundumque uelit spectare cadentem
> expers iste metus? quis, cum ruat arduus aether,   290
> terra labet mixto coeuntis pondere mundi,
> compressas tenuisse manus?

Thus Shackleton Bailey and most of Housman's witnesses. However, ZM have *complosas* or *complossas*, which latter Housman adopts commenting '**compressas** ... edd. plerique, non apte, compressas enim manus tenet qui opem ferre potest nec uult. *complosas* participium, ut Lucr. I 140 *sperata* (quam spero), sine praeteriti temporis notatione ponitur, ut sit *complosionem manuum tenuisse*, id est cohibuisse, abstinuisse a manibus complodendis'. Housman's views are seen more clearly in his lecture notes, transcribed below. However, the justification of *complossas* is (to put it politely) forced in the extreme, while *compressis manibus* was a proverbial expression for standing idly by[39] and goes very well with *expers*.

Choice of conjecture

When editors judge that no authoritative ms offers acceptable sense, they must adopt an emendation. As one would expect, Housman's judgement in such matters was excellent, and Fraenkel (1926, 506-7 = 1964, II 278-9) well notes the careful (but unsurprising) attention that he gives to the conjectures of Bentley.[40] It is perhaps of most interest to discuss passages on which Housman and Fraenkel disagreed.

7.19-24. Pompey dreams about Rome and his earlier triumphs, anxiously:

> seu fine bonorum
> anxia <u>uenturis</u> ad tempora laeta refugit,   20
> siue per ambages solitas contraria uisis
> uaticinata quies magni tulit omina planctus,
> seu uetito patrias ultra tibi cernere sedes
> sic Romam fortuna dedit.

Bentley, followed by Housman and Shackleton Bailey, conjectured *mens curis*, perhaps the most brilliant conjecture in Lucan. Housman, after noting that one set of scholia contains a reference to *mens*, observed 'non illa quies quae 21 sq. contraria uisis uaticinari solere dicitur uenturis anxia erat, sed sopitus ducis animus; et tribus enuntiatis aut tria subiecta requirimus aut unum. quamquam ipsum per se sane quam aptum est *uenturis*'. Fraenkel (1926, 507 = 1964, II 279), seizing on Housman's last remark, supported the paradosis, holding 'dass man die Antithese *anxia uenturis ad tempora laeta refugit* unter keinen Umständen zerstören darf'. In view of what Housman says, I should gladly sacrifice the antithesis to gain better sentence-structure.

Sometimes, however, Housman ignored conjectures of Bentley that may well be true.[41]

5.169-72. The Pythia is filled with Apollo:

> bacchatur demens aliena per antrum
> colla ferens, uittasque dei Phoebeaque serta   170
> erectis discussa comis per inania templi
> ancipiti ceruice rotat...

Neither Housman nor Shackleton Bailey deems Bentley's *corda gerens* for *colla ferens* worthy of mention; but Fraenkel (1926, 507 = 1964, II 280) well asked what *aliena ... colla ferens* was meant to mean, especially with *ancipiti ceruice* following. The paradosis is not certainly corrupt: 'with her neck under possession' is the answer given in Duff's Loeb, *alienus* having the sense 'not under one's control'; and Professor Reeve suggests that, if the text be sound, Lucan would have wanted us to understand *alienum iugum collo ferens*. However, *corda* is found twice in the passage of Virgil (*A.* 6.49, 80) that has influenced Lucan, and with it the picture has a proper gradation and repetition is avoided.[42]

Fraenkel drew attention also to some conjectures by others which Housman might have adopted.

4.593-7. The Antaeus episode begins:

> 'Nondum post genitos Tellus ecfeta gigantas
> terribilem Libycis partum concepit in antris.
> nec tam iusta fuit terrarum gloria Typhon   595
> aut Tityos Briareusque ferox; caeloque pepercit
> quod non Phlegraeis Antaeum sustulit aruis.'

Housman writes '**595** pro *terrarum* anonymus Burm. obs. misc. crit. ii p. 193 *genetricis*; sed uide 643 *terris*, 650 *terras*, 653 *terris*'. Fraenkel (1926, 509 = 1964, II 281), in one of his most incisive comments, wrote 'Darin ist *terrarum* unerträglich. Die von Housm. beigebrachten Belege für den Gebrauch des Plurals von terra innerhalb dieser Partie helfen garnichts; die Erde, deren ἄγαλμα Typhon ebenso wie Tityos und Briareus genannt wird, muss an dieser Stelle als wirkliche Person bezeichnet gewesen sein, nur so bekommt auch das folgende *pepercit* sein Subject'. Shackleton Bailey rightly needed no more convincing.

Housman's own conjectures

In one of his most wounding remarks Housman described the conjectures made by (the still living) H.W. Garrod as 'singularly cheap and shallow'; a few pages later he went on to write that '[t]he first virtue of an emendation is to be true; but the best emendations of all are those which are both true and difficult, emendations which no fool could find'.[43] Housman's conjectures in Lucan (which, as in his Juvenal and Manilius, he conveniently signalled with an asterisk) are never shallow and are often true.

Fraenkel (1926, 509-10 = 1964, II 281-2) gave unqualified approval to conjectures made by Housman at 1.234, 3.159, 5.430, 6.782, and 9.368 (this last not promoted by Housman beyond his apparatus); all are adopted by Shackleton Bailey. The first will serve as well as any other to illustrate Housman's brilliance in conjectural emendation.

1.233-5. Caesar has just crossed the Rubicon, declaring his determination to fight, and has marched through northern Italy by night. Day, a gloomy day, now breaks:

> iamque dies primos belli uisura tumultus
> exoritur; seu sponte deum, seu turbidus auster
> inpulerat, maestam tenuerunt nubila lucem.   235

As we have seen, Housman had proposed *sed* for the first *seu* already in 1903. In the apparatus of his edition he now offers a full explanation, observing that the train of thought (*iamque dies oritur: tenuerunt nubila lucem*) is defective, that *sed* is needed (as Housman says, 'dies exoritur illa quidem sed nubibus obscurata'), that the first *seu* can be omitted in expressions of this kind (he cites Lucr. 3.132-3, Hor. *Carm.* 1.32.6-8, and Verg. *A.* 12.685-6 *auulsum uento, seu turbidus imber / proluit*), and that the postulated corruption is easy. One should not be deceived into thinking that it required no great ability to change *seu* to *sed*; on the contrary, it is testimony to Housman's powers of concentration that he was the first to see that the paradosis was wrong.

However, it will again be more instructive to discuss conjectures impugned by Fraenkel than those that have proved uncontroversial.

1.223-7**. Here is how Hosius lets Caesar cast his die:

> Caesar, ut aduersam superato gurgite ripam
> attigit Hesperiae uetitis et constitit aruis,
> 'hic', ait, 'hic pacem temerataque iura relinquo;   225
> te, Fortuna, sequor; procul hinc iam foedera sunto.
> credidimus fatis, utendum est iudice bello.'

Heinsius saw that the perfect tense of *credidimus* produces nonsense: if Caesar in the present abandons *pax* and *iura* in order to trust Fortune, it is absurd for him then to say that he 'has trusted his fates', when *fatis* has a meaning little different from *Fortuna*. Heinsius' own conjecture, *credimus en fatis*, is sensible and respectable and deserved better than to be ignored by Hosius. Housman's *credidimus satis his* (with a full stop placed after *sequor* and a semi-colon after *sunto*) is a magnificent divination, both giving excellent sense (*his* refers back to *foedera* and contrasts strongly with *bello*) and being diplomatically plausible (*his*

77

could easily have been omitted by haplography and *s* and *f* are regularly confused).[44] Fraenkel (1926, 510 = 1964, II 282) defends the paradosis thus: 'd. h. "wir haben uns auf die Schicksalssprüche verlassen [vgl. z. B. Verg. Aen. 10, 67 *Italiam petiit fatis auctoribus*], jetzt muss der Krieg als Richter entscheiden", entscheiden nämlich über die *fides* der *fata*, durch die Caesar zum Bürgerkriege getrieben worden ist.' This cannot be refuted, but it is hard to see how anyone could divine that war was to be *iudex* not of Caesar's cause (the obvious meaning) but of *fata*. Reviewing contrasting defences of the paradosis, Shackleton Bailey first rejects Getty's (in this the perfect is referred to the present: 'my trust has always been in my destiny and still is'),[45] and then terms Fraenkel's *mirabiliora*, the comparative not being unjust.[46]

2.550-4**. Pompey expostulates that, when the fates wanted to join Caesar to Camillus and other heroes, he has chosen to behave like *populares* who had to be killed, for example Lepidus (put down by Catulus) and Carbo and Sertorius (put down by Pompey himself):

> quamquam, siqua fides, his te quoque iungere, Caesar,   550
> inuideo nostrasque manus quod Roma furenti
> opposuit. Parthorum utinam post proelia sospes
> et Scythicis Crassus uictor remeasset ab oris,
> ut simili causa caderes, qua Spartacus, hostis.

> qua ... hostis *WC* : quod ... hosti *ZM*

With this text, Pompey regrets to have to link Caesar with the likes of Carbo and Sertorius (whom he himself had put down) and that Rome has put Pompey himself in the way of Caesar's madness. Rather, he wishes that Crassus, who had defeated the slave Spartacus, had not died in Parthia: since Caesar's *causa* is similar to that of the slave Spartacus, he like Spartacus should die an enemy of Rome. Housman with justice remarked 'inepte editur *ut simili causa caderes, qua Spartacus, hostis*, neque enim, ut hostis fieret Caesar et simili ac Spartacus causa caderet, Crasso reduce opus erat; nequid de *simili qua* pro *simili eius causae qua* posito dicam'. Housman lists two shallow conjectures: Schrader had proposed *illi* for *hosti(s)*, Francken *quo ... ense* for *quod/qua ... hosti(s)*; he acidly remarked 'neque diu deerit qui *qua ... hasta* coniciat'. His own solution is both more economical and cuts deeper. He proposed *quoi* (i.e. *cui*) ... *hosti*, which he glossed 'ut, quoniam causa tua similis est, ab eodem quo Spartacus hoste [that is, Crassus] prosternerere'. This gives good Latin (Housman quotes parallels for both the dative *hosti* and *simili causa* as ablative absolute) and changes but one letter of the reading of ZM.

Fraenkel (1926, 510-11 = 1964, II 283-4) objected that elsewhere Housman did not value Z and M very highly; that the point of the sentence should be that Caesar is being termed a *hostis patriae*; that the weight of the sentence falls on *hosti(s)*, which ought therefore to refer to Caesar; and that *causa cadere* is a technical term from law (Fraenkel additionally noted some other legal technical terms in Lucan missed by commentators) and that its point here is that both Caesar and Spartacus were *hostes* of the Roman state. To which one may retort[47] that there is no reason why the truth should not be found in ZM (see, e.g., verse 570 on the same page of Housman's edition); that, with Housman's conjecture, the weight that *hosti* has to bear only reinforces the clever point (Caesar is worthy, like Spartacus, not of a Pompey as an opponent but a Crassus); that without Housman's conjecture Pompey's whole reference to Crassus is largely gratuitous;[48] that to make Pompey describe Caesar and Spartacus as enemies of Rome is to make him say something very obvious; that the fact (if it be a fact)[49] that *causa cadere* is technical is an instance of Fraenkel's judgment being affected by his learning, since even with Housman's conjecture the technical sense could be felt.[50]

Sometimes, however, Fraenkel is right against Housman.

5.611-13. Lucan, vying with his uncle to produce the most cataclysmic storm yet unleashed in Latin literature, has just said that the *pelagus* had remained in its place (*mansisse loco*). However, he goes on to say that some seas were transported from one region to another:

> nam parua procellis
> aequora rapta ferunt (*sc.* uenti): Aegaeas transit in undas
> Tyrrhenum, sonat Ionio uagus Hadria ponto.

Housman comments thus on the paradosis: 'maria alia aliis minora sunt, paruum nullum est (nisi forte Oceano collatum, quod nunc non fit), nedum quae hic rapta dicuntur Tyrrhenum et Hadriaticum, hoc loco poeta parua fateretur. opponuntur inter se *pelagus*, hoc est mare uniuersum, et singulae eius partes quamuis ingentes, quae ueri superiectione fidem et modum egressa uento abreptae esse finguntur'. He therefore conjectured *priua*, and Shackleton Bailey follows. However, after Lucretius *priuus* is not found in Latin poetry with this sense,[51] and Fraenkel (1926, 511 = 1964, II 284) correctly objected: 'nur hätte er (sc. Housman) nicht bezweifeln sollen, dass Lucan in der ihm eigenen übertreibenden Art die Einzelmeere im Gegensatz zu dem gesamten *pelagus* als *parua aequora* bezeichnen kann, und hätte nicht das stilwidrige *priua* einführen sollen.' *priuus* was doubtless lodged in Housman's capacious memory from his very good knowledge of Lucretius, on whom he lectured; this is a good example of his cleverness mastering his judgement.

4.715-19. Juba is pleased that Curio had defeated Varus:

> tristia sed postquam superati proelia Vari   715
> sunt audita Iubae, laetus, quod gloria belli

sit rebus seruata suis, rapit agmina furtim
obscuratque suam per iussa silentia famam
hoc solum metuens incauto ex hoste uideri.

ex *Z²*: ab *WC* uideri *Z¹*: timeri *Z²WC*

ab is unmetrical after *incauto*. Hosius failed to realise that the one thing Juba feared was not that Curius should *see* him (flat and unpointed) but that he should *fear* him. Grotius and Cortius did realise this, but Housman adorned their favoured *hoc solum metuens incautus ab hoste timeri* with 'inepte', not altogether unfairly. He printed his own *incauto metuentis* (agreeing with a putative genitive inherent in *suam*) for *metuens incauto*, but Anderson (1927, 29) rightly objected that this is solecistic when the possessive pronoun refers to the subject of the sentence. The conjecture is anything but shallow, but, again, this is an instance of Housman's being overimpressed by his own ingenuity. However, Fraenkel's feeling for style deserted him, too: he thought that Grotius' reading 'ist echt lucanisch zugespitzt' but failed to see that *hoc solum* has greater force with *incauto*. Even though the corruption of *ex* to *ab* is odd (as Housman observed), the simplest, and most pointed, solution is *hoc solum metuens incauto ex hoste, timeri*, adopted by Shackleton Bailey. That Housman knew in his bones that he was wrong is suggested by his later marginal comment ?*metuens sibi* (i.e. *hoc solum incauto metuens sibi ab hoste, timeri*), which gives good sense but has an unacceptable elision and is less economical than what Shackleton Bailey prints.

Now a passage (6.518-20) in which Fraenkel proposed his own conjecture. Erichtho emerges from tombs:

> si nimbus et atrae
> sidera subducunt nubes, tunc Thessala <u>nudis</u>
> egreditur <u>bustis</u> nocturnaque fulmina captat.   520

Housman was unhappy with *nudis ... bustis* ('busta enim cur nuda, hoc est opinor spoliata, hic appellentur non satis apparet') but was not convinced that *pedibus* for *bustis* (Burman) was the answer. Håkanson (1979, 43) thought that *nudis* meant 'unprotected' or 'bare', Shackleton Bailey (1981, 57) more probably that '[t]he tomb was bare because the witch had thrown out its contents when she took up her lodging in it' (cf. 511-12). We may agree with both that Fraenkel's *Thessalis udis* (1926, 508 = 1964, II 281) is an almost comically tasteless conjecture.

Deletions

Housman's preface (xviii-xxii) shows that there is an uncomfortably large number of lines which have only a slender foothold in the tradition; and a vexing consequence of the contaminated ms tradition of Lucan is that one is deprived of the help of a stemma in deciding whether to excise verses which appear in only a minority of PGUV. Many verses had been excised by Hosius and previous editors, but Housman's own attitude, as in his edition of Juvenal, was to be very cautious about excising anything except the most obvious interpolation. In this he has been followed by, for example, Shackleton Bailey, and, suspicious though one may be, it is rare that suspicion can be backed up with conclusive arguments against Lucan's authorship.[52]

Perhaps because he was denied the gift of textual divination, Fraenkel throughout his career was an enthusiastic hunter for interpolations,[53] with success in *Phoenissae* but less happily in *Choephori* and Petronius.[54] In Lucan, most of the lines for whose deletion he argued remain in Shackleton Bailey's text. One example will show why. At 7.87-92, reluctantly urged on by a speech of Cicero, Pompey agrees to fight:

'si placet hoc' inquit 'cunctis, si milite Magno,
non duce tempus eget, nil ultra fata morabor:
inuoluat populos una fortuna ruina
sitque hominum magnae lux ista nouissima parti.   90
testor, Roma, tamen Magnum quo cuncta perirent
accepisse diem.'

Verse 90 is omitted in ZM. Housman says nothing, but Fraenkel (1926, 520 = 1964, II 294) says 'meinem Stilgefühl ist diese schlaffe Ausweitung nach dem monumentalen Verse 89 *inuoluat populos una fortuna ruina* unerträglich, ich urteile genau wie Cortius: "ignavus versus est et ab glossatore effictus"'. On the contrary, the climax works well spread over two verses, and *parti* (referring to just the losing side) contrasts effectively with *populos* (between them both sides involved all nations). Many of Fraenkel's arguments against other passages are similarly insecure.

In his discussion of interpolation Fraenkel (1926, 517-27 = 1964, II 291-303) made two valid objections to Housman's procedures. First, that in defending poorly attested verses Housman's arguments for their omission through purely palaeographical reasons were sometimes flimsy;[55] in this Fraenkel must be right. Second, that Housman took no interest in how texts of Lucan in late antiquity may have appeared. Housman had conceded (xxx) that some blemishes in the text of Lucan may have been due to the imperfect revision of the text at the author's death. Fraenkel developed this further, hypothesising that the author or his first editors passed on a text that included lines by Lucan either imperfectly worked into their context or left as possible alternatives to those in the text; that these were marked by an obelus or the like in ancient copies; that both the varying response of late antique and early mediaeval scribes to these marks and subsequent contamination explains the erratic distribution of many of these lines in the mediaeval manuscripts; and that ZM more than other witnesses reflect these ancient obeli. The hypothesis is bold, may seem far-fetched, and Fraenkel undoubtedly pushed it too far; yet it has some merit because it explains the presence in some witnesses of verses (e.g. 6.556, 7.796) for the interpolation of which there is no obvious reason.

Abuse

An elaborate edition with apparatus criticus and commentary was produced in 1896 and 1897 by C.M. Francken. Hardly a page of it can be read without anger and disgust. Francken was a born blunderer, marked cross from the womb and perverse; and he had not the shrewdness or modesty to suspect that others saw clearer than he did, nor the prudence and decency to acquaint himself with what he might have learnt from those whom he preferred to contradict ... The width and variety of his ignorance are wonderful; it embraces mythology, palaeography, prosody, and astronomy, and he cannot keep it to himself ... For stupidity of plan and slovenliness of execution his apparatus criticus is worse than Breiter's apparatus to Manilius; and I never saw another of which that could be said. (*Lucan*, xxxiv-xxxv)

Thus runs one of Housman's best-known criticisms of a dead scholar. Yet, more secure in his own eminence than he had been a quarter of a century earlier, and with no need to justify his earlier views (contrast the final volume of commentary on Manilius), he reined back his notoriously polemical style. Though jibes,[56] jokes,[57] and adverse criticism abound, one must in general search elsewhere for his cruellest witticisms. Contemporary reviewers,[58] however, objected above all to his treatment of Hosius, whose errors are noted time and again in the apparatus criticus.[59] Since he owed his information about the mss almost entirely to Hosius, Housman here combines ingratitude and poor manners. As Fraenkel (1926, 531 = 1964, II 307-8) observed, Housman should have contented himself with a somewhat fuller version of the general remarks about Hosius that he makes in his preface.[60]

VII

The discussion above has given some of the reasons why it is said that Housman's Lucan and Fraenkel's review show the difference between a great critic and a great scholar; but it must not be forgotten that Fraenkel is sometimes right against Housman.

According to Williams (1970, 426), 'the victim greatly admired' the review.[61] That there is any evidence for this assertion seems doubtful, since (as we shall shortly see) Housman professed agreement with Fraenkel on only one trivial matter.[62] Nevertheless, any author is bound to be flattered when he reads in the second sentence of a review that his book is a *Meisterwerk*; and Housman must have realised that a 35-page, closely argued review in a prestigious new German periodical was a very great compliment. When Fraenkel sent him a copy of his review, he replied thus:[63]

Eduardo Fraenkelio s.d.
A. E. Housman.   accepi, uir doctissime, beneuole missam censuram tuam nec minus beneuole scriptam. laudes nimias esse intellego, partim etiam falsas, nam quod in IX 766 extat scripsisse Lucanum nec dixi nec credo.[64] reprehensionum, qui hominibus insitus est amor sui, ne unam quidem iustam esse agnosco, nisi quod recte interpungis IX 491;[65] omninoque uos censores in eo errare soletis quod uobis me magis circumspecti uidemini, estis autem multo minus. occurrit exemplum in ipso limine positum; ego enim id, quod tu p. 501 refutandum sumis, non dixi, sed, quid dicerem, accurate definiui praemissis uerbis 'Of these manuscripts', quos quinque numero inter se comparare, nulla ceterorum ratione habita, institueram.[66] item quae p. 504 de 'Housm. s. XVIII' scripsisti non scripsisses nisi paginae XVII oblitus esses.[67] sed haec ne longius excurrant subsistam, si prius gratum donum pensare conatus ero admonitione. igitur cauendum est ne nunc odio librorum MZ non minus peccetur quam antea amore; sunt enim nullis secundi.[68] multum mali feci cum Manilii Gemblacensem interpolatum esse ostendi coram hominibus qui Charydin [*sic*] uitare non possent nisi ita ut ad Scyllam confugerent.[69]   Oct. I an. 1926

VIII

Since the majority of those who can read Latin have never found much of interest in Manilius, it took the publication of Lucan to consolidate Housman's reputation. Other reviews were laudatory,[70] and W.M. Lindsay wrote 'Housman has at last made good. His Lucan is A 1'.[71] In 1930 he finished his commentary on Manilius. Despite the failure of his second book, *Iktus und Akzent im lateinischen Sprechvers* (Berlin, 1928), Fraenkel's reputation likewise grew: he published many articles, including the often cited papers on 'Kolon und Satz', and moved in 1928 to Göttingen and then in 1931 to Freiburg im Breisgau. The racial policies of the Nazis led to the next communication between the two men.

Forced in 1933 to resign his professorship, Fraenkel lectured in Scandinavia and Oxford, vainly looking for a secure position.[72] In August 1934 he was elected to a Bevan scholarship by Trinity College, Cambridge. Though better than nothing, the position was unsatisfactory, and he was preparing to look for a post in the United

States of America when A.C. Clark resigned from the Corpus Christi Professorship of Latin at Oxford. Fraenkel applied on 20 November 1934, submitting testimonials from a glittering array of scholars, including C.M. Bowra, W.M. Lindsay, E. Löfstedt, E. Norden, J. Wackernagel, and Housman himself.

Housman's reply (12 November) to Fraenkel's request for a testimonial may be found at Burnett 2.447.[73] He made it plain that he wanted Fraenkel to be successful, and Fraenkel seems to have responded with a modest reply.[74] The testimonial itself, dated 17 November 1934, may be found at Burnett 2.448; though more famous than any other reference written on behalf of an applicant for a classical position in the United Kingdom, its final sentence still bears repetition: 'I cannot say sincerely that I wish Dr Fraenkel to obtain the Corpus Professorship, as I would rather that he should be my successor in Cambridge.'[75]

In those years the electors to the Corpus Chair could move swiftly, and soon Housman was writing this letter, previously unpublished:

Trinity College | Cambridge
13 Dec. 1934

Dear Fraenkel,
    Though we shall be sorry to lose you from Cambridge, I must not let that prevent me from writing to congratulate you on your success.
Yours sincerely
A. E. Housman

The appointment upset some of those in Oxford who favoured the candidacy of E.A. Barber, a past and future editor of Propertius of modest distinction. The *Sunday Times* of 16 December 1934 carried an ignorant article of protest. Housman was asked by Oxonians to intervene, and his elegant response (Burnett 2.456-7) concluded with the crushing words: 'I do not know who the other candidates were, but they cannot have been Latinists of European reputation; for no Englishman who could be so described was young enough to be eligible'.[76]

For that Christmas Fraenkel and his family remained in Cambridge,[77] but he soon moved to Oxford,[78] where *Rome and Greek Culture* (Fraenkel 1934 = 1964, II 583-98), his inaugural lecture as Corpus Christi Professor of Latin, was delivered on 13 February 1935. He sent Housman a copy that was accompanied by verses in which Housman is described as ποιητής τε μέγας κριτικῶν τε μέγιστος.[79] Housman's response has not before been published.[80]

Trinity College | Cambridge
17 Feb. 1935

Dear Fraenkel,

My hearty thanks to you for sending me your inaugural lecture together with your amicable and accomplished verses.

It is full of the most varied interest, and I especially admired p. 30.[81]

I have been asked by Stanford University in California for my opinion of H. Fränkel, and I hope that they may find him at least a temporary post.[82]

I recollect that you wished to have offprints of some of my recent writings and I have now looked them out.[83]

Yours sincerely

A. E. Housman

Housman's health was already failing, and within fifteen months he would be dead. In June he was sent to the Evelyn Nursing Home, Cambridge, and from there he went to recuperate, first with the Withers family and then at the home of his sister-in-law Jeannie Housman.[84] There he wrote for the last time to Fraenkel, a note hitherto unpublished.[85]

Lower House, Tardebigge, Bromsgrove

It was kind of you to make enquiries after me and send me peaches when you were in Cambridge. I am now moving about in the country, and getting rid of the enfeebling effects of the nursing home.

Yours

8 July 1935   A. E. Housman

Since Williams (1970, 417 n. 2) tells us that Fraenkel had photographs of Leo, Pasquali, and Blakeway on his desk, and of Mommsen and Wilamowitz on the walls of his library, let it be said also that he possessed a very good photographic copy of Dodd's pencil portrait of Housman, the man who had helped him significantly but unobtrusively on his arrival in England.[86]

IX

Housman and Fraenkel, both prodigiously learned and hard-working men, invite comparison with each other:[87] colleagues briefly at Trinity College, and linked by the correspondence discussed in this essay, the one was indisputably the most important scholar to have held the chair of Latin in Cambridge, the other in Oxford. Housman was by far the superior textual critic: unlike Fraenkel, he had astonishing success in conjectural emendation, and, again unlike Fraenkel, he rarely allowed his learning to cloud his judgement in consideration of ms readings and the conjectures of others. Fraenkel edited with commentary only one classical work of any length (*Agamemnon*),[88] and, within seven years of its appearance, his publisher had issued a rival commentary that was often sharply critical of it; Housman's Lucan and Manilius advanced knowledge further and are still today the editions in which many people choose to read these poets. It is probably fair to say that Housman had the more penetrating intellect, was capable of more precise thought, and was therefore the finer scholar; but in so saying one runs the risks of forgetting first that it is easier for the textual critic than for the literary critic or ancient historian to achieve results that are immune to fashion (readings and conjectures are either right or wrong; literary and historical judgements often are not) and, second, that textual criticism is only one branch of the study of the ancient world.

And textual criticism was only one of Fraenkel's interests. Whereas Housman's work looked back to earlier times in which most classical scholars explicated in grammatical terms the text of their author and tried to emend it where it was inexplicable, Fraenkel drew his strength from the great German tradition in which classical philology embraced also the study of history and culture. Born in the capital city of *Altertumswissenschaft*, he brought to England the supremely compelling outlook of Mommsen (the greatest classical scholar of Housman's time)[89] and of his own teacher Wilamowitz, an outlook that saw the different branches of the study of the ancient world as a unity. Housman's precision and mastery still inspire awe; but when Fraenkel – in, for example, *Agamemnon* or the review of the Harvard Servius – uses the combined firepower of all the branches of classical knowledge that he commanded,[90] he too provides a remarkable spectacle that may inspire emulation. Sometimes Fraenkel's literary, like his textual, judgement went astray (his interpretations of the character of Agamemnon and of Horace's relationship to Augustus suggest a simplistic attitude to authority), but who could forget the way in which he brings to life Plautus, or many poems of Horace, or *Adeste hendecasyllabi* and the other poems of Catullus about which he wrote?[91] Housman deployed his knowledge of Latin idiom as though it were evidence to help solve riddles: in *Beobachtungen zu Aristophanes* and elsewhere Fraenkel delighted to illustrate idiom because it was the living speech of Greeks and Romans;[92] in *Kolon und Satz* he uses his knowledge of linguistics to bring to life the manner in which the ancients articulated their sentences.[93] No sensible person should wish that Housman had wasted his talent in writing papers that he was not suited to write; but the paradox remains that, despite being himself a creative artist of a standing higher than all other classical scholars, he could not bring ancient authors to life in the manner that Fraenkel managed. In Lucan, as we have seen, he found rhetoric, epigram, and an editorial challenge; from 'Lucan als Mittler des antiken Pathos' we learn that rhetoric and epigram served to express the passion of a young poet who had something important to say.

Appendix

Transcribed here are some comments from Housman's lectures, now preserved in Cambridge University Library, mss add. 6878 (Lucretius and Lucan, mostly general introductory material), 6887 (Books 1 and 7.1-390), 6888 (Books 2 and 3.1-380), 6889 (Books 3.381-4.300), 6890 (Books 4.300-824 and 5), 6891 (Books 6 and 7.390-872, 6892 (Books 8 and 9.1-522), 6893 (Books 9.523-1108 and Book 10). They take the form of a commentary on the text. The comments on rectos consist for the most part of translations and grammatical comment (but with occasional remarks on other matters, including textual problems); those on the facing versos report ms readings and deal with textual problems. Sometimes there are additions to the original drafts, usually in pencil. Writing inside square brackets [ ] is my own. Where Housman underlined, I have italicised, sometimes standardising his practice.

1.227 (ff. 15ᵛ-16ᵛ) *credidimus*, where *credimus* would be expected, caused Heinsius to propose *credimus en* and the scholiast to say 'deest *nos*'. But apart from the tense, the sense of *credidimus fatis* is unsuitable. The necessity of resorting to the arbitrament of war is not caused by Caesar's trust in fate; it is caused by the failure of negotiations: *credidimus satis <his>*. S and F often confused even in Virgil's capital MSS. When, by corruption, a word has changed its quantity, the scribes will mend the metre by omission or insertion, as at 209. Man. 2.114 *materiaeque datum est* [with *cogi*, the next word in Manilius, added in pencil] M, *que fatum* L, then *que* erased. 673 *satis haec* same place in verse.

[These remarks are supplemented by pencil annotations: 'Petron. 122.174 and Mart. 1.42.4 MSS' opposite the first line of the note. Then 1.134-5 'multumque priori | credere fortunae' opposite the second sentence. Then 'Sen. H.O. 275 *satis, fati*' opposite the sentence discussing confusion of *s* and *f*.]

1.333 (ff. 23ᵛ-24ʳ) *tamen* cannot look back to what has preceded: it looks forward to (*quamuis*) *tam longa*: 'when will his tyranny, though so long, nevertheless end.' Every *tamen* implies a *quamuis*, and every *quamuis* a *tamen*. We generally omit the *tamen*, and so do the Romans sometimes, as in 354 *quamquam caede feras, mentes* (*tamen*) *frangunt*. But sometimes they omit *quamuis* instead, as in 378 ~~Prop. 2. 34. 5~~ ~~(quamuis) trux, tamen a nobis mitem domandus (??) eris 'I shall have to tame you first, headstrong though you are'~~ *inuita peragam tamen omnia dextra*. Then the *tamen* sometimes stands in the place where you expect to find the *quamuis*, as in Verg. Aen. 3.341 *ecqua tamen puer est amissae cura parentis*, i.e. *quamuis amissae*. Stupid editors pass this idiom over without understanding it, and clever editors often want to alter it, as Bentley here conj. *tandem*.

[Pencil annotations include 292 (this opposite 354) and 7.786, 5.102, 8.229, Cic. *Phil.* 1.7 'quae *tamen* urbs *mihi coniunctissima* ... me retinere non potuit'. S. *Tr.* 1115 is quoted, too, but deleted; Housman adduces it more appositely in his note on Man. 4.413]

2.174-6 (f. 16ʳ) a. Usual punctuation, comma after *pendit*, makes *umbris* dative, and *piacula* apposition to *inferias*, to which it adds little.

    b. Bentley makes *forsan nolentibus umbris* parenthesis and ablative, removes comma after *pendit*, and encloses between commas *non fanda piacula*, again apposition.

    c. I think there should be no commas and the construction is 'cum uictima Marius, umbris forsan tristis inferias nolentibus (abl.), pendit inexpleto non fanda piacula busto.' Thus the apposition is avoided.

2.292 (f. 26ʳ⁻ᵛ) *compressas* is paralleled by Liu. 7.13.7 'quid enim aliud esse causae credamus, cur ueteranus dux, fortissimus bello, *conpressis*, quod aiunt, *manibus* sedeas', and it signifies sitting inactive without lifting a finger. But that notion is not here in point: no one could dream of trying to make himself useful when the sky is falling. In the day of judgement we shall not be expected to behave as if the house were on fire, catching the stars in blankets and pumping water on the comets. The sense required is not that of sitting inactive but of standing unmoved, and that sense is given by *complosas* [added in pencil at this point are 5.201-2, Lucr. 1.140 *sperata uoluptas*, and ?Mart. 8.78.10 *spectatas ... feras*], and the phrase means *tenuisse complosionem manuum*, to check the action of striking the hands together – a sign of agitation, e.g. Petron. 137.1 'illa *complosis manibus* "scelerate" inquit "etiam loqueris"', when Encolpius has killed the sacred goose.

    compressas arose from *complossas*, apparently the original reading of M.

2.554 (ff. 51ᵛ-52ʳ) [lengthy lemma omitted] 'that you might fall, a public enemy, in such a case as did Spartacus'. *causa* is condition, position, situation; here the guilt of brigandage. Tac. hist. 4. 46 *neu pari causa disparem fortunam paterentur* 'when this guilt was no greater and no less'. The words *causa qua Spartacus* could mean 'at the hands of the same agent' i.e. Crassus, and, if they could, *simili* would have to be *eadem*. Therefore, if the text is right, the verse contains no motive for wishing that Crassus were here: Pompey can himself satisfy its requirements, or anyone else who defeats Caesar. The sense demanded is 'that he who defeated Spartacus might defeat you'; so Schrader altered *hostis* to *illi*. But the *hosti* of Z, with *quoi* for *qua* or *quod*, ['cf. Quintilian, and 541 quom' here written in pencil above the line] gives this sense in a more pointed form: 'that, being a brigand like him, you might be overthrown by the same adversary as Spartacus' i.e. Crassus.

For the dative see 547. [Below this '5.521 *quem* dabat alga, *toro*' is written in pencil]

4.253 (f. 62ᵛ) *facie* fortasse Z certe cod. coll. Trin., *faciem* MPGUV. Though most editors read the acc., they do not defend it. Certainly the ablative is usual: the thes. ling. Lat. has 7 examples of *ponere in conspectu*, none of *-um* [6.159 written beside this note in pencil.]

6.550 (ff. 54ᵛ-55ʳ) *quodcumque* MZPGUV, *quocumque* N, *quacumque* Grotius and almost all editors, without cause. *quicumque* and *quisquis*, like 'whoever' in English, are often used where it is neither easy nor natural to supply an antecedent, so that they are equivalent to *si quis*: just as *si quis* on the other hand is often used where it natural to translate it as a relative. [7.703 is written in pencil in the margin.] Luc. 1.383-4 'tu *quoscumque* uoles in planum effundere *muros* | his aries actus disperget saxa lacertis', it is just possible but not at all natural to supply *eorum* with *saxa*. Hor. serm. 2.5.51-2 '*qui* testamentum tradet tibi *cumque* legendum, | abnuere et tabulas a te remouere memento' it is impossible to supply an antecedent: 'whoever offers to show you his will, be sure to decline,' i.e. 'if anyone' does so.

6.498-9 (f. 51ʳ) Verg. A. 3.56 '*quid* non mortalia pectora *cogis?*', Liu. 6.15.13 'uos *id cogendi estis*'.

6.582 (f. 58ʳ) The construction is *uetuit Philippos transmittere bella*, 'forbade Pharsalia to let war go past it'. Compounds of *mitto* often have this sort of force: Liu. 21.24.5 *reguli Gallorum ... cum bona pace exercitum per fines suos ... transmiserunt*, Stat. Theb. 12.746 *ferrum ... umero transmisit Iapyx* 'had his shoulders pierced by the spear' [7.623 written in pencil in the margin.]

Notes

1. A friend once observed that to pass judgement on Housman requires a certain arrogance. Since the arrogance is compounded here by writing also about Fraenkel (whom I never knew) when many of his pupils are still alive, let me say that nothing inspired me more with a love of Latin literature and with the desire to become a classical scholar than my reading Fraenkel's *Horace* when at school; and in recent years nothing has reminded me more of my own philological shortcomings than studying Housman's Lucan. With regard to both men, I quote the wise words of a humane Greek: οὐ γὰρ εἰ τῇ δυνάμει λειπόμεθα Θουκυδίδου τε καὶ τῶν ἄλλων ἀνδρῶν, καὶ τὸ θεωρητικὸν αὐτῶν ἀπολωλέκαμεν. οὐδὲ γὰρ τὰς Ἀπελλοῦ καὶ Ζεύξιδος καὶ Πρωτογένους καὶ τῶν ἄλλων γραφέων τῶν διωνομασμένων τέχνας οἱ μὴ τὰς αὐτὰς ἔχοντες ἐκείνοις ἀρετὰς κρίνειν κεκώλυνται, οὐδὲ τὰ Φειδίου καὶ Πολυκλείτου καὶ Μύρωνος ἔργα οἱ μὴ τηλικοῦτοι δημιουργοί (Dion. Hal. *Thuc.* 4). I am grateful to Mr D.J. Butterfield and Professors J. Diggle and M.D. Reeve for improving an earlier draft of this essay

and to Mr J. Reid, Archivist of Corpus Christi College, Oxford, who allowed me
to transcribe the letters of Housman first published here.

2. Shackleton Bailey 1981, 57 n. 2. Shackleton Bailey, who preferred the
plain 'critic' to 'textual critic', himself ran a seminar comparing the two; see
Thomas 2008, 8.

3. *Man.* I, xvii.

4. Burnett 2.64.

5. Housman, review of J.P. Postgate, *Corpus Poetarum Latinorum*, fasc. III.,
CR 14 (1900), 465-9 = *CP* 525-31.

6. Heitland 1901. The article is a poor advertisement for Heitland's
scholarship. In its second paragraph it contains the sentence: 'It may well be
that what commends itself to the judgement of the modern scholar as the better
reading is not (even though that scholar be infallible) what the author wrote'.
Housman takes up the theme in his own final sentence: 'If my infallibility, that
is to say the care with which I think and write ...'.

7. Housman (n. 5 above) = *CP* 532-5.

8. Housman, *Man.* I, 59 (on 1.657). The conjecture is discussed below.

9. The lecture courses given by Housman in Cambridge are listed by Gow
1936a, 60-1.

10. The comments on 6.498-9 and 582 transcribed below are examples of
matter not repeated in the edition.

11. In the preface to his Loeb edition J.D. Duff notes his debt to Housman's
edition (which indeed he does follow closely) and that he had attended
Housman's lectures and borrowed some turns of phrase from them. When I have
compared Duff's edition with Housman's notes, I have found that the renderings
borrowed are usually limited to a phrase in length: I noticed no full sentences
taken from Housman.

12. Housman, 'Lucan vii 460-5', *CQ* 15 (1920), 172-4 = *CP* 1043-5.

13. See Graves 1979, 235, Burnett 1.558.

14. Sir Frederick Macmillan's elegant letter to Housman on 22 December
1926 may be read at Nowell-Smith 1967, 243.

15. For text and commentary see Burnett 1.642.

16. Fraenkel 1924 = 1964, II 233-66.

17. Shackleton Bailey conveniently notes divergences from Housman's text
with an asterisk, of which I counted about 130. However, these include some
uncertain emendations in passages that Housman thought corrupt but left
unemended and some conjectures of Housman's that Housman did not print.
Given the bulk of scholarship since 1926 and the difficulty of Lucan, this
number is very small. Housman changed Hosius' text in about 260 places
(Anderson 1927, 28). Goold's Manilius is in similar thrall to the mature
Housman; see Shackleton Bailey 1979, 161.

18. In addition to Fraenkel, note esp. Anderson 1927.

19. Those who want to read Lucan in the text that approximates more
closely than any other to what the poet wrote should read him in one of these
editions; but, apart from their excellent text and bibliography of textual work on
Lucan, these volumes contains little of interest. By contrast, although
Housman's text is occasionally inferior, his apparatus contains something of
interest on almost every page.

20. Nevertheless, it is a pity that he who passed so much time in France did
not seek to discover the readings of the early Paris lat. 7900A.

21. But Håkanson 1979, 31-2 suggested plausibly that a true reading in ZM
(*sola* rather than *sole*) has been excised at 6.622.

22. For more on Housman's remark see Reeve's chapter.

23. On M see also the interesting remarks of Fraenkel 1926, 498, 502 = 1964, II 268, 273-4.

24. For criticism of Housman's paragraph see Gotoff 1971, 5-6.

25. See esp. Fraenkel 1926, 501-2 = 1964, II 272-3.

26. I take much further a passing remark of Gotoff 1971, 6.

27. This memorable expression is taken from J.B. Hall in Reynolds 1983, 144 (but I have no evidence that Hall's use of it with regard to Claudian's mss is unfounded).

28. Tarrant's article is the easiest starting point for the study of Lucan's mss. That Housman's main business escapes virtually unscathed from Gotoff's researches is well shown by Håkanson 1979, 26-30; see too Shackleton Bailey 1988, v.

29. For such emendations see on, e.g., 1.542; 2.554, 701-2; 4.793; 6.287; 7.691-6, 701; 8.619; 9.36, 161, 179, 471, 762; on 9.228 the paradosis in the Bern scholia is defended.

30. Further examples at, e.g., 1.145, 147, 176, 262-3, 267, 337; 2.195, 204, 276-7, 711, 714; 3.149 (here the *adnotationes* seem to have the true reading); 4.82, 102, 203, 204; 5.205, 218, 330, 668; 6.1, 194, 195; 7.436; 8.309-10, 335, 517, 519, 621; 9.83, 104, 105.

31. From many notes see those at, e.g., 1.231, 249, 349, 378, 652, 691; 2.27; 4.796; 5.166; 8.204, 251.

32. Very many other notes could be cited; for example those at 1.102-3, 637, 649-50; 5.120, 315, 473, 615, 680-1; 6.124; 8.133-7, 225; 9.125.

33. However, Heyworth 2007, 131 has rightly challenged Housman's explanation of Lucr. 3.553 and Ov. *Am.* 1.8.20. In the marginalia to his own copy Housman added in ink Ov. *Her.* 4.31 (a doubtful parallel), 16.238 (vulnerable to the objection raised by Heyworth), and Man. 5.553 (see Housman's own note); and then in pencil Plaut. *Stich.* 124 *tamen cum res secundae sunt*, Ov. *Her.* 16.238 *tamen ... dissimulatus*, Stat. *Silv.* 4.2.43-4 *tamen dissimulatus*, Priap. 2.4-5 *tamen ... non uirgineum*, Luc. 3.763 *tamen ... si* (later crossed out), Ov. *Nux* 153 *tamen ... admissa*. In the comment on this passage in his lectures (reproduced below) Housman observed that stupid commentators ignore the idiom, clever ones try to emend it. It would be invidious to list those whose notes ignore it, but the discussion of these uses of *tamen* at *OLD s.v.* 4 is very muddled. There is more material, not well categorised, at Mulder 1954, 245 (on *Theb.* 2.392) and Bömer 1969-86, I 327 (on *Met.* 2.337). Fraenkel, too, was interested in the unusual placement of resumptive particles after a concession: see 1964, I 98-9 on ὅμως.

34. Other long notes with material on idiom include 6.550** (*quicumque* without antecedent), 7.323-5 (double zeugma), and 9.463 (on unusual placement of *quoque*).

35. From many other examples of repunctuation see, e.g., on 1.8-10, 367-72, 441, 664-5; 7.699-700, 8.400-1, 9.482.

36. Fraenkel cited 7.658 as one of the very few passages for which Housman's punctuation is faulty. Neither scholar convinces and the text seems to be corrupt: see Shackleton Bailey's apparatus.

37. See Housman's letter quoted below.

38. See Housman's and Fraenkel's discussion; the verses are deleted by Shackleton Bailey, who does not punctuate them with Fraenkel.

39. See Fantham 1992, 133 and Oakley 1997-2005, II 163.

40. See also Anderson 1927, 28.

41. For another good example, see Mayer 1979, 351-3.

42. Earlier Fraenkel (1924, 240 = 1964, II 246) had tacitly printed *corda* from Bentley's conjecture. However, *corda ferre* seems to be unparalleled, and, if one prints *corda*, one should perhaps print also the idiomatic *gerens* (Val. Fl. 4.158, Mart. 10.103.12, 12.44.2, Ambros. *Ep.* 9.62.20).

43. *Man.* V, xxv, xxxiv.

44. In his lecture notes Housman says that the confusion occurs even in capital mss.

45. If Lucan wrote as Getty suggested, his expression would have been very hard to understand (perhaps not a decisive objection with this poet) and very pedestrian and tautologous (which is decisive).

46. Anderson 1927, 28 approved the conjecture, somewhat reluctantly.

47. For a different defence of Housman, see Håkanson 1979, 36-8.

48. I have borrowed this argument from Håkanson.

49. Fraenkel's view was disputed by Håkanson, perhaps wrongly.

50. Shackleton Bailey follows Housman.

51. See *TLL* X.2 1417,9-45.

52. However, he was the first to excise 7.161, 388, and 746 *nec* – 749 *duces*, pointing out at xxii-xxvi the difficulties caused by these lines; the second of these is rejected by Fraenkel (1926, 512 = 1964, II 285), the third praised, but none is accepted by Shackleton Bailey, perhaps rightly.

53. See Lloyd-Jones 1971, 639 = 1982, 258; also Horsfall 1990, 65.

54. See, respectively, Fraenkel 1963, 1950, 815-28, and in Müller 1961.

55. On Housman's liking for such explanations, see Reeve's chapter.

56. E.g. that on *Überlieferungsgeschichte*, mentioned above.

57. The best is at the expense of Housman's own hero (xxxii): '[t]he characteristic which Napoleon so much admired in Turenne, that he grew bolder as he grew older, was not for Bentley a fortunate endowment'.

58. See, e.g., the review of O.L. Richmond (published anonymously) of 22 April 1926 in the *Times Literary Supplement*; Anderson 1927, 33 has an excellent concluding paragraph.

59. See for example at 2.425, 432-4; 3.106-7; 4.57; 5.140; 8.59, 118-19, 505, 523; 9.104.

60. Where his comment is judicious and, though firm, is not rude.

61. This may be the source for statements to this effect in other, later memoirs of Fraenkel.

62. Nor is it likely that a man so shy as Housman would have said this to Fraenkel in 1934 or 1935.

63. This letter is reproduced in Burnett 2.627-8 from the draft (or, conceivably, copy) filed in Trinity College, adv.c.20.25. I have transcribed from the version that Fraenkel received, now to be found in Corpus Christi College, Oxford, Ms. 551/AI/1. This version avoids the three errors noted by Burnett but imports the slip noted below. In other respects the two versions are identical.

64. Housman reacts to Fraenkel 1926, 530 = 1964, II 306).

65. See above.

66. Housman refers to his list of places where one of ZPGUV was alone in the truth. It is not obvious that Fraenkel's criticism is unfair.

67. Fraenkel 1926, 504 = 1964, II 276 says that Housman cited Leo 'auf dem Umwege über Schanz'; Housman points out that he cited Leo in his own right on the previous page. Though Fraenkel had made a slip, it is revealing of Housman's character that he thought such a trifle worth his attention.

68. This warning seems slightly unfair, given what Fraenkel 1926, 519-20 = 1964, II 294 says about ZM.

69. This reflects one of Housman's current concerns. After finishing his Lucan he was devoting his energies to completing his greatest monument, the edition and commentary on Manilius. In the final volume, published in 1930, he looks back over the editing of Manilius in the period 1903-1930, and unleashes one of his more venomous tirades against Thielscher and others who had used his proof that the Gemblacensis was interpolated as an unjust reason for despising it (*Man.* I, xxiv-xxviii (for the initial proof) and *Man.* V, vii-xiii (for the subsequent tirade)).

70. Note esp. Anderson 1927.

71. Quoted by Bowra 1966, 253. I am grateful to David Butterfield for reminding me of where I had read this.

72. This paragraph draws on Williams 1970, 9.

73. The instruction to be addressed as 'Dear Housman' will amuse anyone who has been lectured by his seniors on the merits of such an address.

74. So I deduce from the first sentence of the covering letter to Housman's testimonial: see Burnett 2.447.

75. It and the preceding sentence were quoted in print first by Williams 1970, 421.

76. The letter is printed also at *CP* 1277. On these events, and on Fraenkel's arrival in Oxford, see Bowra 1966, 299. Alexander Souter wrote to Fraenkel to congratulate him and to Housman (in response to Housman's letter to *The Sunday Times*) to tell him that he, too, had been a candidate. On Christmas Day Housman wrote a kindly reply, observing *inter alia* that Souter was a Scotsman (Burnett 2.457-8).

77. See Housman's letter to Souter.

78. For a not altogether kind description of his first days in Oxford, see Trevor-Roper 1974, 405-6.

79. They are printed at Fraenkel 1964, II 599.

80. Like the other unpublished letters of Housman to Fraenkel it may be found at Corpus Christi College, Ms. 551/A/I/1. The footnotes are mine.

81. P. 30 (= 1964, II 597-8) contains these words: 'The Romans became the saviours of our culture because they did not imagine that to profit selfishly from Greek culture was sufficient, and because they, or at least the best among them, turned themselves towards Greece in willing surrender. In the building of their state they did not in the long run allow foreign ideas to interfere, and in their empire they fashioned an armour which, if sometimes irksome, was yet a trusty protection to guard the body of Mediterranean culture. But for the life which they wished to live within their state and their empire they claimed no kind of national or racial self-sufficiency. They were magnanimous enough to realise what they lacked themselves, and strong enough not to be afraid of foreign strength. With sure instinct they were aware that, after the Greeks had discovered the Kosmos and the ἀρχαί of human life and work, to succeeding generations there was given the alternative either to adapt what the Greeks had discovered and formulated or to remain barbarians.'

82. Hermann Fränkel (1888-1977), a classical scholar best known for his work on Homer, Apollonius of Rhodes, and Ovid, was born a few weeks after Fraenkel, whose sister he married. Like Fraenkel, he was forced to leave Germany because of the racial policies of the Nazis. He was appointed to a permanent position at Stanford.

83. Oddly, these seem to be missing from Fraenkel's collection of off-prints, now housed in the Sackler Library, Oxford.

84. For Housman's visit to the Evelyn Nursing Home and his subsequent recuperation, see, e.g., Withers 1940, 104-14, Graves 1979, 260, and Burnett 2.478-83.

85. As perusal of Burnett shows, the use of the bald 'Yours' (perhaps explained by the informal note which contains no address) is very unusual for Housman. For another note written at the same time see Burnett 2.482.

86. The photograph is of the version of the portrait made for St John's, Oxford. It was presented by Prof. Edward Fraenkel (Fraenkel's son) to Queens' College, Cambridge (where Edward Fraenkel had been a Fellow); Prof. Diggle kindly showed it to me. That Housman had been given at least two photographs of this drawing is revealed by his letters to F.W. Hall and Arnold Rubin, at Burnett 1.625, 629, 2.138.

87. See, e.g., Shackleton Bailey 1973, 190, Horsfall 1990, 63, Nisbet in Nisbet and Russell 2007, 224 'Bentley and Housman ... Greats and Fraenkel'.

88. Fraenkel 1950.

89. Prof. Reeve recalls hearing Fraenkel describe Mommsen as the greatest classical scholar since Scaliger.

90. Fraenkel 1948 and 1949 = 1964, II 339-90 and Fraenkel 1950.

91. *Plautinisches im Plautus* is now available in an English translation (Fraenkel 2007); Horace: Fraenkel 1957; Catullus, most conveniently in Fraenkel 1964, II 86-129.

92. Fraenkel 1962.

93. Fraenkel 1932 and 1933 = 1964, I 73-130, 131-9, and 1965.

5

Housman and Ovid's *Ibis*[1]

G.D. Williams

A.E. Housman published his first words on Ovid's *Ibis* in 1883, his last in 1921.[2] In 1894 he published his own recension of the poem in the second fascicle (pp. 590-5) of the first volume of J.P. Postgate's *Corpus Poetarum Latinorum*. Twenty-one years then passed before Housman published the first in a triad of articles which explicated his editorial choices in that 1894 recension. 'Ovid, *Ibis* 512 and *Tristia* III 6 8' (1915) was followed by 'Transpositions in the *Ibis* of Ovid' (1918) and then by 'The *Ibis* of Ovid' (1920);[3] the last in particular, his final major writing on the poem, has to a large extent shaped later critical attitudes towards this most difficult of Ovid's works. In the melancholic mindscape of the exilic poetry which Ovid composed in Tomis (modern Constanza on the Romanian coast of the Black Sea) after he was relegated from Rome by Augustus in 8 AD, the *Ibis*, modelled on a now lost Callimachean original from which it takes its name, stands out as an artistically contrived explosion of manic rage against Ibis, a pseudonymous enemy. Ibis' alleged crimes against Ovid (11-22) are first avenged by an elaborate set of curse-rituals (29-250) before the poet embarks on, and gradually loses himself in, a vast catalogue of imprecations (251-638), each of them portending its own exquisite punishment, and all of them delivered to intimidating effect in a cloud of learned obscurity. The importance of Housman's work on the *Ibis* rests in large part on the sheer acuity that he brought to bear on specific problems of textual emendation, transposition and the elucidation of Ovid's *arcana* in the catalogue; but he also radically challenged complacent attitudes to the poem by questioning the meaning and function of Ovid's curse-catalogue, and also Ibis' very existence, in ways unparalleled in previous scholarship. In section I below we sample the prevailing climate of scholarship on the *Ibis* that preceded, and to no small degree provoked, Housman's contributions to the field; our guide is Robinson Ellis, whose Oxford edition of the poem, with introduction and commentary in Latin, was published in 1881. We then turn in section II to a closer appraisal of Housman's three articles of 1915, 1918 and 1920, and of their originality as a body of work that transformed

Ibis-study. Finally, the consequences of that transformation for later scholarship are briefly assessed in section III.

I

By his own account Robinson Ellis was first led to serious engagement with Ovid's *Ibis* when, after the publication of his Oxford commentary on Catullus in 1876, he was exploring the Bodleian's treasures and came upon the *Fabularius* (1273) of Konrad of Mure (1210-1281);[4] or, more precisely, Ellis fell upon the version of the *Fabularius* published in 1470 by Bertold Ruppel of Basel under the title (as Ellis gives it in short form) of *Repertorium vocabulorum exquisitorum*.[5] An encyclopedic lexicon that alphabetically listed the names of (*inter alia*) many figures drawn from Greco-Roman mythology and history, the *Fabularius* 'was particularly designed as a complete guide to the reading of the *auctores*, especially the poets', Ovid prominent among them.[6] Konrad frequently quotes passages from the *Ibis* to provide illustration of the names he catalogues; and he often offers (or attempts) elucidation of the mysteries that are encased in couplet after couplet of Ovid's obscure imprecations against Ibis. True to his commitment to advancing the claims of manuscript research on Greek and Latin authors,[7] and partly in response to K.R. Merkel's 1837 edition of the *Ibis*,[8] Ellis sought out new mss for the poem. He duly claims credit for bringing to light two mss belonging to the tripartite 'first family' of codices, both of which he dates to c. 1200.[9] Because of this early date he attaches special importance to these two mss, and also to the ms (with its attendant scholia) on which Konrad drew in his *Fabularius* – for Ellis, a 'good' ms which 'in some cases ... seems to have preserved the true reading where Merkel's mss are misleading'.[10] This respect for Konrad's early source leads to special treatment in Ellis' edition of the *Ibis*, where he holds that 'everything bequeathed by Konrad is to be set out in the *apparatus criticus*'.[11]

Ellis' earliest publication on the poem, 'On the *Ibis* of Ovid' (1877), offers a sequence of case-studies on individual couplets to demonstrate (*inter alia*) the high value that he attaches to the ms of the *Ibis* used by Konrad. Along the way, Ellis himself reveals the mindset that Gilbert Murray was succinctly to capture in his obituary after Ellis' death in 1913:

> The riddles of mythological and historical allusion which constitute the greater part of [the *Ibis*] provided just the most suitable material for Ellis's enormous knowledge of recondite literature as well as for his curious ingenuity.
>
> Ellis cared, of course, for literature ... But as material to work upon he seems actually to have rather avoided great literature. He liked the rare rather than the good. His object was not the desire to elucidate a great writer, but rather *the artist's delight in working at difficult material*. He

liked fixing a reading, puzzling out a difficulty; whether the result was of much value or not did not seem to trouble him. There is something of the same indifference to practical results in his method of annotation ... In the same spirit he was always impatient of those over-practical scholars who liked to base a text on the one best MS., rejecting as useless all the rest. An instinct told him they were wrong, and he always rejoiced when he discovered a good reading in a MS. of late date or low reputation. *He was not characteristically a scientific scholar.* He had no power of going straight to the heart of a subject by a bold hypothesis which he then followed consistently. His arguments were often not very clear or effective. One felt in his work no great commanding force of intellect. One felt only that he knew Latin wonderfully, understood it, and loved it; that his instinct was apt to be a safer guide than another man's well-documented reasoning ... *Ellis was essentially an artist.*[12]

Many of these attributes are well exemplified by his 1877 treatment of lines 539-40, which Merkel prints as follows, accepting the conjecture of Paul Léopard (1510-67) in the hexameter:

> conditor ut tardae, Blaesus cognomine, Cyrae
> orbis in innumeris inueniare locis.

The mss offer variants in *conditor/cognitor*, *tardae/tardus* and *laesus/blaesus*, but *Cyrae* is Léopard's importation for mss *mir(r)e/murrae/myrre* (= *Myrrhae*). The allusion in Merkel's text is then to Aristoteles Battus, founder of Cyrene,[13] allegedly labeled βάττος/*Blaesus* ('the stammerer') 'because of his being tongue-tied' (*propter linguae obligationem*, Just. 13.7.1);[14] the pentameter, and also *tardae*, refer to his many wanderings before finally settling in Cyrene. An 'ingenious' reading, concedes Ellis; but its implausibility begins with the fact that Cyra 'is nowhere used as a synonym for Cyrene'.[15] Building instead on the second of two explanations of the couplet given by Konrad of Mure's entry s.v. *Leius*,[16] Ellis detects an allusion to Cinyras, father and (unbeknown to him) incestuous lover of Myrrha. He tentatively proposes to read as follows:

> cognitor ut tardae laesus cognomine Myrrhae
> orbis in innumeris inueniare locis.

'Like the discoverer of the lingering Myrrha, when the fraud of a name deceived him, may you be found wandering in exile from country to country':[17] Ibis is to become a second Cinyras, whom Konrad (unlike Ovid) represents as a mendicant wanderer, *uagus et profugus*, after the terrible truth is revealed.[18]

Ellis' diffidence in venturing this interpretation is reflected in his 1881 edition: there, he prints Merkel's reading and reports his alternative proposal in the apparatus criticus, where he refers back to his 1877 article.[19] Fifteen years were to pass before Ellis wrote again of lines 539-40 in his 'New remarks on Ovid's *Ibis*' (1896), on this occasion to take issue with Housman's very different interpretation of the couplet. If Ellis' 1877 treatment of the lines bears witness to what Murray characterised as his 'curious ingenuity' and 'the artist's delight in working at difficult material',[20] and if he indulges the problem rather than setting himself to solve it with a keen efficiency, then Housman reveals a very different aptitude in his pithy '*Ibis* 539',[21] published when he was 24 and had recently taken up his clerkship at the Patent Office. Two strong objections to the Battus-interpretation of Merkel after Léopard are set out without fuss: (i) amid so many curses of such extreme physical cruelty, Battus' wanderings appear oddly tame as a punishment for Ibis; and (ii) that the pentameter refers to dismemberment is surely indicated by the parallel that Housman adduces at *Trist.* 3.9.27-8 *atque ita diuellit* [sc. Medea] *diuulsaque membra per agros / dissipat in multis inuenienda locis*. Ellis' own proposal that the couplet alludes to Cinyras is passed over in a telling silence. Housman reads:

> conditor ut tardae, laesus cognomine, Myrrhae,
> orbis in innumeris inueniare locis.

With minimal fanfare he elucidates the couplet by reference to C. Helvius Cinna, neoteric poet and tribune, who was lynched by the Roman mob when, after Julius Caesar's funeral, he was mistaken for Caesar's enemy, the praetor L. Cornelius Cinna: 'may you be torn in pieces like the author of the Zmyrna[22] that was nine years in writing, brought to grief by his cognomen of Cinna'.[23] The identification of the poet Cinna with the murdered tribune has been disputed in modern scholarship, but it has been forcefully vindicated by T.P. Wiseman,[24] who nevertheless ignores 'the strongest evidence in its favour',[25] the Ovidian couplet as elucidated by Housman. Led by Virgil's allusion to Cinna in the *Eclogues* in c. 40 BC (*nam neque adhuc Vario uideor nec dicere Cinna / digna*, 9.35-6) to suppose that the poet Cinna was alive after 44, Housman himself treads carefully in speculating on the origin of the Ovidian identification: 'Whether Ovid dreamt that the tribune and the poet were one, or whether he was humouring a popular fancy, or whether these lines are not Ovid's, let others say'.[26] But when he briefly returned to the couplet in 1920, he drew on the work of others to support the *fact* of the historical identification;[27] and he also attended to a detail unaddressed in his note of 1883.

In the *apparatus* of his 1894 recension Housman conjectured *urbis* for 540 *orbis*, to the effect of 'may you be found [torn to pieces] in countless parts of the city'; as he himself was to acknowledge in 1920, *urbis* was in fact already 'cited from two MSS by Heinsius and Merkel'.[28] 'I do not think it necessary' to read *urbis*, he declares;[29] but the mss' confusion with *orbis* is easily explained, *urbis* naturally complements the allusion to murder *at Rome* in 539, and, for all its own 'iperbole poetica',[30] it shows more restraint than the arguably overblown *orbis*. Along with the almost universal agreement that the reference in 539 is to the poet Cinna,[31] *urbis* has since been printed in the editions of S.G. Owen (1915), F.W. Lenz (1937), A. La Penna (1957) and G.P. Goold (1979). For present purposes, however, the choice between *urbis* and *orbis* is of interest because of Ellis' 1896 critique of Housman's 'highly ingenious interpretation of 539, 540'.[32] The shining correctness that later editors were to see in Housman's 1883 elucidation was differently perceived by Ellis, who holds that '[a]s far as I know, one, and only one, passage has been definitively settled since 1881': lines 517-18.[33] His objection to Housman's interpretation of 539-40 rests on – and it seems *only* on – his own resistance to reading *urbis*: he hesitates to accept any confusion of *urbis/orbis* 'in such excellent MSS as G and T of the *Ibis*'; and so, '[i]f *Orbis* is genuine, it is difficult to see how the poet could be described as "found in countless places of the *world*" because he was torn to pieces in the streets of *Rome*';[34] hence the allusion apparently cannot be to Cinna. The (overblown) hyperbole in *orbis* for which Housman evidently made allowance[35] quite escapes the literal-minded Ellis, who persists in 1896 with the same deeply learned but still more deeply submerged approach that he first took to the mysteries of the *Ibis* some 20 years earlier.

Ellis' natural affinity was to the world of the earlier humanists whom he lists and appraises in the preface to his 1881 edition – fellow competitors in the Olympic-like challenge[36] of construal and demystification that Ovid's curse-catalogue lays down to scholarly savants across the ages. For all his 'modern', transforming effect on *Ibis*-study generally, Housman too was a formidable contender in this arena of traditional *interpretatio* and elucidation – but a contender who was fully 'a scientific scholar' in comparison with the kind of artist that Gilbert Murray discerned in Ellis.[37] Murray makes no allusion to Housman in his obituary of Ellis, but it is hard not to detect in Murray's description of what Ellis was *not* an oblique summation of what Housman *was*. That 'great commanding force of intellect' that Murray found lacking in Ellis' control of argument[38] is already evident in Housman's tightly constructed note of 1883. Whereas Ellis 'would often write a long note which led to no definite result, provided it gave scope for real erudition and ingenuity',[39] the young Housman of 1883 characteristically goes straight to the heart of his subject, neither parading nor concealing his formidable learning[40] – an indifference to display which meant that the true depth of erudition informing his 1894 recension lay implicit and concealed until his articles of 1915, 1918 and 1920 proved revelatory. And whereas Ellis relished the task of mss collection and collation, Housman's brisk effort to separate the wheat from the chaff ('But the MSS on which we depend for the tradition of what Ovid wrote are the seven which I selected in my recension of 1894')[41] marks him out by Murray's criteria as a 'practical' scholar, of a breed different from those persistent enough to seek 'a good reading in a MS. of late date or low reputation'.[42]

Before Ellis' death in 1913 Housman had been relatively restrained in his criticisms of Ellis' scholarship, and not insensitive to the effects of his attacks,[43] but in later years his contempt flowed forth more freely and harshly.[44] His low opinion was formed early: already, under the pseudonym Tristram in *The Eleventh Eclogue* (1877), he portrayed Ellis and Henry Nettleship, the two candidates then vying for the Chair of Latin at Oxford, 'with witty unfairness, displaying them as petty controversialists with a remarkable, and very unfortunate, command of pedantic language'.[45] At a more personal level, Ellis may also have incurred the young Housman's lasting resentment because it was on Ellis' advice that the Oxford University Press refused to publish Housman's Propertius.[46] For present purposes, however, Housman's general disdain finds scathing but witty expression in the elegiac couplet of his own that he appended to the text (p. 41) in his copy of Ellis' *Ibis* edition – a couplet purporting to be Ibis' reply to Ovid:

> At, precor, ultores in me mala carmina facta
>   Ellisio tradant emaculanda dei.

2 commaculanda *al.*[47]

'But, I pray, may the avenging gods hand the noxious curses written against me over to Ellis for cleansing'; or (the point of the alternative proposal in the mock *apparatus*) should that be 'hand over to Ellis for *contamination*'? On either reading – the irony of *emaculanda* gives way to blunter insult in *commaculanda* – the *Ibis* suffers at Ellis' hands, destined as it is for Ellisius rather than Elysium. But beyond the specific weaknesses that Housman perceived in Ellis' editorial work, Ellis conveniently represents for now a time-honoured orthodoxy of approach to the poem – an entrenched, even complacent mindset – against which Housman militates in his own vigorous writings. Who is Ibis? What had he done to provoke Ovid's curse against him? What can we infer from the Ovidian poem about the nature, length and metre of the Callimachean original on which it is purportedly modeled? Ellis usefully surveys earlier opinion on these and other questions and offers his own theories on (e.g.) the identity-problem; he interestingly describes the biology and habits of the ibis, and also its ancient reputation, and he painstakingly surveys the possible range of sources on which Ovid may have drawn in compiling his curse-catalogue.[48] Despite his contributions on these fronts, however, he works within the familiar terms of debate handed down from one scholarly generation to the next;[49] he offers nothing in the way of a creative response to the curse-catalogue in particular, but approaches it, as his predecessors had, as a sequence of textual puzzles that tested his learning and taxed his ingenuity.

In fundamental contrast to Ellis, Housman approaches a problem not according to traditional or conventional criteria, but very much on his own terms. Consider lines 291-2:

> utque parum mitis, sed non impune, Prometheus
> aerias uolucres sanguine fixus alas.

Several important mss transmit *parum mitis*, a reading which yields something approximating to 'poco docile, troppo ribelle', even though *mitis* is strained in this sense.[50] Ellis duly prints *parum mitis* in his 1881 edition but reports the conjectures of F. Sanctius, F.A. Riese and K.R. Merkel in his *apparatus*. Of these, he regards Sanctius' *parum Metes* (out of Greek Μῆτις, to the effect of 'lacking in wisdom') with special favour in his commentary because of its ironic play on Prometheus' name;[51] and in 1896 he went on to propose the ingenious but far-fetched *poru metis* (= Greek πόρου μῆτις) on the basis of a possible allusion to the Platonic *Symposium* (Poros/Resource is cast as the son of Metis at 203b3), whence *poru metis* allegedly represents Prometheus as 'the craftsman of resource', 'inventive genius of supply'.[52] More sober is S.G. Owen's *parum inmitis* ('Prometheus was not, like Zeus, *inmitis* to mankind, but was considerate'),[53] which he prints in his 1915 Oxford Classical Text. Housman's different intervention, however, changed the focus of the problem by approaching it from outside the closed arena of conjecture and counter-conjecture. In his 1894 recension he brackets lines 291-2; already, he records in 1920, the lines were condemned by Salvagnius and Bentley – a deletion approved by J. Schrader on the grounds that Ovid 'does not say the same thing twice in these curses'.[54] The case for deletion is invisible in the critical mainstream represented above by Ellis and Owen, but Housman succinctly revives it in reviewing those instances where the same character is twice named or signified in the *Ibis*, but differently killed or persecuted in the two instances.[55] But the two imprecations that befall Prometheus at 291-2 and then 543-4 are identical – a singular repetition that breaks the Ovidian rule, and therefore one of the two couplets *cannot* be authentic. To the independent-minded Housman the uncertain reading of line 291 is irrelevant to the *real* problem, which he perceives exactly as it was, and not as others preferred it to be;[56] yet the couplet is standardly retained by later editors, usually with a non-committal nod to Housman's proposal – although La Penna for one is inclined to accept it.[57]

II

It was in 1891,[58] some four years after J.P. Postgate's first correspondence with him,[59] that Housman embarked on editing the *Ibis* for Postgate's *Corpus Poetarum Latinorum*. That Housman was actively engaged with the *Ibis* by the autumn of that year is confirmed by the enquiries that he made of Robinson Ellis' mss collations – enquiries reflected in three surviving letters written by Ellis on (respectively) 18 and 20 October 1891 and 21 March 1892, and in one extant reply from Housman on 30 October 1891.[60] That he did not embark on the work before 1891 can also be inferred from his later allusion, in his 'Transpositions in the *Ibis* of Ovid' of 1918 but apparently written in 1916, to the quarter-century that had passed since he first turned his mind to the *Ibis*.[61] C.O. Brink asserts without argument that Housman contributed his edition in 1893;[62] but that it was in production in the summer of 1894 is shown by a postcard from Postgate to Housman of 8 August concerning the printing of the apparatus to line 512.[63]

After publishing his recension, which differs from Ellis' text in more than 80 places,[64] Housman had intended, he claims, 'to put together a paper discussing various problems which the poem presents, and in particular defending and explaining my alterations of its text'.[65] In the event, he was distracted by other interests,

> and the editors of Ovid were left staring at a set of very puzzling objects, – conjectures which I had proposed because I had read the *Ibis* with attention, and whose cause and aim were obscure to those who had not.[66]

Housman turned the time-lapse between his 1894 recension and his three elucidatory articles of 1915, 1918 and 1920 to creative advantage; or so it would appear from the tempting parallel to be drawn between the mysteries of Ovid's curse and those of Housman's own *Ibis*. Ibis, we are to imagine, is confronted with a set of barely penetrable *arcana*; in his different way Housman's recension confronts *his* readership with what he ostentatiously casts as a secondary set of obscurities. So in 1915:

> In 1894 ... I changed the *uiro* of u. 512 to *Iouis*, citing Hor. *carm*. II 17 22-4 'te Iouis impio / tutela Saturno refulgens / eripuit'; and editors of Ovid cannot imagine why. Mr Ehwald in 1902 ... enquired 'aber was hat Horat. II 17 22 mit unserer Stelle zu thun?', and Mr Owen in 1914 ... 'but what has the star of Jupiter to do with Simonides?'. When these scholars ask me these questions, they are not beseeching me to lighten their darkness; nothing is further from their desire ... They assume without more ado that there is no answer, and that my conjecture is therefore wrong.[67]

And in 1918:

In my recension of the *Ibis* ... I transposed four distichs, 135-40 and 459 sq., and suggested the transposition of three more, 181 sq., 203 sq., 409 sq. Perhaps, after two-and-twenty years, it is time to unravel the mystery of this behavior, and disclose my inscrutable reasons for resorting to the most unpopular of all methods of emendation.[68]

As if providing *his* 'victims' with much-needed illumination, and as if (like Ovid) the all-controlling master of the situation, Housman channels his characteristic acerbity towards a refreshing (and fitting) combativeness within *Ibis*-study that is missing in the more sedate researches of an Ellis. And if the Ovidian curse was launched in response to intolerable provocation, Housman was seemingly provoked from his long silence on the poem by a particular irritant of his own: S.G. Owen's 'Notes on Ovid's *Ibis*, *Ex Ponto Libri*, and *Halieutica*' (1914). Housman's low opinion of Owen had already found harsh expression in his 1903 review of Owen's Oxford edition of Persius and Juvenal.[69] Owen's 1915 Oxford edition of Ovid's exilic corpus receives similar treatment from Housman,[70] who nevertheless tellingly pays no serious attention to Owen's *Ibis*: since the poem goes unannounced on Owen's title-page, 'so it shall' in Housman's review.[71] For now, however, our focus is on Owen's 1914 article.

Housman's 'Ovid, *Ibis* 512 and *Tristia* III 6 8' (1915) takes its start, as we observed above, from the apparent consternation of Ehwald and Owen as to why he cites Hor. *Carm.* 2.17.22-4 in support of his proposed *Iouis* for the transmitted *uiro* in the following couplet:

> lapsuramque domum subeas, ut sanguis Aleuae,
> stella Leoprepidae cum fuit aequa Iouis.

'May you enter a house doomed to fall, as did Scopas, the seed of Aleuas, when the planet Jupiter was propitious to Simonides, son of Leoprepes'. According to the familiar story, the poet Simonides, while dining at the house of Scopas, was summoned to the door by two youths, the Dioscuri; he thereby survived the sudden collapse that killed Scopas and his other guests.[72] How, then, is Housman's *Iouis* to be justified? In response to Owen's 1914 defense of *uiro*, he unleashes a force of argument and learning that makes Owen's treatment appear unscientific and ill-informed by unfortunate comparison. '"*Stella*" is usually explained as the constellation of the Dioscuri, Gemini,' writes Owen, who deems this explanation 'unsatisfactory, for the function of that constellation would appear to have been to promote unity among friends'.[73] Manilius' editor would agree that there cannot be any allusion to the Dioscuri here, but he goes more directly to the heart of the matter: interpreters who 'mistake *stella* for the constellation Gemini, the third sign of the zodiac,' are misguided because (i) 'it was no sign of the zodiac that came to the door and called for Simonides, any more than it was a form of electricity; it was a pair of travel-stained young men on horseback'; and (ii) *stella* in any case simply 'does not mean a constellation: the examples alleged in the dictionaries are all false'.[74] Owen understands *stella* 'to mean Simonides' own natal star',[75] but Housman brooks no nonsense: 'there can be no allusion to that astrological entity which is called in English the natal star. "Natal star" is a translation of *natale astrum* or *sidus natalicium*, and it means one of the twelve signs of the zodiac. But *stella*, as I have said, does not mean a sign of the zodiac; and moreover the signs of the zodiac are neither *aequa* nor *iniqua* and do not rescue anybody from anything'.[76] Yet Owen claims to find the natal star at *Ibis* 209-10 *natus es infelix, ita di uoluere, nec ulla / commoda nascenti stella leuisue fuit*[77] – only for Housman to offer the corrective that '"planet" is what *stella* most often means in astrology, and what it means' in 209-16,[78] where the planet/*stella* of 210 takes its place alongside (e.g.) Venus and Jupiter (211) and Mercury (213-14). Owen claims that *uiro* is 'emphatic, "the illustrious man", as in Lucret. III.371, *Democriti quod sancta uiri sententia ponit*';[79] and he seeks support for this emphatic reading by drawing on Housman's own words of 1901 on the Lucretian line (Lucretius' *uiri* 'means a right worthy man, like ἀνδρός in Soph. Aiax 817 and elsewhere').[80] As if directly responding to Owen's citation of his 1901 words, Housman in 1915 restates that same position on the Lucretian line (*uiri* at Lucr. 3.371 has 'the pregnant force of "worthy wight" as a formal civility to a respected antagonist'),[81] but as a prelude to showing why *uiro cannot* carry equivalent weight at *Ibis* 512: 'But there is no similar reason why Simonides should be singled out from the multitude of his peers to be designated as Ovid never designates anyone else'.[82]

For Housman, *uiro* is 'an unexampled redundancy' after the patronymic *Leoprepidae*,[83] and *stella* no zodiacal sign but a planet in 512; *uiro* is a corruption of a word that gave definition to *stella*, which is surely awkward if left absolute.[84] At every stage his argument is brisk, precise, forceful. But which planet is meant? The benign Jupiter, 'Saturn's especial foe';[85] through Jupiter's benign influence, Simonides is saved from a peril – the collapse of houses – that is among those that 'both in ancient and in medieval astrology [are] laid to the account of Saturn'.[86] Housman's impressive case is supported by the same error – *uiro* for an oblique case of *Iuppiter* – that he would similarly correct at *Tr.* 3.6.8 *cognita sunt ipsi, quem colis, ista uiro/Ioui*,[87] only for him then wittily to sketch the defence that he anticipates for the mss' *uiro* in the *Tristia* instance (Augustus is cast as *uir* elsewhere in the exilic poetry ...) in merely mortal editors: 'This defence ought to satisfy quite a large number of their readers; for there are millions of mankind who can no more detect *ignoratio elenchi* than if they were editors of Ovid'.[88] The condescension that surfaces throughout Housman's 1915 piece is unattractive; and yet Owen's clipped and confident stance in his 1914 article ('But what has the star of Jupiter here to do with Simonides?')[89] arguably meets its just desert in Housman's withering tones ('But it is time to be telling Messrs Ehwald and Owen exactly how the planet Jupiter was concerned in the rescue of Simonides').[90] Housman's *Iouis* may yet be resisted, not least on the grounds that it implies a special Jovian intervention on Simonides' behalf; yet on a narrower interpretation of the astrological protocols, Jupiter's neutralising effect on malign Saturn should work to avert the general collapse, not to save Simonides in particular.[91] In most modern editions *uiro* is still cautiously retained, although *Iouis* is printed by Goold.[92] But whether or not Housman's argument ultimately convinces, his erudite demystification of *Iouis* takes on a life of its own as a work (or performance) of highly creative scholarship – another striking example to support J.D. Morgan's observation (à propos of Housman's elucidation of 539-40) that 'modern writers on ancient literature who dismissively regard Housman as merely a *Wortphilolog* do so at their peril'.[93]

Owen again draws his ire in another area where Housman transformed the landscape of *Ibis*-study. At last, after nearly a quarter century, Housman took it upon himself in his 'Transpositions in the *Ibis* of Ovid' to demystify the textual rearrangements in his 1894 recension. His approach is liberated from any undue deference either to ms authority or to standard editorial practice; in this article, Owen is cast as part of a complacent or backward-looking opposition which offsets, and defines, Housman's new precision of diagnosis and treatment. On occasion Housman can perhaps be too clinical. Take lines 139-40:

> tecum bella geram; nec mors mihi finiet iras,
> saeua sed in manis manibus arma dabit.

Housman was not the first to detect a problem of coherence between lines 139-40 and 141ff.,[94] but his solution – to transpose lines 135-40 to between lines 44 and 45 – was certainly novel. The problem as he perceived it is that in lines 139-40 'Ovid declares that his warfare with Ibis will persist even when both of them are dead';[95] shade will battle shade beyond the grave. In lines 141ff., however, Ovid suddenly envisages a different scenario: his own ghostly shade is set to persecute the evidently *still living* Ibis; for '[s]uch phrases as 143 *ueniam ... umbra* ... are merely comical if they describe one spectre trying to haunt another spectre'.[96] Then to line 153 (*Stygiis erumpere nitar ab oris*): 'If Ibis as well as Ovid is dead, this can only mean that Ovid's ghost will turn tail on Ibis' ghost and make a bolt for the upper air'.[97] And on 161-2: '*uiuus agitabere* and *uita futura est*, and in verse 140 [Ibis] was already dead and disembodied. O grave, where is thy victory?'[98] But if lines 135-40 are transposed, '[a]ll inconsistency is ... removed: Ovid says in 131-4 that while his life lasts he will hate his adversary, in 141-58

105

that when dead he will haunt him as a ghost; the death of Ibis is not contemplated till 161; his funeral follows in 163-72, and only in 173 does he reach the world below'.[99] Moreover, the examples of perpetuity in lines 135-40 sit well enough in their new context: after expressing his unceasing hatred through the adynata of lines 31-44, Ovid reverts to the perpetuity topos to declare endless war both in life (cf. *donec mihi uita manebit* 43) and in death (cf. *nec mors mihi finiet iras* 139).

This transposition admirably restores consistency to Ovid's plan of vengeance against his enemy: his undiminished hatred in life (131-4) will be perpetuated by his avenging shade in death (141ff.). But by removing the apparently ill-fitting allusion to Ibis and Ovid as shades locked in post-mortal combat, Housman arguably imposes on the avenging persona's imagination a disciplined logic that is out of step with the bizarre manoeuvres that characterise the curse as it gradually gathers momentum. Our avenger's indiscriminately directed prayer to any god who will heed him (67-88) gives way to his grotesquely imagined role as a priestly master of ceremonies who perverts all normal ritual in readying Ibis for human sacrifice (89-106). His subsequent recourse to every kind of commonplace imprecation (107-26) is then answered in his own certainty that his prayers will be granted (127-8) – a solipsistic vision of full satisfaction that takes another irrational turn if (*pace* Housman) we retain the contradiction between lines 139-40 on the one hand (Ibis and Ovid both dead) and 141ff. on the other (Ibis yet lives).[100] Housman diagnosed a real difficulty; yet he perhaps resorted too quickly to surgical correction of the poet's designedly irrational persona, as did those before him who had sought to resolve the difficulty through emendation.[101] But whether or not we accept his proposed transposition,[102] his argument is based on an alertness of perception that sees discomfort where Owen finds relatively smooth progress: 'In the first couplet [139-40] Ovid says that death will not end his wrath, but will furnish his spirit with merciless arms against the spirit of his enemy. This idea is repeated in the next couplet [141-2] with redundancy characteristic of Ovid.'[103] By emphasising repetition between the two couplets, Owen quite fails to address, or even acknowledge, the essential point that Ibis miraculously returns from the grave to live again in 141-2. In turning on this myopia ('"the next couplet" is the critics' horizon, and if they read as far as the third couplet they would lose sight and memory of the first'),[104] Housman targets a more general mindset very different from the restless acuity on display in his 1894 recension: 'I am the first editor who ever did read the *Ibis*, and down to this year 1916 I am the last.'[105]

Housman's transpositions have enjoyed a mixed reception among later editors,[106] but they invariably offer a bracing challenge to complacency. Perhaps the single most impressive stroke in his recension is to transpose three couplets – 459-60, 439-40 and 461-2, in that order – to between lines 338 and 339.[107] In a single ms lines 439-40 ('May Ibis die as Phalaris did in his brazen bull') occur in two places, after 437-8 (another allusion to death in Phalaris' bull) and before 339-40; in the latter case, lines 439-40 are joined by 461-2 before 339-40. In the other six mss on which Housman draws, lines 439-40 are found in one or the other of these two positions: which is the more correct? For Housman, lines 437-8 and 439-40 cannot originally have been set in juxtaposition to each other because of their common reference to Phalaris' bull; although the two couplets differ in their precise nuances of punishment for Ibis, Ovid's practice elsewhere is to separate, not directly to juxtapose, cognate allusions.[108] Hence the provisional case for locating lines 439-40 before 339-40; but what then of lines 461-2? The allusion there is to Apollodorus, the notoriously cruel tyrant of Cassandrea:

> aut, ut Cassandreus domino non mitior illo,
> saucius ingesta contumuleris humo.

> Or, as he of Cassandrea, who was no less cruel than that tyrant,
> may you be wounded and buried under the high-piled earth.

If this couplet is retained in its conventional *sedes*, the allusion in *domino ... illo* is hard to explain in its immediate context. But Ovid brings Apollodorus and Phalaris together elsewhere (cf. *Pont.* 2.9.43-4); if on that analogy lines 439-40 and 461-2 are read before 339-40, the allusion in *domino ... illo* (461) is then conveniently to the Phalaris of 439-40. The difficulty of interpreting *domino ... illo* in its original *sedes* is matched by a similar problem in lines 459-60:

> solaque Limone poenam ne senserit illam,
> et tua dente fero uiscera carpat equus.

> And, that Limone alone may not experience that punishment,
> may your flesh too be torn by the horse's savage tooth.

The terrible fate that befell Limone, the daughter of Hippomenes,[109] finds no immediate parallel in the lines preceding line 459; hence the strained case for taking the phrase *poenam ... illam* as a proleptic allusion to the pentameter, and not to a preceding verse.[110] But if 459-60 are transposed along with 461-2, Limone's fate follows neatly after that described in 335-6, and a fitting referent is found for *poenam ... illam*:

> utque nouum passa genus Hippomeneide poenae   335
>   tractus in Actaea fertur adulter humo,
> sic, ubi uita tuos inuisa reliquerit artus,
>   ultores rapiant turpe cadauer equi.

> And as, when the daughter of Hippomenes suffered a new kind of
>   punishment,
>   her illicit lover is said to have been dragged over Attic soil,
> so, when your odious life has left your limbs,
>   may avenging horses drag your filthy corpse.

In line 459 '*poenam ... illam* will refer to the *nouum ... genus ... poenae*
of 335; and nothing could be more apt and harmonious. Ovid first
imprecates on Ibis the doom of Limone's paramour, and then the doom
of Limone herself.[111] How did Housman's proposed ordering of the text
– 337-8, 459-60, 439-40, 461-2, 339-40 – become displaced? He
ingeniously posits that the scribal eye slipped from 336 *humo* to 462
humo, with the inadvertent omission of the eight intervening lines. The
error was discovered, and 337-8 inserted into the margin; restriction of
space caused the remaining six lines to be appended to the end of the
poem, from where they were later wrongly reintegrated into the curse-
catalogue.[112]

Housman's overall case is compelling, but for present purposes his
conclusions are less important than the methodological rigour – his
control of the ms evidence – that guides his entire approach to
transposition. His procedure is scientific and exact where Owen's, in his
1915 Oxford edition, appears imprecise and susceptible to half-truth:
Owen 'prints 339 immediately after 338, and lets his readers suppose
that he is obeying the MSS, when in truth he is obeying one MS and
disobeying six. He places 439 sq. between 438 and 441, and lets his
readers suppose that the MSS do so, when in truth half the MSS place
them elsewhere ....'[113] By such comments Housman effectively asserts
the superiority of his 1894 recension over its 1915 challenger; and
despite the favorable reception of Owen's edition elsewhere,[114] his
injudiciousness continues to be targeted in 'The *Ibis* of Ovid' (1920). In
this, Housman's most wide-ranging publication on the poem, his
analysis and attempted ordering of the most important mss (seven in
number) according to their relative quality gives way first to a seminal
disquisition on Ovid's avoidance of repetition in his curse-catalogue; and
then to discussion of his preferred readings in thirteen couplets or
passages, before he ends by remarking on the poem's *raison d'être* and
the different motives generating its different halves (1-250 and 251-
644). He self-consciously introduces this article as his last word on the
poem ('I will now take leave of the poem by adding a series of remarks,
general and particular, upon matters which may still seem to need
explanation or discussion');[115] and he ends with appropriate closure,
killing off Ibis in the last pages of his article with a deadliness quite
beyond Ovid's curses.

III

In dismissing Ibis as a fiction, Housman dispenses once and for all with the literalist approach to the poem that Ellis had unquestioningly perpetuated:

> Who was Ibis? Nobody. He is much too good to be true. If one's enemies are of flesh and blood, they do not carry complaisance so far as to choose the dies Alliensis for their birthday [219-20] and the most ineligible spot in Africa for their birthplace [221-2]. Such order and harmony exist only in worlds of our own creation, not in the jerry-built edifice of the demiurge. *Nor does man assail a real enemy, the object of his sincere and lively hatred, with an interminable and inconsistent series of execrations which can neither be read nor written seriously.* To be starved to death and killed by lightning, to be brayed in a mortar as you plunge into a gulf on horseback, to be devoured by dogs, serpents, a lioness, and your own father in the brazen bull of Phalaris, are calamities too awful to be probable and too improbable to be awful.[116]

The death-stroke was not just to Ibis, but also to the complacency of previous scholarly generations for whom Ovid was evidently attacking a real enemy. After Housman's pronouncement, those scholars who would remain committed to the fact of Ibis' existence have had to justify their approach in the face of his telling objections;[117] and the burden is on them to show how Ovid's curses *can* be either read or written seriously. As soon as Ibis is viewed as a figment, the curse is also easily explained away as a mere literary exercise that makes no pretension to doing real harm to anyone. For Housman, the first 250 lines constitute a 'masterpiece'[118] of literary cursing that gives climactic expression to Ovid's increasingly bitter remonstrations against an unnamed addressee (or addressees) in *Trist.* 3.11, 4.9, and 5.8. But then a drastic change of direction after line 250:

> From that point onward the poem is merely a display of erudition. Ovid, at the date of his exile, was bursting with information rather recently acquired. In his young days he had by no means been a learned poet; and Propertius, in the season of their sodality, must often have exhorted him to lay in a larger stock of those examples from mythology with which his own elegies are so much embellished or encumbered. But by the time he was fifty he had at his disposal more examples from mythology than he knew what to do with. His studies for the metamorphoses and some of his studies for the fasti (notably in the aetia of Callimachus) had furnished him with a far greater number of stories and histories than could be crowded into those two poems; and he felt the craving of the ὀψιμαθής to let everyone know how learned he had become. Here was his chance: history and mythology alike are largely composed of misfortunes as bad as one could wish for one's worst enemy; and he could discharge a great part of his load of knowledge through the channel of imprecation.[119]

This characterisation of the curse-catalogue as a mere *jeu d'esprit* has been faithfully echoed in later *Ibis* scholarship[120] – an orthodoxy of viewpoint that might itself convey the impression that modern criticism of the *Ibis* began and ended with Housman.

But we may yet take issue with Housman's insistence that Ovid's imprecations 'can neither be read nor written seriously', and that a poem addressed to a fictional enemy *must* lack any 'real' hostile purpose. Already in the *Tristia*, the Ovidian persona's reluctance to name his Roman addressees, allegedly through his fear of endangering them through named association with him, creates an air of mystery and even paranoia, as if the marginalised exile begins to see threats and vulnerabilities where there may or may not be real dangers. Uncertainty on so many fronts suggestively fuels this state of suspicion and unease. Does his wife remain loyal? Can he still count on the goodwill and practical support of this friend or that? Will that practical support ever win him a recall from Tomis? Has the imperial heart softened towards him or hardened against him? Amid these uncertainties, he paradoxically finds consolation in the very Muses who have destroyed him (cf. *carmen demens carmine laesus amo*, *Tr.* 4.1.30); his love-hate relationship with the Muses alternates between deep frustration and still deeper gratitude and reliance, so that 'although at times I curse (*deuoueo*) my poems and my Muses, whose injury to me I cannot forget, yet when I have fully cursed them (*cum bene deuoui*) I still cannot live without them' (*Tr.* 5.7.31-3). In his self-characterisation here, Ovid *needs* the outlet that cursing provides, as if that outburst releases a pent-up psychological tension in his isolated and vulnerable exilic persona. On this approach, his initial skirmishes with his unnamed enemy or enemies in the *Tristia* (3.11, 4.9 and 5.8) build tensions that finally explode some four years into his exile in the *Ibis*,[121] where the search for Ibis' 'true' identity is arguably irrelevant: whoever (if anyone) Ibis might conceivably be – and the extraordinary range of his alleged offences against Ovid in lines 11-22 suggests that his criminality is much too versatile and evil to be true[122] – what matters more is that the exilic persona perceives (or merely imagines?) itself to be under persistent attack in distant Rome. What matters on this approach is the possibility that the Ovidian persona targets a *supposed* enemy, truly 'the object of his sincere and lively hatred', but a phantom object who represents any and all of Ovid's real or imagined persecutors.

We may agree with Housman, then, that Ibis is nobody and yet still take Ovid's curse seriously as an artistically contrived explosion against a world that has disowned him. If the first 250 lines constitute a masterpiece of vitriol in which the poet runs through a medley of familiar curse-strategies, many of them in conformity with Hellenistic precedent,[123] his persona loses itself after line 251 in a solipsistic fantasy of revenge. There, in the seemingly limitless flow of his imprecations, his cursing imagination knows no bounds either to Ibis' suffering or to its own inventiveness: the 'seriousness' of the curse-catalogue lies precisely in the manic psychological condition that it represents before (we anticipate) Ovid's persona eventually tires and reverts in cyclical fashion to its normative melancholic state in exile.[124] What gives the *Ibis* overall coherence between the two halves so clinically distinguished by Housman is the gradual movement from Ovid's relatively controlled persona early in the curse to his *un*controlled abandon in the dream-like present of the catalogue. From this perspective, the curse-catalogue is not *merely* a display of erudition, but one that is meant to intimidate Ovid's (fantasy) enemy by fostering in him an ominous sense of foreboding as he patiently struggles to decode each new awfulness that awaits him. The whole experience is evidently unreal, but Housman's version of that unreality – the *Ibis* as the show-piece of an ὀψιμαθής brimming with learning – is not, perhaps, the only option before us as we try to take stock of this extraordinary poem: the *Ibis* may yet be chillingly 'real' in the strained but still life-like psychology that drives Ovid's cursing persona.

Notes

1. All references to the text follow the numeration of Housman 1894. For help and advice on numerous fronts, I am most grateful to James Zetzel and the editors.

2. For present purposes his blistering review of Rostagni 1920 (Housman 1921, 67-8 = *CP* 1049-50) need not detain us below, despite the interest of Rostagni's spirited rejoinder (1922, 76-80).

3. Respectively, Housman 1915a, 31-8 = *CP* 905-12; 1918, 222-38 = *CP* 969-81; 1920, 287-318 = *CP* 1018-42.

4. For background, Meier 1997, 114-15, and now van de Loo 2006, vii-lxxxii.

5. For the full title and details of the 1470 publication, van de Loo 2006, lxvii.

6. Meier 1997, 114. The lexicon was in fact the largest by far of three constituent parts of the original *Fabularius*; within that section, the mythological entries (80-90% of the whole) far outweigh the historical (see van de Loo 2006, xix-xx).

7. Cf. his words to the Oxford University Commission as reported by Clark 1913/14, 519: 'During the last thirty years all, or nearly all, the principal contributions to an enlarged knowledge of Greek and Latin authors have been based on an investigation of MSS of a minute and laborious kind unknown before. It has been my own aim as a scholar to show that research in this department of Philology is not confined to the Continent, and that Englishmen are able to appreciate the treasures which lurk in their national collections or in the private libraries of individuals.'

8. Cf. Ellis 1881, v.

9. Cf. Ellis 1881, liv: 'Sed ut G [= Cambridge, Trin. Coll. 1335], sic T [= Tours 879] hactenus latuit: neque ego citatum eum a doctis memini'. For the tripartite

division of the mss concisely surveyed, Tarrant in Reynolds 1983, 273-5 and Richmond 2002, 477-80.

10. Ellis 1877, 244; cf. Ellis 1881, liii-liv.

11. Ellis 1881, liv: '... omnia in apparatu Critico edenda duxi quae Conradus tradiderit' – an achievement for which Ellis is not slow to claim credit (ibid.: 'pro quo gratos lectores me habiturum confido, praesertim qui ea primus exhibuerim').

12. Murray 1913, 286-7 (my emphasis). Ellis' work on the *Ibis* reflects a broader eccentricity (cf. Murray 1913, 287: 'Oxford is full of stories of his quaint sayings, his oddities, and his weaknesses. That was the outer surface.') which itself had a troubling history, including an attempt on his life by shooting himself in the forehead with a revolver on 16 January 1869 (see Hopkins 2005, 257-8). In relating the circumstances of the shooting in a letter to Florence Nightingale, a sympathetic and concerned Benjamin Jowett writes that Ellis 'has been for the last 7 years really insane, living ... in a state of divided consciousness, & in the most aweful suffering. During the last year he appeared better because he never spoke of his misery. But on Friday night he could endure no longer ...' (Quinn and Prest 1987, 158 no. 184). One might speculate on a further dimension to Ellis' interest in the *Ibis* in light of Jowett's further remarks in a separate letter to Nightingale: 'Do you know that poor Mr. Ellis appears to have fired a ball at the side of his right eye into his brain, & scarcely to have injured himself? He has partially lost the sight of his right eye but this so far appears to be all. *He told me that he did it under the impression, which he has had for years, that some one was going to put him to a horrible & cruel death.* When he found that he had not succeeded, he ran out to the Surgeon at 5 oClock in the m^g. He is wonderfully good & patient and perfectly rational ...' (Quinn and Prest 1987, 159 no. 185; my emphasis). In other correspondence with Nightingale, Jowett reports (19 February 1869) that '[t]he surgeon who attends him says that he expresses regret that he did not succeed. The ball has been at last extracted & the eye sees nearly as well as ever' (cited at Hopkins 2005, 258); by October 'his mind appears decidedly better' (Quinn and Prest 1987, 178 no. 213); and (14 January 1870) '[o]ur mad friend has really been appointed [Professor of Latin] at the London University – I suppose that they did not know. His mind has been far better since his attempt, now just a year ago ... My hope of him is that his insanity belongs to a particular time of life' (Quinn and Prest 1987, 183 no. 223).

13. For the birth-name Aristoteles cf. Pind. *Pyth.* 5.87; for the foundation c. 630, Hdt. 4.155-8 with *CAH* III² 3.135-6, 256-7.

14. But cf. Hdt. 4.155: by one tradition the young Battus was so called because he was 'weak-voiced and stammering' (ἰσχνόφωνος καὶ τραυλός), but for Herodotus he acquired the name only after arrival in Libya, where the word for king was 'battus' (Λίβυες γὰρ βασιλέα βάττον καλέουσι).

15. Ellis 1877, 252.

16. van de Loo 2006, 353.131-8.

17. Ellis' rendering (1877, 252-3).

18. van de Loo 2006, 353.137-8. In Ovid, it is *Myrrha* who becomes the wanderer (cf. *uagata*, *Met.* 10.477, *errauit*, 479) after fleeing from her angry father (472-6).

19. Ellis 1881, 34.

20. Murray 1913, 287, as quoted above.

21. Housman 1883, 167 = *CP* 9.

22. Cf. Cat. 95.1-2; Zmyrna a variant of Myrrha.

23. Housman's own summation (1883, 167 = *CP* 9).

24. Wiseman 1974, 44-6, supported by Morgan 1990, via reference to Housman on *Ibis* 539-40.

25. Hollis 2007, 18 (further, 38 on 7c).

26. Housman 1883, 167 = *CP* 9.

27. Housman 1920, 315-16 = *CP* 1040.

28. Ibid., 316 (cf. 293) = *CP* 1040 (cf. 1023). For mss *urbis*, also Winstedt 1899, 396 with La Penna 1957, 143 in app. and p. cxxiv.

29. Housman 1920, 316 = *CP* 1040.

30. La Penna 1957, 143.

31. But for colorful distraction cf. Rostagni 1920, 36-8, reading *cognitor ut tardae laeuus cognomine Myrrhae* (Cinyras *laeuus cognomine* because his name [after Gk κινυρός] presaged misery upon revelation); briskly countered by André 1963, 52-3 n. 2.

32. Ellis 1896, 178.

33. Ibid., 178.

34. Ibid., 185-6; Ellis' emphasis.

35. I.e. by not deeming it 'necessary' to read *urbis*; cf. André 1963, 53 n. 2 ('La leçon *urbis* ... n'est pas nécessaire; ... *Orbis* est une hyperbole').

36. Cf. Salvagnius (Denis Salvaing de Boissieu, 1600-83) in the preface to his *Commentationes in Ibin* (1661), subsequently reprinted in the fourth volume of P. Burman's *P. Ovidii Nasonis opera omnia* (Amsterdam, 1727): wrestling with Ovid's obscurities is like entering an Olympic contest ('plurimi ... in hoc poëmatio, tanquam in Olympico stadio, non citra pulueris tactum desudarunt', p. 3 Burman). For Ellis' broader engagement in his 1881 *Ibis* edition with the humanist past, Williams 1996, 1-3.

37. Cf. Housman 1893, 128 = *CP* 347, eschewing an *over*-scientific eclecticism while also attacking the opposite extreme, Ellis presumably his unspoken target (cf. Naiditch 1988, 45): '... and there is *the born hater of science who ransacks Europe for waste paper that he may fill his pages to half their height with the lees of the Italian renascence ...*' (my emphasis). The editors of Housman's collected papers date this 1893 article to 1894 (*CP* 314), but see Naiditch 1995, 149.

38. Murray 1913, 286 (cited above).

39. Ibid.

40. Cf. Shackleton Bailey 1959, 796.

41. Housman 1920, 289 = *CP* 1019.

42. Murray 1913, 286. Cf. S.G. Owen's biting characterisation (1904, 126) of 'Mr. Housman's well-known eclectic idiosyncrasy as to editing, and his avowed disinclination to allow preponderating authority to one MS or group of MSS' (itself with sharp answer in Housman 1904, 228 = *CP* 618); Owen continues with 'Mr. Housman ... seems to think that a critic can declare by intuitive insight that this or that reading is right, taking now from a pure and now from a vitiated source. So that the ultimate court of appeal is not the MSS but the critic, not the MSS but Mr. Housman'.

43. Cf. Burnett 1.179-80 (Housman to Walter Ashburner, 6 July 1905): 'If you were here [sc. in England], your valuable advice would be sought on an important question, for I hear that Ellis [then 71] is asking undergraduates and other persons whether they think that he had better marry. I have not seen him for some time, and I fear I am rather in disgrace at present through having reviewed his last edition of Catullus [Housman 1905, 121-3 = *CP* 623-7] in a

manner which inspires deep indignation among the correspondents of the *Oxford Magazine*'.

44. See Naiditch 1988, 48-50.

45. Naiditch 1988, 34. For the poem and its prolegomena, published in *Ye Rounde Table* 1.6 (22 June 1878) 87-90, see Naiditch 1988, 34-41 and Burnett 1997, 230-5 with 525-8 for commentary.

46. See Naiditch 1988, 42, citing Gilbert Murray: 'Bobby told me he did not think it was a good edition at all. "But to encourage Housman I wrote him a long letter carefully explaining all my reasons for thinking him wrong". But, said Bobby, gazing at me with pained astonished eyes, "he did not like it at all!".' I am most grateful to Christopher Stray for his report *per litteras* of materials in the Oxford University Press archives which detail Ellis' involvement in, and payment for (two guineas), adjudging Housman's Propertius for the Press.

47. The couplet is printed by Burnett 1997, 289 with brief commentary on 564.

48. Ellis 1881, xix-liii.

49. Further, Williams 1996, 3.

50. La Penna 1957, 62 – but less far-fetched than Ellis' rendering of *parum mitis* as 'that failed in his philanthropy' (1881, 118, elaborated thus: 'Volebat Prometheus beneuolus esse ... hominibus, igni inuento, reuera autem nocebat ...').

51. Ellis 1881, 118.

52. Ellis 1896, 181.

53. Owen 1914, 255.

54. Housman 1920, 297 = *CP* 1025, citing Schrader ('in his Diris poeta bis idem non dicit'; 'Ovidius iisdem exemplis in breui carmine non utitur').

55. Ibid., 297-8 = *CP* 1026; cf. La Penna 1957, xlix-l.

56. Cf. Shackleton Bailey 1959, 796, albeit there on Housman's *Manilius*.

57. La Penna 1957, 63, holding 'probabile l'espunzione del distico'; Goold 1979, 256 brackets the couplet.

58. Naiditch 1995, 73-4.

59. See Naiditch 1988, 75-7.

60. For Ellis' letters, Naiditch 1988, 42-4; for Housman's reply of 30 October 1891, Burnett 1.71. The fifth and last letter that survives of their correspondence was written by Housman on 1 May 1907 (Burnett 1.207).

61. See Naiditch 1995, 73-4.

62. Brink 1985, 154.

63. See Naiditch 1988, 78 nn. 30-8; 1995, 73 n. 1.

64. Cf. Housman 1920, 293 = *CP* 1023.

65. Ibid., 287 = *CP* 1018.

66. Ibid.

67. Housman 1915a, 31 = *CP* 905.

68. Housman 1918, 222 = *CP* 969.

69. Housman 1903, 389-94 = *CP* 602-10. Cf. also Housman 1904, 227-8 = *CP* 617-18; 1915b, 40-6 = *CP* 964-8. The latter article is dated to 1918 by the editors of Housman's collected papers (see *CP* 964), but it was in fact published three years earlier; see Naiditch 1995, 149.

70. Housman 1915c, 60 = *CP* 903-4.

71. Ibid. Cf. the gentler formulation closing Alton's more benign review (1916, 232): 'Is it due to oversight that the *Ibis* is not mentioned in the title?'.

72. Sources: La Penna 1957, 133-4.

73. Owen 1914, 257.
74. Housman 1915a, 33 = *CP* 907.
75. Owen 1914, 258.
76. Housman 1915a, 33-4 = *CP* 908.
77. Owen 1914, 258.
78. Housman 1915a, 34 = *CP* 908.
79. Owen 1914, 258.
80. Housman 1901, 264 = *CP* 541.
81. Housman 1915a, 32 = *CP* 906.
82. Ibid.
83. Ibid. Along the way Housman discredits an alleged parallel for *uir* qualifying a patronymic by brilliantly modifying the punctuation at Sil. 13.800 to read ... *ire uiro. stupet Aeacide* ... (accepted by Delz 1987, 355).
84. Cf. Kenney 1959, 40: '*uiro* is not itself admirable, and what of *stella* absolute? It is *not* here 'come a 210' [La Penna 1957, 134 on 512]'.
85. Housman 1915a, 36 = *CP* 910.
86. Ibid.
87. Ibid., 37-8 = *CP* 911-12.
88. Ibid., 38 = *CP* 912.
89. Owen 1914, 258.
90. Housman 1915a, 36 = *CP* 910.
91. So La Penna 1957, 135.
92. Goold 1979, 278.
93. Morgan 1990, 559.
94. Cf. Schenkl 1883, 264, quoted by Housman 1918, 231-2 = *CP* 976.
95. Housman 1918, 230 = *CP* 975.
96. Ibid., 230-1 = *CP* 975-6.
97. Ibid., 231 = *CP* 976.
98. Ibid.
99. Ibid., 232 = *CP* 976-7.
100. For the approach, Williams 1996, 61-2.
101. So *inde meis* manibus arma dabo Schenkl 1883, 264; *innocuis* manibus arma dabit Merkel 1884, III.107, adopted by Mozley 1947, 260 (but *in manes* Goold 1979, 244; cf. next n.).
102. La Penna 1957, lxxxii-iii commends it ('probabile') but, adjudging it 'not strictly necessary', he hesitatingly retains 135-40 before 141; but cf. Goold 1979, 238 (135-40 'plausibly transposed by Housman after 44').
103. Owen 1914, 254.
104. Housman 1918, 232-3 = *CP* 977.
105. Ibid., 231 = *CP* 976.
106. For a judicious overview, La Penna 1957, lxxvi-lxxxiv.
107. Explication in Housman 1918, 222-9 = *CP* 969-74. The transposition is accepted by La Penna 1957, 82-3 (cf. lxxviii-lxxxi) and commended by Enk 1959, 367 in his review of La Penna; it is endorsed but not printed by Goold 1979, 260.
108. Housman 1918, 225 = *CP* 971.
109. Her father had discovered her seduction by an adulterous lover; for the legend, La Penna 1957, 81.
110. For Housman 1918, 227 = *CP* 973: 'this [a forward reference in *poenam ... illam*], though possible, is not natural, and is contrary to the analogy of *domino ... illo* in 461'.
111. Housman 1918, 227 = *CP* 973.
112. Ibid., 228-9 = *CP* 973-4.

113. Ibid., 229 = *CP* 974.

114. E.g. Alton 1916, 229-32, beginning 'Mr. Owen's services and merits are too well known to need recapitulation ...'.

115. Housman 1920, 287 = *CP* 1018.

116. Housman 1920, 316 = *CP* 1040; my emphasis.

117. So, e.g., La Penna 1957, xiii-xvi; André 1963, xviii-xix.

118. Housman 1920, 317 = *CP* 1041; also Enk 1959, 368-9.

119. Housman 1920, 317-18 = *CP* 1041-2.

120. E.g. Wilkinson 1955, 356-7; Kenney 1982, 454; Mack 1988, 42.

121. For the *Ibis* composed no later than 12 AD, La Penna 1957, vii-xi (probably 11 AD); André 1963, vi-vii.

122. On this point, Williams 1996, 20, 118.

123. Exhaustively demonstrated by Watson 1991.

124. For the approach, Williams 1996, 121-9.

6

Housman on Metre and Prosody

D.J. Butterfield

One of the most scientific fields in which Housman left his mark was the study of ancient metre. Throughout his career he repeatedly demonstrated his conviction that a deep knowledge of Latin and Greek metrics, applied with common sense, is a necessary tool for any textual critic of poetic texts. In this chapter I shall address the primary areas in which Housman contributed to the study of ancient metre and prosody. In attempting to assess the importance of his overall contribution, I will adopt a primarily chronological rather than a thematic approach.

Before turning to Housman's researches, we may briefly consider from what source his metrical knowledge initially came. At Bromsgrove (1870-7), he would not have progressed far beyond the canonical rules for verse composition (largely restricted to Greek iambic trimeters and the Latin dactylic metres)[1] and there is no record of lectures during his time at Oxford that would have instructed him in more recherché metrical knowledge. Yet it is clear from his confident disparagement of the metrical practice of other scholars in some of his early writings that, in both languages, he had found access to a higher authority.[2] It seems a safe presumption that Housman first learnt more advanced aspects of Greek metre from the work of J.H.H. Schmidt (1830-1913) but refined his knowledge by close use of individual commentaries and his own careful analysis of choral stanzas; the commentaries of Porson, Hermann and scholars working in their wake would have provided instruction about most of the intricacies of the iambic trimeter.[3] Nonetheless, it is striking to what extent Housman generally avoided employment of metrical jargon or annotation in his discussions; the one obvious exception, his 1898 '[Bacchylides] Ode XVII' (*CP* 455-64), I shall briefly discuss below. In his treatment of various aspects of Latin metre, the only sources for which he showed obvious respect in his early work are Lucian Müller's *De re metrica* (Leipzig, 1861; 1894[2]), Lachmann's Lucretius (Berlin, 1850) (and to a lesser extent Munro's Lucretius (Cambridge, 1864; 1866[2]; 1873[3]; 1886[4])) and occasionally the conclusions of Haupt, Meineke and certain German theses. Beyond these, Housman must have instructed himself in the minutiae of ancient metre by close and wide-ranging reading of Latin poetry; the fact that he did nevertheless disagree so often with these esteemed figures evinces the independent fruits of this private research.[4] I have found in Housman's discussions no positive mention of lexica (general or metrical), verse graduses or compositional handbooks.[5] Incidentally, there is no evidence in his academic papers, extant lecture notes and correspondence that he ever took any real interest in the historical origin and development of ancient metres or (to any serious degree) ancient pronunciation (cf., e.g., *CP* 960).

*

Housman's earliest articles, i.e. those of the 1880s, concerned almost exclusively the Greek tragedians, Propertius and Horace.[6] Accordingly, the metrical points he treated in Greek concerned aspects of choral lyric (especially responsion) and details relating to the tragic trimeter; metrical points arose rarely in his Horatian work and only occasionally in his series of Propertian emendations. As regards his earlier publications, therefore, although metre is occasionally discussed when it is the reason for emendation, there is no clear evidence of its being an area of particular interest for Housman (contrast Walter Headlam (1866-1908), for whom it evidently was *ab initio*). We may, however, reference a few small discussions. In his 'On certain corruptions in the *Persae* of Aeschylus' of 1888, Housman dismissed (*CP* 18-19) the lengthening of τε before mute-cum-liquid (here κλ-) at A. *Pers.* 664 (dochmiac) and many competent judges have since followed him (cf. Barrett ad E. *Hipp.* 760 and p. 435, and Diggle 1994, 386 with n. 79), though not necessarily preferring his emendation (καινὰ γᾷ) to Enger's (αἰανῆ). In his 'Horatiana [III]' of 1890, objection is made (*CP* 149) to the elision at Hor. *S.* 2.6.29 of *rem* (introduced by Bentley's emendation) at 4s before a short syllable, a point that had already been sufficiently discussed by Arthur Palmer.[7] In 'Manuscripts of Propertius [II]' (of 1893) he correctly objected (*CP* 287) that the lengthening of *-er*, as presented by the mss at Prop. 2.28.29 is unexampled in the poet.[8] His statement (*CP* 280) upon *Capanei irato* (Heinsius : *magno* mss) at Prop. 2.34.40 is worth quoting for its restraint: 'It is however uncertain whether Propertius would venture to elide this diphthong in a Greek name. Seeing that even before a short syllable he employs the very rare elision of a long Greek vowel in II xxviii 19 "Ino etiam", he may be thought capable of eliding before a long syllable even the diphthong, which after all is not a Greek diphthong: but it is perhaps safest to suspend judgment.' There can be little doubt that, if he had returned to discuss this emendation in later life, Housman would have dismissed wholesale the unparalleled elision of *-ĕī* in synizesis.

By the time he had obtained his professorship at University College, London, and had come to specialise in Latin scholarship from the mid-1890s, Housman had evidently refined his knowledge about the metres in which those authors most interesting to him composed: dactylic hexameters and elegiacs. The fruits of his deeper study into this metrical form first appeared clearly in his series of articles entitled 'Ovid's *Heroides*', published throughout *CR* 11 (1897). Housman here showed that his knowledge of Ovidian compositional style was sufficiently thorough to allow confident discussion of a number of refined points concerning elision in his poetic corpus. I focus on three such instances.

(i) Housman argued (*CP* 401-2) against the text of *Her.* 10.85-6 (*forsitan et fuluos tellus alat ista leones* / *quid scit an et saeuas tigridas insula habet*) on grounds of syntax (*habet* in lieu of *habeat*) and metre (elision at 4w in the pentameter). Having transposed *forsitan* and *quis scit an*, thereby permitting the indicative *habet* to stand, he nonetheless rejected the support of what he took to be the sole Ovidian parallel for the elision, *resistere equos* at *Tr.* 4.2.54, on the grounds that it was 'penned at Tomi and taken straight from Propertius [3.4.14]'. To remove the metrical fault he offered no proposal of his own but expressed sympathy with Gronovius' *forsitan et saeuam tigrida Naxos habet*. In this instance editors have not generally followed his practice, perhaps because they also know of the pentameter close *addere aquas* at *Pont.* 1.8.46 (which is universally retained) and mistakenly believe it to be adequate support for *insula habet*.[9] Other critics are more attracted to *quis scit an et saeuam tigrida Dia* [i.e. *Naxos*] *ferat* (certainly better than Heinsius' *saeua tigride Dia uacet*)[10] of the *ed. Etonensis*. Bentley's deletion of the couplet, however, is not the act of a wild man.

(ii) Housman was also right to reject 12.65 in its transmitted form (*orat opem Minyis. petit altera et altera habebit*) on the grounds that it is 'un-Ovidian in metre' (*CP* 404). Although he provided no explicit reason for this assertion, he probably doubted specifically the elision at 4w (made all the more improbable by its combination with the commoner, but still rare, elision at 5w).[11] Housman's instinct was correct on this point:[12] elision at 4w never occurs in Tibullus, only twice in Propertius[13] and only eight times in the mss of Ovid's vast corpus (some 22,000 elegiac verses). Crucially, the seven secure Ovidian examples all involve enclitic -*que* (*Am.* 1.9.41, *Her.* 9.39, 12.63, *Tr.* 3.2.9) or the proclitic pyrrhics *nisi* (*Her.* 21.5) and *sine* (*Fast.* 1.111, 3.727); the eighth transmitted instance (*Her.* 8.73 *aequora ab hospite*) should be removed by reading Heinsius' singular *aequor*.[14] Housman suggested *alter petit, impetrat alter*, a conjecture which has been praised or adopted by numerous subsequent editors (e.g. Palmer 1898, Shuckburgh 1910 and Goold 1977b).

119

(iii) A third discussion of Ovidian elision concerns the closing hemiepes of 20.178 (*certe ego saluus ero*), upon which Housman observed that '[t]he elision of a long syllable in the latter half of a pentameter occurs nowhere else in either Ovid or his imitators (15.96 is to be emended away)'[15] (*CP* 419). The assertion is correct; perhaps it is uncharitable to infer that Housman's expression, avoiding any comment on Propertius or Tibullus, signalled that he was in doubt as to their practice or believed that they did so elide long syllables. At any rate, the one possible example (Prop. 4.1.36) he prints in its emended form with *longa* (recc.) for *longe* at *CP* 39.[16]

We may note finally his discussion (*CP* 409) of Wakker's emendation of *legeres etiam* at *Her.* 15.41 to *legerem etiam*: 'There is no such verse [i.e. exhibiting true caesural hiatus] in Ovid;[17] the two examples in Propertius are very soon emended;[18] the one example in Tibullus is hard to emend, but his MSS are almost the worst in the world.'[19] Housman's elegant suggestion *sat iam* (with *legerem*) has been accepted by a number of subsequent critics.[20]

*

In the same year scholars across Europe set upon emending the odes of Bacchylides, discovered in papyrus in 1896.[21] Within a series of articles published in early 1898, Housman and his colleague at UCL, Arthur Platt, arrayed themselves on a particular metrical point against Kenyon, Jebb, Herwerden, Blass and Tyrrell (*inter alios*) by denying that the final syllable of the line in his odes is in reality *anceps*.[22]

Subsequent scholarship upon Bacchylidean metre has judged largely in favour of Housman and Platt: for the most part, Bacchylides employed close correspondence in his metrical schemes, avoiding *ancipitia*. His practice necessarily varies according to the metrical base of each ode and also to its position in each colon. The pair therefore pushed their case too far in denying any instances of *syllabae ancipites*, with the result that they came to emend away supposed instances of non-correspondence owing to their ignorance of certain prosodic licences available to Bacchylides, such as the artificial doubling of a final ν, ρ and σ[23] or lengthening of a vowel (such as bacchiac μινύθει at 3.90). Accordingly, many of their emendations are misjudged where the transmitted text can be shown to scan. Yet the victory is largely theirs.[24]

To consider a single instance, we may briefly inspect the metre of 11.119:

> ἄλσος δέ τοι ἱμερόεν
> Κάσαν παρ' εὔυδρον πρόγο—
> νοι ἐσσάμενοι Πριάμοι' ἐπεὶ χρόνῳ   120

βουλαῖσι θεῶν μακάρων
πέρσαν πόλιν εὐκτιμέναν
χαλκοθωράκων μετ᾽ Ἀτρειδᾶν.

πρόγονοι ἐσσάμενοι has been suspected for two reasons. Firstly, syntax: it is impossible to construe the clause without a finite verb; secondly, metre: the appearance of βροτῶν (35) and κάμοῡ (76; the latter syllable long according to the prosodic licence mentioned above) at the corresponding place of the two preceding epodes proves the second omicron of πρόγονοι to be untenable; furthermore, synaphea at this place in the epode is unexpected. Housman rightly raised the metrical objection, adopting Platt's πρὸ γουνοῖ᾽ and following it with ἑσσαν ἔμεν. He proceeded to develop his argument as follows, however: 'Since we learn from this passage that synaphea exists between the seventh and eighth lines of the epode, it follows that κάμον in 77 is unmetrical',[25] which he replaces with Platt's κάμοντ',[26] conjectured at his own prompting.[27] Were this same malpractice committed by another scholar, i.e. emendation on the basis of another, inherently corrupt passage, Housman would doubtless have rebuked the culprit with some severity.

In a note of three months later (*CP* 465-9), Housman instead emended δέ of 118 to τε and Κάσαν πάρ᾽ to κά πευσαν, thereby restoring ἐσσάμενοι in 120.[28] This second treatment of the passage shows, however, a further evolution in Housman's thought. For, having rebuked Blass and Wilamowitz for their belief in the possibility of a short syllable at the close of 119, he embarked (*CP* 466) upon a brief discussion of this particular point. He compared as parallel to these scholars' poor method the perverse acceptance of transmitted instances of anapaestic third feet in iambic trimeters of Attic tragedy, explicitly citing Porson's rigorous dismissal of these anomalies in the famous preface to the second edition of his *Hecuba* (Cambridge, 1802). Observing that 11.119 should match 11.35 in scansion, he conceded 'there is another way of scanning 77 to match 35, not indeed a legitimate way, but at any rate a less outrageous one. It is to reckon the -ον of κάμον as long.' Housman distanced himself, however, from adopting this theory, offering it to a generic second person: 'The hypothesis that a short final syllable can be lengthened even at a point which is not the end of a measure has a large number of MS corruptions to support it, and will help you to defend ... πόλιν at 114, μεγαίνητε at III 64, ἀπωσάμενον at V 189 and ἐσθλόν XIV 3.'[29] Housman therefore implied that these instances are genuine manuscript errors (and indeed he had emended them away in his first *CR* paper upon Bacchylides at, respectively, *CP* 449, 444, 446 and 452) but subsequent critics typically retain all as prosodic (rather than metrical) 'lengthenings' (and instances such as νασιῶτιν̄ 10.10 and δόμοῡ 17.100 could also be compared).[30] The fact that Housman allowed himself to record this comment may betray his partial uncertainty in this difficult field.

In the duel of metrics that the Bacchylides controversy engendered, Housman explicitly rebuked Jebb as an unqualified metrist,[31] having thought little since his early years of the Greek professor's metrical competence.[32] Although the sensitive Jebb was evidently wounded, and felt maltreated by Housman, he seems later to have sympathised with some of Housman's metrical assertions. In his edition of Bacchylides (Jebb 1905), although he continued to accept *syllabae ancipites* with evidently excessive leniency, he termed Housman's ἀπωσαμένους 'attractive' (p. 104), accepted his νόσων for νούσων at 1.170, and in the end declared the transmitted πρόγονοι to be 'impossible' at 11.119-20. Indeed, Jebb's final conjecture on this last passage above does satisfy Housman's metrical strictures: πρὸ ναοῖ' with Wilamowitz' ἑσσαμένων (cf. his *Appendix* at 481-3).

Outside this particular instance, Housman's ability to handle Bacchylidean metre with confidence is well evidenced by his clear and calm summary of the metre of *Ode* 17 (*CP* 455-64), which lays out its schema in a format that has only undergone minor rearrangement in subsequent, twentieth-century discussions. With this self-assured treatment we may compare Housman's tongue-in-cheek but nonetheless rather resigned observation about two earlier lyricists: 'versifiers are divided into two classes, one of which contains Pindar and Aeschylus, and the other the rest of mankind' (*CP* 459).

*

By the turn of the twentieth century Housman's interest and proficiency in metre had become manifest to all. Nonetheless, at no point in the rest of his career did he devote prolonged research to any explicitly metrical topic. The closest he came to a sustained analysis is the '*nihil* in Ovid' dispute (on which see below); two landmark articles (to which I will also come), both entitled 'Prosody and Method', were as much concerned with methodological approaches to metrical questions as they were with furthering research in the field. Accordingly, in order to trace his further contribution to metrical studies, one must work carefully through the pages of his editions (*Man.* I-V, *Juvenal*, *Lucan*) as well as the numerous minor observations in his later articles.

We may at this medial point in Housman's career take stock of how he regarded the contemporary state of metrical studies in Classical scholarship. His view of metricians (or 'metrists', as he typically termed them) was generally disapproving and many well-known scholars came under his lash. Friedrich Marx 'attempts to play the metrist without success' (*CP* 672, in a two-page attack on his metrical shortcomings as Lucilian editor); Friedrich Vollmer is 'certainly not a metrist' (*CP* 771);

J.P. Postgate (who came to publish one of the few twentieth-century British manuals on Latin metre (see n. 4)) is often treated harshly on metrical matters (e.g. 'Dr Postgate has shown on other occasions that his ear for the Latin iambic is not perfect, and some of his conjectures here [Phaedrus *OCT*, 1920] are metrically insecure or vicious' (*CP* 1010)); the young Cyril Bailey is mocked for a metrically anachronistic emendation.[33] The contemporary English-speaking world is more than once reprimanded for its poor metrical knowledge, most strikingly in 1924: 'German tiros can learn metre from experts; it is in Mr [E.T.] Merrill's country [i.e. the United States] and mine that tiros are instructed by their fellow-tiros ... Competent authority speaks with one voice, and provokes a babel of dissent from the Anglo-Saxon race, which will not study metre and yet presumes to have opinions upon it' (*CP* 1092).[34] Even scholars of earlier centuries could not escape criticism: in one sentence (*CP* 1138) Gronovius is declared to have been an 'imperfect metrist' and, more mercifully, Markland's (knowledge of) prosody is downcast as 'not that of a Bentley or Dawes'. Nonetheless certain figures do receive clear praise as to their abilities in the field: Lucian Müller, author of one of the most important books on Latin metre yet written, is a 'consummate metrist' (*CP* 662) and Paul Maas 'a genuine metrist'[35] (*CP* 1118); Lachmann (mostly from material contained in his Lucretian commentary) is cited *passim* as a metrical expert, grimly contrasted with the decadent practices of later generations. In his Cambridge lecture notes on Plautus (University Library, Cambridge, mss add. 6882, II p. 4; cited by Naiditch 1988, 222 nn. 70-6) Bentley is praised as the greatest metrist of the modern age.

To return to Housman's subsequent (i.e. twentieth-century) metrical work, we may first take note of a surprising feature that runs contrary to, or at any rate sits uncomfortably with, his rigour in treating metrical matters. This is his willingness, throughout his career, to accept individual metrical anomalies as legitimate licences rather than to posit scribal corruption. Although it would be a cavalier and fallacious dogma with regard to metrical and poetic licences to ordain '*si semel, numquam*', and thus emend away each individual and unparalleled anomaly, in a number of instances I do not find myself particularly convinced by Housman's defence of unique metrical irregularities.

For instance, we find him accepting (*CP* 512) the sole transmitted instances of hypermetre in both Germanicus (*Arat. fr.* 4.73) and Lucretius (5.849): modern editors do not accept the former instance and I have argued (albeit contrarily to most scholars) against the veracity of the latter.[36] Housman likewise believed (*CP* 145) in the contraction *singlariter* at Lucr. 6.1102, although there is no other example in Classical Latin literature of *-ngul-* contracted to *-ngl-*.[37] Such open-armed acceptance of contracted forms led him to conjecture (ibid.) the hapax *crepuscla* (< *crepusculum*) at Hor. *S.* 1.8.36, a suggestion that has not found approval.[38]

In his note upon Man. 1.194 (*nec uero tibi natura admiranda uideri*) Housman conceded that there is no other verse in Manilius with parallel rhythm. Yet, despite his acknowledging that Lachmann (*ad Lucr.* 6.1067) and Ellis (*CR* 7 (1893), 311) produced a more natural rhythm by their simple transpositions (the former also supported by the reading of m v and (according to Housman) k), he kept the text unchanged in his later *Man. ed. min.* as he had previously in *Man.* I. Goold's decision to accept Ellis' version of the line in his Teubner text seems rather more prudent. Housman likewise supported the single (and conjectural) instance of a monosyllable elided before a dactylic word in Manilius (4.46 *quod, consul totiens, exul, quod <de>* [add. Bentley] *exule, consul*), just as he retained the sole transmitted instance of a long elided monosyllable at Luc. 1.334 (upon which he added no note in his *Lucan*).

It is also surprising that Housman's close familiarity with the nuances of elegiac metre did not lead him to discuss or (it seems) suspect the usage of unelided *atque* in elegiac poetry. Further, he even introduced the word in a preconsonantal position in his conjecture at Prop. 4.5.20; although the emendation was made as an undergraduate or in the years soon after his graduation (see *CP* 38), he still explicitly supported this conjecture in 1894 (*CP* 329).[39]

On the other hand, Housman was perhaps correct to resist emending away apparently unmotivated metrical rarities in his note at Man. 5.634, where he refused to transpose the word order *sub tali tempore*, which is contrary to Manilius' usual practice of placing the preposition between modifier and noun (if the order is metrically equivalent; cf. *tali sub tempore* at 5.699). With poetic hyperbole, he demands 'huc huc cito conuenite quotquot ubique estis Cortii Marxiique nec poetam se liberum hominem existimantem ... tuleritis.'[40] Citing 1.624 (*per gyri signa*) and 2.195 (*cum uernis roribus*) as sufficient parallels for the transmitted text, he then concludes bitingly: 'quae tria exempla, si ingeniosus essem, aut transpositis uerbis emendarem adderemque "nur so konnte Manilius schreiben", aut nauiter extare negarem, aut causas fingerem a libero arbitrio remotas; nec tamen, nisi etiam Germanus essem, laudarer.'[41] His defence of the only perfect forms in *-ĕrunt* at Man. 2.877 (see n. ad loc. and also the addendum in *Man.* V) and at Luc. 4.771 (retained without a note) seems similarly right-minded.

In two instances does Housman retain the 'lengthening' of a short closed final vowel in the arsis of the line: at Man. 1.10 (*das animum uiresque facis ad tanta canenda*) and 876 (*numquam futtilibus excanduit ignibus aether*). The former, non-caesural, example is less easy to stomach and, notwithstanding his assertion ad loc. that 'certe aptissimum est *facis*', it may well be that emendation is required.[42]

Although the latter could indeed be a Lucretian or Virgilian reminiscence,[43] it could easily be removed by reading *canduit*, 'shone', preceded by a particle such as *quia* (in third position at 1.336 and 2.728).[44]

Housman also showed prudence in defending the elision of (probably dactylic) *ducito* in the fifth foot at Man. 3.423, upon which he offered a magisterial note on the correption of -*ō* that repays close study. It was nonetheless bold of him, on the basis of the two elisions of cretics ending in -*um* at 5.536 (first foot) and 735 (fifth foot), to employ the same licence, though admitting that it is 'duriuscula', in his supplement at 2.937a (*asperum iter temptans Aries qua ducit Olympum*).

A symptom of the influence that both Lachmann and Munro had upon Housman in metrical matters is evidenced by his conjecturing the archaic pronominal form *ibus* as a pyrrhic at Lucr. 2.462: this form, unattested in Lucretius, had been conjectured by one of the Vossii at 2.88 but also by Lachmann and Munro elsewhere in the poem, all improbably. Had Housman investigated the metrical properties, and dates of occurrence, of this particular pronominal form in Latin literature, or reflected upon its morphology (which demands *ībus*), it would have become clear how improbable it was that Lucretius ever used this form.[45]

*

We may now turn to a metrical debate at the centre of which Housman found himself. In an article of 1916 entitled 'Notes on Ovid', he had referred (*CP* 925) with tacit approval to Lachmann's well-known note on Lucr. 1.159 (separately expressed in Lachmann 1876, II 159), in which it is alleged that, for Ovid, disyllabic *nihil* was of iambic scansion[46] and that there is no genuine evidence for its employment as a pyrrhic in his work. In the wake of Lachmann's controversial assertion, Merkel had cited *Tr.* 5.8.2 (*te quoque sim, inferius quo nihil esse potest*) and Mueller *Tr.* 4.8.38 (*mitius immensus quo nihil orbis habet*). For his own part, Housman dismissed as spurious the distich containing the former pentameter and suggested emending the latter by transposition (*immensus quo nil mitius orbis habet*). Although Housman does not explicitly state that he was convinced by Lachmann's reasoning, he was evidently not averse to it. Three years later, however, he came to expand upon this precise question in '*Nihil* in Ovid' (*CP* 1000-3). He there somewhat misleadingly states, 'I ... concluded that judgment of the controversy must be held in suspense' (*CP* 1000), for no such conclusion was evident in his earlier discussion. He continued, 'I can now settle the question by means of an observation which I ought to have made before, and so indeed ought Lachmann.' Housman's procedure was laudably simple and convincing: he collected all examples of *nil* or *nihil* in the latter half of the first foot in Ovid and found that, of the 21 such instances, the mss present *nihil* in eighteen. Furthermore, emending *rethei* (=*Rhoetei*) at *Ib.* 284 to *Hercei* on grounds of sense, and positing *nil* as a scribal error for *nihil* at *Met.* 13.266 and *Fast.* 1.445, it emerges that all instances of the word in this *sedes* are the pyrrhic *nihil* placed in prevocalic position. Since Ovid did, however, place other monosyllables preconsonantally in this same location, the highly probable inference is that, at least in the latter half of the first foot, he did not want to use monosyllabic *nil* when a disyllabic byform stood as a viable alternative. Housman rightly concluded that the motivation for this decision must have been a desire to procure an initial dactyl in the hexameter and pentameter.[47] Yet since *nil* is found alongside *nihil* in preconsonantal position in the latter half of other feet, Housman left the question open as to whether Ovid did place *nil* prevocalically in such *sedes*.[48]

Housman's remarks stirred J.P. Postgate to an attack on his method (1920, 52-63). This salvo failed to appreciate Housman's particular point and instead, in a misguidedly patronising tone, merely reasserted the long-held but still unproven suspicion of many scholars that Ovid did not use *nil* in prevocalic position in the latter half of any foot. This unhelpful challenge was rightly rebuked by Housman in an article entitled '*De nihilo*' (*CP* 1012-15). Yet neither this, nor Postgate's subsequent rebuttal,[49] brought an advance in metrical knowledge and need not concern us here.[50]

Although Housman definitely emerged better from the fray, it is to be regretted that he did not investigate the manuscript evidence for preconsonantal *nec* vs *neque* (the closest analogue to prevocalic *nil/nihil*) with regard to Ovid's practice in the latter half of the first foot, although manuscript evidence would have been even less trustworthy on this point. The closest he came to such an enquiry is found in a note upon the two forms ad Luc. 1.439, an author whose practice with regard to *nihil* is clearly summarised in a note ad 6.819.[51]

Yet Housman was ever-conscious of his careful methodology in these matters. In the latter stages of his career, he recorded his own conception of the relationship of metrical and grammatical rules with manuscript evidence in his masterly 1921 lecture to the Classical Association, 'The application of thought to textual criticism' (*CP* 1058-69):

> There is one special province of textual criticism, a large and important province, which is concerned with the establishment of rules of grammar and of metre. Those rules are in part traditional, and given us by the ancient grammarians; but in part they are formed by our own induction from what we find in the MSS of Greek and Latin authors; and even the traditional rules must of course be tested by comparison with the witness of the MSS. But every rule, whether traditional or framed from induction, is sometimes broken by the MSS; it may be by few, it may be by many; it may be seldom, it may be often; and critics may then say that

the MSS are wrong, and may correct them in accordance with the rule. This state of affairs is apparently, nay evidently, paradoxical. The MSS are the material upon which we base our rule, and then, when we have got our rule, we turn round upon the MSS and say that the rule, based upon them, convicts them of error. (*CP* 1066)

And, shortly after:

One of the forms which lack of thought has assumed in textual criticism is the tendency now prevailing, especially among some Continental scholars, to try to break down accepted rules of grammar or metre by the mere collection and enumeration of exceptions presented by the MSS. Now that can never break down a rule: the mere number of exceptions is nothing; what matters is their weight, and that can only be ascertained by classification and scrutiny. (Ibid.)

In two articles of 1927-8, Housman magisterially puts into practice what he regarded as the correct *modus operandi* for analysing apparent metrical or prosodic anomalies. The first such article, 'Prosody and method [1]'[52] (*CP* 1114-26), served as a diatribe against those scholars who assailed established rules of metre and grammar by merely looking for counterexamples in manuscript evidence. Housman's chosen point of focus was the 'lengthening' of open short final vowels in preconsonantal position at the penthemimeral caesura, and his primary object of attack was Theodor Birt, who had asserted (1913, 72) that this was a legitimate licence for Classical poets. Housman prunes Birt's nineteen varied examples by removing those excluded by virtue of better manuscript witnesses or their sphere of occurrence (epigraphic evidence being dismissed as too insecure) and those that can be explained away for other reasons (e.g. when they precede mute-cum-liquid).

He explicitly formulated (*CP* 1117) the sound rule that no manuscript anomaly can be treated as significant if it is also accompanied by bad grammar or bad sense or both; an impartial critic would disregard such instances, since the metrical irregularity could be part of the same corruption. This important point he explicitly demonstrated by considering Prop. 4.5.64 (transmitted as *per tenues ossa sunt numerata cutes*), a line he showed both to contain barbarism (*cutes* as plural for singular) and to be devoid of sense. In the end, Housman whittled down Birt's proffered instances to eight and added five of his own. Six of Birt's remaining eight he suggested could be emended away with relative confidence (*Ciris* 189, Prop. 2.13.35, Tib. 1.7.61, Verg. *A.* 3.464, 12.648, Ov. *Am.* 3.7.55), leaving the two early instances (Enn. *Ann.* 139 and the *Epigramma Plauti* ap. Gell. 1.24.3), where their composers perhaps did adopt Graecising licences. By contrast, he here made no attempt to emend away his five additional instances drawn from Classical authors (Macer 8 Bl., Verg. *A.* 1.501, Prop. 4.1.101, Tib. 3.12.19, Man. 4.478). We should note, however, that the last (*et sexta et decuma et quae ter quinta notatur*) Housman had printed in 1920 with Bechert's *tibi* inserted after *ter*; in the addendum upon 4.419 at the close of *Man.* V, he had also expressed an opinion that Morel's (in reality Aldrovandri's) *tellus* for *terra* at Macer 8 Bl. could be correct. It should nevertheless be left as a curious fact that the easy emendations available for the three remaining instances, unique in each author, were not explicitly embraced by Housman, neither here nor elsewhere: Prop. 4.1.101 *facito* (Lachmann) for *facite*; Verg. *A.* 1.501 *deas* (Fω and Macr. 5.4.9, 13.8) for *dea* (MPR) and Tib. 3.12.19 (*ut* post *grata* add. Eberz). Housman rather ended by asserting, 'my object has not been to controvert the opinion that short final vowels were lengthened; it has been to show how flimsy is the evidence arrayed in support of that opinion, and to reprobate the temper of mind which finds such evidence sufficient' (*CP* 1125). Such restraint, even in this didactic context, is surprising.

The second article of the same name ('Prosody and Method II: The metrical properties of "gn"' (*CP* 1136-46)) focused upon the question of '*gn*' making position, and therefore again addressed, as Housman acknowledged, more as a matter of metre than prosody. He begins by observing how Lucian Müller's rule (1861, 315-16), that in dactylic poetry no short open final vowel remains short before initial *gn*-, has been inappropriately assailed by later scholars. He proceeds to mock the fact that Gustav Friedrich is treated as a metrical expert,[53] attacking the poorly selected or illusory examples that he cites to counteract Müller's rule, some being conjectural, others of an epigraphical nature. The discussion proceeds by separating with clarity occurrences of *gnatus* and *natus*, then moves to Greek words either beginning in *cn*- or containing -*cn*-.[54] The piece serves as an exemplary instance of Housman's sound methodology and clear-headed logic in this difficult field.

*

In spite of his increasingly authoritative voice on metrical matters, Housman did appreciate that there were advances yet to be made in ancient metre. In a letter of 1920 (Burnett 1.430) to Gow, who had presumably enquired about what potential metrical study it might be worthwhile for him to undertake, Housman showed a clear sense of what interesting queries remained to be tackled. He suggested investigating the elision of -*m* before long vowels and diphthongs, expanding upon Lachmann's celebrated note ad Lucr. 3.374. 'Or you might take I. Hilberg's *Gesetze des Wortstellung im Pentameter des Ovid* and try how far they apply to pentameters of the other poets if true.[55] / Or the employment, in Attic tragedy for instance, of forms mostly used for metrical convenience, in places where metre does not require them; e.g. λαόσ in Eur. frag. 21.1.' In the end Gow undertook no such investigation, and Housman evidently did not see the work as sufficiently important or original for him to carry it out himself. He was also explicit, even to his adversary Postgate, about matters on which he was undecided: in the same letter cited previously (n. 4), Housman showed acceptance about the limits of metrical knowledge, confessing his general aporia about the Alcaic: 'The Alcaic stanza is one of the worst puzzles, and even Schroeder, who usually talks like the Pythia on her tripod, is evidently uncomfortable about it ... I have no clear notion of the extent to which Aeolic lyricists thought they might depart from homogeneity.'[56]

As a final remark on Housman's metrical studies, it cannot escape notice that he had little interaction with early scenic poetry.[57] A cursory search for such playwrights in the index to *CP* shows that his textual focus very rarely fell upon these authors and, when it did, it almost never strayed from Plautus' senarii. Perhaps this arose from a lack of interest in the subject matter of such literature, perhaps from comparative frustration or apathy at the great flexibility of most of these metrical forms which rendered them relatively resistant to rigid rules.[58] Nonetheless, Housman's lecture notes on Plautus (University Library, Cambridge, mss adv. 6882), delivered in 1932, make clear that he had worked up his knowledge not only of the playwright's corpus but also of early Latin metre to a formidable standard (see especially ibid., chapters III and IV). Incidentally, it is indicative that, when he closes his discussion with a list of six useful books for Plautine metre, he makes no mention of W.M. Lindsay's *Early Latin Verse* (Oxford, 1922). By contrast, C.F.W. Müller's *Plautinische Prosodie* (Berlin, 1869) is hailed (II 8) as 'the great landmark in the study of Plautine metre'. At any rate, it is clear that Housman had no desire to engage with intricate matters of early scenic metre outside the lecture room.

I have said almost nothing so far on Latin and Greek verse composition, the quintessential exercise of the nineteenth-century British schoolboy and undergraduate (and very often the academic and gentleman). In contrast to his evidently very close familiarity with metrical matters, Housman had a comparative lack of interest in this then-flourishing field.[59] Leaving aside the well-known tangent of his Cambridge Inaugural, which does not reject the practice of the art form but rather its utility for improving scholars' prosody and metrics, I know of no instance in which Housman discusses verse composition.

Excluding his longer textual supplements in Latin and Greek poets, only seven specimens of Housman's verse composition survive.[60] The earliest (presumably composed in late 1881 or early 1882) is a translation into hendecaysllabics of Venus' song from the fifth act of Dryden's *King Arthur* (1691).[61] The opening lines (*O, quot fert Thetis, insularum ocelle / O domus venerum cupidinumque*) mark Catullus as the imitated poet, although Housman's employment of a trochaic base in six of the sixteen lines (four of the first five lines) is a proportion unparalleled even in Catullus' latest hendecasyllables. Deservedly most famous is Housman's emotive elegiac poem of fourteen couplets prefixed to *Man.* I. Burnett (1997, 289-91) has provided an apparatus detailing Housman's first and second drafts, which is instructive in showing the genuine labour behind the composition. The poem evinces formidable poetic skill and judgment but also a notable detachment from the British compositional ideal of Ovidian elegiacs and instead contains many elements reminiscent of Propertius' earlier poetry (cf., e.g., lines 8 and 28 and the comparatively frequent use of inter-couplet enjambment).[62] Notwithstanding the poem's power, most contemporary judges, even accepting Propertius as Housman's closest Classical model, would not have welcomed his *periturene* of line 21: there is no parallel for *-urĕne* in Classical dactylic poetry, nor indeed of *-urĕue, -urăne* or *-urĕue* (but cf. *perituraque* at Stat. *Theb.* 10.594). Furthermore, I am yet to find a Classical poetic instance of *-ne* appended to any vocative singular of the masculine second declension. In Housman's own interleaved copy of *Man.* I (Trinity College, Cambridge, adv.c.20.40) there is evidence that he had later become aware of this infelicity, for he noted alongside the line 'II 479 audireque / Cic. n.d. 1. uarietatene / carm. epigr. 251.2 uenerandeque'.[63] That his closest poetic parallel is drawn from an epigraphic poem of the third century AD underlines the inelegance of the collocation.[64]

The five other extant pieces are all original compositions: an offhand elegiac quatrain (beginning from an interrogative version of Man. 4.794) recorded later in the same volume of Manilius (xxi); the elegiac distichs against Ellis (quoted in Williams' chapter) and Phillimore (quoted in Heyworth's chapter); the elegiac couplet sent in 1922 to A.B. 'The Ram' Ramsay (Burnett 1.508) to celebrate the latter's fiftieth birthday;[65] finally, most entertaining of all, a spoof prize poem of 29 hexameters – and one dactyl – entitled 'Nonae Novembres [*sic*]'.[66] This piece was perhaps written by Housman for his own amusement when he invigilated the 'Original Latin Verse' exercise for University Scholarships at Cambridge on 12 January 1912, at which 'Nonae Novembres' was one of five available topics (see Burnett 1997, 567). The poem plays deftly throughout with variable scansions, some legitimate, some reflecting a student's uncertainty (e.g. *Păpă Pāpă Păpā* (9)) when '*sunt misero mihi lexica longe / lexica sunt longe, custos prope*' (14-15). Of the truly horrific hexametric close *et Guido Faux*,[67] Housman adds the following mock note of an optimistic candidate: 'The metre is expressive of horror'. The piece ends with the start of a new paragraph of epic resonance: '*Ergo ubi*', to which the simple note is appended: 'No more time'.[68]

*

It may be regretted by some that Housman, unlike Wilamowitz or Lindsay or Fraenkel (not to mention Bentley and Porson), never more explicitly formulated, in positive terms, his wider views on ancient metre and poets' individual compositional strictures. Perhaps the fact that he evidently brought together most of his own knowledge from his private reading and hard grafting left him naturally disinclined from the production of any comprehensive treatment of the topic (we may compare his almost pervasive disapproval of Classical handbooks). Yet despite never having collected his views in any given place, the conclusion seems impossible to resist that, although Housman cannot be lauded in historical terms as a great proponent of metrical theory, not only his knowledge of, and sensitivity to, classical poetry, but also his care, judgment and logical rigour in applying it, must stand at the very fore among twentieth-century scholars.[69]

Notes

1. It is worth noting that Housman was evidently considered a good enough judge in the field by his Classics master Herbert Millington (1841-1922) to have proof-read his *Translations into Latin Verse* (London, 1889), cf. '[Housman's] keen eye and sound learning have detected not a few blemishes which might have disfigured these pages' (ix).

2. Indicative are Housman's early annotations in Jebb's *Translations into Greek Verse* (Cambridge, 1873), preserved at St John's College, Oxford (Housman Cabinet 2): after 'tried' in Jebb's statement (viii) 'The metres into which I have tried to do "Abt Vogler" are those of the Fourth Pythian', Housman has added 'and failed'. Scansions are marked as incorrect in a number of compositions, both Greek and Latin, that follow. For Housman's further disparagement of Jebb's metrical knowledge, see Stray's chapter in this volume.

3. Housman recorded in 1888 that the metrical notation of Schmidt was 'familiar to Englishmen' (*CP* 62). Schmidt's work, *Die Kunstformen der griechischen Poesie und ihre Bedeutung* (4 vols, Leipzig, 1868-72), was made familiar to the English-speaking world largely through the translation of J.W. White, *Introduction to the Rhythmic and Metric of the Classical Languages* (Boston, 1878; 1902[2]). The implication is that Wilhelm von Christ's, *Metrik der Griechen und Römer* (Leipzig, 1874; 1879[2]) did not significantly develop the theories of Schmidt.

4. Writing even in 1915 to J.P. Postgate (Burnett 1.341-2), Housman states, 'I don't think you have asked me before about works on Latin prosody since L. Mueller; anyhow, I know of none, and have not seen [F.E.] Plessis' book [*La Poésie latine* (Paris, 1909), not his edition of Horace, as suggested by Burnett's n. ad loc.].' If 'since L. Mueller' means after the first edition of *De re metrica*, then the work of Christ (see prev. n.) is being explicitly ignored (unless Housman limited his statements to works concerning prosody alone, unlike Mueller's). Two British manuals upon Latin metre and prosody appeared soon after the writing of his letter: W.R. Hardie's *Res Metrica* (Oxford, 1920) and J.P. Postgate's own *Prosodia Latina* (Oxford, 1923): there is no evidence that Housman held either in high esteem. His reception of R. Klotz's *Grundzüge*

altrömischer Metrik (Leipzig, 1890), K. Rupprecht's *Einführung in die griechische Metrik* (Munich, 1924; 1933²), F. Crusius' *Römische Metrik: eine Einführung* (Munich, 1929) and O. Schroeder's *Grundiss der griechischen Versgeschichte* (Heidelberg, 1930) is not known, although his passing mention in 1915 of Schroeder's view on the Alcaic (cited later in this piece) implies that he was not impressed by the over-confident tone of Schroeder in his *Vorarbeiten zur griechischen Versgeschichte* (Leipzig, 1908). Perhaps nothing can be concluded from the fact that Housman's copy of J.W. White's *The Verse of Greek Comedy* (London, 1912; Trinity College, Cambridge, adv.c.20.19) shows no sign of having been worked through beyond the introduction.

5. His opinions on Lewis and Short and, once it began to appear in 1900, the *TLL* are denigratory as to their utility on prosodic matters. In an unpublished letter of 15 November 1929 to R.W. Chapman [OUP archives: OP1728/12941], Housman writes, 'to remove the actual errors in Lewis & Short, though no light task, should be practicable; and if only the false quantities were corrected, and "relative" amended to "interrogative" in the hundreds of places where it should be, that would be something'. In 1907 he had written, 'I turn to the thesaurus linguae Latinae, though with no high hopes of enlightenment on a point of metre' (*CP* 700; cf. also *CP* 1116 n. 1).

6. The sole exceptions in print are one-page notes on Ov. *Ibis* 539 (*JPh* 12 (1883), 167 = *CP* 9) and Isoc. *Paneg.* 40 (*CR* 2 (1888), 42 = *CP* 22) and his 'Notes on Latin Poets [1]' (*CR* 3 (1889), 199-201 = *CP* 106-9, treating Pers. 3.43 (cf. also *CR* 3 (1889), 315 = *CP* 110-11), Mart. 12.3.4 and Juv. 9.143, 7.22 and 15.75).

7. Palmer 1883, n. ad loc.

8. Likewise true but then already well-known is Housman's passing comment ad Prop. 2.5.3 (*CP* 284) upon *mihi* and *mi*, viz that Propertius 'never uses the latter form except under metrical necessity'.

9. Remarkably, in a commentary on the book running almost to 600 pages (Gaertner 2005), not a word is said about this metrical anomaly.

10. For, as Samuel Parr rightly objected in a rambling letter on the Latin subjunctive of the early 1820s to James Pillans (Johnstone 1828, VII, 552), *uacat* bears the undesirable implication of an insular want or need of tigers; the text is nonetheless printed by Knox 1995. It is only just to recall that Heinsius did close his own critical note thus: 'Si quis meliora excogitarit, ei ego libens adsurgam et gratulabor.'

11. Platnauer 1951, 85 records that Ovid elided a short -*a* five times in this position (four of which are neuter plurals).

12. Although I say 'instinct', Housman made clear on more than one occasion his lack of confidence, notwithstanding his self-evidently acute ear as an English poet, in determining the minutiae of ancient metrics aurally: 'I have little faith in MSS and still less in my own ear, but as they here gave the same counsel I thought there might be something in it' (*CP* 1015); 'When Mr Friedrich says of [Hor. *S.*] II 5 28 "auch klaenge *sine natis* (ne-na) viel weniger gut", he displays that enviable fineness of ear which is peculiar to bad metrists' (*CP* 1140 n. 1); ad Prop. 3.16.7, considering the variants *si haec distulero* and *si distulero haec*: 'either elision is admissible, and a modern ear is incapable of judging which an ancient would prefer' (*CP* 281).

13. At 3.9.39 and 3.21.11, neither passage emended elsewhere by Housman and both probably correct.

14. For further discussion see Platnauer 1951, 84-5, and, for the addition of further examples, see Reeve 1973, 327.

15. Reading *uerum* (F) *ut amere* (de Vries) for *sed te ut amare* of most mss.

16. On the basis of these solid metrical foundations, Housman was able 30 years later rightly to castigate Schneidewin, Friedlaender and Postgate for their each introducing elisions in the syllable at the third longum of the former hemiepes of the pentameter into post-Catullan poets (*CP* 1119 n. 2).

17. Therefore he implicitly rejects *Her.* 8.71 and 9.131.

18. Prop. 2.15.1 (*o me felicem! o nox mihi candida! et o tu*), where Housman emended (*CP* 32) all three instances of *o* to *io* (with deletion of *et*), and 3.7.49 (*sed thyio thalamo aut Oricia terebintho*), although this instance should probably be retained as a Virgilian reminiscence (*A.* 10.136 *inclusum buxo aut Oricia terebintho*). We must therefore presume that Housman took Passerat's *curuas* as assured at 3.7.29. This shows a certain *volte face*, for Housman had already objected that P's correction of *illam* to *ante illam* at Prop. 2.32.45 is '[a]n obvious and perhaps unnecessary conjecture' (*CP* 343).

19. 1.5.33 *et tantum uenerata uirum, hunc sedula curet*, where *nunc* of the Hamburgensis is often read for *hunc*. As an example of metrical methodology in this field that would have made Housman's head spin, I suggest F. Cairns, 'Tibullus 2.1.57-8: problems of text and interpretation' in Radke 1998, 47-54.

20. The two Manilian instances (1.795 and 4.661) he had dismissed at *CP* 409, suggesting *haud indigna* (for *magna*) and accepting Isaac Vossius' *Latias* respectively.

21. For further discussion of this scholarly episode see Stray's and Leach's chapters.

22. Platt certainly began in a sufficiently polemic tone: (on the need to emend νούσων to νόσων at 1.170) 'A Scotch friend (they do not teach the elements of Greek verse in Scotland, I believe, nor apparently in some other places) entreats me to explain *why*? I do not wish to insult the readers of the *Review* by explaining the elements of verse to *them*; let my inquisitive friend look up some introduction to the subject' (*CR* 12.1 (February 1898), 58 n. 1).

23. Cf. West 1980, 16.

24. For a fuller discussion of this topic see Maas 1914/21 and, in a more limited metrical context, Barrett 1956, 251 = Barrett 2007, 317-18.

25. *CP* 450.

26. A suggestion which Jebb rejected at *CR* 12.2 (March 1898), 126, and Platt reaffirmed at *CR* 12.4 (May 1898), 214.

27. Cf. Platt at *CR* 12.1 (January 1898), 61: 'It was Professor Housman who pointed out to me that the last syllable must be long.'

28. *CP* 465-6.

29. In the same *CR* volume (12.4 (May 1898), 214 n. 2) Platt also made a similarly partial concession, albeit on slightly different grounds: 'Better to say the last syllable of κάμον is lengthened by metrical ictus (I do not believe in it myself, but see Gildersleeve on *Pyth.* iii. 6).'

30. R.Y. Tyrrell, though an early public champion of Housman, was an ardent member of the pro-*anceps* corps. He allowed himself a tangent on the matter at the end of his anonymous review article upon Kenyon's edition (*Quarterly Review* 187 (1898), 422-45 at 443-4); the article was published under his name in Tyrrell 1909, 134-70. He used 11.119 as a primary example of his (unnamed) opponents' methodological weakness: 'The [transmitted] reading is undoubtedly sound ... The true state of the case is that πρόγονοι here is right and indispensable, and that a short syllable at the end of a line corresponds strophically to a long one here as in some fifty other places in the poems. To make the poems before us conform to the rules laid down in some treatises on metre, we must either rewrite the poems or rewrite the treatises.'

31. For relevant quotations, see Stray's chapter. Diggle 2007, 163 n. 42, has rightly commented that 'Housman would have regarded the ability to say things about metre which are both true *and new* as rare indeed. His concern here [when treating the metre of Bacchylides] is not with novelty ... but with understanding.'

32. Cf. n. 2 above. For Jebb's indirect attack upon Housman and Platt as inexperienced in verse composition, and thereby more removed from the poetic author under discussion himself, see also Stray's chapter.

33. In his review of the first edition of his Lucretius *OCT* (Oxford, 1900), Housman closes by stating that Bailey 'prints only one emendation, and it is *intust*. Better one than two' (*CP* 524). With good reason is the introduction of the early Latin fusion of *-us* and *es(t)* rejected in Lucretius, who provides no compelling evidence for the licence. In a letter in my possession of 1900 from J.S. Reid to J.P. Postgate, it is remarked upon this review that 'Housman is doubtless right in his estimate, but he might have treated a young scholar a little generously'.

34. Compare his contemptuous dismissal of a fellow Briton in a letter of 1923 to Ernest Harrison (Burnett 1.539): '[Aeschylus'] Ag[amemnon] 239 has no[t] 'metrical flaw' [quoting a manuscript submitted to *CQ* by D.S. Robertson but not published] except in the imagination of the ignorant and immodest Agar, and similar folk.' English knowledge of metre is rightly rebuked for its general failure to advance in the hundred years following 1825 at *CP* 1271. His general aside ad Man. 4.597 ('neque ista rei metricae peritia huic aetati parum conuenit, quare huius libri u. 174 *praecōcia*, u. 800 *sŭrrepta* [both unmetrical] coniectatum uidimus') is without any explicit geographical rider. For Housman's low opinion of W.M. Lindsay as a metrician, see my other chapter in this volume at pp. 206-7.

35. This complement implies that Housman found much to praise in Maas 1927 and perhaps Maas 1914/21.

36. See Butterfield 2008a, 118-20.

37. See Butterfield 2008b, 640.

38. Housman declared, 'he who will object to the cacophony of *scl* must first emend 'Ascli' in Sil. Punic. VIII 438.' This comment is of little force, for the latter word is a proper noun and the language of Horace's *sermones* is much removed from that of Silius. For the collocation of consonants, reference could instead have been made to forms of *discludere* (and its cognates) and Persius' curious onomatopoeic neologism *scloppo* (5.13). Housman's bold declaration ad loc. ('Whether this shorter form of the word [*crepusclum*] occurs elsewhere I do not know, nor does it matter') may fairly be branded rash, when introducing into an author as much read and imitated as Horace a form not found elsewhere.

39. For the use of *atque* in the primary Latin poets, see Butterfield 2008c.

40. His obvious model is the Petronian Sotadean 23.3.1 *huc huc <cito>* [suppl. *L. Mueller*] *conuenite nunc, spatalocinaedi*, mischievously associating Cortius, Marx and those of their school with an inherently insulting term. I see that this parallel was noted by Hunt 1994, 101.

41. Housman's frustration with other scholars' short-sightedness about the history of metrical knowledge is well exhibited by his comments on the tendency of Classical Latin poets to avoid filling the latter half of the third foot with a monosyllable and the fourth foot with a spondee, but rather reverse the two: 'One of [Cortius'] hobbies [22 references in Lucan are then provided] is what modern Germans call 'lex Marxii', because they never heard of it before 1922.

Mr Marx's true merit is to have collected exceptions and to have tried, with partial success, to classify them.' (*Lucan*, xxxii n. 1); on Heraeus' note ad Mart. 3.15.1 '*quam tota* ... quod ... lex Marxii ... falsum coarguit' he exclaims 'Marxii forsooth! see Cortius on Luc. IV 476, where this verse is cited' (*CP* 1102). Housman showed his unwillingness to apply this rule across the board not only in the Manilian instances discussed above but also in his note ad Luc. 7.369 (*credite pendentes e summis moenibus urbis*): 'e om. M, post *summis* add. M². nequem moueant quae Marxius Cortii placita aemulatus abhandl. d. Saechs. akad. XXXVII 1 p. 212 disputauit, adscribo, praeter uersum quem ille inani antitheti nomine iactato amoliri conatur IX 29 *post Magni funera*, hos duos, VII 619 *per cuius uiscera*, VIII 49 *de falso coniugis*.' In a similar vein, we may also compare Housman's mocking Vollmer and Jebb for their ignorance of one of the key precepts of Dawes' *Miscellanea Critica* at *CP* 1139 n. 2.

42. However, neither Burton's reworking (*facis et uires*) nor Lachmann's alteration of the verb to *excis* can be deemed attractive.

43. The collocation *ignibus aether* is first found in Virgil (*A.* 1.90) and the conceit of the following lines (877-9) of the *defessus arator* urging on *maerentes ... iuuencos* is reminiscent of the close of Lucretius' second book (1160ff.).

44. We may also compare Housman's willingness not only to accept iambic *eis* of G L at Man. 2.744 (a scansion not attested in Classical dactylic poetry) but also to introduce it at 2.542 (his own emendation) and 377 (Bentley).

45. See further Butterfield 2008d, 189-90. For similar scepticism about Housman's introducing (*CP* 437) by conjecture a second instance of sigmatic ecthlipsis into a single Lucretian hexameter (5.1442), see Butterfield 2008d, 197 n. 31, 203 n. 61; on his believing (Burnett 1.303) in the scansion *remigī oblitae* (6.743), see Butterfield 2008a, 120-1.

46. *Tr.* 5.14.41, *Pont.* 3.1.113, *Met.* 7.644, 10.520 (s.v. l.) and, as emended by Housman, *Met.* 14.24.

47. From the statistics provided by Platnauer 1951, 36-7, it emerges that Ovid opened 85.4% of his hexameters with dactyls and 83.3% of his pentameters.

48. At the close of the piece he allows himself a tangent upon Juvenal's usage: in only three instances does the word form the latter half of first foot at 6.331, 7.54 and 13.18 and all the mss support *nihil*. In his *Juvenal*, however, he printed prevocalic *nil* in the latter half of the second foot at 15.88 and of the third foot at 6.58 (see his note upon the latter).

49. *CR* 35 (1921), 23-5. Postgate's tone is comparatively bitter, although he rightly disparages Housman's apparent sympathy with Lachmann's thesis as late as his mid-50s: 'Had instruction been my object, I should have sought an apter pupil than a scholar who has taken over twenty years to learn that in Ovid the last syllable of *nihil* was normally short' (23).

50. Naiditch 1988, 88-9, is right to record that Housman probably saw no scholarly profit or defensive need in continuing the debate.

51. Housman argued that, since scribes wrote *nil* for *nihil* much more rarely than the converse error, in those instances where the mss favour *nil* in prevocalic position in the latter half of the verse, we should follow this shorter rather than the disyllabic form. This occurs in the fourth foot (8.665, 858, 9.854, 10.96, 335, 366 but not 7.268) and the third (7.88 but not 8.315 and 10.189).

52. Housman had already delivered a paper to the Cambridge Philological Society on 26 October 1911 entitled 'On prosody and method with reference to a supposed anomaly of scansion in Statius' (cf. *CP* 1259); see Naiditch 2005, 50f.

53. 'Since it thus appears that the country of Lachmann and Meineke regard Mr Gustav Friedrich as an authority on prosody, to that fount of doctrine let us go' (*CP* 1136). Housman's own copy of Friedrich's Catullus (Leipzig, 1908), preserved at St John's College, Oxford (Housman Cabinet 1), is filled throughout with spirited attacks on his metrical decisions.

54. Housman's landmark 1910 article 'Greek nouns in Latin Poetry' (*CP* 817-39) brought ample progress in analysing the prosody of words of Greek origin (cf. also *CP* 699).

55. These last two words again demonstrate Housman's reluctance to pass judgment one way or the other on intricate metrical matters which he had not personally investigated to his satisfaction.

56. Housman did not prominently advertise his occasional retractions of metrically improbable conjectures, for natural reasons. In two instances his recanting occurs explicitly in the light of another scholar's metrical observations: at Juv. 6.O8 (*CP* 621 n. 1) he rightly concedes that his 'conjecture *turpi* <*et*>... is upset by the observation of L. Kiaer (de sermone Iuu., Hauniae 1875, p. 14) that Juvenal does not admit elision at this point in the verse'. Similarly, at Man. 2.831 (*hunc penes* [Housman : *tenet* mss] *arbitrium uitae, hic regula morum est*), Housman in his original note ad loc. (*Man.* II) had transposed *est* to after *uitae*, thereby obviating the hiatus. Yet in the addendum upon the line at the rear of *Man.* V (145f.) he argues (explicitly in the wake of Leo's *Plautinisches Forschungen* (Leipzig, 1892; 1912²) that, although Manilius twice elided the dative *-ae* (5.476 and 508, both at 2s), the hiatus transmitted at 2.831 should be accepted because he nowhere elided the homophonous genitive termination (*stellae* at 2.747 being emended to Bentley's *stella*). In this latter instance, the change of tack is misguided, for the hiatus is unwelcome (Housman's comparing the anaphora and hiatus at Ov. *Met.* 14.832 *o et de Latia, o et de gente Sabina* does not seem *ad rem* owing to its exclamatory nature) and *uitae* would not suffer elision but rather *est* aphaeresis.

57. As a result of his specialising in Latin literature in the mid-1890s, Housman of course diminished his opportunity to discuss matters of Greek metre outside Attic tragedy and Bacchylides.

58. Compare the criticism of Skutsch 1985, 697, that Housman, like Lachmann, did not sufficiently understand *breuis breuians* when arguing, in 1907, against dactylic *sicuti* at Enn. *Ann.* 549 Sk.

59. See the brief comments in Hopkinson's chapter and Naiditch 1988, 182-3. Housman did have some success in composition prizes whilst at Bromsgrove (see Naiditch 1988, 5-6) and at the end of the nineteenth century taught at least one pupil (Miss A.M.B. Meakin) verse composition at UCL (see Naiditch 1988, 128).

60. This is the answer to the first query posed by Shackleton Bailey 2003, 194.

61. The poem was first printed in *The Bromsgrovian* 1.4 (25 May 1882), 92; the orthography was presumably not Housman's.

62. The closing word of the poem *sodalicii*, though found in Catullus (100.4) and Ovid (*Tr.* 4.10.46) but not Propertius, bears the hallmarks of the last, insofar as it demonstrates the uncontracted genitive in *-ii*, not securely attested for Latin nouns in poets before Propertius, and stands as a non-Hellenising pentasyllable at the close of the pentameter (only in 0.1% of Ovidian pentameters).

63. Although we find Housman recording the well-known avoidance of *-que* in Ovid and Virgil at *CP* 269 and ad Man. 2.479, his earlier drafts contained *reditureque* as well as *peritureue*.

64. Housman himself explicitly dismissed epigraphic poetry as a reliable source for Latin metre at *CP* 1116: 'Inscriptions are a garden of illiteracy where anyone who relishes violations of metre or accidence or syntax may fill his hands with nosegays of all the horrors dearest to his heart; they will lengthen any short syllable to please Mr Birt and shorten any long syllable to please Mr Lindsay'; cf. also *CP* 1137.

65. *Multa decem lustris addantur lustra precantur / Arietis Housmanus Gouius Harrisonus.* The employment of *arietis* as a dactyl, contrary to the eschewal of the word in its oblique cases by the Augustan elegists, can be excused owing to the nature of the piece and the addressee.

66. These Latin compositions, excepting those against Phillimore and for Ramsay, can be found at Burnett 1997, 289-92.

67. *Faux* is simply Fawkes once the unreformed pronunciation of Latin is employed.

68. Housman evidently worked through his copy of Postgate 1922, preserved at the Lilly Collection at Bryn Mawr (PN 241.P6), but the occasional annotations rarely concern metrical matters *per se*. I thank Paul Naiditch for making a full list of these marginalia available to me.

69. I am grateful to Chris Stray, James Diggle, Neil Hopkinson and Paul Naiditch for helpful comments and corrections.

7

Dust and Fudge: manuscripts in Housman's generation

M.D. Reeve

'Nothing is much better known in the province of Plautine metric than H.A. Koch's paper in the *Neue Jahrbuecher* for 1870, vol. 101, headed *uoxor = uxor*. There are ten or twelve verses in Plautus, spoilt by hiatus as they stand, which would be rid of this disfigurement if *uxor* began with a consonant: in such places Koch would introduce the form *uoxor*, which is actually proffered by B, the codex uetus Camerarii, at *Truc.* 515 and *Trin.* 800.'[1] After disposing of *uoxor* on metrical grounds, Housman goes on to derive its occurrences in B from an old spelling, in capitals *VCXOR*, for which he cites analogies chiefly from the late-antique manuscripts of Virgil. That he was right has never been questioned, nor should it ever be.

No editor of Catullus, however, has followed him at 64.237, where for *aetas prospera* Avancius had proposed *sors prospera*, Lambinus *fors prospera*, and Baehrens *lux prospera*.[2] 'Now *fors* is not at all like *aetas* but very like *pros*: it may be then that *aetas prospera* is an attempt to emend *pros aetaspera*, which in its turn is a letter-for-letter corruption of *fors decxstera*.' As *aetas prospera* is neither unmetrical nor ungrammatical, most editors still keep it despite its poor sense, but anyone inclined to emend it will probably try, as Housman did, to account for it. Baehrens 'rejects his [own] idea as too remote, but perhaps *lucx* fell out after *duce*, and *aetas* was interpolated from 232'.[3]

Explaining presumed corruptions has a long history. Bede on *Acts* 28.11:[4]

> *Navigavimus in navi Alexandrina quae in insula hiemaverat cui erat insigne castrorum*] Credo primitus *insigne Castorum* esse positum, sed vitio librariorum *r* litteram adiectam, sicut *frustra* panis pro *frusta* et *adpropriat* pro *adpropiat* saepe scriptum in antiquissimis exemplaribus invenimus.

Salutati in 1403 on the earliest literary reference to Florence or its inhabitants, Plin. *Nat.* 3.52, where he knew only the dominant reading *Fluentini*:[5]

Fluentini profluenti Arno appositi forte corruptum est et scribi debuit *Florentini*, quodque sequitur *profluenti Arno appositi* non minus librariis dare potuit corrumpendi materiam quam auctori 'profluentis' vocabulo ei quod *Fluentini* dixerat alludendi.

Valla in the 1440s on what Panormita and Fazio did to the *codex regius* of Livy at 21.57.5-6:[6]

Omnes igitur clausi undique commeatus erant, nisi quos Pado naves subvehere. Temporium prope Placentiam fuit ...] Vos nihil aliud quam dempsistis illud *T*, ut *Emporium* tantum esset, non intelligentes litteram illam ad precedentem pertinere dictionem et quia figure maiuscule erat fuisse apicem cum littera coniunctum scriptumque reliquisse auctorem *subveherent*.

When Beatus Rhenanus in 1526 published notes on the text of Pliny's *Natural History*,[7] he made a systematic attempt to account for corruptions. Here he is on a passage right at the outset where he earns a mention in any recent apparatus, *Praef.* 1:[8]

Ut obiter molliam Catullum] Sic omnes docti legunt. Vetus codex manu scriptus habet, *ut obicere molliam Catullum*. Apparet a Plinio fuisse scriptum, *ut obiter emolliam Catullum*. Hinc autem erroris occasio nata est, quod librarius eruditionis expers, quales apud nos hodie typographorum sunt operae, cum videret *e* primorem huius verbi *emolliam* syllabam paulo fortassis seiunctiorem a reliquis, putavit cum *obiter* proxime praecedente dictione coniungendam, et *obitere* scripsit. Alius paulo doctior, et idcirco magis damnosus, videns *obitere* minime latinam esse vocem, audacter, sed periculose elemento *t* in *c* mutato, ex *obitere*, fecit *obicere*. Facilius autem fuisset erratum deprehensum, si *obitere* sinistra diligentia non fuisset in *obicere* versum. Porro cum elegantius, tum multo significantius est *emolliam* in hoc loco, quam *molliam*. Nam *e* praepositio non solum gratiam, sed et vim quandam addit.

At Cat. 64.237 no one appears to have discussed Housman's proposal, but four objections might be levelled at it, three specific and one broader: that there is nothing wrong with *prospera*; that *fors dextera* is unparalleled in classical Latin; that actually *fors* is not much like *pros* either; and that more than anything else ingenuity in postulating a graphic corruption seems to have driven this attempt at improving on earlier conjectures.

To take the last first, 'a surgeon', George Goold remarks in connection with transposition in Propertius, 'may mend a broken leg in ignorance of the cause of the fracture',[9] and despite emulating Housman's critical approach he regrets his appeal to graphic corruptions, for instance on Ov. *Rem.* 492: 'Housman's *niue* (for *tuae*) is palaeographically neat, but bespeaks that anxious adherence to the ductus litterarum whose seductive powers over men like Scaliger and Porson distressed him so greatly [*Man.* V, xxxiv-xxxv]. O Alfred, Alfred! The Romans no more said *frigidior niue* than we say "colder than snow".'[10] Palaeographically neat? 'Conjectures which stick close to the MSS are neat if true, but if not true they are not even neat.'[11] In his own notes on passages of Ovid and Propertius, Goold often suggests a process of corruption, usually graphic at least in part. 'Of course information about letter-forms, abbreviations, and common corruptions,' says Robin Nisbet, 'never comes amiss ... We should start from the thought, as the best critics advise; yet in real life we usually find ourselves playing with the letters as well'.[12]

How much like *pros*, then, is *fors* ?

Ham.	Do you see yonder cloud that's almost in shape of a camel?
Pol.	By the mass, and 'tis like a camel, indeed.
Ham.	Methinks it is like a weasel.
Pol.	It is backed like a weasel.
Ham.	Or like a whale ?
Pol.	Very like a whale.[13]

One cannot read far in the *Classical Papers* without meeting lists of corruptions taken to be graphic, which some of them unquestionably are, but contemporaries raised two objections, albeit not directed explicitly at Housman: 'la rareté des fautes purement graphiques',[14] and the need to take account of chronology and stratification.[15] Housman acknowledges the latter principle, but not before ignoring it in his discussion of Hor. *Carm.* 3.11.18.[16] As for the former, he proposes *coniugis* for *uirginis* in a passage of Phaedrus and alleges a graphic confusion also found at Ov. *Met.* 15.836,[17] but the corruption there of *sancta cum coniuge* (the empress Livia) to *sancta cum uirgine* in some manuscripts seems likelier to have had a devotional cause and so to belong in the category of what he elsewhere calls untimely reminiscences.[18] Yes, he did postulate other causes of error too, as a glance at the long entry 'manuscripts, errors of' in the index to the *Classical Papers* will show.[19]

One cause not separately listed there is homoearchon, invoked at Luc. 9.664-5 'because that is a longer and nobler name than fudge': so Eduard Fraenkel,[20] turning back on Housman his provocative reference to 'an idle and pretentious game in which Lucan's less serious critics find amusement, and which they call *Ueberlieferungsgeschichte*, because that is a longer and nobler name than fudge'.[21] The target was not new. 'I have no inkling', he had written 20 years before, 'of *Überlieferungsgeschichte*':[22]

141

> And to the sister science of *Quellenforschung* I am equally a stranger: I cannot assure you, as some other writer will assure you before long, that the satires of Juvenal are all copied from the satires of Turnus ... It seems ... as if a capacity for these two lines of fiction had been bestowed by heaven, as a sort of consolation-prize, upon those who have no capacity for anything else.

He was attacking there the notion that Juvenal had been edited in late Antiquity by the Nicaeus mentioned in subscriptions, and when a similar notion about a recension of Lucan made by the Paulus mentioned in subscriptions brought him back to the matter, he recalled that in 1905 he 'dismissed it in a few derisive words', namely those just quoted, 'which echo for ever in the memory of Mr W.M. Lindsay'.[23] Lindsay, that is, had no capacity for anything but *Überlieferungsgeschichte*.

Doubtless that oblique insult was Housman's response both to Lindsay's review of his Juvenal and to the extravagance of his claims for *Überlieferungsgeschichte*. In the review, after explaining away three variants of *recentiores* or *deteriores* that Housman had favoured, Lindsay said this:[24]

> But if definite proof be required in each of these cases, it can be obtained only by a thorough investigation of the mediaeval transmission of Juvenal's text [with this footnote: Mr Housman's sneer at 'Ueberlieferungsgeschichte' (p. xxviii) refers, I suppose, to the ancient transmission of texts].

Then, when Ludwig Traube died in 1907, Lindsay provided *CR* with an obituary, which invited readers into the 'new world of study' that Traube had opened up, for instance in his work on the transmission of the *Regula Benedicti*:[25]

> Had he been spared until he had completed his 'Palaeographische Forschungen', we should have had a full and final account of Latin Manuscripts, their peculiarities of script, the scriptorium from which each has come, the mediaeval scholars whose influence they shew. But now, all this work will have to be done by others. And who is competent to take Traube's place? He had an unrivalled knowledge of the literary life of the Middle Ages, so that a mediaeval MS. of a Latin classic appeared after his handling of it in quite a new light. The Berne MS. of Horace and Servius was shewn to be a copy of an original which emanated from the circle of Sedulius, that Irish scholar who, with a band of compatriots, visited the monastery libraries of Europe in the ninth century, imparting and receiving the best instruction of the time. The Berne Valerius Maximus was traced to Lupus, the learned Abbot of Ferrières, who had recorded in the margins the variants from a MS. of Julius Paris's Epitome. The Vatican Livy was revealed as a transcript made by certain monks of Tours from the Paris Puteanus. How different all this was from the lifeless accounts of these MSS. given in the prolegomena of previous editions![26]

Different too, he might have added, from the *Überlieferungsgeschichte* of the *Appendix Vergiliana* as Emil Baehrens had conceived it while Traube was still a child: nothing there about the historical context in which any of the extant manuscripts was written.[27] In the meantime, Housman had replied more politely but no less categorically to another of Lindsay's claims:

> Professor Lindsay says in *C. Q.* XI p. 41 that with the help of the *thesaurus* Latin scholarship is now becoming easy, and that textual emendation will become equally easy when certain advances have been made in palaeography. No advance in palaeography will ever make textual emendation easy, because textual emendation depends much less on palaeography than on several other things, the chief of which is the textual emendator; and for a like reason Latin scholarship will never be made easy by any dictionary, much less by such a dictionary as this.[28]

Lindsay's best rejoinder would have been to ask Housman what he meant by a term of approval that he often used, 'scientific'.[29]

Time, however, had changed Housman's target. 'No self-respecting woman was ever seen in 1866 without a crinoline, and no Munich professor at this moment', namely 1907, 'can publish a classic without a scheme of *Textgeschichte*'.[30] He was reviewing a Teubner edition of Horace by Friedrich Vollmer, born in 1867, who in 1905 became Ordinarius at Munich after a spell as Generalredaktor at what Housman later called the ergastulum there – the *Thesaurus Linguae Latinae*.[31] Traube too held a chair at Munich, the first in Germany of Lateinische Philologie des Mittelalters, but his other institutional responsibilities lay with an enterprise nowhere mentioned by Housman, the *Monumenta Germaniae Historica* in Berlin, where in 1898 he took over from Theodor Mommsen the running of the section devoted to *auctores antiquissimi*.[32] In the report that he delivered when he stepped down, Mommsen discussed the selection of authors, which excluded two more important for German history than the rest put together: Tacitus and Ammianus. Excluded why? Because their editorial foundations had already been laid. 'Dagegen war für alle oben genannten Schriftwerke [thirteen volumes of them] die handschriftliche Grundlage der Feststellung bedürftig.'[33] The enterprise went back to 1826, and its first two directors, G.H. Pertz and G. Waitz, had already announced the same policy and themselves done much towards carrying it out for a number of medieval works.[34] Of Mommsen's last contribution to the series, *Libri pontificalis pars prior* (1898), one of his successors had this to say:[35]

> Im Januar 1896 begab er sich noch einmal nach Italien, um einige Handschriften teils neu, teils nachzuvergleichen ... Der Text hatte durch die Benutzung der Pertzischen Kollation des Codex Neapolitanus und einer anderen italienischen Handschrift auch gegenüber der Ausgabe

Duchesnes, deren Verdienst Mommsen voll anerkannte, erheblich gewonnen. Die klug ausgedachte Editionstechnik mit einer Fülle kleiner Zeichen und Randbemerkungen mochte anfangs verwirrend wirken, war aber bei einiger Aufmerksamkeit bequem zu übersehen und bot dann eine so vollständige Einsicht in die Entstehung und Überlieferung des Textes, wie sie aus der französischen Ausgabe kaum ebenso sicher zu entnehmen war.

Mommsen thanked Traube for help (and 'indices ... confecit optimae spei iuvenis Felix Iacoby'). The transmission in Antiquity of Homer and the tragedians had occupied Wolf and Wilamowitz,[36] but Traube devoted himself to the transmission of Latin works in late Antiquity and the early Middle Ages. The opening footnote of his monograph on the *Regula Benedicti* is a warm acknowledgement:[37]

Ulrich von Wilamowitz-Moellendorff hat in vielen seiner Schriften einzelne Textgeschichten und auch theoretische Erörterungen über das Wesen der Textgeschichte gegeben. Ihm bin ich, wie immer, zu besonderem Dank verpflichtet.

In range, however, the bridge was not Wilamowitz but Wilamowitz's father-in-law, Mommsen.[38]

The *auctores antiquissimi* include several poets of late Antiquity, among them Dracontius, edited by Vollmer with a dedication to Traube;[39] but outside astronomy Housman paid little attention to late poets. Furthermore, the kind of editing that exasperated him had different roots. 'A.E. Housman, in the traditions chosen by him as a whetstone for his critical acumen, seems to have come across the worst possible combination of late Lachmannianism and conservative criticism.'[40] Far from encouraging a full investigation of textual traditions by the genealogical method that came to bear his name, Lachmann's practice led to the search for a 'best' manuscript, which some editors then followed through thick and thin.[41] There were also practical advantages in cutting down on manuscripts, 'travel grants being much rarer than nowadays and photography still in its infancy'.[42]

In his determination to use the full spread of serviceable manuscripts, Housman more closely resembled the editors of the *Monumenta*, but he had fewer resources to call on. Mommsen remarked that only a national institution could fund the 'diplomatische Kritik' required by the *Monumenta*,[43] Lindsay that 'Traube was, unlike most foreign scholars, wealthy enough to visit all the important libraries of Europe and make a prolonged study of their manuscript treasures'.[44] Up to the turn of the century German scholars could still arrange to have manuscripts transferred for collation, and not just to an accredited library: four manuscripts of Jordanes, among them one from the Cambridge college where Housman later held his chair, went up in smoke at Mommsen's house in 1880 while he was preparing his edition.[45] From abroad Housman borrowed only Loewe's collation of M, preserved at Göttingen, towards his edition of Manilius.[46] Towards his editions of Juvenal he used O at Oxford and T at Cambridge and consulted seven manuscripts at the British Museum, where he also consulted A of the *Appendix Vergiliana*; towards his edition of *Ibis* he used G and H at Cambridge; and towards his edition of Manilius he consulted the Caesenas on the spot and perhaps H, presumably at Cambridge.[47] He also consulted published facsimiles,[48] and photographs that he ordered can still be used.[49] For preference, though, he availed himself of collations made by other scholars, especially Carl Hosius. Hosius published at 22 the collations of Juvenal in his dissertation and at 25 the collations of Lucan in his *Habilitationsschrift* – no mean feat, even when contemporaries had already done some of the work.[50] Housman supplemented such collations more by requesting information than by inspecting the manuscripts on the spot or in reproduction.[51] That did not prevent him from harping on the desultoriness and inaccuracy of some collators, especially Robinson Ellis, or from expressing disdain for such labours:[52]

> To examine 'plurimos Iuvenalis codices' was not necessary: it was enough to cast an understanding eye on the collations of Hosius and especially on the excerpts of Jahn.

> For the readings of M I depend on others. This MS [of Manilius, Madrid Nac. 3678] is a bad sailor, and has not forgotten the Armada: it will travel to Germany and Italy, but to England it will not travel; it is also modest, and dislikes to be photographed; and I am not disposed to learn a fresh language with a poor literature, and undertake a long journey to an uninviting capital, merely in order to settle a question of so little practical importance as the question whether V is or is not a copy of M.

> The fact is that Mr Ellis does not collate MSS: he transcribes from them, without reference to any particular text, such things as attract his attention.

> I did not yet know, what subsequent experience taught me, that he never in his life collated a MS nor even grasped the meaning of the word *collation*.

> I do not intend to collate the MSS myself, nor do I urge any other scholar to that undertaking, unless he thinks he can find nothing better to do.

In this disdain he had company: Wilamowitz derided *mataeoponia* and *codicum sordes*, spoke of collation as *codicum corradere lectiones*, and declared that he had no relish for a diet of library dust.[53] People had once boasted of rescuing forgotten texts from dusty libraries,[54] and collation is a more demanding task than scholars who disparage it appear to imagine.[55]

It is no surprise, then, that Housman caricatured both the Lachmannians and the other school:[56]

> The student of an ancient text has two enemies. There is the devotee of system who prefers simplicity to truth, and who having learnt from Madvig and Bekker the great lesson of our century, *magnam et inconditam testium turbam ad paucos et certos esse redigendam, a quibus ceteri rem acceperint*, selects his few witnesses without ascertaining if they were really the informants of the rest, constructs a neat apparatus at whatever cost to the text of his hapless author, and seeks to overawe the timid by sonorous talk about 'sanae artis praecepta omnia'; and there is the born hater of science who ransacks Europe for waste paper that he may fill his pages to half their height with the lees of the Italian renascence, and then by appeals to the reader's superstition would persuade him to hope without reason and against likelihood that he will gather grapes of thorns and figs of thistles.

Five years later, however, 'Nemesis ... brought out from the arsenals of divine vengeance, if I may so describe the Bodleian library,' ancient interpolations in Juvenal's sixth satire;[57] and if, as is commonly said, in a tradition riddled with contamination inherited truth may lurk anywhere,[58] it is hard to see how a point can be fixed beyond which an investigator would be hoping 'without reason and against likelihood' for useful returns.[59]

Three of the four texts that Housman edited have traditions of that kind, and the limits that he imposed on his apparatus laid him open to charges of misjudgement in recension, as when Eduard Fraenkel cited from other manuscripts of Lucan omissions that he believed to be right[60] or L. Håkanson argued that at 6.622 *sola* should have been reported from ZM and indeed put in the text;[61] but if they had been forced to state their policy for a recension of Lucan, how would it have differed from Housman's? and which has dated more, the apparatus of Housman's Lucan or Fraenkel's ideas about ancient editions?[62] No more in Ovid's *Ibis* or Juvenal has Housman's recension been overtaken by work done since. For the narrower tradition of Manilius a stemma can be drawn up of the authoritative manuscripts, though he preferred to express it in words. He would have drawn it up sooner if he had not relied at first on collations made by others, and further witnesses of value have since emerged;[63] but nothing has overturned his analysis, and closer acquaintance confirmed his suspicion that one *recentior* descended partially and another wholly from M.[64] Though he did not edit *Culex*, he took enough interest in its recension to order photographs of V and Γ from Rome, and they enabled him to prove what he had already guessed from the sketchy information available to him, that V was the source of the Vossianus reported by Baehrens.[65] True, his most detailed analysis of a textual tradition misfired, and not just because he contented himself with manuscripts already in play:[66]

Troppo spesso ... Housman fonda il giudizio circa i rapporti tra i testimoni su una valutazione di 'superiorità' di una lezione su un'altra motivata dalla sua maggiore vicinanza a congetture moderne, le quali ovviamente partivano da quella stessa lezione. Tipico giro vizioso, che nulla toglie, sia detto per inciso, all'acume e alla lucidità insuperata con cui decine di ardui passi properziani vengono discussi e non di rado chiarificati.[67]

The editorial project went no further, however, and so Housman's Propertius became the most famous edition not to be found on the shelves of a library.

How much does it matter, then, that Housman professed to regard *Überlieferungsgeschichte* as fudge? In discussing the relationship between M and V of Manilius he drew an argument from *Überlieferungsgeschichte*:[68]

Of the Asconius which Poggio discovered about the same time [as the exemplar of M] there were made no fewer than three copies – one by Poggio himself, one by Zomini, and one by Bartolomeo da Montepulciano; and we have no right to presume that the Manilius, on the contrary, was copied only once.

Yet the profession was no pretence:

The only object of seeking and collating manuscripts is to restore the author's text, to recover what he said.[69]

On the contrary, manuscripts yield evidence of other things too. In Britain and America through pupils of Traube's, in Italy through Pasquali's *Storia della tradizione e critica del testo* of 1934,[70] the interest taken in that evidence continues to bear fruit.[71] Anyone tempted to reprove Housman for not sharing it, though, should flip the coin and ask how often these days any interest in textual criticism accompanies it. The question would not have embarrassed the admirer of Traube and Pasquali as well as Housman who delivered this verdict on Housman's editions:[72]

Altrove [outside Propertius], e segnatamente nelle edizioni maggiori (Giovenale, Manilio, Lucano), valutando codici in prevalenza medievali Housman si dimostra maestro anche di *recensio*, e anche in tradizioni fortemente contaminate è in grado di districarsi magistralmente o almeno di fare il punto della situazione, nei limiti, beninteso, di ciò che gli è noto. Si sa che non si dava molto da fare per indagare sulla tradizione manoscritta, in ispecie sui *recentiores*, in ciò aderendo a quella che chiamava 'the great lesson of our [scil. XIX] century', ossia 'magnam et inconditam testium turbam ad paucos et certos esse redigendam, a quibus ceteri rem acceperint'. Ma poi, fatta la scelta dei *codices potiores*, i loro rapporti vengono sviscerati con il massimo rigore; sicché è falsa l'immagine di uno Housman tutto concentrato sull'attività emendatoria.

No suggestion here that by setting his face against *Überlieferungs-geschichte* Housman fell short of his aims.

Two other British Latinists were born within fourteen months of Housman and died within ten months of him: Lindsay and A.C. Clark.[73] Lindsay's editions of Festus, Nonius, Isidore's *Origines*, Martial, Plautus, and Terence, are still in use, though reservations are often expressed about his Plautus and Terence[74], but only Martial of these authors much engaged Housman in print. For once compliments sweetened his strictures:[75]

> Students of Martial now live in an age which was begun by Professor Lindsay's edition of 1903, one of those works which are such boons to mankind that their shortcomings must be forgiven them. All that energy could do in the investigation or skill and industry in the collation of MSS was done, and the fruits of his labour were condensed in an apparatus criticus of the most admirable lucidity. It is true that one was obliged to form one's text for oneself, but without Mr Lindsay that would not have been possible.

Cicero and Asconius engaged him even less than Plautus and Terence, and Clark's name appears in only two of the *Classical Papers*;[76] but he was a capable critic who made intelligent use of *Über-lieferungsgeschichte* and important contributions to it, and his editions not only stood out in the first batch of Oxford Classical Texts but have carried their years well.[77] If Housman is thought to offer a model both too narrow and too daunting, future editors will not go far wrong if they follow in the footsteps of A.C. Clark.[78]

Notes

1. *CP* 175 (1891).

2. The passage does not come up in either version of Avancius' *Emendationes* (Venice, 1495, 1500[2]), but the acknowledgement to him in the Aldine (Venice, 1502), where *sors prospera* appears in the text, suggests his authorship. Housman attributes *fors* to him, but Lambinus proposed it in his Horace (Lyon, 1561) II 13, on *Sat.* 1.1.2.

3. Nisbet 1978, 111 = Nisbet 1995, 99. Baehrens's conjecture is also accepted by Trappes-Lomax 2007, 192-3. On Baehrens, 'who with one hand conferred on the Latin poets more benefits than any critic since Lachmann and with the other imported ten times as many corruptions as he removed' (*Man.* I, xliii), see D.R. Shackleton Bailey, 'Emil Bährens (1848-1888)', in Hofmann 1990, 25-37 = Shackleton Bailey 1997, 346-60. More about him below (n. 27).

4. M.L.W. Laistner, *Bedae venerabilis expositio Actuum apostolorum et retractatio* (Cambridge, MA, 1939) 88 = *CCSL* CXXI (Turnhout, 1983), 96-7.

5. The remarks appear in his reply to Antonio Loschi's *Contra Florentinos invectiva*; I consulted it in Laur. 90 sup. 41.2, where they occur on f. 70r. See now S.U. Baldassari, '*Contra maledicum et obiurgatorem*', in Teresa De Robertis, G. Tanturli & S. Zamponi (edd.), *Coluccio Salutati e l'invenzione dell'Umanesimo* (Florence, 2008), 171-3. Modern editors of Pliny read not only *Florentini* but also *praefluenti*.

6. M. Regoliosi (ed.), *Laurentii Valle Antidotum in Facium* (Padua, 1981), IV iv 42 p. 334.

7. *In C. Plinium* (Basel, 1526), reprinted in editions (Heidelberg, 1593; Geneva, 1615).

8. I take the opportunity of restoring to A. Turnebus, *C. Plinii Secundi Veronensis in XXXVI libros Naturalis historiae praefatio* (Paris, 1556) ff. 2r, 6v-7r, a conjecture that modern editors print later in the sentence, *nugas esse aliquid meas putare*, for which Th. Mommsen, *Hermes* 1 (1866), 128-9, thanked Haupt.

9. Goold 1966, 96.

10. Goold 1965, 104, wittily quoting from *A Shropshire Lad*.

11. *CP* 1095 (1925).

12. Nisbet 1991, 66, 90 = 1995, 339, 361.

13. *Hamlet* III ii 393-9.

14. Havet 1911, §§578-86; similarly, with reference to the *Historia Ecclesiastica* of Eusebius, E. Schwartz cited by Pasquali 1934, 137. Havet's book and W.M. Lindsay's *Introduction to Latin Textual Emendation* (London, 1896) were reviewed for *CR* not by Housman but by J.P. Postgate: 25 (1911), 218-23, 11 (1897), 408.

15. Traube 1909/20, III 112-14, 'Paläographie und Überlieferung'.

16. *CP* 96 (1888), 3 (1882).

17. *CP* 661 (1906).

18. *CP* 436 (1897). At Plin. *Nat.* 23.53 Le Mans 263 (s.xii) and some later manuscripts read *Palestina* for *pestilentia*.

19. See also Briggs 1983, 268-77. S.P. Oakley, *A Commentary on Livy* II: *Books VII and VIII* (Oxford, 1998), gives further bibliography on polar errors in his note on 7.26.9, where the manuscripts are divided between *superum* and *inferum*. A presumably authorial one comes to hand in the *Times* for 31 October 2008, 41, under the headline *Phoenicians live on*: 'Ancestors of the Phoenicians, believed to have been wiped out [really?] when Rome destroyed Carthage in 146 BC, are still living in Mediterranean regions, according to researchers who found a genetic marker in the male chromosome.'

20. Fraenkel 1926, 518-19 = Fraenkel 1964, II 292-3.

21. *Lucan*, xiii.

22. *Juvenal*, xxviii.

23. *Lucan*, xvii.

24. *CR* 19 (1905), 465.

25. 'Textgeschichte der Regula S. Benedicti', *ABAW* III 21 (1898), 599-731; revised version *ABAW* III 25.2 (1910). Pasquali 1934, 120 described the study as 'classica per l'abilità con la quale è sfruttata ogni testimonianza e ogni indizio interno', but K. Zelzer, surveying recent work on the transmission of the *Regula* in Chiesi and Castaldi 2004, 366-89, at 377, says that Traube did not take enough manuscripts into account.

26. Lindsay 1907, 188-9. 'Perhaps Livy,' he went on to say, 'is the Latin author for whom Traube did most'; Traube's study of the transmission, *ABAW* III 24 (1904), 1-44, was the broadest in scope before the many contributions of Giuseppe Billanovich from 1951 to 1992 and beyond – an article that he drafted in the mid 1990s was published after his death, *Studi Petrarcheschi* n.s. 14 (2001), 199-221.

27. *JCPh* 111 (1875), 137-51, especially 137-44, 150-51. Baehrens had a nose for manuscripts of importance; see my remarks in Reynolds 1983, 424 n. 18, and Reeve 1991, 455 n. 9. See also n. 3 above.

28. *CP* 954 (1918); similarly 1058 (1922). G. Viré, *Informatique et classement des manuscrits: essai méthodologique sur le de astronomia d'Hygin* (Brussels, 1986), 76-9, 93, still hoped for enlightenment of Lindsay's kind from increasing refinement of the categories drawn up in works such as Havet 1911.

29. *CP* 11, 18, 134, 151, 216 n. 1, 233, 347, 929, 1058 (the much quoted definition of textual criticism); sarcastic at 497, 533, 602.

30. *CP* 772 (1908).

31. *Juvenal²*, lvi, from his Cambridge inaugural of 1911. On Vollmer's career see H. Rubenbauer's obituary, *BJ* 202 (1924), 68-103.

32. Bresslau 1921, 651. On Traube see also P.L. Schmidt, 'Ludwig Traube als Latinist' in Calder III et al. 2000, 491-503.

33. Mommsen 1899, 9-12. The transmission of Ammianus had been discussed not only by Mommsen himself, *Hermes* 6 (1872), 231-42, 7 (1873), 91-101, 171-5, but also by Traube, *Mélanges Boissier* (Paris, 1903), 443-8 = Traube 1909/20, III 33-8, and the baton passed to a pupil of Traube's, C.U. Clark.

34. G. Fiesoli, 'A colloquio con Timpanaro: note a margine di storia della tecnica filologica' in Ghidetti and Pagnini 2005, 199-225, at 209-24.

35. Bresslau 1921, 653.

36. *Prolegomena ad Homerum* (Halle, 1795); *Einleitung in die attische tragödie* = *Euripides Herakles* I (Berlin, 1889), 120-219 'Geschichte des tragikertextes'.

37. Op. cit. (n. 25), 694.

38. Schmidt 1988, 233-4.

39. *Auct. ant.* XIV (1905) il. Bresslau 1921, 651 reports that Buecheler arranged the commission for him.

40. Schmidt 1988, 233.

41. Schmidt 1988, as regards Lachmann an important discussion of S. Timpanaro's book *La genesi del metodo del Lachmann* (Florence, 1963; Padua 1981²; 'corretta con alcune aggiunte' 1985), now available in an annotated translation by G.W. Most, *The Genesis of Lachmann's Method* (Chicago, 2005); in the title of the original article, *SIFC* 31 (1959), 182-228, 32 (1960), 38-63, *metodo del Lachmann* more suitably appeared in inverted commas. See also Schmidt 1995, 12-14, and Fiesoli 2000.

42. Schmidt 1988, 233.

43. Op. cit. (n. 33), 10.

44. Lindsay 1907, 189.

45. M.R. James, *The Western Manuscripts in the Library of Trinity College, Cambridge* III (Cambridge, 1902) 284-5; Bresslau 1921, 538-9. The closing words of Mommsen's preface, *Auct. ant.* V (1882), lxxiii, draw a veil over the incident. Buecheler secured manuscripts of Juvenal from Munich and Leiden for use at Bonn, Hosius manuscripts of Lucan from Bern and Montpellier for use at Bonn and Münster: C. Hosius, *Apparatus criticus ad Iuvenalem* (Bonn, 1888), 1, first ed. of Lucan (Leipzig, 1892), xii-xiii, third ed. of Lucan (Leipzig, 1913), xxx. K. Mayhoff collated at Dresden the Bambergensis of Plin. *Nat.* 32-7: ed. vol. V (Leipzig, 1897), v. Wilamowitz consulted at Göttingen a manuscript of Callimachus from the Bibliothèque Nationale, Paris: *Callimachi Hymni et Epigrammata* (Berlin, 1897²), 11. Housman arranged to consult at Cambridge University Library manuscripts from Holkham Hall and the Bodleian: *CP* 1020, *Man.* V, xxxvii. Changes of ownership apart, single manuscripts now travel only for exhibitions, collections only for cataloguing and then only in the same country.

46. The statement at *Man.* V, 101 is ambiguous, but see his letter of 1 May 1907 to Robinson Ellis (Burnett 1.207).

47. Postgate 1905, V viii-ix, *Juvenal*, ix; *CP* 707 n. 1, 778; *CP* 1020; *Man.* V, xvii, 104 n. *. Paola Errani of the Malatestiana kindly tells me that Housman consulted the Caesenas of Manilius (S.25.5) on 11 April 1912.

48. *CP* 312 (Catullus), 464 (Bacchylides), 480 (*Heroides*), 970 n. 1 (*Ibis*).

49. For Manilius those of MLGVRU and the Cusanus, for *Culex* those of V and Γ (*CP* 773, 776), are in Cambridge University Library, 899 a 394-402. Another reference to photographs (borrowed): *CP* 1020 (T of *Ibis*).

50. Another author whose editing his collations still influence, but less beneficially, is Lucretius; see Reeve 1980a, 28 and 2005, 136-7.

51. I am on much the same ground here as Nisbet 1989, 286-7 = 1995, 273-5.

52. *Juvenal*, vi, *CP* 704 (1907), 777 (1908), 1019 (1920), 1022 (1920).

53. *Callimachi Hymni et Epigrammata* (n. 45), 5, 13; *Bucolici Graeci* (Oxford, 1905), vii; *Aeschyli Tragoediae* (1914), x.

54. See for instance the letter of Cencio Rustici's quoted by A.C. Clark in his edition of Asconius (Oxford, 1907), xi-xii.

55. Halporn 1984, 110-11, 114-17, has good remarks on the hazards and difficulties. Except in the dreariest of texts, I enjoy collating, because I always set out with hypotheses that I want to test and one meets an interesting range of scribes, from the canny or conscientious to the comically or calamitously inept (to say nothing of artistry).

56. *CP* 347 (1894).

57. *Juvenal*, xxix.

58. R.J. Tarrant concludes his entry on Lucan in Reynolds 1983, 215-18, as follows: 'For the present an editor must regard any reading or variant not an obvious blunder that is found in one or more of the ninth- and tenth-century manuscripts as potentially ancient'. The restriction of date probably reflects ignorance of the many later manuscripts rather than anything established or assumed.

59. In my edition of Vegetius (Oxford, 2004), xxvii, I warned against relying on probability even in tackling a more linear tradition.

60. Fraenkel 1926, 524 = 1964, II 299.

61. Håkanson 1979, 30-2.

62. Of the manuscripts listed by Munk Olsen 1982/9, II 17-83, four not mentioned in Fraenkel's review or in Gotoff 1971 or in the editions of G. Luck (Berlin, 1985), D.R. Shackleton Bailey (Stuttgart, 1988; 1997²), and R. Badalí (Rome, 1992), are Colmar Archives fr. 79 (s.ix¹), Paris B.N. Lat. 8039 (s.ix/x), Paris B.N. Nouv. Acq. Lat. 1907 III (s.ix), and St Gallen 863 (s.x¹). Bischoff 1998, 203 no. 932, adds two more fragments of the same manuscript at Colmar and gives its date as s.ix²/³; St Gallen 863 is illustrated by Chatelain II clv and by K. Schmuki, P. Ochsenbein, C. Dora, *Cimelia Sangallensia: hundert Kostbarkeiten der Stiftsbibliothek St Gallen* (St Gallen, 1998), 114-15, and the whole of it can be viewed at www.cesg.unifr.ch, where it is assigned to s.xi²/⁴ on the authority of A. von Euw, *Die St Galler Buchkunst vom 8. bis zum Ende des 11. Jahrhunderts* (St Gallen, 2008), 504-5 no.146, with plates 731-4 in the second volume.

63. Reeve 1980b, 519-22 (Parma 283, British Library Add. 22808, Gronovius' collation of the lost Venetus). In Trapp 1983, 14, 18, I derived Laur. 30.15 (*CP* 526 'a certain villainous Florentine MS', *Man.* I, xi-xii, V, xvii) from an extant copy of the ed. Bonon. 1474.

64. *CP* 702-9 (1907).

65. *CP* 773-7 (1908). In *Maia* 28 (1976), 239 n. 27, I confirmed his case for an intermediary with the aid of a manuscript unknown to him, British Library

Harl. 2701. The collation that he went on to offer is criticised as too selective by G. Orlandi, *Filologia Mediolatina* 4 (1997), 29 n. 96 = Chiesa et al. 2008, 155 n. 96.

66. *CP* 232-304, 314-47, 351-68 (1893-5).

67. G. Orlandi, *Filologia Mediolatina* 2 (1995), 15 = Chiesa et al. 2008, 107. The central question, what a medieval reader was capable of conjecturing, is discussed by Orlandi in 'Lo scriba medievale e l'*emendatio*', *Filologia Mediolatina* 14 (2007), 57-83 = Chiesa et al. 2008, 209-32.

68. *CP* 702-3 (1907).

69. *Lucan*, v, quoted with approval by Shackleton Bailey 1987, 90 n. 3.

70. Wilamowitz and Traube receive the longest entries in the 'Indice degli studiosi' that Pasquali added to his second edition (Florence, 1952), 519-25. An assessment from outside Italy: J. Irigoin, 'Giorgio Pasquali, storico e critico del testo' in Bornmann 1988, 101-13.

71. A vigorous account of aims and achievements is R.H. Rouse's chapter 'The transmission of the texts' in Jenkyns 1992, 37-59; see also Schmidt 1995. For 40 years now the standard British work of *Überlieferungsgeschichte* has been L.D. Reynolds and N.G. Wilson, *Scribes & Scholars* (Oxford 1968, 1974[2], 1991[3]; translated into Italian, French, Spanish, Greek, and Japanese); see also Reynolds 1983, which combines textual and historical evidence in summarising the textual traditions of Latin authors from Plautus to Apuleius and beyond. In Germany the greatest monument of *Überlieferungsgeschichte* in the same generation is P.L. Schmidt's book *Die Überlieferung von Ciceros Schrift 'De legibus' in Mittelalter und Renaissance* (Munich, 1974); he has also written some of the condensed entries on transmission in P.L. Schmidt and R. Herzog, *Handbuch der lateinischen Literatur der Antike*, the new Schanz-Hosius (Munich, 1989-). I discussed some questions of principle in *RFIC* 115 (1987), 436-40 and *JRS* 90 (2000), 196-206.

72. Orlandi, op. cit. (n. 67) 16 = Chiesa et al. 2008, 107-8.

73. *BJ* 262 (1938) includes obituaries not only of Lindsay by H.J. Rose (15-28) and of Clark by C.J. Fordyce (108-13) but also of Hosius by J. Martin (65-72).

74. On the transmission of the *Origines* see now V. von Büren, 'La place du manuscrit Ambr. L 99 sup. dans la transmission des *Étymologies* d'Isidore de Séville', in Ferrari and Navoni 2007, 25-44, on Lindsay especially 27 n. 14, 28-9.

75. *CP* 1099 (1925).

76. *CP* 378-9 (1896), 873-9 (1913).

77. S. Rizzo, *La tradizione manoscritta della* Pro Cluentio *di Cicerone* (Genoa, 1979) 21; M.D. Reeve in Reynolds 1983, 96.

78. For comments and suggestions I thank Stephen Heyworth and Stephen Oakley, for corrections and references David Butterfield.

Part II

HOUSMAN'S SCHOLARLY ENVIRONMENT

8

Housman and R.C. Jebb: intellectual styles and the politics of metre

C.A. Stray

One of the most striking developments in classical scholarship in the late nineteenth century consisted of the discovery of papyri of Greek literary texts previously known only through scattered references and quotations in other works.[1] Several of these papyri were bought by the British Museum: the *Athenaion Politeia* and the mimes of Herondas in 1890, and the poems of Bacchylides in 1896. In each case, Frederic Kenyon of the Museum's Department of Manuscripts prepared a publication; and in the case of the *Ath. Pol.* and Bacchylides, published the *editio princeps* at great speed. The texts were then descended on by the classical scholars of several countries, in what one of them, Otto Crusius, described as an 'acerrima velitatio'.[2] Those responsible for publications in progress, liable to instant outdating, sought to report the new discoveries and make sense of them. For example, in 1891 the second volume of the revised edition of William Smith's *Dictionary of Greek and Roman Antiquities* was moving toward publication under the editorship of George Marindin.[3] Seizing the opportunity, Marindin wrote and commissioned articles on the *Ath. Pol.* and added them in an Appendix.[4] Among the contributors to the volume was Richard Jebb, who wrote the articles on 'Theatrum' and 'Tragoedia'; the editor/contributor relationship was resumed in 1898. At this point, Marindin was editor of the *Classical Review*, having succeeded its founding editor J.B. Mayor in 1893, and thus presided over the flurry of 'Notes on Bacchylides' which began to appear in the February issue of the journal. It was this series of notes which brought Housman into conflict with Jebb, the most celebrated Greek scholar in Britain, well known for his edition of Sophocles (1883-96) and already established as a leading national spokesman for the humanities.[5]

The aim of this chapter is to examine the dispute between Housman and Jebb over the text of Bacchylides. My concern is not to establish who was, in any sense, 'right', but to explore the nature and context of the dispute.[6] This was not simply a disagreement between two individuals over a text, but a conflict of intellectual and cultural styles, of institutional locations and of generations. Further, the dispute was conducted in a relatively new arena: in the pages of a journal founded in the previous decade to encourage open scholarly discussion in Classics by the frequent and regular publication of signed reviews. In the first half of the century, reviews had usually been anonymous, but from the 1860s on, it had become more common for writers to declare themselves.[7] At this point, in the late 1890s, the long nineteenth-century history of debates in such general reviews as the *Edinburgh Review* (founded in 1802) and the *Quarterly Review* (1809), the *Athenaeum* (1828) and the *Academy* (1869) was giving way to the interchanges in such scholarly journals as the *Journal of Philology* (1868), the *Journal of Hellenic Studies* (1880) and the *Classical Review* (1887).[8] The persistence of scholarly review and debate in the general reviews named above was due in part to their frequency of publication, *ER* and *QR* both being monthlies (despite the latter's name), *Athenaeum* and *Academy* weeklies.[9] *CR* was better placed to function as an arena of debate than *JPh* and *JHS*, because it appeared frequently (every month except August and September) and regularly.[10] As *JHS* was an annual and *JPh* an (erratic) bi-annual, *CR*, which began by publishing in nine months of the year, had a distinct advantage over them in reporting discoveries and promoting debate.

What literature there is on Housman's relations with other scholars has largely focused on his own involvement;[11] in this chapter Jebb's papers are drawn on to show what was happening on the other side of one particular dispute.[12] What emerges is a story of alliances and exclusions, of ideological commitments, and of editorial mediation behind the scenes.

Co-operation and contest: assembling Bacchylides

The Bacchylides papyrus reached the British Museum early in December 1896; two weeks later, on the 23rd, Frederic Kenyon of the Museum's Department of Manuscripts, whom Jebb had earlier helped with the publication of a papyrus of Herondas, reported the acquisition and asked for his help in preparing the *editio princeps*. On 11 January 1897 Jebb inspected the papyrus for the first time, and he and Kenyon then compared notes while the latter was preparing his edition. This appeared in December of the same year; Jebb's full edition, with lengthy introduction, text, facing prose translation and notes, was published shortly before his death in December 1905.[13] This procedure replicated that followed for the *Ath. Pol.*, whose *editio princeps* was issued by Kenyon in 1891 (with help from J.E. Sandys), followed by a full edition by Sandys (1893).[14] It is worth noting, however, that the timing and editorial policies differed in the two cases. Both of Kenyon's editions were met with comments and suggestions in such journals as the

Athenaeum and the *Academy*; but in 1891 this took place during *CR*'s publication season, and the editor J.B. Mayor responded, in the March issue, by merging all the emendations received into one text, into which he incorporated suggestions sent to other journals. In 1898, the spate of suggestions began in January, a month in which *CR* was not published.[15] The editor G.E. Marindin published proposals as a collection of 'Notes' by individual scholars, though he added footnotes which added cross-references. This strategy may have been dictated by a concern to bring out the February issue at speed; and it is clear from R.Y. Tyrrell's letters to Jebb (quoted below), which begin on 7 February, that the issue had been published before then. The effect of this presentational strategy, it could be argued, was to highlight the role of individual scholars in offering emendations.

The appearance of Kenyon's *editio princeps* of Bacchylides provoked a flurry of responses from the scholars of several continents.[16] In the 'Notes' which were published in classical journals, general reviews and the transactions of learned societies, certain tensions can be observed. Each author wanted to help in the common quest, but also hoped to be the first to make a successful point. As the Notes accumulated, disputes broke out between the authors of rival (or identical) conjectures, and the corpus of comments expanded and changed. In England, emendations were published in the general cultural journals the *Athenaeum* and the *Academy*, and then in *CR* from February 1898, with Housman taking a leading part.[17] He had already acquired a reputation for polemical acerbity, as in his controversy with J.P. Postgate over the MSS of Propertius in 1895. In the previous year Postgate had published a pamphlet on the MSS of Propertius (Postgate 1894) which commented more than once on Housman's work. Housman responded in *CR* in February (9 (1895), 19-29) with a tone of tired reproof: 'Dr Postgate makes his mistakes with a tranquil air of being in the right which is likely enough to satisfy students not possessing my weary familiarity with the subject' (22). In the April issue (178-96) Postgate gave a long and crushing reply, remarking *en passant* that Housman, who had 'rated half the scholars of Europe', was now 'sore at reproof' (180).[18] Housman was clearly bruised; his publication rate slowed, and he turned to writing poems, in part, apparently, because of the impact of Postgate's response.[19]

Jebb too had had considerable experience of controversy. Always sensitive to criticism, he tended to assume that it was personally motivated, especially in the cases of J.P. Mahaffy, A.H. Sayce and Heinrich Schliemann. Jebb was more likely to strike in defence than in attack, but was a skilled and determined adversary. In 1876, though infuriated by a savage review of his *Attic Orators* which he was convinced came from Mahaffy's pen, he told Alexander Macmillan that '... silence is wisest, and I shall say nothing'.[20] Jebb's response to

Housman's criticisms of his Sophocles edition has been concisely described by Naiditch (1988, 178): 'He acted as if they had never been published.' Housman's article on *Oedipus Coloneus*[21] was liberally sprinkled with digs at Jebb: 'This breakneck asyndeton is accepted ... by no modern editor but Prof. Jebb' (182-3); 'Mr Jebb, from information privately received, knows ...' (190); 'Prof. Jebb quite mistranslates' (191); 'Mr Jebb wrongly translates' (198); and most wounding of all, '... to find Mr Jebb saying "the reiterated πολλά is effective" would be astounding if one had not often observed that a conservative critic writing for a conservative public is apt to grow careless how he defends a text which most of his readers are willing and eager to accept without any defence at all' (205-6). Still other such remarks were suppressed by Housman: for example, in his copy of Jebb's Sophocles *OC* he wrote on lines 438-9, 'I do not possess the esoteric knowledge of rhythm which I so often admire in Prof. Jebb and other editors; but what rhythm has to do with the question I cannot imagine.'[22] On the flyleaf of his copy of the third edition of Jebb's *OT*, he transcribed part of a letter by Edward Fitzgerald:

> This Wright edits certain Shakespeare Plays for Macmillan: very well, I fancy, so far as notes go; simply explaining what needs explanation for young Readers, and eschewing all <u>aesthetic</u> ... observation. It is safest surely to give people all the <u>Data</u> you can for forming a Judgment, and then leave them to form it by themselves.

The implication is presumably that this is what Jebb should have done, but did not.[23]

Bacchylides reborn

The first batch of 'Notes on Bacchylides' appeared in *CR* 12.1 (February 1898), 58-83; they consisted of comments on Kenyon's edition by nine scholars, including Platt (58-63) and Housman (68-74). Both men criticised Kenyon's and Jebb's metrical analyses, Platt declaring that '[t]he defect of the edition is the faulty manner in which the metre is treated' (58), and accusing Jebb of twice suggesting readings which made 'ridiculous poetry' (61). In his own notes (68-74), Housman included an acerbic paragraph (68-9):

> One does not like to look a gift horse in the mouth, and one cannot fairly expect a palaeographical expert to be a metrical expert as well: non omnia possumus omnes. But there must be quite half a dozen scholars in England who understand these matters, and it surprises me that Mr Kenyon could get none of them to help him. The consequence is that his text contains at present a good many metrical solecisms: some of these are introduced by his conjecture, and three or four supplementary violations of metre are proposed in the notes by Professor Jebb. The

schemes prefaced to the odes are often incorrect: the marks of quantity placed above lacunae are even worse, and have led Mr Nairn to make two unmetrical conjectures in the last number of this Review. Mr Kenyon says that ode III is logaoedic: the strophe is, but the epode is dactylo-epitrite. He says that XI is logaoedic with dactylo-epitritic lines interspersed: it is purely dactylo-epitrite from beginning to end. He says that XIII is logaoedic: it is dactylo-epitrite with no logaoedic elements at all. He says that XVII is paeonian: it ought to be, but as Mr Kenyon prints it it is neither that metre nor any other. It is the more deplorable, because Mr Kenyon and Mr Palmer and Prof. Jebb have all three done a great deal to restore the text: some of Palmer's corrections in particular are admirable for their simplicity and certainty.

This is not in Housman's most brutal style; but since Kenyon's preface had made it clear[24] that Jebb had helped Kenyon with his text, Housman's reference to 'quite half a dozen' clearly excluded Jebb from the group of competent metrists. The wound is deepened by the provocative avoidance of specificity for the 'three or four supplementary violations', which made impossible a clearly-targeted defence. Even the final compensatory praise singles out Palmer, leaving Jebb and Kenyon below the salt.

Housman suggested that one reading 'proffered by Messrs Jebb and Blass' was 'an amazing solecism'.[25] Jebb picked up on this remark in the next issue of *CR*, declaring that the offending reading was that of the MS and that Housman's remarks were misleading: 'To say nothing of courtesy, this is a breach of fairness.' In his peroration, Jebb responded to Housman's remarks on the availability of proficient metrists:

As we know that one distinguished College in Gower Street already claims two of these, there are only four left for the rest of England; and no one of any modesty could feel hurt at being left out of such a group.[26]

In his discussion of the controversy, James Diggle remarks that 'Housman had phrased his insult carefully, and Jebb, through incomprehension or wilfulness, did not take his meaning.'[27] In other words, Jebb took 'quite half a dozen' to mean 'very few', not 'quite a few'.[28] Incomprehension is however vanishingly unlikely: Jebb *did* take Housman's meaning, though he pretended otherwise. Parrying an insult with a show of humility, he pointed out that Housman's formulation implied the arrogant claim that he and Platt made up a third of the body of proficient metrists in England. Far from missing Housman's point,[29] he saw it and dodged the blow.

Some of the issues underlying the question of metrical proficiency can be seen in the final words of Jebb's response to Housman in March 1898:

> It is indispensable to study metres in technical hand-books; but it is also good to aim at acquiring, by writing in those metres, some insight into their spirit, some perception of their rhythm, some sympathy with their flexible movement, some ear for their music; something, in a word, which is nearer to their essence than a doctrine which, when separated from the discipline of taste and feeling, may sometimes incur the danger of becoming rashly dogmatic and pedantically rigid.[30]

Despite the rhetorical softening of 'sometimes' and 'danger', this represents a measured defence of aesthetic insight as against rule-bound analysis. And this is what we might expect from Jebb, who was not only a specialist in Greek poetry, but also a virtuoso composer: a man to whom the intricacies and subtleties of Greek metre were second nature. In 1873 he had published a Pindaric version of Browning's difficult poem 'Abt Vogler', the first item in his *Translations into Greek and Latin Verse* (Cambridge, 1873).[31] In 1888 he had composed a Pindaric ode to celebrate the 800th anniversary of the foundation of the University of Bologna, which had excited much admiration.[32] Now he circulated a Pindaric version of an ode by the Italian poet and classical scholar Giacomo Leopardi, to mark the centenary of his birth on 29 June 1798.[33] This substantial piece of work resembles the two earlier compositions in its virtuoso employment of a difficult metre, but at 35 stanzas is longer than either of them. Jebb was perhaps responding in part to the Gower Street criticisms of his metrical knowledge: declaring, by doing, that he was a master of the kind of metre in which Bacchylides had written.[34] If so, the choice of Leopardi, whose fame rested on both poetic and scholarly excellence, was an apt one. We should also notice the striking parallel with Housman's course of action in the wake of Postgate's onslaught three years earlier. Both men turned to composition in verse after a bruising encounter. The languages were different – English for Housman, Greek for Jebb; and so too the function – solace in one case, assertion in the other – but the similarities are nonetheless worthy of remark.

Taste vs doctrine: rallying the aesthetes

Jebb's correspondence with his friends and allies Henry Butcher and Robert Tyrrell throws considerable light on their shared approach to the text and on their attitude to Housman and Platt.[35] On 7 February 1898, Tyrrell wrote:

> I do not at all like the tone adopted by Platt and Housman in the CR.[36] It vulgarises classical criticism, and reminds me of 'Henry' and 'Edmund' in the 'World' and 'Truth'.[37] Moreover, it is downright stupid to talk of 'solecisms' when the Editor rightly presents us with the reading of the Ms.; still more stupid (if not malicious) to involve in the responsibility those who have assisted him by their suggestions. Many of the

suggestions made by Platt and Housman are interesting enough; but surely you cannot, apostrophising a River, say σοὶ ποταμοί. Again, πρὸ γουνοῖ' is quite abnormal.[38] I do not believe in their metrical theories at all. The last syllable seems to be common, unless you resort to wholesale correction. They seem to have pinned their faith to some obsolete book like Boeck[h].[39] I hate the very sound of such words as paeons and epitrites.[40]

And in response to Jebb's reply, on the 9th Tyrrell wrote:

The views which I expressed ... about the γῆς ὀμφαλός[41] at Gower St coincide with yours. Something must be done to stop this dictation. It is quite unscientific to resort to wholesale emendation to carry out the rules of some obsolete treatise on which Gower St nourishes its youth sublime ... I would welcome an edition of Bacchylides with commentary ...

On the previous day, Butcher had written in similar vein:

... I have glanced through the papers on Bacchylides, and read enough of Platt & Housman to make me long to punch both their heads. The arrogance of that pair! Nothing could exceed the badness of their taste & tone. As for the metrical question,[42] I don't believe it is the simple thing they imagine. My own impression is that the last syllable of the verse must be anceps in Bacchyl., & that otherwise you must resort to wild conjecture & correction. But, it would need a very close study to establish that fact. ... To lay down the law in the jaunty manner of P & H is sheer impudence & nothing else.

On the 17th Tyrrell wrote again:

I have stood up for the common syllable at the end of the lines in Bacchylides in my article;[43] but don't you think something ought to be said in the CR? The fact is, the Gower St theory is borne out only by one strophe and not in the whole set of poems, and they only 5 lines long! The rest either exhibit a common syllable, or are not applicable, being either non-antistrophic or corrupt. The second ode with its str. and ant. of 5 lines is actually the only one which conforms to the Gower St view! Is it not monstrous that this should be treated as the norma and all the rest treated as deviations tortured into conformity?

The ranks of battle were thus clearly drawn up: Jebb on one side, with his allies Kenyon, Butcher and Tyrrell; on the other, Housman and Platt. Tyrrell's vehement backing of Jebb, however, contrasts strikingly with his history of support for Housman from 1887 onwards; support which seems to have resumed after Jebb's death in 1905.[44] The position of Jebb's younger colleague Walter Headlam (fellow of King's College since 1890) was somewhat ambivalent. Toward the end of 1891 he had created a minor sensation by issuing a pamphlet against Jebb's pupil and Trinity colleague Arthur Verrall denouncing his editing of

Aeschylus.[45] Earlier the same year, he had publicly criticised Jebb's competence at metrical analysis in a review of the latter's edition of the *Philoctetes*, though he had subsequently offered a private apology.[46] Surviving letters from him to Jebb show that they often discussed the text of Bacchylides.[47] On 17 August 1898 he wrote offering some conjectures; his accompanying comments are largely supportive of Housman's suggestions. On one of Jebb's proposals, he commented: 'The brevity of style would be startling in any author, but strikes me always as foreign to B's manner – easy, fluent, facile, luminous, but mechanical, it seems to me, and lacking personality.'[48]

On reading Housman's criticisms in the February issue of *CR*, Jebb wrote to the editor George Marindin, asking him to secure the details of his alleged metrical blunders from Housman; Housman duly supplied them, and Marindin sent them to Jebb on 8 February 1898. Jebb also sent Marindin letters from Butcher, Kenyon and Tyrrell; presumably not for publication, but to bolster his case that Housman was misbehaving. Marindin replied on the 10th with a judicious letter:

> I return Professor Tyrrell's PS with many thanks ... When you set all together the 5 passages from Professor Housman's article they present a worse appearance than they do when scattered through a long article which on many points expressly endorses your views. At the same time I quite agree with you in disliking his style: it is certainly not one which I should adopt or recommend for imitation. But I ... think that you overrate its importance on these particular points and his animosity. I did not know till you told me that there was any reason for supposing an animus against you on Professor Housman's part – had I known it I should have thought it best to cut out a good deal that remains, even though I trust that there was no such personal feeling in his mind when he wrote. I did know that you had had a controversy with Platt, and for that reason I abstained from asking him to review the forthcoming Bacchylides when I heard from you that you had had a large share in the Editio Princeps. I think (as the point is raised) that I disagree, editorially, with you in thinking that your position <u>enhances</u> the offence. On the contrary the cases where I should be most careful to interfere are when the person assailed by a violent or 'bludgeon' style of review is a young or unknown scholar, of honest intention, who has not the same power of holding his own; and may be rushed or wounded by the attack. However that is an academic question which need not be discussed. It is certainly preferable (as Grote once pointed out to Shilleto) to be courteous in controversy.[49]
>
> As to προ γουνοῖ', I wrote to Platt before I had his MS printed, dissenting from his suggestion, not on the grounds of metre (about which I do not feel sure myself), nor of palaeography, but simply because I cannot conceive how an ἄλσος can be in front of a γουνός. It seems to be a contradiction of terms, and I am old fashioned enough to think primarily of sense – one might as well talk of a man's coverts lying not far from his estate.[50]

Feb. 11. I had got so far and now I have two other sets of enclosures which I return with many thanks to you for sending them (Tyrrell, Butcher & Kenyon). First let me say that I shall feel quite justified in holding back the March number a little if necessary to give you time for your article. Feb 19th which I think you suggested will do quite well for the MS to come. Is that too soon for convenience? I feel that this meeting of parliament must have curtailed your time for literary work.

I can quite endorse what Butcher says of Heberden's knowledge of metre (which he has also studied from the musical side).[51] I think he has (as have Platt and Housman) studied the German writers, who as usual, think that they only know the subject – but your own authority should be as good as the German,[52] and you have composed too in Pindaric metre largely which to my mind is the only method of being really at home in a metre.

A variegated professoriate

Professor Jebb and Professor Housman make an odd couple, as different as their respective chairs. Jebb exemplified the high cultural ground occupied by late-Victorian Hellenism, becoming as he did in the 1890s a leading spokesman for humanistic scholarship. It was to Jebb that the Chancellor of the Exchequer turned after the coronation of Edward VII for advice on the lettering on the British penny, to reflect the King's title: 'Edward VII by the Grace of God of the United Kingdom of Great Britain and Ireland [and of the British dominions beyond the seas] King, Defender of the Faith, Emperor of India' – the text in parenthesis being newly added. Jebb's suggestion, which was adopted, was to add 'OMN' to the existing wording, so as to read BRITT OMN REX. [53] Spy's cartoon of Jebb in 1897 was captioned 'Ajax MP', referring to the publication of the final volume of his Sophocles edition. In newspaper reports, Jebb was commonly referred to as 'Professor Jebb, MP'; and though many Oxbridge dons holding chairs would have hesitated to use the title 'Professor', Jebb had for fourteen years been Regius Professor of Greek at Glasgow, where the professoriate was part of the city's social and cultural elite.[54] His return to Cambridge to take up its own Regius Greek chair in 1889 might in retrospect seem part of an irresistible rise; but it had been delayed for some years by the failure of Benjamin Kennedy, the previous incumbent, to retire or die. Nevertheless, his ascent from Trinity College, Cambridge, to Glasgow and then back again represented the triumph of an acknowledged talent; a talent not only for Greek scholarship, but also for the assembly of articles, editions and other books which were very carefully targeted at scholarly and general audiences. There was more to his rise than this, however: at Macmillan's dinners from the late 1860s on he met Arnold, Browning and other cultural luminaries,[55] acquiring contacts which could be reinforced and extended at the Athenaeum (to which he was elected in 1881) and the House of Commons (from 1891).

While Jebb was at Glasgow, Housman went to Oxford, and as is well known, in 1881 'failed to obtain Honours'. The causes of his failure have been much disputed,[56] but a salient feature of it was shared with many other schoolboys who entered Oxford after a thorough grounding in linguistic scholarship. The first part of their course (Mods) represented a continuation of school work, and indeed the best-trained among them could mark time. The second part (Greats), however, took them into new territory – ancient history and philosophy – and many fell at this hurdle. Had Housman been sent to Cambridge, he could have taken the still mainly linguistic Part I of the Classical Tripos and obtained a degree on the strength of it. If he had continued to Part II, first examined in 1882, he would have been obliged to take Section A (Literature: compulsory till 1895), itself mostly textual, and could then have chosen, for example, Comparative Philology. It is not entirely misleading, then, to describe Housman as a Cambridge man who went to the wrong place.[57]

In the 1880s, Jebb was in Glasgow, earning a substantial salary; he worked on his Sophocles edition in Cambridge in the free months of the year (April-September), but was obliged to endure the long, dark northern winters.[58] Meanwhile Housman worked as a clerk at the Patent Office by day, earning less than a tenth of Jebb's salary, and at the British Museum in the evenings, where the winter dark was banished by the recently-installed electric lighting.[59] The articles he published from 1882 onwards led in 1892 to his election to the chair of Latin at UCL. Had UCL not been in London it would have been seen as a provincial university, such as Owens College (later the University of Manchester) or Mason College (later the University of Birmingham). While some of its academic staff might be men (only) of some distinction, it was not uncommon for graduates to go on to Oxford or Cambridge to take a further bachelor's degree.[60] Yet while the social and cultural distance between Cambridge and London was considerable, there were substantial linkages between them. The chair of classical literature at King's College had been held by Joseph Mayor (of St John's) from 1870 to 1879; on his resignation he was succeeded by George Warr (Trinity), who had been a lecturer at King's College since 1874.[61] Trinity College men had played a large part in the early days of UCL (till 1836, known as the University of London), and its founding classical professors, Thomas Key and George Long, were both Trinity men. In Housman's time as Professor of Latin, John Postgate of Trinity held the chair of Comparative Philology, though this involved no more than a weekly visit from Cambridge. Both Arthur Platt and his predecessor in the Greek chair, William Wyse, had been fellows of Trinity. From 1882 Housman contributed articles to the *Journal of Philology*, co-edited from Oxford and Cambridge but predominantly from the latter; in 1889, the year in which Jebb returned to Cambridge as Regius Professor of Greek, Housman joined the Cambridge Philological Society.[62] Six years after Jebb's death in 1905, Housman arrived at Trinity as Professor of Latin, joining Jebb's successor in the Greek chair, Henry Jackson, who as well as being a long-term friend and rival of Jebb's had also been among Housman's strongest supporters in his candidacy for the Latin chair. The links and differences between Housman and Jebb are thrown into a stronger light by the sequential relationship between their lives and careers. Platt's previous Cambridge links had led him at one point to publish a verse polemic against an Oxford don, John Cook Wilson, who had criticised another Trinity classicist, Richard Archer-Hind. Platt's verses ended, 'But what to do with facts that prove adverse? / Cook, Wilson, COOK!'[63] Again, the nexus of oppositions is complex and changing: the defender of Cambridge against Oxford becomes the metropolitan critic of a Cantabrigian eminence.

The founding of the *Classical Review* provided a new arena in which Housman and Jebb were able to publish and potentially to interact. Though the initial proposal for a journal came from Oxford, the crucial editorial and organisational initiative was provided by Joseph Mayor of King's College, London, trained in Cambridge and the younger brother of the much better known John Mayor, Professor of Latin 1872-1910. The editorial preface to the first number of *CR* declared that one of the reasons for founding the *Review* was that 'English scholarship has produced up to the present time no journal of frequent or even regular issue which devotes itself to the different requirements of classical students'.[64] The original plan was that the *Review* should be printed by Cambridge University Press and managed by a group of scholars who would both contribute and referee articles; the printing plan fell through but the informal co-operative was assembled. One of the interesting aspects of the formation of the group was that with solidarity came the possibility of exclusion. Jebb's friend Robert Tyrrell urged that their *bête noire* John Mahaffy of TCD should not be listed in the roll of contributors.[65] On its founding the *Review* joined *JPh* and *JHS* in providing a common ground for scholarly discussion, extending them not only by including reviews, but in allotting a certain portion of its space to American contributions.[66] In the later 1890s it provided the ground on which Jebb and Housman engaged in mutual criticism. The discovery of Jebb's papers has made it possible to look behind the scenes, at least on one side of the debate. In his correspondence we can see his allies rallying to his side to battle the Gower Street 'gang', and the editor of the *Review* mediating between Jebb and Housman, carrying messages between men who were reluctant to engage in direct communication. We have also witnessed Marindin's careful editorial interventions. He appears to be on Jebb's side in spirit, but is determined to see fair play and to keep to a neutral position. Not long afterwards, he sent in his resignation; a letter to Jebb of 30 July 1898 reports this and explains the difficulties of the editorial role – especially for a retired man living in the country.[67] The difficulties of coping with fractious and thin-skinned contributors, we might suspect, also influenced his decision.

Conclusion

Several issues can be identified in the account given above. At the heart of the dispute are of course the questions, What did Bacchylides write? How good a poet was he? How does he fit into, or change, our picture of Greek lyric poetry? But a host of other issues cluster around these. We have seen that the co-operative search for the answers to the question generated dispute as well as solidarity. Indeed, the two are complementary, since scholars whose approaches or doctrines (or generations, or institutions) are held in common often rally together against others. In the tussle between the Gower Street 'gang' and the older generation represented by Jebb and his allies, age, institutional loyalty and intellectual style overdetermined the course of controversy. The protest by Butcher and Tyrrell against the dogmatic insistence on specific metrical values by Housman and Platt represented a defence of a gentlemanly ideal of freedom and flexibility against a newer, more professional notion of scholarship. It was only too apt that the seniors centred their case on the *syllaba anceps*, an example of indeterminacy. The issue can be seen in the final words of Jebb's response to Housman in March 1898, quoted above. Reading Jebb's remarks, one wonders at his swallowing of J.H.H. Schmidt's metrical theories in his Sophocles edition;[68] something one might see as the triumph of systematic rigidity over aesthetic freedom. But Housman himself seems to have accepted Schmidtian notation, if not perhaps his theorising: 'It is possible,' he wrote, 'for anyone to follow as I do the practice of J.H.H. Schmidt and yet to diverge in many points of detail.'[69] Though it is not obtrusive in his correspondence with Jebb, Headlam too had his own metrical master-theory, that of 'appropriate form', which linked different metrical forms with moods, genres and even Greek ethnic groups.[70] Hardly had Jebb finished following one metrical systematiser, on Sophocles, than he began to listen to another, on Bacchylides.[71]

If Jebb's coda encapsulates the gentlemanly doctrine of aesthetic scholarship, his invocation of 'courtesy' and 'fairness' points to the overlap of scholarly norms (fairness in representing the views of others) and wider social norms (courtesy in dealing with others); and the remarks of Tyrrell on vulgarisation reflect his resentment at the perceived invasion of a public discussion of high culture by the 'new journalism' of the 1880s. Jebb's correspondence with T.H.S. Escott, editor of the *Fortnightly Review*, in the early 1880s reveals a shared concern to replace the vulgarisation they associated with J.P. Mahaffy by a higher scholarly popularisation to which Jebb himself would contribute.[72] In September 1897, Jebb had remarked to Gilbert Murray, who had sent him his first book, *Ancient Greek Literature*, 'I imagine that you have more sympathy than I have with the style of the New Journalism.'[73] The controversy over Bacchylides' text, then, was also a struggle over how scholars should conduct such debates. Murray and Housman, though friends, took very different views on this, and on the relationship between scholarship and its audiences.[74] Thus it is that Jebb, who regarded Murray as a vulgar populariser, was himself seen in much the same light by Housman, who in one of his notebooks wrote, around the turn of the century, that Jebb was 'the Lewis Morris of classical scholarship'.[75] Sir Lewis Morris was a popular late-Victorian poetaster whose fame, second only to Tennyson's, came from his talent for writing fluent, vaguely uplifting doggerel.[76]

In the previous decade the *Classical Review* had been founded to promote discussion between classical scholars, but Jebb's experience of being attacked anonymously had something to do with it. It was then based on a group of some 80 scholars who wrote for it and advised on submissions; and there were attempts to discourage contributions by some people (e.g. Mahaffy). By the late 1890s, the journal had passed into new editorial hands and was more detached from its original steering group. As Jebb found, Marindin was a neutral editor who was concerned to see fair play, and did not share Jebb's sense of outrage at the *lèse majesté* aimed at the Regius chair by the Gower St irregulars.

Behind the system of scholarly discussion and mutual criticism promoted by the review stood a specifically Cambridge tradition of which Jebb was almost certainly aware. It stems from the thinking and practice of John Grote, brother of the historian, fellow of Trinity and Professor of Moral Philosophy from 1855 till his death in 1866. Grote promoted discussion in the Grote Club, which continued after his death. He also pleaded for free and fair discussion in his response to Shilleto's pamphlet against his brother George's history (see n. 49). The tradition was invoked by A.B. Cook's piece 'Criticism criticised' published in the *Cambridge Review* in 1892, following his comment on the Headlam/Verrall tussle which had come out in the same journal not long before.[77] In the 1850s, as we have seen, Cambridge and London had been the poles of the controversy; in the 1890s, they were so once again.

The controversy between Jebb and Housman was conducted, as I have suggested, in an evolving scholarly sphere shaped by the development of universities and journals. Its course and tone, however, also owed much to the characters and strategies of the two men. As Mahaffy had remarked long before, Jebb tended simply to ignore those with contrary opinions. Certainly he only refers to Housman's publications on Sophocles once in the seven volumes of his edition.[78]

Paul Naiditch has remarked that 'One method that Jebb employed was to give no publicity to those he opposed'.[79] That is true, though if we wrote 'those who opposed him' we would come closer to identifying Jebb's original motivation. His morbid sensitivity to criticism, often remarked on in his lifetime, led him to see enemies wherever he found critics; his letters are full of denunciations of those he presumed to be the authors or inspirers of anonymous attacks on his work. As he rose to prominence, this defensive posture took on the arrogance of high position. Thus, as we have seen, he suggested to Marindin that Housman's offence in criticising him was compounded by his (Jebb's) position as Regius Professor of Greek. Looking from the other side of the debate, we might think that Housman's acerbity was sharpened by his awareness of Jebb's position, not just as Regius Professor but also as spokesman for the humanities.

In April 1898 Theodore Reinach wrote to thank Jebb for his 'Bacchylidea', a contribution to a festschrift for Henri Weil. After listing several points of disagreement with Jebb, he concluded gracefully, 'However, opinions are free and it is the privilege of such charming poets to form a link, even by their obscurities, between the scholars of Europe.'[80] *C'est magnifique, mais ce n'est pas la guerre philologique.*

Notes

1. For earlier acquisitions, including the Bankes Homer (1821) and Hyperides (1847), see Turner 1968, ch. 2.

2. Neil 1893, 315. Neil's review deals with BM publications and with editions and recensions by Rutherford, Crusius and Buecheler.

3. Marindin was an Eton and King's college man. After his (early) retirement from Eton in 1887 he took on several editing tasks.

4. Vol II, 1063-73. The articles were by Marindin, his co-editor William Wayte, and Hermann Hager.

5. Jebb was knighted in 1900; in 1902 he was elected a founding fellow of the British Academy (which he had helped to set up); OM in 1905. On Jebb's Sophocles, see Easterling 1999, Stray 2007.

6. For a more detailed evaluation of the metrical issue, see Butterfield's chapter on Housman's metrics.

7. See Buurma 2005. The *Cornhill Magazine*, founded in 1860, had made the rejection of anonymity a cornerstone of its policy. Jebb had often agonised over anonymous reviews of his work, ever since the reception of his *Attic Orators* (London, 1876).

8. To this list one can add the *American Journal of Philology* (1880). In the case of the Bacchylides papyrus, some of Housman's emendations were sent to the (weekly) *Athenaeum*, while Butcher published a review of Kenyon's edition in the April issue of the *Quarterly Review* (187 (1898), 422-45).

9. The two *Reviews* published longer pieces, often of 20 pages or more; contributions to the weeklies were much shorter. The contrast persisted in the debate on Bacchylides, with short notes and letters in *Athenaeum* and *CR* and a 23-page article by Tyrrell in *QR*.

10. *JPh* appeared irregularly, and apparently became more irregular after 1897 (see n. 56 below).

11. The major exception is Naiditch 1988, which remains an essential guide to much of the evidence. It is however difficult to evaluate some of his references, which do not separate out major from trivial evidence: see my review (Stray 1990).

12. The few references to Jebb in Housman's letters do not refer to their differences on Bacchylides.

13. Jebb's annotated copy of Kenyon's edition survives in the Research Library, UCLA, Special Collections PA3943.A2 1897. Later responses by Kenyon to Jebb's queries about the papyrus are in Amherst College library, Misc. Mss K.

14. Kenyon's edition of *Ath. Pol.* had also provoked a flurry of 'Notes': *CR* 5 (1891), 105-19, 175-82, 224-9, 269-70.

15. In 1891 ten issues were published, but the January and February issues appeared as a unit in February. From 1895, nine issues appeared, beginning with a single issue in February. Throughout the 1890s, no issue was published in August, September or January.

16. 'In 1898 even the dullest classical journal seethed with excitement because the poet Bacchylides had just risen from his grave and become audible' (Burnett 1985, 1). For a typically vivid response by the least dull of editors, see B.L. Gildersleeve's 'Brief mention', *AJP* 18 (1897), 492.

17. In December 1897 and January 1898 he had published letters in the *Athenaeum* suggesting readings in the text (Burnett 2.101-2, 104). Burnett's edition has rightly been praised for the 'degree and care of annotation characteristic of both volumes' (J. Vaio, *CR* 58.2 (2008), 603); but the annotation of these letters consists in identifying the *Athenaeum* references; the reader is left in ignorance of the purchase and publication of the papyrus, and of the subsequent discussion to which Housman's letters belong.

18. The *Cambridge Review* (16 (1894-5), 318) commented editorially on the issue of *CR* that '[t]he most noticeable and regrettable feature of the number is a controversy on the MSS of Propertius. The tone of the discussion between two well-known scholars cannot be too strongly deprecated.' See Naiditch 1988, 79-84; and on Housman's polemics generally, Naiditch 1995, 52-69.

19. See S.C. Cockerell's report of a conversation with Housman in 1911: Richards 1941, 436. Housman's publication slowed markedly (only two articles in the following 23 months: (Naiditch 1988, 83). His review of Postgate's Propertius in the October 1895 issue of *CR* (9, 350-5) was free of acerbity; it is surprising that the review was commissioned from him.

20. Jebb to Macmillan, 22 March 1876; BL Add. MS 55125, partially published in Nowell-Smith 1967, 151. The review, in the *Spectator* of 25 March, was followed a week later by a milder review, signed by Mahaffy, in the *Academy* of 1 April. This makes it less likely that the earlier review was by him. Cf. Stanford and MacDowell 1971, 160-1.

21. 'The *Oedipus Coloneus* of Sophocles', *AJP* 13 (1892), 139-70 = *CP* 181-208, to which page references refer.

22. Housman's copy is held in the library of St John's College, Oxford.

23. My thanks to David Butterfield for reporting the inscription to me. Fitzgerald was writing to Fanny Kemble on 1 October 1880 (W.A. Wright (ed.), *The Letters of Edward Fitzgerald to Fanny Kemble 1871-1883* (London, 1895), 175). The reference is to William Aldis Wright's celebrated edition of Shakespeare; on which see G. Taylor, *Reinventing Shakespeare: A Cultural*

History from the Restoration to the Present (London, 1990), 184-90; D.J. McKitterick, *History of Cambridge University Press II: Scholarship and Commerce 1698-1872* (Cambridge, 1998), 392-6. Wright was the librarian of Trinity College, Cambridge, and well known to Jebb (they both appear in the 1860s group photograph reproduced as the frontispiece in Stray 1999). There are multiple ironies here: not only was Wright the editor of the letter which refers to him, his edition of Shakespeare may well have influenced Jebb's Sophocles edition: Stray 2007, 86, 88.

24. 'Professor R.C. Jebb ... saw the proofs from the earliest appearance of the text in type, and has most readily and freely contributed suggestions and advice at all subsequent stages' (Kenyon 1897, lii).

25. Platt remarked that it was 'the most remarkable Greek I have seen since looking over the London B.A. pass papers': *CR* 12 (February 1898), 63.

26. 'Notes on Bacchylides', *CR* 12 (March 1898), 130, 132.

27. Diggle 2007, 163.

28. The semantic field of 'quite' is heavily mined; but the usage here is *OED*'s I.3.e (adverb); it is now usually negative ('not quite half a dozen'), but Housman's comments are comfortably within a period of positive usage quite a century long.

29. This is Naiditch's conclusion (1988, 183).

30. *CR* 12 (March 1898), 132-3; cf. Naiditch 1988, 182-3.

31. He sent a copy to Browning, who replied, 'I am ... very proud of the Greek dress you make my poem wear so prominently on its first page. I thank you indeed for almost giving me the right to admire my own work, which I shall henceforth associate with yours' (Browning to Jebb, 30 July 1873: Jebb 1907, 144).

32. Jebb 1907, 265.

33. The ode, 'Sopra il monumento di Dante, che se preparava in Firenze', with Jebb's Greek version, was printed privately and circulated to friends in July, then published as 'Leopardi's Ode on the Monument of Dante at Florence', *CR* 12.7 (October 1898), 369-75, and later reprinted in the posthumous edition of his *Translations into Greek and Latin verse* (Cambridge, 1907²), 240-63. The version of 'Abt Vogler' is on pp. 2-15, the Bologna ode pp. 264-73.

34. He sent a copy to Marindin for publication in *CR*; so much is apparent from the latter's reply (30 July 1898; Jebb Papers).

35. Letters to Jebb quoted in this chapter are unless otherwise noted those preserved in his papers, and are quoted by kind permission of his great-nephew Lionel Jebb. An edition of a selection from the correspondence is forthcoming: Stray 2010.

36. *CR* 12.1 (February 1898) included at pp. 58-83 comments on Kenyon's edition of Bacchylides by nine scholars, including Arthur Platt (58-63) and Housman (68-74). Both were rude about Kenyon's knowledge of Greek metre.

37. Henry Labouchere and Edmund Yates, the owner/editors of, and contributors to, their respective journals, *Truth* (founded in 1877) and *The World* (1874). Both men were notorious for the 'new journalism' of society gossip, which prompted a succession of libel suits (one of which led to Yates's imprisonment).

38. Tyrrell was presumably referring to Housman's proposal for Bacchyl. 9.45-6 (*CR* 12 (March 1898), 140). But the deity is addressed as 'σῶν ἄναξ ποταμῶν'; Tyrrell must have thought better of his remark (and with reason), and the point is mentioned neither in Jebb's Notes nor in Tyrrell's article in *QR*. πρὸ γουνοῖ' for the transmitted πρόγονοι (printed by Kenyon) at Bacchyl.

11.119; for further discussion of this passage see Butterfield's chapter on Housman on metre.

39. Presumably August Boeckh's edition of Pindar (1811-21).

40. Metrical feet. The paeon consisted of a long and three short syllables, the epitrite of three long syllables and one short.

41. The 'godless college in Gower Street' is equated with Delphi: cf. E. *Med.* 668. Tyrrell's protest at the assumption of centrality by Housman and Platt is unconsciously ironic, given his own location at what was still, in 1898, the Irish margin of Britain.

42. Whether some final syllables were *syllabae ancipites* or not.

43. The article referred to was 'The poems of Bacchylides', *Quarterly Review* 187, April 1898, 422-45. In it Tyrrell stated that the theory denying the existence of a *syllaba anceps* at the end of a line was borne out only by a single passage of five lines. The proposers of the theory, he concluded, had been led to apply 'wholesale correction in order to bring about a conformity against which the MS – our only evidence – everywhere protests' (p. 443).

44. For Tyrrell's support of Housman, see Naiditch, 1988, 216-20. Tyrrell's article on Bacchylides in *QR* twice commended Housman's ingenuity in textual restoration (440-1). But as is clear from his letters to Jebb, his denunciation of the 'arbitrary correction' following denial of the final *syllaba anceps* (443-4) was aimed directly at Housman and Platt.

45. Headlam 1891. Verrall replied in January 1892 (Verrall 1892); see S. Goldhill, *Who Needs Greek?* (Cambridge, 2002), 232-6.

46. 'Emendation ... is not Prof. Jebb's forte, his chief defects being in acquaintance with two branches of study which must especially guide conjecture – lyric metres and the causes of corruption' (*Cambridge Review* 12 (30 April 1891), 288). Jebb replied (ibid., 7 May 1891, 306) and Headlam responded (ibid., 14 May 1891, 324). Headlam's apology was offered in a letter of 27 November 1891 (Bancroft Library, University of California, Berkeley, ms 92/606z, 2.59; to be published in Stray 2010). He may have sensed impending embarrassment, as his assault on Verrall almost certainly appeared the next month; Verrall got hold of it c. 14 January 1892 (Verrall 1892, 5).

47. Amherst College Library, ms J3Z He. Headlam's rapprochement (rehabilitation?) is reflected in the period 1899-1905 by a shift from 'Dear Prof. Jebb' to 'Dear Jebb'. In January 1899 he sent suggestions to Tyrrell for approval before trying them on Jebb – perhaps to show Jebb he was now collaborator rather than critic. Both Headlam and his erstwhile opponent Verrall attempted to be unprovocative when standing for the Greek chair in 1906: cf. Stray, 'Flying at dusk; the 1906 praelections' in Stray 2005, 1-12, at 6.

48. Headlam to Jebb, 17 August 1898.

49. Marindin refers to the controversy between two Cambridge scholars, the well-known classical coach Richard Shilleto and the Trinity philosophy don John Grote, in 1851. Shilleto attacked the treatment of Cleon in vol. 6 (1848) of George Grote's *History of Greece* (12 vols, London, 1846-56); Grote denounced the attack on his brother's book as unfair. Shilleto's motivation, as he admitted himself, was as much political as academic. It also had overtones of academic politics, including a Cambridge vs London tension which anticipates that between Jebb and Housman: see Stray 1997. Marindin may have known of the incident through Cambridge oral tradition, but it is also possible that he was told of it by his predecessor in the editorship of *CR*, J.B. Mayor, who was John Grote's nephew and the custodian of his memory: see Gibbins 2007.

50. See Jebb 1905, 482 for a discussion. Marindin wrote from a rural address and, one suspects, from personal experience. His assumption seems to be that one looks from one's dwelling, across open ground (a garden?) to a peripheral wooded area (covert = a thicket, where game might shelter from the guns of the owner and his guests.) From this viewpoint, culture is nearer than nature; a relationship reversed if a grove is in front of open ground.

51. Charles Heberden, of Brasenose College, Oxford, had published school editions of Euripides; in 1908 he brought out a treatise on Dante's metres.

52. Jebb underlined this sentence ('but ... German').

53. Sir M. Hicks Beach to Jebb, 16 August 1901, with Jebb's ms annotation.

54. Replying on 16 July 1875 to congratulations from his publisher Alexander Macmillan on his election, he had commented: 'I believe it was Matthew Arnold who set the example of declining to be called "Professor". It appears to me that, if it is usual to take that style, to decline it is an affectation – just as much as to exact it would be pedantry' (British Library, Add. Ms 55125).

55. On 2 April 1868, he dined chez Macmillan with 'Browning, M. Arnold, Huxley et al. ... I felt very small & rather shy among the celebrities' (letter to his mother of that date). Jebb and Macmillan had first met in October 1865.

56. See Naiditch 1988, 191-203.

57. Cf. his remarks in the 1911 Inaugural on the two styles of mid-nineteenth century scholarship (in Cambridge, 'scholarship with no nonsense about it'; in Oxford, scholarship in which a scientific pursuit is infiltrated by literary study) (Housman 1969, 25-6).

58. His spirits lifted at the point in February when he could work at 8 am without a candle. On 30 January 1880 he wrote to his mother: 'It is always an agreeable relief here when it begins to be daylight at 8 am, as it does about the middle of February.'

59. This had been installed in the Reading Room in 1878, and the opening hours extended from 7 to 8 pm in 1881 (E. Miller, *That Noble Cabinet: A History of the British Museum* (1973), 254-7). Housman secured a reader's ticket early in July 1883: Naiditch 2005, 11-12.

60. The account Housman gave of Platt's teaching could be applied to his own: 'Much of the teaching which he was required to give was elementary, and he seldom had students who possessed a native aptitude for classical studies or intended to pursue them far' (Housman 1927, vii).

61. In his diary (now in the Mayor Papers, Trinity College Library, Cambridge), Mayor wrote on 6 June 1875: 'Philological on Friday. Discussion about Cambridge invasion of London' (referring to the Cambridge Philological Society).

62. Jebb's inaugural lecture was delivered on 18 October (*Cam. Rev.* 11 (1889-90), 18). Housman was elected to the Philological Society on 7 November and according to Page (1983, 97) attended several meetings. This makes it very likely that he and Jebb were in the same room together, perhaps more than once; but there is no evidence that they actually met.

63. 'A tribute to J. Cook Wilson, Esq', *Cam. Rev.* 10 (1889), 278.

64. *CR* 1 (March 1887), 1. The phrase 'frequent or even regular issue' was aimed at *JPh*, which was notorious for the irregularity of its appearance. In his Housman bibliography, A.S.F. Gow stated: 'After 1897 the *Journal of Philology* appeared very irregularly' (1936a, 65). The list of *JPh* issues given by Naiditch 1998, 661-2, shows that no issues dating from 1902, 1905, 1909, 1911, 1914, 1916 or 1917 were published. Thirty-two contributors were listed in the

prospectus for *CR* circularised in November 1886 (University Library, Cambridge, Cambridge Papers, MR1); which concentrated on the need for a review journal dedicated to Classics.

65. Tyrrell to Jebb, received 25 April 1887.

66. The early volumes of *JHS* carried no reviews; they appeared first in vol. 8 (1887) – influenced perhaps by *CR*. *JPh* had none.

67. His successor was J.P. Postgate, Jebb's pupil and colleague and previously, as we have seen, Housman's antagonist in debate; cf. also Hopkinson's chapter.

68. Wilamowitz, writing to Jebb in 1890 to thank him for his *Philoctetes*, declared that '... on metre I am very far from agreeing with your approach. The conviction acquired by daily habit has made me more attached to tradition than the rules of Schmidt allow you to be.' See Easterling 2005, 42 (giving Wilamowitz's Latin original and the translation I quote here).

69. Housman, 'Notes on Bacchylides', *CR* 12 (March 1898), 137.

70. See Headlam's 'Greek lyric metre', *JHS* 22 (1902), 209-27. The theory was developed and promulgated by George Thomson in his *Greek Lyric Metre* (Cambridge, 1929).

71. See Easterling 2005, 43. She aptly quotes Dale (1968, 14) on the subjectively-based grand theories which litter the history of classical scholarship. In an age of recycling, we badly need a cultural history of classical metric which would take them seriously, rather than relegating them to the litter-bin of history.

72. Escott's initial invitation (14 August 1882) diplomatically singled out Jebb's *Bentley* as a model: 'Its singular thoroughness is a great contrast to many of the monographs & manuals, which are now issued, & it is a valuable contribution to the real knowledge of the public.' Jebb published five articles in the *Fortnightly Review* in 1883-4.

73. Jebb to Murray, 30 Sep. 1897; quoted by Stray 2007, 6.

74. See M. Davies, 'Gilbert Murray and A.E. Housman' in Stray 2007, 167-80.

75. L. Housman 1937, 88.

76. On Morris, see D. Phillips, *Sir Lewis Morris* (Cardiff, 1981), and Meic Stephens' account of him in *ODNB* (2004).

77. A.B.C., 'Mr. Headlam's "Charge"', *Cam. Rev.* 13 (19 May 1892), 316-17; ibid. (9 June 1892), 364. ('Charge': instruction or admonition, usually issued by a judge or bishop.) Cook was a collateral descendant of Grote.

78. On the other hand, Housman's conjectures appear frequently in his edition of Bacchylides. Jebb's ms notes for this are preserved at Amherst College Library: ms J3nb (13 vols). Also held there are letters from Kenyon (1900-05) concerning the text of Bacchylides.

79. Naiditch 1988, 177.

80. Reinach to Jebb, 6 April 1898. *Mélanges Henri Weil* (Paris, 1898) appeared later in the same year, to mark Weil's 80th birthday: Jebb's 'Bacchylidea' can be found at pp. 225-42.

9

Housman and J.P. Postgate

N. Hopkinson

John Percival Postgate, perhaps the most prominent champion of Classics in Britain in the late nineteenth and early twentieth centuries, maintained relations with Housman that were at times affable, often uneasy, occasionally vituperative. It was hardly surprising that these two middle-class, non-public-school Latinists from the Birmingham area,[1] both students of Propertius and later of Lucan and Manilius, both Professors at University College, London and later colleagues at Trinity College, Cambridge, both sarcastic, irascible, bristling and moustachioed, should not go through life without conflict.

Postgate was born in Birmingham in 1853. His father, a physician, campaigned tirelessly against the adulteration of food. The son would later show a comparable zeal for reform in Classics.[2] After King Edward's School, Birmingham, he entered Trinity College, Cambridge. In spite of severe toothache during his final examinations, he graduated as eighth Classic in 1876. His conventional academic career began with six years as a private coach at Cambridge (1876-84). In 1878 he was elected to a Fellowship at Trinity, and in 1884 to a Lectureship there. In 1880 he applied for the Chair of Latin at University College, London. By then he had published only a pamphlet entitled *Notes on the Text and Matter of the Politics of Aristotle* (Cambridge, 1877), and he did not secure the post; but the Electors were so impressed by his qualifications that they created for him a Chair of Comparative Philology. As it turned out, his publications in this field were not as significant as his work on the Latin poets,[3] but he held the Chair until his move to Liverpool in 1909. Since the duties were very light and residence in London was not required, he was able to combine the post satisfactorily with his work in Cambridge.[4] In 1891 he married a former pupil, Edith Allen, sister of T.W. Allen, later the Oxford editor of Homer.[5] Two of their six children would publish valuable memoirs. As a father Postgate emerges as not untypical of his time and class. He was short and stocky, remote but not unkind, unpredictably vehement, stubborn, and (because money had always been in short supply when he was young) parsimonious.[6] He was agnostic, and in politics a high Tory. As a colleague he is described by his obituarist S.G. Owen as 'full of literary enthusiasms' and 'absolutely honest in criticism'; he adds that 'despite his angular personality he had a quite exceptional attractiveness'.[7]

The details of Housman's early career are well known. He was born near Bromsgrove, Worcestershire, in 1859. His father was a solicitor, and the household was conventionally middle-class. His mother died when he was twelve. From school in Bromsgrove he entered St John's College, Oxford, in 1877. After a First Class in Mods, something more serious than toothache caused him to fail in Finals, and he spent the years 1882-92 as a Civil Servant in the Patent Office in London. His leisure hours were devoted to study in the Reading Room of the British Museum.

By the year 1892 Housman's labours had resulted in a number of textual articles on Greek and Latin poets, including Propertius.[8] Supported by testimonials from an impressive range of British and foreign scholars, he applied for the vacant chairs of Greek or Latin at UCL, expressing a preference for that of Latin. The election has been studied in detail by Paul Naiditch (Naiditch 1988). Postgate, who was a member of the committee, must have supported Housman for the Chair of Latin; indeed, it may have been he who informed Housman of the vacancy.[9] The two had corresponded for some years, and Postgate had asked Housman to edit Ovid's *Ibis* for his *Corpus Poetarum Latinorum*.[10] Postgate will have had reason to be satisfied that the Chair of Latin was now held by a scholar of great promise. But he had already had need of forbearance. In 1887, in an article entitled 'Emendationes Propertianae', Housman had taken him to task for a conjecture:

> It makes nonsense of the whole elegy from beginning to end ... If this is the attention to context with which conjectural emendation is practised, no wonder that many students of the Classics regard it as a game played merely for the amusement of the conjectural emendator.[11]

In general, however, Postgate does not emerge badly from this article. In 1889 the two had an almost polite disagreement in the *Classical Review* over a passage of Persius.[12]

Characteristic features of their scholarship are already clear very early in the careers of both Postgate and Housman. While almost all Housman's work is either tacitly or explicitly *editorum in usum*, Postgate aimed for a wider audience. In 1888 he collaborated with the headmaster C.A. Vince on *The New Latin Primer* (1890[2], 1918[3]),[13] which aspired to rival Kennedy, and in 1889 *Sermo Latinus: a Short Guide to Latin Prose Composition* appeared, which gives an insight into his method of teaching and his efforts to enliven a subject found dull by many.[14] He was in the vanguard of those who wished to introduce a more correct pronunciation of Latin into British schools, and he was associated with the efforts of W.H.D. Rouse to teach by the Direct Method.[15] His texts, too, were intended for wide circulation. In 1881 he published, in the 'Red Macmillan' series, *Propertius: Select Elegies*; in addition to a conventional commentary, he provided a 148-page introduction containing a sort of literary-critical evaluation of the poet's style. The book was described by Housman in 1895 as 'the best explanatory commentary [which these poems] yet possess'.[16] In 1889 he produced for G. Bell & Sons an elegant pocket edition of Catullus.[17] Later he would edit Tibullus for Macmillan (1903, 1910[2], 1922[3]) and for the Loeb series (1913), Books 7 and 8 of Lucan for the Pitt Press Series (1896, 1913[2]; 1917), which was designed for school and university students, and Tibullus (1905, 1914[2]) and Phaedrus (1919) for the Oxford Classical Texts, a series which nowadays is felt by students to be formidably austere, but which was intended to help form a cheap basic Classical library.[18] The five fascicles of the *Corpus* appeared between 1893 and 1905, and the work was subsequently available in two stout volumes. Today it is hard to conceive how these unwieldy small folios, with their 1,200 pages of tiny brevier print in long double columns, could have been thought a work of utility and a public benefit.[19] Purchasers will have included not only libraries and professional scholars, but also perhaps undergraduates, classically educated gentlemen and clerics, and even imperial administrators with limited library space. That such portmanteau works could sell in no small quantities is shown by W. Dindorf's *Poetae Scenici Graeci*, containing the plays and fragments of the Attic dramatists, of which there were six editions between the years 1830 and 1885.

Housman and Postgate corresponded on classical matters and served together on committees at University College.[20] Soon, however, their bitter dispute over the textual tradition of Propertius would entertain and offend readers of the *Classical Review*. In 1892-3 Housman published in the *Journal of Philology* three long articles entitled 'The manuscripts of Propertius';[21] beneath the title of the first part is printed the ominous and prescient *sententia* of Publilius, *nimis altercando ueritas amittitur*. In 1894, Postgate published 'On certain manuscripts of Propertius', an 82-page pamphlet in which he praised Housman's work but courteously disputed his conclusions. Housman replied with a ten-page article in the February 1895 issue of the *Classical Review*, in which he treated Postgate and his arguments with characteristic asperity,[22] concluding 'this ends what I have to say on Dr Postgate's spirited attempt ... to re-establish chaos among Propertius' mss'. In the April issue Postgate gave an intemperately indignant and at times rather heavy-humoured response; typical of his polemic is the attempt to turn his opponent's words against himself.[23] Housman had complained:

Were it not for the humour of the situation, I might well resent the tone of placid assurance in which *I*, who think before I write and blot before I print, am continually admonished by the author of this pamphlet.[24]

Postgate replies:

There *is* humour in the situation; but not what Mr Housman supposes. The humour is this, that Mr Housman, who has rated [i.e. berated] half the scholars of Europe, should himself be so sore at reproof and should expect his indignation to move the readers of the *Classical Review*.

Here are some further specimens of his polemic:

He again perverts my argument in this passage ... To make unlike like by confusing the circumstances seems to be out of many Mr Housman's favourite paralogism (178 n. 2).

Had the cabman of the story been a Propertian scholar, he would surely have called Mr Housman a 'harbitrary cove' (179).[25]

The speculation what scholars would or would not hold were the manuscripts of Propertius other than they are, is an airy field where Mr Housman may disport himself at will (183).

The starveling theory then is his own, not that of Baehrens, on whom he would father it (183 n. 1).

Mr Housman vapours here as follows ... (183 n. 2).

He corrects, forsooth, my words into the form he desires them to assume (184).

These trivial accusations come from a scholar who has appropriated my observations on the confirmations of F by L. I too 'acquit him of any intention either to garble or plagiarise; but he has done both' (185).[26]

Of the contumelious reference here ... I intend to make Mr Housman ashamed (180 n. 2).

This was the end of the controversy. Postgate, who had the last word, might have been felt by many readers of the *Classical Review* to have had the best of the dispute. Later researches have confirmed that his view of the manuscripts is more likely to be right than that of Housman, and Housman may himself have come to recognise this.[27] The edition of Propertius' text which he had probably already completed remained unpublished, and after his death it was destroyed.[28] Except for reviews, he subsequently published on Propertius only one brief article.[29] In 1911 he told Sydney Cockerell that most of the poems in *A Shropshire Lad* had been composed 'in the first five months of 1895 at a time of ill-health, and partly perhaps as a reaction from a learned controversy in which he was then engaged'.[30] And so Postgate was perhaps responsible, or at least in retrospect seemed to Housman to have been responsible, for the excited mental state that produced his best-known work.

The first two fascicles of Postgate's *Corpus*, which appeared in 1893 and 1894, included his own texts of Catullus, Propertius and the fragments of Ovid, and Housman's *Ibis*. The Propertius was issued separately by the same publishers, and Housman reviewed it in the *Classical Review* in October 1895. Though critical of many details, he was surprisingly generous (or ostentatiously fair-minded), concluding with the words, 'the general result is a text which I should call not only nearer but much nearer to the truth than any which has gone before it'.[31] He acknowledges that the large pages of the *Corpus* provide 'too good an opportunity to miss' for presenting transpositions, a controversial feature of Propertian textual criticism which both he and Postgate favoured.[32] There is no mention of recent disagreements.

But if it was indeed the case that the controversy with Postgate led to his writing poetry, Housman must have felt particularly aggrieved when six years later, in an article which was in part a vindication of his text of Propertius against some of Housman's strictures, Postgate mockingly quoted passages from *A Shropshire Lad* to illustrate the dangers of misplaced hypercriticism:

> Now there is a strong family resemblance between this criticism and the immortal Lord Dundreary (a creation of the late Mr Sothern not yet, I hope, forgotten) upon certain of our English proverbs. '*Birds of a feather | Flock together*. Absurd, 'pon my word. *Flock together*; of course they do. It would be a dashed silly bird that would go and flock in a corner by itself!' The same treatment may be applied to any kind of literature with interesting results, as for example to the following:
>
>> Now, of my threescore years and ten,
>> *Twenty* will not come again.
>
> Nor will the 'fifty' for that matter. Or to the following:
>
>> Buoyed on the heaven-heard whisper
>> Of dancing leaflets whirled
>> From *all* the woods that autumn
>> Bereaves in *all* the world.

Why not 'From all woods in the world' or 'From the woods in all the world'? δὶς ταύτην ἡμῖν εἶπεν ὁ σοφὸς. – ∪ –.[33]

The Greek quotation, 'The wise X has said the same thing twice', is from a well-known scene in Aristophanes' *Frogs* in which Euripides ludicrously accuses Aeschylus of pointless repetition. The omitted word is Αἰσχύλος (Aeschylus), but Postgate presumably invites the supplement 'Housmanus', which happily has the same scansion.[34] Housman, who by now was occupied with other authors, published no response.

Postgate published his edition of Lucan Book 7 in 1896 and continued work on the *Corpus*, for which he went on to edit Grattius, the fragments of Lucan, Columella Book 10, Nemesianus' *Cynegetica*, and (jointly with G.A. Davies) the *Siluae* of Statius. In 1897 appeared his *Silua Maniliana*, a small volume of conjectures written in Latin.[35] At about the same time Housman, too, had begun work on Manilius,[36] and his edition of Book 1 was published in 1903. In the second section of the Introduction he surveys the work of previous editors and critics. Postgate was not likely to be flattered by his own brief appearance:

> Foremost among the critics who have written on Manilius since the time of Jacob stands Theodor Breiter ... The merits of Robinson Ellis will be thought quite equal to Breiter's by readers who get their knowledge of his conjectures from this edition and do not consult the book from which they are taken, his Noctes Manilianae published in 1891 at Oxford: these students too may wonder why it is that I comment sharply enough upon several of Mr Breiter's errors but never even mention any of Mr Ellis's. The third work of criticism demanding separate notice is J.P. Postgate's Silua Maniliana published at Cambridge in 1897.[37]

The juxtaposition of Postgate's work with that of Ellis, about which readers are invited to suspect the worst, is bad enough; but the self-conscious omission even to engage with the book suggests not restraint from controversy so much as a determination to spare its poor author and a fastidious reluctance to engage with it further.[38]

Postgate, who was the British scholar best qualified to review *Man.* I, did not do so,[39] but he may have found it impossible to secure any other reviewer. In the February 1904 issue, under the heading 'Briefer Notices', he wrote as follows:

> In the uncertainty whether an adequate notice of Prof. Housman's Manilius I will yet be forthcoming for the Classical Review, a brief account of its contents may prove acceptable. The text of I and II 1-3 together with a Latin commentary take up 83 pages, emendations of books II, III and IV 16 more, and the Index what remains of the 103. The commentary which is in Latin is critical and explanatory and only incidentally illustrative. The following figures will give a rough notion of the constitution of the text. It deviates from the MS tradition or traditions in some 160 readings of which, the round 100 belongs in roughly equal parts to Scaliger, Bentley and the remainder of Manilian scholars. The rest are corrections of the editor's own, distinguished by a star. In addition to the Latin commentary and a text thus reformed the purchaser acquires an ample Introduction dealing with the history and condition of the text and the proper method of emending it, written for the most part in English and in the slashing style which all know and

few applaud. In its pages a number of contemporary scholars, chiefly Germans and notably Mr. R. Ehwald and Mr. F. Vollmer, the choice of five Universities as editor of the new Latin Thesaurus, are roughly handled. Before it stands a dedicatory poem to a friend who is described as 'harum litterarum contemptor' from which we cull the following dubitation of immortality

> o uicture meis dicam periturene chartis,
> nomine sed certe uiuere digne tuo.

The volume – a well printed one – is the most substantial English contribution to the criticism and elucidation of Manilius since the time of Bentley.

This Notice, though it refrains from polemic, is not without irony, and not only in the suggestion that Housman has offended every competent reviewer. When Postgate describes Housman's conjectures as 'distinguished by a star' (that is, an asterisk), he mockingly makes a connection between the poem and the ambitions of its Editor. And he implies a strange inconsistency in Housman, who expressed contempt for reputable scholars while dedicating his book to a man who despised Latin studies.[40]

The dedicatory poem to *Man.* I was almost the only Latin verse published by Housman. It seems extraordinary that a scholar who was both a notable English poet and a rigorous student of the Latin language, one moreover who was inspired to study Classics by reading *Sabrinae Corolla* and who in his Cambridge inaugural defended the art of verse composition,[41] who wrote whole volumes of commentary on Manilius in a vigorous and stylish Latin prose when he might have composed them in English, and many of whose predecessors and contemporaries, including his inspiration Munro, produced elegant collections of such work, should have published no other Latin verse. Gow says, 'he had little taste for it himself'.[42] Housman's move directly from the Patent Office to a professorship in London, and later to a chair at Cambridge, meant that he was never called upon to teach verse composition to an advanced level, and to produce the 'fair copies' which the dons of Oxford and Cambridge would collect as books of 'versions'. But it is a thousand pities that Housman never produced a volume of this sort. Postgate did produce such a work, *Translation and Translations: Theory and Practice* (London, 1922); it contained versions, written over a period of 50 years, both into and out of Greek and Latin prose and verse, together with a 100-page introduction reflecting at perhaps unnecessary length on the challenges and compromises inherent in such exercises.

In 1899, stimulated by the discovery in Oxford of a new passage in the sixth satire, Housman turned his attention to the text of Juvenal. In 1903 he was asked by Postgate to edit Juvenal for the *Corpus*,[43] and in

1905 both that text and his separate edition *editorum in usum* were published. He continued to work on the second volume of Manilius, which would appear in 1912. Postgate meanwhile was active in administration and in championing the cause of Classics for the twentieth century. He edited the *Classical Review* from 1898 to 1907. More significantly, he published in the popular *Fortnightly Review* in 1902 an article entitled 'Are the Classics to go?'[44] The Education Act of that year had given the government new powers of intervention, and there was concern that Classics would be afforded fewer hours in the curriculum. Postgate advocated less translation into Latin and Greek from English authors, more original composition, versifying to be restricted to the keenest students, and less teaching of obscure points of grammar. Eager that there should be a body to represent the subject, in 1903 he and E.A. Sonnenschein founded the Classical Association, which has continued now for more than a century to represent Classics throughout the British Isles. The Association bought up the copyright of the *Classical Review* and established a new journal, the *Classical Quarterly*, for longer articles, the *Review* in future being reserved for reviews and short notes. Postgate was Editor of the *Quarterly* for its first three years (1907-10).[45] Housman kept aloof from the Association, except to deliver to it as guest speaker 'The application of thought to textual criticism' at Cambridge in 1921.[46]

In 1909, at the age of 56, Postgate accepted the Chair of Latin at the University of Liverpool. The reasons for his move are not recorded, but it seems likely that he was keen to exercise his talents in a new field and to champion Classics away from its heartland in London and Oxbridge.[47] He may also have been attracted by the salary: by 1919 professors at Liverpool on average earned £1,000 per year.[48] He could look forward to retirement back in Cambridge, since he was by now a Life Fellow of Trinity. Nevertheless, his move is surprising for at least two reasons. First, his colleague at Trinity J.G. Frazer had very recently accepted the offer of a Chair of Social Anthropology at Liverpool, and had hated life there so much that after only five months he returned to Cambridge. Secondly, the Professor of Latin at Cambridge, J.E.B. Mayor, had reached the age of 84, and that Chair might soon become vacant. Still, Postgate went ahead with the move. He will have heard other, more positive, accounts of Liverpool;[49] and perhaps he was resigned to the fact that Housman would eventually obtain the Cambridge appointment.

Mayor died on 1 December 1910. It is unfortunate that no official record or minutes of the 1911 election survive. The candidates were not asked to give a public lecture, as had happened in 1906 with the Regius Professorship of Greek,[50] or even to supply testimonials.[51] Postgate was the strongest internal candidate; J.S. Reid, who worked on prose authors, and J.D. Duff also stood.[52] But Housman was more famous, and potentially more controversial. Whether other candidates were considered is not known. Of the twelve Electors, six were ex officio: the Vice-Chancellor (R.F. Scott), the Regius Professor of Greek (H. Jackson), the Public Orator (J.E. Sandys), the Professor of Sanskrit (E.J. Rapson), the Professor of Latin at Oxford (R. Ellis) and the Headmaster of Shrewsbury School (C.A. Alington). The six Electors nominated by the Board of Classics were T.R. Glover, E. Harrison, W.T. Lendrum, J.T. Sheppard, A.W. Verrall and L. Whibley.[53] It is known that Jackson and Verrall were in favour of Housman,[54] and that Lendrum persuaded Whibley to vote for him.[55] Ellis, now aged 77, had both corresponded amiably with Housman and suffered from his reviews.[56] At any rate, even if there were objections among some of the Electors to the appointment of an Oxford man (the previous holders of the chair, Munro and Mayor, had been products of Cambridge), it seems that they did not agonise for long, since the announcement was made on 18 January 1911, the date of the first and only meeting of the Electors.[57]

The inaugural lectures of Postgate at London and of Housman at Cambridge, both of them aimed at a general audience, form a telling contrast. In Postgate's lecture, 'Dead language and dead languages, with special reference to Latin' (1909), is clearly to be seen the new professor's concern to proselytise for his subject and to make the study of Latin seem both relevant and interesting. Giving examples from Chaucer and the Authorized Version of how easy it is to misunderstand archaic language, he shows that for us early English is 'dead'; he argues that Latin lives on in the modern Romance languages; he emphasises the debt owed by our civilisation to the Romans; and he praises the 'monumental' quality of Latin. Housman, in 'The confines of criticism' (1911), begins with a generous appraisal of Kennedy, Munro and Mayor before addressing the 'two diverse evils' of an over-reliance on literary appreciation of texts (the English scholar's 'besetting sin') and an unthinking reliance on method (characteristic of German scholarship).[58] Housman aims to delimit his subject; he wishes to establish the proper function of a professor of Latin. Postgate is concerned to make Latin of interest to the wider world. But one suspects that Housman's performance was the more memorable. Henry Jackson and J.M. Image, who were present, described it as 'excellent' and 'brilliant'.[59] Postgate's regular lectures at any rate are said to have been drawlingly monotonous.[60]

Postgate can hardly have been surprised at Housman's election, but family sources record his bitter disappointment.[61] He devoted himself however to teaching and administration at Liverpool, publishing his Tibullus for the Loeb series (1913), an edition of the eighth book of Lucan (1917),[62] the OCT Phaedrus (1919) and, among other articles, the entry 'Textual criticism' for the eleventh edition of the *Encyclopaedia Britannica* (1910-11). The Phaedrus was reviewed by Housman, who contrasts the 'diffidence and flexibility' necessary in an editor of this text with Postgate's 'sanguine and stubborn' nature and his 'iron resolve'.[63] Although Housman is here referring to Postgate's editorial practice, he is reflecting also on the temperament of Postgate the man.[64]

In 1920 Postgate retired to Cambridge. Trinity had at that time only about 65 Fellows, and he and Housman, who lived in the College, must have encountered each other at meals fairly often. But the prospect of familiarity did not prevent further conflict. In 1919, Housman published '*Nihil* in Ovid', an article in which he argued that in the second half of the first foot, in order to introduce an initial dactyl, Ovid always used *nihil*, never *nil*.[65] Postgate claimed that Ovid was not pursuing a dactyl, but avoiding *nil*.[66] Housman replied in an article pointedly entitled 'De nihilo'[67], in which he enquires, after quoting Postgate's modified definition of the phenomenon, 'Has Dr Postgate any news from the sick bed of our beloved sovereign Queen Anne?'[68] Postgate elucidated his view under the title '*De nihilo nil*', speaking of Housman's 'brilliant logomachy' and complaining that his 'immediate object was not to set out the truth, but to discredit a rival attempt to ascertain it'.[69] That he quotes by way of conclusion some of Housman's wittiest sentences shows a touch of polemical naïveté. In this controversy Housman seems to have been correct within the narrow limits which he imposed; Postgate's thesis is separate, and more contentious.[70] Housman drafted a reply but did not publish it.[71]

In 1923 Postgate produced for Liverpool University Press *A Short Guide to the Accentuation of Ancient Greek*. The claim on the title-page, *in usum doctorum*, is a hit at Housman. In his copy, now in the library at Trinity College (adv.c.20.57), Housman has written 'From *doctus* or *doctor*?'; and it is indeed unclear whether the meaning is 'for the use of scholars' or 'for the use of teachers'.[72] Given Postgate's past history of useful introductory works, one might have expected teachers to be meant. He states, 'this book has been composed in the first instance for English students of Greek' (p. 80), and by 'students' he seems to mean undergraduates, though he says also that he despairs of teaching them accents when pronunciation in Britain is so perverse.[73]

Housman's Lucan appeared in January 1926, a few months before the death of Postgate. Again there is a long introduction with a survey of previous work on the text. Postgate had less claim to inclusion here than in the introduction to *Manilius* I, since his editions of Books 7 and 8 were not primarily textual. But he can hardly have rested quite content when he read:

> I pass over Weber's perfectly useless edition of 1821 and come to the handy text and notes produced in 1835 by C.H. Weise. His recension is ludicrous ... But ... of all Lucan's editors he is the most careful and consistent. Weise's text ... was reproduced ... by C.E. Haskins as the peg

on which to hang an English commentary, superficial indeed and unlearned, but helpful to beginners and not wanting in common sense.[74]

Postgate, not dignified with a mention even in company with Haskins, might have wondered for a second time whether or no a damning *praeteritio* is preferable to complete oblivion.

Postgate was still mentally and physically vigorous when on 15 July 1926 as he left his home in Brookside, Cambridge, his bicycle was in collision with a steam lorry.[75] His last words, 'Take me to Addenbrookes; I have a subscription there', have led to the suggestion that he died a victim of his own parsimony; but in fact the accident happened an equal distance from two hospitals. The other of these, the Evelyn Nursing Home,[76] a few hundred yards to the south, was the scene of Housman's death ten years later.

In the antechapel of Trinity College distinguished Fellows are commemorated by brass plaques inscribed in Latin. Housman's, composed by Gow, is on the south wall. In fifteen lines it refers to his poetry, his introduction of a new rigour in editorial practice, and his intolerance of those who could not match his own standards.[77] Directly opposite on the north wall, beneath Jackson and Jebb, is Postgate's memorial. It is unique in its brevity and in having been designed by the honorand himself.[78] Its expression is more suited to a gravestone than to a commemorative tablet:[79]

> IOHANNES PERCIVAL POSTGATE. SOCIUS
> Natus est a.d. ix Kal. Nov. Mdcccliii
> Obiit Id. Iul. Mdccccxxvi
> Nobis meminisse relictum[80]

The form of his name is that given on the title-page of his scholarly monument, the *Corpus Poetarum Latinorum*.[81] In death as in life, these two combative Latinists keep a wary distance.[82]

*

In his relations with Housman Postgate fared better than some other Latinists: he engaged robustly and not without success in controversy, and published articles and reviews by Housman while deprecating his 'slashing style'. For Postgate textual criticism was one interest among many, and he no doubt recognised Housman's pre-eminence in that field. Housman for his part, though he clearly felt himself to be Postgate's superior in intellect, did not express for him, either before or after his death, anything like the contempt which he felt for Owen or Ellis.[83] It may be the unfortunate lot of all Housman's adversaries to be known to the wider public only as the victims of his invective and criticism; but Postgate, though he may have foreseen that such would be his fate in the long term, had reason to feel that in the opinion at least of his fellow scholars he had emerged not without credit from his dealings with the arch-tormentor.

If Postgate instead of Housman had been elected Professor of Latin at Cambridge, the Classical course might have developed in a different direction. Housman punctiliously fulfilled the duties of lecturing and examining, and devoted the rest of his time to research. Postgate, a keen administrator who had strong views about the merits of composition and translation for weaker students, might well have introduced reforms. At that time, for the first two years of the course candidates expended most of their efforts on prose and verse composition and unseen translation. Postgate, who in devising syllabuses was willing to compromise in the interests of the non-scholarly majority, might have persuaded his colleagues to make Part I of the Tripos less like school work and more stimulating for those not destined for academic life. As it was, Housman's fame and example meant that philological and textual study remained at the heart of the curriculum in Cambridge until the reforms of the 1960s.[84]

Notes

1. On the new generation of Classicists from day schools in the late nineteenth century see Stray 1998, 145. Sonnenschein, who together with Postgate founded the Classical Association, was another.

2. Cole 1949, 5, John Postgate 2001, 62-8.

3. The best known of his philological publications is his treatise on the Greek accents. He contributed a curious preface to M. Bréal's *Semantics: Studies in the Science of Meaning* (Eng. trans., London, 1900), viii-lix; he does not much engage with the book, but discusses at length the terms rheme and epirrheme, which were in use by the Prague School. Appended (311-36) is a lecture given by him at UCL on 6 October 1896, entitled 'The science of meaning'. This science is revealed to be Rhematology. In 1924 Postgate published in Prague a lecture entitled 'The syllable in English', in which he deplores the fact that phoneticians have neglected to define the English syllable.

4. Naiditch 1988, 77-8 with n. 30-7.

5. She studied Classics at Girton College 1882-5. In 1887 or 1888 Postgate had proposed to another pupil from the same year group, Edith Annie Sheldon, who broke off the engagement 'at the eleventh hour' (Girton College Papers GCPP Strong 2/1 File 1 (1879-89)). The file contains several letters from Postgate to Eugénie Sellars, who helped revise the *New Latin Primer*.

6. His children remembered his parsimony without pleasure. He would stint on coal and electric light for their nursery and scrape what he considered excess butter from their bread (Cole 1949, 4-6). Whenever possible he travelled by bicycle. He kept up a strict correspondence over money with his son Raymond when he was an undergraduate at Oxford. In his will he specified that not more than £15 should be spent on his funeral. The most notable instance of his irascibility was his virtually disinheriting Raymond and his sister Margaret for their socialism and unsuitable marriages.

7. Owen 1926, 346.

8. On his emendations in Greek drama see Diggle 2007.

9. Naiditch 1988, 77.

10. See Williams' chapter in the present volume.

11. On 1.1.33. The article is *CP* 29-54; quotation from p. 53.

12. *CR* 3 (1889), 199, 275, 315 (= *CP* 110-11).

13. At around the same time (1885) Jebb delegated to the schoolmaster M.A. Bayfield an abridgement for schools of his commentary on the *Oedipus Tyrannus*.

14. He recommends reading a passage of a Latin author carefully and then, after an interval, trying to reconstitute it with the help of a translation (14). In Trinity College his practice was to compile on a blackboard a composite version from suggestions offered by the class (9-10). In his enthusiasm he disparages the teaching of French and German: 'Politically, their importance is lessening year by year before the growth of the Anglo-Saxon race, and it will not be long before Englishmen will (except for special reason) as little think of learning either of them as they now do of learning Dutch or Welsh' (6 n. 2). A key for teachers was provided.

15. For Latin the Direct Method seems to work only with the most brilliant of teachers; on Rouse, who was one such, see Stray 1992. Postgate attempted it at home, notably at Sunday lunch, but succeeded only in traumatising his daughter Margaret. When he tried to teach her Latin verse composition (probably not via the Direct Method) she found him 'exacting and irritable' (Cole 1949, 5-6). Perhaps he had more success with the children who left no memoir.

16. *CP* 369. Naiditch 1988, 90 remarks that the commendation is less than effusive; but cf. Burnett 1.58.

17. Housman had sent to Postgate a list of corrections to the apparatus criticus of this edition, now preserved among the Carter Collection at the University of Austin, Texas (information kindly supplied by David Butterfield).

18. Whitaker 2007. In 1960, for example, the dust-jackets of OCTs announced, 'Volumes bought at school should serve as the beginning of a small library which will be used by its possessor throughout school and undergraduate life; and be a better stimulus to literary interest than annotated editions of the parts of an author's works which are set for the next examination.' In the April 1900 editorial of the *Classical Review* Postgate gave a qualified welcome to the proposed series, noting that several of the advertised editors were not known to be expert on the authors they were to edit.

19. W.M. Lindsay, reviewing the final fascicle in *CR* 19 (1905), 462, says the *Corpus* is 'as universally known and commended as the Encyclopaedia Britannica', but Ellis had complained about the small print at *CR* 8 (1894), 302.

20. Naiditch 1988, 79.

21. *CP* 232-76, 277-304, 314-47. Postgate had forwarded the manuscript without success to the Syndics of the Pitt Press and had asked Henry Jackson to write a letter of support (Cambridge University Library Pr.B.13.9.59; I owe this reference to Professor D.J. McKitterick). It was turned down also by Macmillan and Oxford University Press.

22. *CP* 351-68.

23. For another example of this tactic, see below.

24. *CP* 366.

25. The reference is to John Forster, the biographer of Dickens, who is said to have been so called by a cabman exasperated at his contrary nature.

26. This is a quotation from Housman, *CP* 367.

27. Goold 2000, 140-1. On the work of Postgate and Housman on the manuscripts of Propertius see Butrica 1984, 6-8.

28. Cf. Naiditch 1988, 41 n. 10-16, Gow 1936a, 12: 'At his death there was found among his papers a complete transcript of the text, with apparatus, written in the exquisitely lucid script which he employed where special accuracy was required of printers'. F.H. Sandbach told me that one morning, I suppose in 1936 or 1937, Gow showed him this transcript and told him that he would burn it that afternoon.

29. 'A transposition in Propertius', *CP* 880-5.

30. Letter to the *Times Literary Supplement*, 7 November 1936, reprinted in Richards 1941, 436.

31. *CP* 377.

32. *CP* 374.

33. The two articles entitled 'Vindiciae Propertianae' appeared in *CR* 15 (1901), 40-4, 406-13; the quotation is from p. 407. Postgate cites *A Shropshire Lad* II and XLII (Burnett 1997, 4, 44); the italics are of course his.

34. Arist. *Ran.* 1154. That Postgate spelt the Latinised form thus is shown by *Mnem.* 52 (1924), 21 *excogitauit Housmanus*. (In the *Corpus* he does not use Latin forms of the names of contemporary scholars.) Housman at first used this form himself (Burnett 1.518), but he came to prefer *Housmannus* (Praef. ad *Man. ed. min.*, viii n. 1).

35. The book was in part a response to R. Ellis' *Noctes Manilianae* (Oxford, 1891).

36. Naiditch 1988, 84-5 n. 30-15.

37. *Man.* I, xxii.

38. Note the parallelism in sentence structure: 'published in 1891 at Oxford ... published at Cambridge in 1897'.

On Housman's restraint as a polemicist see Naiditch 1988, 89 n. 30-22, and on this passage ibid. 90-1, Goold 2000, 149. In *Man.* V, xvii-xviii, Housman tabulates the number of emendations by each critic that he has adopted into his text of Manilius. Eight are by Postgate, sixteen by Ellis, twelve by Breiter (and 238 by Bentley).

39. This can hardly have been because he felt that the Editor of *CR* ought not to indulge in controversy: only two years before he had had no compunction in publishing 'Vindiciae Propertianae' (see above).

40. The dedicatory poem is printed at Burnett 1997, 289-91 (cf. 565-6); see also Harrison 2002. Quite where the irony lies in the 'dubitation of immortality' is less clear, though the concluding paragraph suggests that Postgate feels the work will indeed bring fame to its author. Does he object to the Latinity, or to the sound of the couplet? The fact that he does not mention the name of Moses Jackson suggests that he has not noticed, or is not critical of, the biblical allusion: Jackson is *nomine ... uiuere dignus* because the name Moses means 'saved from the water' (Exod. 2.10).

41. Housman 1969, 17-18.

42. Gow 1936a, 77 n. 3. He would probably have mentioned the fact if compositions had been found among Housman's papers on his death.

43. *Juvenal*, v; cf. Naiditch 1988, 85-6 n. 30-16.

44. *Fortnightly Review* n.s. 72 (1902), 866-80.

45. On the Classical Association see Stray 2003; on its foundation, ch. 1.

46. He was reluctant to do even this: Burnett 1.469.

47. J. and M. Postgate 1994, 31. No relevant records survive in Liverpool.

48. Kelly 1981, 197.

49. However, he had access to other, more positive, accounts: 'Inevitably, most of the College staff came from the older universities. Of the 30 non-medical professors appointed during this period [1892-1903] 20 came from Oxford or Cambridge; and of the 13 who came from Cambridge 9, including the three Principals, were former students of Trinity College' (Kelly 1981, 92). On Postgate and Frazer see Ackerman 1987, 54; on Frazer's time at Liverpool, ibid., 207-14. He went there in part to oblige his wife, and also in hopes that from that great port he might send out expeditions to gather anthropological data. But he pined for Cambridge, and was much exercised about the removal of his enormous library. He continued to hold the Chair, without giving lectures or taking a salary, until 1922 (ibid., 333 n. 39).

50. Stray 2005.

51. *Cambridge University Reporter* 13 December 1910 'Candidates are requested to send in their names to the Vice Chancellor on or before Monday, 9 January 1911'; cf. Gow 1936a, 33.

52. On Reid see Naiditch 1988, 242-3; he had sponsored Housman in his application to UCL in 1892. On Duff see Naiditch 2006.

53. University Library, Cambridge, O.xiv.56.

54. Naiditch 1988, 212 on Verrall and 165-72, esp. 168 with n. 58-2, on Jackson.

55. Naiditch 1995.

56. Though Naiditch 1988, 47 points out that while Ellis was alive Housman treated him with 'comparative mildness'.

57. The election of an Oxonian proved controversial for a reason that could hardly have been foreseen. It was proposed immediately afterwards that apart from the Vice Chancellor there should no longer be ex officio members on the Board of Electors (*Cambridge University Reporter* 21 February 1911, 643). To this it was objected by S. Gaselee that (i) it was insensitive to remove the Headmaster of Shrewsbury from the Board while there still remained alive family members of B.H. Kennedy, in whose honour the Chair had been established in 1869, and that people had given money to endow it on the understanding that the Electors should include those present ex officio; and (ii) that such a precipitate change would make it appear that the intention was to prevent the election of another Oxonian (Alington, as well as Ellis, being from that university). (*Reporter* 7 March 1911, 698-9). The vote, on 16 March 1911, was 39:19 in favour of reform (*Reporter* 21 March 1911, 769).

58. Housman 1969, 35-6.

59. J. Carter in Housman 1969, 7-8.

60. Owen 1926, 346.

61. Cole 1949, 6: 'Looking back, I see my father as in some ways an unfortunate man, disappointed, in spite of the estimation in which he was held, of his highest academic aspirations – he wanted above all things to be Professor of Latin in his own University, but the post went to A.E. Housman'; Naiditch 1988, 87-8 with n. 30-21; J. and M. Postgate 1994, 31: 'It was a tremendous blow to J.P.' The Postgates add, '[h]e was a bitter man, too. Sir John Barnes told us that "when J.A. Duff [i.e. J.D. Duff] ... voted for Housman ... Postgate never spoke to Duff again, although they had previously been friends and colleagues for many years"' (ibid.) But the story should be linked to Duff's candidature, since he was in no position to vote. It was probably just after his election that Housman was invited to dinner by the Postgates; he was remembered by their son Raymond, who would have been aged 15 in 1911, as 'an indeterminate-looking man with a scraggy moustache' (R. Postgate 1958, 379). It is perhaps as well that Housman's impressions of the visit are not on record.

189

62. Housman is thanked in the Preface (v).

63. *CP* 1007-11.

64. According to Owen 1926, 345-6, Postgate attributed his stubbornness to 'Yorkshire blood'.

65. *CP* 1000-3.

66. 'On some quantities in Phaedrus', *Hermathena* 19 (1922), 52-63.

67. *CP* 1012-15.

68. *CP* 1013.

69. *CR* 35 1921, 23-5.

70. In the versions in *Translation and Translations* Postgate does not use *nil* in the second half of the first foot: p. 161 no. 51 *aut nihil aut feruens tu bibe, caute, merum.*

71. Naiditch 1992, 88. In spite of this controversy Housman granted Postgate permission to reproduce his 'Epitaph on an Army of Mercenaries' in *Translation and Translations*, published in 1922 (174-5).

72. The volume contains a few other notes by Housman. On p. 50, for example, where a conjecture of his is said by Postgate to involve a false quantity, Housman writes, '*petitio principii*'.

73. The book played a surprising role in the reconciliation of Postgate with his son Raymond: 'He invited me, without any warning, to dine with him in London University ... As we parted, I said ... that I hoped he would some day come to dine with me and my wife. "Ah", he said, and his face was very kind, "I will send you a full set of my studies on Greek accents. I will sign it". He did; I have it still' (R. Postgate 1958, 379).

74. *Lucan*, xxxiii.

75. At this time he was living at 16 Brookside, Trumpington Road (opposite the Leys School). Owen 1926, 338: 'He swerved into the lorry which was proceeding in the same direction, probably (though the evidence at the inquest was conflicting) being confused by a motor-cycle which passed just at the same time. The intimidating noise caused by that sort of dangerous and distracting vehicle may well have alarmed the old man and deprived him of his nerve just at the moment when it was most needed.' The inquest is reported in the *Cambridge Daily News* of 17 July 1926. He died of 'contusion of the brain and shock'. No one was held to blame.

76. The Evelyn was more than a nursing home; operations were performed there. Many Fellows of Trinity had subscriptions at the Evelyn, so that Postgate had good cause to fear misdelivery.

77. HOC TITVLO COMMEMORATVR | ALFRED EDWARD HOUSMAN | PER XXV ANNOS LINGVAE LATINAE PROFESSOR KENNEDIANVS | ET HVIVS COLLEGII SOCIVS | QVI BENTLEII INSISTENS VESTIGIIS | TEXTVM TRADITVM POETARVM LATINORVM | TANTO INGENII ACVMINE TANTIS DOCTRINAE COPIIS | EDITORVM SOCORDIAM | TAM ACRI CAVILLATIONE CASTIGAVIT | VT HORVM STVDIORVM PAENE REFORMATOR EXSTITERIT | IDEM POETA | TENVI CARMINVM FASCICVLO | SEDEM SIBI TVTAM IN HELICONE NOSTRO VINDICAVIT | OBIIT PRID. KAL. MAI. | A.S. MDCCCCXXXVI AETATIS SVAE LXXVII (Clackson 1990, 98).

78. The names of composers are not of course recorded on the plaques.

79. There is no gravestone: Postgate was cremated – at Golders Green (*Cambridge Daily News*, 22 July 1926) – in accordance with his instructions (see n. 6 above).

80. Clackson 1990, 88.

81. The quotation seems unexceptionable so long as one 'remembers' only Postgate and not the fact that in Statius the words conclude a passage describing the winsome attractions of a *puer delicatus*: Stat. *Silu.* 2.1.55. Postgate had jointly edited these poems for the *Corpus*. Postgate narrowly escaped memorialisation by Housman. The Agenda for the Memorials Committee meeting of 3 August 1926, suggests that Housman be asked to compose the inscription; but the Minutes record that the Committee agreed to follow the wording suggested by Postgate. It seems quite possible that Postgate, anticipating that Housman would be asked and determined to avoid a final and all too long-lasting appraisal by him, determined to forestall this by putting forward his own composition. That in turn would account for the unusual brevity: self-praise would have seemed inappropriate, and would probably have been unacceptable to the Committee.

82. The contrast between the two personalities is clear also from their final instructions. Postgate left £100 to pay for a volume of collected articles (which never appeared): 'I hereby direct my executor to permit ... Thomas William Allen [his brother-in-law] to republish in collected form any addresses essays articles or "papers" of mine already published as after consultation ... he shall ... deem suitable for republication.' Housman specified precisely the opposite: 'I expressly desire and wish my desire to be made as widely known as possible that none of my writings which have appeared in periodical publications shall be collected and reprinted in any shape or form' (*CP* vii).

83. David Butterfield draws my attention to two brief sallies after Postgate's death. At *Juvenal*[2], xlviii, Postgate is said to have shared the general 'ignorance and bewilderment' about the Oxford fragment until it was explained by Housman; and in 'Prosody and method', published in 1927, he mentions a conjecture made by Postgate in ignorance of a metrical rule (*CP* 1119 n. 2).

84. A judicious appraisal of Housman's influence is to be found in Wilkinson 1974.
For details of and bibliography for the life of Postgate I am much indebted to Stray's articles in the *Dictionary of National Biography* and the *Dictionary of British Classicists*, and to Naiditch 1988, 74-91. For their comments on this piece I should like to thank Stephen Heyworth, Paul Naiditch and the editors.

10

Housman and W.M. Lindsay[1]

D.J. Butterfield

Since the death of Hugh Munro in 1885, the achievements of two British Latinists, A.E. Housman, the subject of this volume, and W.M. Lindsay (1858-1937), 'stand out like Bentley's Digamma'[2] above their compatriots.[3] This chapter will compare the careers of the two scholars, their points of significant overlap and difference and, as far as the evidence allows, the relationship between their scholarly activities.

A brief survey of the career of Lindsay is required at the outset.[4] Wallace Martin Lindsay was born the son of a Scottish Free Church minister at Pittenweem, Fife, on 12 February 1858. He passed through Edinburgh Academy and matriculated at Glasgow University in 1874. He *proxime accessit* to the winner of the classical exhibition at Balliol, Oxford, in 1876 but succeeded in winning the coveted Snell exhibition to the college in the following year. He passed through Mods and Greats without any apparent problem but without major successes[5] and, having duly 'crammed', achieved one of the few firsts in Greats in the same year that Housman was infamously 'ploughed'.[6] After graduation Lindsay travelled to 'the more congenial atmosphere'[7] of Leipzig University for two semesters, where he attended the lectures of Ribbeck on Latin, Curtius and Brugmann on Sanskrit, Celtic and Greek, and Gardthausen on palaeography. On his return to Oxford in 1883 he took up a fellowship at Jesus College,[8] a position which he held until 1899. During his first two years as a fellow, however, he took the decision to work as an assistant of W.Y. Sellar, the Professor of Humanity at Edinburgh (1863-90), until he was made a tutor at Jesus in 1884.[9]

Lindsay's work at Oxford demonstrated his remarkable diversity: a school edition in 1887 of Plautus' *Captiui* at the behest of his former Balliol tutor, Evelyn Abbott, papers on early Latin and its relationship with Celtic, early Latin metre (especially the Saturnian), papyri (Latin and Greek), a major volume on the Latin Language which made his name on the Continent,[10] handbooks on Latin inscriptions and errors in Latin manuscripts[11] and detailed work on the codices of Plautus. Further, he produced material for William Smith's *Dictionary of Greek and Roman Antiquities* (3rd ed., London, 1890) and Nettleship's projected Latin dictionary[12] as well as bringing to press the incomplete work on Nonius I-III of his former tutor J.H. Onions. Two other significant volumes were refused by the Clarendon Press.[13] His specialist lectures appear to have been limited to Greek and Latin palaeography; his tutorial commitments, however, would have covered the typical range for the period, with particular focus upon translation and composition in the ancient languages.[14] Towards the close of his Oxford years, in 1898, Lindsay 'spent the happiest time of his life' lecturing upon Plautus for a year at Harvard. Having returned to Oxford, he was made Senior Proctor in 1899.

The major landmark event in Lindsay's career occurred in the same year when, after trying and failing to acquire other Chairs of Latin,[15] he was elected to the Professorship of Humanity at St Andrews, a post he held until his death 38 years later. Although the position provided a fixed burden of lectures on a variety of topics, Lindsay's productivity remained exceptionally high. He founded *St Andrews University Publications* and, over the next 29 years, wrote – or contributed the majority of material to – fourteen of 28 volumes, six being the short-lived journal *Palaeographia Latina* (1922-9), a series also founded by Lindsay (at the instigation of Franz Ehrle). Lindsay's monographs included important research on the textual history of Plautus, Martial and Nonius, Plautine syntax, early Irish and Welsh scripts and Latin glossaries. He replaced his earlier and confessedly unsatisfactory work on Plautus' *Captiui* with a full-scale edition and commentary (Cambridge, 1900), his only literary comment in print, and edited Nonius (Teubner, Leipzig, 1902), Martial (OCT, 1903), Plautus (OCT, 1904-5), Isidore (OCT, 1911), Festus (Teubner, 1912, and *Glossaria Latina* 4 (1931)), Julian of Toledo's *De uitiis et figuris* (*St Andrews University Publications* 16, Oxford, 1922) and Terence (with R. Kauer, OCT, 1926), all of which are supported by comparatively accurate and comprehensive *apparatus critici* and therefore continue to serve a purpose in the classical world, albeit to varying degrees. His palaeographical and codicological researches culminated in a major work on scribal abbreviations in Latin manuscripts of the eighth and ninth centuries, *Notae Latinae* (Cambridge, 1915). He oversaw and edited much of *Glossaria Latina* (5 vols, Paris, 1914-34), a major edition of Latin glossaries designed in many respects to better that of Goetz and Loewe (7 vols, Leipzig, 1888-1923), and, in a quite different field, produced as the result of 30 years' research, *Early Latin Verse* (Oxford, 1922). Throughout his career he dispatched relentlessly a series of articles and reviews across the full spectrum of his research to the major British, Continental and American classical journals, often writing in German, French, Italian and Latin;[16] only from the late 1920s, when his deafness made conversation and research particularly difficult,[17] did this steady stream of articles begin to dwindle. He was killed aged 79 and still in good health[18] on 21 February 1937, when knocked down by a motor-car driven by a student at the university. He was elected a fellow of the British Academy in 1905 and an honorary fellow of Jesus, Oxford, in 1928.

No one can doubt the breadth and lasting significance of Lindsay's work. Indeed, I do not believe that any other British Latinist, *uiuis exceptis*, has ever worked at the forefront of Latin linguistics, metrics, palaeography and codicology and also edited texts of classical and mediaeval Latin. It is perhaps because most of his research dealt with the fundamental groundwork on which future scholarship would build that his name is now not more prominent and recognition of his contribution is generally below the mark. The same, of course, could be said of certain aspects of Housman's work.

Similarities

One can readily adduce a great number of similarities between Housman and Lindsay, over and above their similar backgrounds,[19] almost identical lifespans and identical spells as Oxonian undergraduates.[20] Both were fiercely and independently driven in their research, pursuing lines of investigation that they realised sorely needed work. Both came to specialise in the study of Latin texts, after wider research interests in their earlier years. Both devoted almost all their energy to their studies, a situation aided by their remaining bachelors (and suitably catered for) throughout their lives and not pursuing administrative work beyond what was necessary for their posts.[21] Both were happiest when engaged in research unaided[22] and did not gain particular repute as lecturers or tutors.[23] Both berated in print the laziness of their contemporaries.[24] Both avoided aesthetic comment upon Latin literature and rarely ventured into wider exegesis, concentrating their energies instead upon the factual elements of scholarship. Both were prepared to provide funds for their own publications in order to produce the desired results.[25] Finally, both steered clear of the popularising of classical education and almost always wrote for expert audiences.[26]

Although it may be said that the research interests of Robinson Ellis and J.P. Postgate were closer to Housman's, much of Lindsay's career stands parallel to his. Yet there are significant points of difference, not only in smaller details (e.g. the Latin authors they primarily tackled) but also in their fundamental outlook upon dealing with Latin texts. In brief, Lindsay was convinced that recension of a text was of primary importance, combined with as accurate a reconstruction of its manuscript history as was possible from detailed codicological examination; a concomitant conservatism made him reluctant to consider seriously any textual corruption that lacked an obvious palaeographical motive. Housman, on the contrary, acknowledged the necessity of recension, but regarded conjectural criticism as a primary desideratum for improved literary understanding, a task based upon deep resources of factual knowledge but always requiring sound logic and sparks of *ingenium*. Whereas Lindsay felt a natural urge to defend manuscript readings, Housman's bolder approach and constant suspicion that scribal error had occurred allowed him to achieve wider aims by the movement of boundaries that emendation allowed. As is evident from my earlier chapter in this volume, Housman's willingness to emend where probability allowed gave him the vantage-point to delineating major metrical and grammatical points. A 'love of truth' has been attributed deservedly to both scholars.[27] None the less, Lindsay's truth was sought on strictly empirical grounds, with more solid rewards for success, whereas Housman was prepared to find his answers in the abstract, typically without the luxury of proof of their validity.

There exists a spectrum of potential relationships between such a pair of hard-working, ambitious and manifestly accomplished Latinists with so different approaches to ancient texts. At one extreme, each could acknowledge the achievements of the other and make appropriate use of what was best from their united scholarship, or, at the other end, the two could stand firmly in conflict and artificially polarise their outlooks as 'correct' and 'incorrect'. In truth, both were touched by feelings at either end of this spectrum.

Direct contact

Let us turn to contact between the two Latinists. The pair studied at Oxford between 1877 and 1882[28] and almost certainly heard the same lectures. However, there is no evidence that they knew each other or that their social interests overlapped.[29] It is possible that Housman first noticed Lindsay's name when it appeared in the small First Class for Greats (see n. 6). After their undergraduate years, there is no real likelihood that they ever had occasion to meet:[30] there is no evidence that Lindsay ever attended the Cambridge Philological Society (of which he was not a member),[31] nor does his research appear to have brought him to University College, London or Trinity College, Cambridge during his life. Further, I have found no indication that he made social visits to colleagues or old friends in London or Cambridge. Housman was not a Fellow of the British Academy and was rarely involved with the Classical Association. Whereas Lindsay scoured the Continent in search of manuscripts, Housman to my knowledge only once entered a library on his cultural tours.[32]

Nevertheless, three items of direct contact survive: two letters from Housman to Lindsay,[33] and one postcard from Lindsay to Housman. The earliest extant evidence of interaction[34] between the two men is a letter of 12 December 1901 (Burnett 1.134), in which Housman responds to a

196

(lost) letter from Lindsay concerning an emendation at Mart. *Spect.* 21.8 that Housman had proposed in *CR* 15 (1901). Lindsay, then preparing his Oxford Text of the author, had evidently written to Housman to enquire whether he thought his emendation παρ' ἱστορίαν (for the impossible *ita pictoria*) was improved by παριστορία, as suggested by S. Allen at *CR* 15 (1901), 231-2. Housman dismisses this alteration as impossible, though he 'knew that it was [true]' that someone would make the conjecture in his wake. This tersely-written postcard, lacking any opening or closing salutation and any hint of friendliness, could hardly have warmed Lindsay's heart.

The second item of correspondence is more expansive: a letter of 5 February 1903 (Burnett 1.141) that summarises Housman's opinion of Lindsay's *Ancient Editions of Martial* (*St Andrews University Publications* 2, Oxford, 1903), which the latter had sent to him on its publication. Lindsay presumably hoped that his rigorous and formidable recipient would welcome what he himself saw as breakthrough research and a lasting contribution to the textual criticism of Martial. Housman evidently did not see the work in the same light: his own copy[35] contains a number of spirited annotations[36] on points of disagreement and the work appears to have enjoyed only a single read-through. In his letter, Housman politely states that he does not accept Lindsay's primary thesis, namely that the three branches of the tradition of Martial reflect different editions stretching back to Antiquity. He proceeds to point out that a number of textual discrepancies which Lindsay treated as significant could be explained with comparative ease as the results of *saut du même au même*, with subsequent expansion to repair metre. Housman concludes in measured terms: 'But no one can say that you put forward your opinion with any undue confidence; and the details you give are most interesting.' Posterity has seen Lindsay's work in a much fairer light, acknowledging that it did indeed represent a significant step in firming up the recension of Martial's tradition, although his optimism about authorial variants was probably excessive.

Perhaps Lindsay also sent Housman his similarly-structured *The Ancient Editions of Plautus* (*St Andrews University Publications* 3, Oxford, 1904) in a renewed attempt to win him over. At any rate, no letter or inscription accompanies Housman's copy (also preserved at St John's) and Housman's occasional notes again suggest a single cursory and unimpressed read.[37]

More correspondence (now lost) must have occurred prior to this letter for, in the preface to Lindsay's 1903 edition of Martial (p. [xvii]), a footnote is appended to the statement '[v]irorum doctorum coniecturas tam paucas in apparatu critico apparere nequis miretur' that states 'Housmani benevolentiae acceptas refero duas Marklandi (ad V xxxviii.7 et II lxvi.4), quae sunt in margine libri, olim Marklandi, nunc

Gualteri Ashburneri.' Housman returned the book to Walter Ashburner on 17 November 1898 (cf. Burnett 1.112). Since these conjectures were not published by Housman until 1907,[38] he presumably forwarded the notice of them to Lindsay around the turn of the century.

The sole extant communication from Lindsay to Housman, a brief postcard dated 21 May 1920, sheds little light:[39] 'I have got photographs of the pages of Vat. Lat. 1469 which contain the asbestos Glossary. They show: Abruptus : per vim raptus. I am trying to find out the sources of this Glossary, but have not yet succeeded. / Hardie's "Res Metrica" is published. It will, I hope, usher in a new appreciation of classical metre.'[40] The context of the note was presumably that Housman had written to Lindsay, as the undoubted expert on glossaries, to enquire whether any light could be shed from that field upon the spelling of the past perfect participles of compounds of *rapio*. Housman had touched upon this matter in his commentary ad Man. 3.352 and he perhaps wanted specific information to treat the variants *abruptis* and *abreptis* in his forthcoming text at Man. 4.643 (although he does not there record Lindsay's information).

Conflict in print

It was not until 1905, with both scholars in their mid-forties, that Lindsay and Housman first met head-on in the public domain. Owing to his experience with the manuscript tradition and editing of Martial, Lindsay reviewed the fifth fascicle of Postgate's *Corpus Poetarum Latinorum* (London, 1905), in which J.D. Duff's edition of Martial appeared, along with Housman's Juvenal (also issued separately in the same year) and Postgate's Nemesianus.[41] In order to express his views on the work of Duff in his wake (as Duff had on his own Oxford text),[42] Lindsay also had to deal with Housman's major contribution in the same fascicle. In doing so, it was little more work to review at the same time Housman's separately-published edition, which was larger only in terms of its preface. (Nemesianus was lamentably ignored.) Lindsay's review of Housman's work is mixed, praising its clarity and scope but ignoring most emendations and deploring certain aspects of his approach.[43] Most obvious is his lament about Housman's manner of dealing with recent scholars of repute. He writes of 'the unfortunate style in which [the preface] is written' (464), to which the following footnote is appended: 'I suppose it is useless to express a wish that Mr. Housman would cease to speak about veteran scholars of eminence, like Buecheler, Vahlen, and Friedlaender, in that fashion.' Of more import to Lindsay, however, was a passing remark made by Housman (*Juvenal*, xxviii):

'Nothing,' I hear it asked, 'about Nicaeus? Nothing about Epicarpius, nor Heiricus, nor the long-resounding name of Exuperantius?' No, nothing. The truth is, and the reader has discovered it by this time if he did not know it before hand, that I have no inkling of *Ueberlieferungsgeschichte* ... It is a sad fate to be devoid of faculties which cause so much elation to their owners; but I cheer myself by reflecting how large a number of human beings are more fortunate than I. It seems indeed as if a capacity for these two lines of fiction had been bestowed by heaven, as a sort of consolation-prize, upon those who have no capacity for anything else.[44]

In his review Lindsay writes (464), 'Mr. Housman's sneer at "Ueberlieferungsgeschichte" ... refers, I suppose, to the ancient transmission of texts'[45] and proceeds to make an observation about a point of detail. Yet there can be no doubt that Housman's dismissal as 'fiction' of a method of investigating texts which Lindsay keenly practised and confidently regarded as of prime importance annoyed the latter significantly. Although in his mid-sixties Lindsay could say that this field was his 'hobby [i.e. obsession] at present',[46] it is an area of study that had greatly interested him since the beginning of the twentieth century. This particular difference in viewpoint as to the importance of the field stood throughout the lifetimes of the two scholars. Housman was only too aware of the effect of his words, and over two decades later he again touched upon the matter in the preface to his Lucan (xvii):

This belief [that all manuscripts of Juvenal ultimately descend from Nicaeus' recension] was accepted by scholars whose analytical faculty did not enable them to detect any error in this reasoning. But Mr Duff in 1898 quietly ignored the whole fuss, and I in 1905 dismissed it in a few derisive words (p. xxviii) which echo for ever in the memory of Mr W.M. Lindsay.

Upon this point the anonymous *CR* obituarist of Lindsay elegantly observed that 'it was characteristic of Housman to think that certain "derisive words" of his echoed for ever in Lindsay's memory; it was characteristic of Lindsay that they did not'.[47] However, a close perusal of Lindsay's articles after 1905 leaves the matter, beyond any possible doubt, in Housman's favour. Naiditch (1995, 77-8) provided a further reference alongside the remark in the 1905 Juvenal review quoted above, namely a passage from Lindsay's review of Clark 1918,[48] but in fact several other passages could be recorded. For instance, 'Apicius' cookery book', a review of Giarratano and Vollmer's edition of Apicius (Teubner, Leipzig, 1922) opens thus: 'When an editor has boasted that he has "no inkling of 'Ueberlieferungsgeschichte'", it seems natural that his divination is now criticised as "mere waste of time" '[49] (*CR* 36 (1922), 131).[50] The close of this same note seems equally to have had Housman in mind: 'Take it for model, ye dilettante editors. And contrast its

199

modest preface with the flamboyant style of X, or Y, or Z.' At times, however, the echo is far more nuanced.[51]

Lindsay viewed textual problems as ultimately a scientific investigation in which palaeography and codicology played the leading roles; in verbal conjecture he had very little interest. His promisingly-entitled *Introduction to Latin Textual Criticism* (London, 1896) is in reality an analysis of corruptions in the text of Plautus under the six headings 'Errors of emendation', 'Errors of transposition', 'Errors of omission', 'Errors of insertion', 'Errors of substitution', 'Confusion of letters' and 'Confusion of contractions',[52] and would have been better named *A Survey of Visually-motivated Scribal Errors in Plautus*.[53] Forms of corruption without a palaeographical or codicological basis are largely ignored, with the result that short shrift indeed is given to any conjectural emendation that strays outside these bounds. The book is certainly useful[54] but serves as only a partial introduction to the field its title claims to embrace.[55]

In a review of 1898, Lindsay indicates the reasoning that underlay his approach: 'It is high time that the old style of baseless emendation were abandoned and that every editor should be able to account on good palaeographical grounds for any corruption which he ventures to ascribe to the traditional text.'[56] This is undoubtedly a misguided application of logic.[57] Perhaps the clearest declaration of his standpoint comes in his *Contractions in Early Latin Minuscule mss* (*St Andrews University Publications* 5, Oxford, 1908), 1-2: 'It is at last coming to be generally recognised that emendations, if they are to be convincing, must conform to the requirements of Palaeography and start from a knowledge of the mediaeval transmission of the text. They must not call into existence, for the sake of the argument, contractions which could not possibly be found in a MS. of the time and the place at which the hypothetical archetype was written.' If such information is securely available, the latter sentence would find agreement with all, Housman included, but the former assertion shows clearly Lindsay's blinkered outlook, unprepared to see beyond palaeographical motivations for transcriptional errors. Housman, by contrast, could never regard palaeography as more than an ancillary tool for textual criticism: in his private notes he averred that '[w]hatever advances may be made in palaeography, Mr Lindsay will still find textual emendation difficult, if not impossible'.[58]

Lindsay consequently felt a fundamental dissatisfaction with conjectural emendation, evident even from his earliest published book[59] to his last printed piece: his autobiography states that '[o]f conjectural emendation "at large" or, as he called it, "feet-on-the-hob emendation" he had always a great distrust'.[60] He certainly did not aim to practise it himself.[61] It was therefore impossible for him ever to welcome wholly the scholarship of Housman, whose primary achievements lay in this field. It was presumably the sheer volume of such textual notes, and the open arms with which they were received by the learned journals of the time, not to mention the low scoring-rate of such suggestions, that irked him so much about the field. Even in his sixties Lindsay could paint the following caricature of the conjectural emendator:

> Those classical scholars who occupy themselves with what is called 'feet on the hob' emendation have a poor opinion of the extant MSS. They sit by the fire with Virgil in one hand and a pencil in the other and jot down in the margin any alteration of a word or line which caprice suggests. When this marginal litter has accumulated they send it, under the misleading title 'Emendations', to an indulgent magazine-editor. If any one thinks it worth while to censure them, they justify their action by some argument like this: 'The transmission of Latin texts was wholly capricious and wholly ignorant; one can have no confidence that the traditional form in which we ourselves re-write the passage was what the author wrote; the form in which we ourselves re-write the passage is just as likely to have been the author's form.'[62]

Although the tone is heavily satirical, the serious intent behind Lindsay's attack is not to be questioned. Yet it is impossible to believe that any contemporary scholar was seriously proposing that modern emendations *tout court* are 'just as likely' to have been the author's words as those transmitted. Instead, the attack underlines Lindsay's distinct refusal to appraise corruptions other than those in which palaeography was the major catalyst for error. Alongside these basic mechanical errors, the significant stages of corruption for him were the transition from one historical script to another and, in particular, the mistaken resolution or misreading of abbreviations unfamiliar to scribes. Undoubtedly these are always important factors in the transmission of any text that does not survive in manuscripts from late antiquity. Yet they can never tell the whole story. For manifold corruptions occur in texts of all natures that lack any palaeographical or physical basis. Psychological slips, or mere acts of carelessness (such as certain forms of transposition), could not be explained by Lindsay's stripped-down inventory. This fact hardly now requires articulation but Lindsay never tackled the matter head-on. The reason is not hard to seek: if the 'rules'[63] of textual criticism are not comprehensive, the science falters and the 'capriciousness' of the art of conjectural emendation gains a foothold.[64]

Lindsay once declared that Traube's 'genius raised 'Ueberlieferungs-geschichte' to an exact science'.[65] As we have seen, Lindsay believed that he had succeeded in such a scientific enquiry into the manuscript history of Martial, thereby securing a very firm basis for Martial's own text. In triumph he wrote that 'the very raison d'être of emendation is called in question' and that '[t]he real field for textual emendation, following its usual methods, is, we may almost say, narrowed to the

Spectacula'.[66] This conviction led to the production of a particularly conservative Oxford text of Martial in 1903. Indeed, as one reviewer noted,[67] Lindsay only recorded one emendation from his own hand, *hic situst* for *his situs* at 11.90.4. Having tried his hand upon the manuscript histories of Martial and Plautus prior to producing his Oxford Classical Texts,[68] Lindsay evidently saw his achievements as the foundation for a new means of textual investigation, in which literary archetypes are to be 'traced back to rival editions of an author which were current in the second, third and fourth centuries'.[69] Such optimism was largely misplaced, for Lindsay's sure achievements with Martial can be attained with few other classical Latin authors.[70]

None the less, such confidence about his method led to an editorial conservatism, which Lindsay rarely discussed directly,[71] although certain points of outlook can be gleaned from his later writings. In a review of 1918, his belief in the inefficacy of British textual scholarship is evident:

> Latin scholarship in this country seems to choose by some perverse habit to make itself barren by restricting itself severely to a path which once offered glorious prospects, but not now – the path of conjectural emendation. To thresh old straw, to re-edit and re-edit the text of Propertius and Catullus and Ovid, with no new materials and no new clue, to fill the pages of learned journals with dogmatic (and eristic) divination, *that* can lead to nothing but vanity and vanity's sequel – vexation of spirit. Can we wonder that so many University lecturers and school-teachers, if they publish anything at all, are content with books for schoolboys or articles which do not rise above the level of the *Times Literary Supplement*?'[72]

Evidently, Lindsay felt that the important work had been done in the field of conjectural criticism. Accordingly, he felt that time, energy and (one imagines) praise were woefully misdirected by his contemporaries. Two years later, during a wandering review of Ernout's Lucretius (Paris, 1920), he praises the existence of the then newly-founded Budé and Paravia series of texts, in the hope that they will limit the publication of conjectures, and wills that Holland start a similar series.[73] This failure to appreciate the skill and ingenuity of verbal criticism performed well, apparently on the basis of the indisputable fact that the great majority of published emendations are not generally deemed by subsequent editors to be correct, permeated Lindsay's view of textual criticism. This almost-pervasive denigration of the field would of course not have gone unnoticed by Housman. Lindsay clearly regarded him as a firm detractor of *Überlieferungsgeschichte* but did he reckon him to be a reckless, unthinking emender? The occasional approval of Housman's conjectures can be found scattered throughout Lindsay's publications[74] but, for the most part, it is fair to regard Housman as the most prominent target of Lindsay's attacks on conjectural criticism.[75]

Yet it was Lindsay, not Housman, who explicitly regarded conjectural emendation and *Überlieferungsgeschichte* as opposing ways of dealing with ancient texts. To return to Lindsay's review of Ernout's Lucretius, the efficacy of these two, supposedly rival, schools is broached.

> It is a debateable point whether Mr. Dull Dog[76] who has mastered the practice of medieval scribes, or Mr. Nimble Wit who cannot read a Ms., is likelier to emend a text. I would bet on Dull Dog, for the tenth and eleventh-century scribes were dull enough, but their familiarity with scribal error made them very fair emendators. But, not to insist on this, are we not all agreed that the best results will come when Nimble Wit acquires Dull Dog's knowledge? Why, then, do our heaven-illumined scholars not study Palaeography? Are they afraid that the work will make their wits dull?

At this point Housman enters the fray, but escapes rebuke:

> Hard work need not have this effect. No harder spade-work has been done by any editor than by the editor of Manilius. Do the *Lines to a Mercenary Army* suggest that dulness has invaded the author of *A Shropshire Lad?*[77]

Housman's dedicated behind-the-scenes drudgery for Manilius clearly earned Lindsay's approval. But one wonders whether the 'spade-work' refers to palaeography or rather collation (from photographs), or even astrology. The context would suggest the first but two years before, in an unnecessarily partisan review of Clark's *Descent of Manuscripts* (cf. n. 48), Lindsay wrote that the 'Cambridge Professor ... will hear nothing of the usefulness of palaeography for the emendation of texts'. He proceeds to imagine a parody of Tenniel's celebrated *Punch* cartoon of Disraeli reading Gladstone's *Juventus Mundi* and Gladstone Disraeli's *Lothair*, in which Housman is pictured reading Clark's work and Clark Housman's *Juvenal*, Housman exclaiming 'Ha! – prosy!', Clark 'Hm! – flippant!'. Lindsay concludes proudly, 'in this case the prosy book will outlive the flippant'. So much then for Lindsay's views about 'the reckless vagaries of conjectural emendation'[78] of the Nimble-wits 'who thrive in our foggy climate and by the canals of Holland'[79] and among whom he certainly did not number himself.

A little further insight into the stand-off between the two scholars can be provided from a controversy concerning the textual history of Varius' *Thyestes*. A substandard article by H.W. Garrod of 1916[80] (declared to be written in 1911) led Housman to chastise his argumentation severely and minutely.[81] Yet Housman's own intervention drew a note from the hand of Lindsay a few years later: 'I read with amusement a recent article in this journal in which the writer severely censured Mr. Garrod's ignorance of the entry in Paris 7530, but revealed his own ignorance by assuming that it was the same scribe of the Paris MS. who had the lost tragedy of Varius before him.'[82] This was direct criticism, then, of Housman's lack of codicological knowledge.[83] Lindsay's objection was on this point correct, for the existence of a similar partial *incipit* in Rome, Bibl. Casanat. 1086 guarantees that the *incipit* in Paris. 7530 is also an apograph. Nevertheless, Housman's mistake was simply ignorance of this manuscript's existence.

The next and last conflict between the two in print is also indicative of their scholarship. By unintentional ring-composition, it again concerned the text of Martial. In an article of 1930 Housman had stated, 'Two editors of our golden age [= Heraeus and Lindsay] retain it [= *drauci* closing Mart. 11.8.1], and without an obelus; for if conservative critics had not strong stomachs they would not be conservative critics.'[84] He proceeded to conjecture the loan-word *dracti* on the strength of its appearance in Greek epigraphy. Lindsay, ever sensitive to criticism, soon after met this challenge to his editorial decision. In 'New light on Festus' (*CR* 26 (1932), 193-4) he adds the note (194 n. 1): 'The leader of this band [of 'our gallant conjectural emendators']85 recently (*C.R.* XLIV 115), after wrongly accusing Heraeus and me of not knowing that *draucus* meant "a strong man," dogmatically divined *dracti* (a word he had found in the new Liddell and Scott) in Martial XI viii, 1: *Lassa quod hesterni spirant opobalsama drauci*. Heraeus and I remembered – but he did not remember – Mart. XIV lix, 1. *Balsama me capiunt, haec sunt unguenta virorum*. Moreover, Heraeus and I knew – but he did not know – the Cyrillus gloss: ΔPAYKION: *monile*.' This dispute happily serves as a prime specimen of the two scholars' handling of a classical text: Housman saw the absurdity in context of *draucus* (a strong-man) and sought out a word of appropriate meaning; Lindsay, ever-desirous to defend the transmitted letters, could only find support for the meaning he desired in a glossary of the sixth century AD, and minded little that 'necklace' barely makes sense in context.[86] Subsequent editors have been almost unanimous in following Housman, one commentator observing simply 'Housman's emendation is certain'.[87]

It is clear that Lindsay's view of Housman throughout his career was an admixture of respect for his achievements through dedicated research, underlying scepticism about his conjectures that stray somewhat from the paradosis, frustration at his lack of concrete respect for palaeography and *Textgeschichte* and, I believe, bitterness that Housman's successes were, at least in his later years, so widely recognised when little heed was paid to his own 'science' of textual transmission.[88] Lindsay was prepared, however, to recognise Housman's achievements, and he could write in 1927 of 'Professor Housman's excellent edition of Lucan'.[89] Indeed, Maurice Bowra[90] ventured to record that 'the learned W.M. Lindsay did not really approve of [Housman] until 1927,[91] when he wrote a postcard to a friend:

"Housman has at last made good. His Lucan is A 1".' If the report is accurate and the expression sincere, 'at last' is a serious indictment of Lindsay's ability to judge the importance of the scholarship of those outside his own fields. Lindsay's last recorded mention of Housman occurs in his positive testimonial for Fraenkel's application to the Corpus Chair (written on 12 November 1934): 'It [= *Plautinisches im Plautus* (Berlin, 1922)] was a book written in "the great style", the style of our own Munro and (when he is not gambolling) of Munro's present successor at Cambridge. In versatility too Prof. Housman can be compared with him; for he is anything but a mere specialist.'[92]

Lindsay through Housman's eyes

It has proved far easier to reconstruct Lindsay's views of Housman than the reverse. Since the focus of this book lies on the latter scholar, however, I will turn in the remainder of this chapter to attempting to reconstruct Housman's views of Lindsay.

Since Housman's first published articles concerned textual criticism of the Augustan poets and Greek tragedians, whereas Lindsay's tackled early Latin philology (including Etruscan), metrics and accentuation, along with codicology, it is little surprise that we have to wait until 1905 for contact between the two scholars.[93] Housman first recorded Lindsay's name in an article published in 1907[94] but first passed judgment on him in his important article 'Greek nouns in Latin poetry from Lucretius to Juvenal', where he called Lindsay 'a child of the age'[95] for regarding *Thyeste* at Mart. 4.49.4 as a vocative form transmitted 'fortasse recte'.[96]

A few years later, Housman privately objected to Lindsay's conduct in a matter relating to Friedrich Leo, the latter's long-standing adversary upon Plautine matters. Lindsay mistakenly asserted on two occasions that Leo had continued to maintain his complex theory about the text of the *Truculentus* in the second edition of his *Plautinische Forschungen* (Berlin, 1912), Leo complained that he had done no such thing at *BPhW* 33 (1913), 128 and Lindsay there responded that he 'must leave it to his readers to decide whether I have been guilty or not'. Housman's objection to this means of treating another scholar is a two-page unpublished manuscript, entitled 'A note on conduct', which was evidently written soon after April of 1913 and survives at Trinity College, Cambridge (Ms a 72.3 [27,40]); cf. Naiditch 1995, 78-9. Housman opens by stating his belief that he should make more widely known to English scholars the dispute that Lindsay had engendered and 'advertise to foreigners that even in controversy about textual criticism we do not all of us think all things lawful'. Housman declares on the strength of the evidence that Lindsay read the book properly only after he had reviewed it, and that he then realised that he had 'calumniated' Leo. The piece ends with Housman observing: 'I showed [Lindsay's sentence quoted above] to a friend and asked him what he gathered from it: he gathered that Mr Lindsay was tranquilly assured of the truth of what he had said.' Truthful, of course, it was not. That Housman chose not to publish in this instance serves as a strong example of his potential faculties of restraint in polemic.

Housman was notoriously wary of lexicographical and other reference tools, not least the *TLL*, a work which Lindsay keenly supported. Indeed, all attempts to systematise and record in full materials that impinged upon conjectural emendation evidently vexed him. In 1918 he opposed Lindsay's assertion that 'Latin scholarship is now becoming [easy] (from A to D) with the help of the *Thesaurus* [= *TLL*]'[97] by curtly asserting that '[n]o advance in palaeography will ever make textual emendation easy, because textual emendation depends much less on palaeography than on several other things, the chief of which is the textual emendator'.[98] Lindsay's interest in such reference tools perhaps inspired his odd closing sentence to an article concerning *cada* as a potential heteroclite neuter plural (*CQ* 12 (1918), 120: 'Will not Professor Housman give us a lexicon to Manilius, *lexicographorum in usum*?' The answer could only ever have been 'No' and it is hard, even in context, to see the purport of the comment. Housman, on the contrary, was able to land a blow in this field by asserting that Lindsay's index to his Isidore (1911) was 'rather Otto's index, which he has taken over without adapting it duly to his own recension or eliminating its misprints and other errors'.[99]

Housman's view of Lindsay as a textual critic and *arbiter emendationum* was obviously low and I know of no praise of a conjecture made by him.[100] Housman, thinking primarily of Lindsay's *Introduction*, had declared in 1922: 'One sees books calling themselves introductions to textual criticism which contain nothing about textual criticism from beginning to end.'[101] A particularly pointed barb can be found in the margin of his copy of Lindsay's Martial OCT (1903).[102] Lindsay humbly opens, '[p]ost egregios labores Schneidewini, Friedlaenderi, Gilberti, non potui sperare me ad emendanda haec epigrammata multum conferre posse.' Housman expands 'ne ante quidem'. Yet this was an edition whose organisation, clarity and general accuracy he praised highly in 1925.[103] The commendation, of course, was not of Lindsay as an editor drawing upon good judgment in his calibration of variants and emendations, but rather as an industrious and skilful collator and distributor of the available codicological evidence. Yet since this is the area of editing to which Lindsay turned his focus, this praise would certainly have brought him some mirth.

Some further insight into Housman's opinion of Lindsay can be gleaned from the field of metrics. In a letter to D.S. Robertson of 9 October 1931 (Burnett 2.260-1), by which time Lindsay had published all that he did on the subject of early Latin metre, Housman objects (260) that Lindsay's book[104] should not be on the reading list since students 'cannot learn [theories about prosody and *Iambenkürzung*] from Lindsay without at the same time being bamboozled'. More direct contact with Housman's opinions on Lindsay as a metrician can be had via the copious annotations in his copy of Lindsay's *editio maior* of Plautus' *Captiui* (London, 1900), presumably made soon after its publication.[105] Although annotations occur throughout the commentary, they primarily concentrate on the massive introductions on prosody and metre (12-102). Commonly the margins contain 'Nonsense' or 'How to scan?'/ 'How do you scan?'.[106] From these notes it is clear that Housman was sceptical about Lindsay's competence in metrical studies,[107] even though it was to early Latin metre that Lindsay limited himself,[108] on which his views were fixed early and remained fiercely resistant to change.[109] Yet there is no evidence that Lindsay, by contrast, regarded Housman as an accomplished metrician.[110]

Conclusion

Clearly no relationship, close or co-operative, was ever forged between these two major scholars. Notwithstanding their similarities, a refusal to accept the importance of the other's field of excellence (i.e. the study of manuscript culture and textual criticism) served to keep the two distant in scholarship, sometimes needlessly. This is to be regretted. Yet how much, we may wonder, *could* a man who sees in his dreams a neglected copy of a sixteenth-century classic with a marginal collation of a lost manuscript,[111] or who imagines with glee an active palaeographical committee directing researchers on missions throughout the world,[112] or who could exclaim in print 'oh what uncials!'[113] ever see eye-to-eye with another who made no direct attempt to seek out new manuscript material?

The differences in the two scholars' approaches had the result that, whereas Housman was intimately familiar with the works of earlier Latinists, whom he regarded as the great fathers of the subject, Lindsay's primary interests in the factual studies of metrics, philology, palaeography and related fields led him primarily to admire contemporaries of his, or at any rate scholars of the nineteenth-century: whereas Housman was largely retrospective with regard to classical scholarship, judging his work against his the benchmark of his predecessors, Lindsay saw himself at the coal-face, always wanting to be 'up-to-date' and looking forward to what remains to be uncovered. The two scholars seem to have looked constantly in opposing directions and never eye to eye.

We may close by returning to the *CR* obituarist, who truly said of Lindsay, 'What was most remarkable in him was that an infinite capacity for drudgery was combined with a happy-go-lucky enthusiasm which enlivened all he did and kept him very young.'[114] His capacity for drudgery cannot be doubted, nor can his sheer enthusiasm for 'Research'. In this field Housman's capacity was also formidable but admittedly lesser. Nor was he a man who felt for ever young. The contribution of both to Latin philology remains undoubtedly immense[115] and it will be difficult for scholars in future to match the achievements of either. None the less, a feeling remains that 'Mr Dull Dog' lacked the imagination, rather than the generosity, to appreciate the flair of 'Mr Nimble Wit'. And in classical scholarship both imagination and flair are sorely underrated virtues.[116]

Notes

1. I am most grateful to Chris Stray, Paul Naiditch, Michael Lapidge, James Diggle, Neil Hopkinson and the librarians of St Andrews University Library, St John's and Merton College, Oxford and Trinity College, Cambridge for their aid.

2. Kenney 1989, 621.

3. The contribution of Postgate, who must stand in third place (excluding scholars born in the twentieth century), was significant but certainly not revolutionary; see Hopkinson's chapter.

4. Unjustly, no biography has been written of Lindsay, who anticipated this oversight by leaving a relatively terse third-person summary of his own scholarly achievements; other than the last three words of the account ('He was unmarried'), he records no details of his private life. H.J. Rose, one of Lindsay's closest friends and colleagues at St Andrews, published the piece (which I shall call 'Autobiography') in its entirety within his obituary (Rose 1937, 487-500). For further discussion of Lindsay, the following accounts are the most useful: Rose 1938, C.J. Fordyce, rev. R.T. Stearn, *ODNB*; Kenney 1989, 621-6; Naiditch 1989 = 1995, 75-9; Lapidge 1991, 23 = 2003, 112; Lapidge 1993, 157-61; Lindsay 1996, ix-xviii; M. Deufert, 'W.M. Lindsay', in Todd 2004, II 583-5; the most instructive of all is Jocelyn 1996 (cf. also the introduction and annotations in Jocelyn 1992).

5. He *proxime accessit* to the winners of the Hertford scholarship (1879) and the Gaisford prize for Greek verse twice (1880, 1881) and was highly commended for the Ireland scholarship (1881).

6. Balliol achieved six of the ten firsts; among the students of other colleges stood A.C. Clark, the future Corpus Professor of Latin (1913-34), and A.W. Pollard, Housman's good friend at St John's.

7. Autobiography, 488. Lindsay showed support for German academic travel for more talented (American) students at *CR* 22 (1908), 25 and indirectly criticised the British post-graduate system at *CR* 12 (1898), 333-4. For further context on his decision to travel in Germany, see Jocelyn 1996, 97 nn. 34 and 106.

8. On the first sheet of Lindsay's manuscript select bibliography reproduced in his *PBA* memoir (now among University Library, St Andrews, Mss 36343), he noted that his Jesus Fellowship began on 21 March 1882. Jocelyn 1996, 105 n. 73 observes that the *Oxford University Gazette* records the election on 5 April 1882; Lindsay, by contrast, spoke of 'gaining' his fellowship on his return from Leipzig (Autobiography, 489).

9. On the first page of his impressive volume of testimonials for the Chair of Humanity at St Andrews in 1899, Lindsay stated that this decision was made 'with the view of gaining more experience in teaching than could be had in Oxford', although this was perhaps a calculated statement in the circumstances.

10. *The Latin Language* (Oxford, 1894), the fruit of ten years' work, was particularly well received on the Continent. It allowed Lindsay to amass the 70-page array of 55 testimonials from across Europe (and the Atlantic) for his application to the St Andrews Chair (see previous note). The German translation of the work by Hans Nohl (Leipzig, 1897), overseen by Lindsay, was for a long time the standard handbook in the German-speaking world. Lindsay's interest in the subject was obviously not exhausted by the work, as he wrote on the flyleaf of his own copy (University Library, St Andrews, ʳPA2080.L5): 'For a second edition, add chapter on syntax'. Since, however, his interests moved on, such a revision never came. By contrast, the school edition of the work, *A Short Historical Latin Grammar* (Oxford, 1895), did enter a second edition in 1915; Lindsay's annotations in his copy of this edition (in my possession) demonstrate a sustained interest in later life.

11. Lindsay 1897 and 1896.

12. See Jocelyn 1996, 102, 114.

13. The first was a bibliographical volume boldly entitled *The Best Books in Classics and Comparative Philology* (refused on 25 March 1885); Lindsay (Autobiography, 490) records with satisfaction that the book, though 'wisely refused', was used by J.B. Mayor in the *Supplement* (1879-96) to the third edition of his *Guide to the Choice of Classical Books* (London, 1885). The second work concerned a survey of the manuscript material of classical scholars in British libraries: in his failed proposal to OUP of c. 1900, made jointly with F.W. Madan, he provided a survey of Heinsius' marginalia in the Bodleian (material in preparation for which survives at both St Andrews and the Bodleian).

14. On the first page of his 1899 testimonial he wrote '[a]t Oxford my College work has comprised all branches of classical education, Greek as well as Latin'.

15. For information in this field I am indebted to the researches of Jocelyn 1996, who discovered that Lindsay unsuccessfully applied for the Chairs of Latin at Queen's College, Belfast, in 1881, Liverpool in 1884, Aberdeen in 1886 and the Chair of Humanity at Edinburgh in 1891 and 1895. It is possible that he applied for a number of other available British Latin Chairs, but not that at University College, London in 1892, to which Housman was of course elected on his first attempt for a post.

16. Lindsay's reputation on the Continent was such that, from 1895 onwards, '[h]e now found himself *en rapport* with Continental scholars and was constantly asked for articles by German magazine-editors' (Autobiography, 492). Housman only published thrice (and in Latin) in Continental journals, most significantly 'Praefanda', *Hermes* 66 (1931), 402-12 = *CP* 1175-84 (after *CR* rejected the piece for its sexual content).

17. In a letter to G. Jachmann of 16 May 1936, cited by Jocelyn 1996, 125 n. 228, he confessed that he was 'too old now to do research'.

18. Lindsay's older sister Elizabeth I.D. Lindsay, with whom Lindsay lived during his St Andrews years and who, like him, remained unmarried, died from natural causes in her 92nd year in 1945.

19. The economic statuses of the Lindsays and Housmans were similar and, though the youngest and oldest children of their families respectively, both experienced the death of a parent in their early years: when Lindsay was six his father Alexander died; Housman's mother Sarah died on his twelfth birthday.

20. Both had even written to H.A.J. Munro in their earlier years: Housman wrote about the text of Horace and Lucretius (see Naiditch 1995, 14-16); Lindsay instead enquired whether any Cambridge pupil of his would be interested in collating, at Friedlaender's behest, the Arundel manuscript of Martial in the British Museum, since 'I have done my best to get some Oxford scholar, but cannot' (University Library, St Andrews, Ms 36326.274: draft of 26 March [1884?]).

21. Gastronomy and Nature in general were Housman's primary diversions from research, Lindsay's was golf. Of foreign countries, France and Italy were great passions of both. Both turned their minds to poetry, one with success to guarantee the immortality of his name, the other as an occasional pastime.

22. The fourth chapter heading of Jocelyn 1996 is 'Lindsay the team-man'. Yet, although Lindsay's involvement and efficacy in numerous group projects is remarkable, rarely did his actual research develop hand-in-hand with another's.

23. Both developed distinctive and engaging prose styles: Housman's English and Latin is manifestly more lapidary and well-balanced, whereas Lindsay's writings in both languages are jauntier and more informal. Particularly striking examples of the latter's Latin can be found in the prefaces to (and occasionally the critical notes of) the volumes of *Glossaria Latina*. The English prose styles of the two can most easily be compared by reading the adjacent autobiographical notes by Housman upon A. Platt and Lindsay upon L. Havet at *CR* 39 (1925), 49-50. The fact that Lindsay is reputed to have composed many of his articles and notes on hotel paper, or upon the backs of envelopes, serves somewhat to explain his less elegant style.

24. Housman *passim*; Lindsay was more restrained but occasionally his distress boiled over: 'The truth is that the Germans are too imaginative for that kind of work [= so-called *Kombinationsforschung*]. And the Americans bind themselves to the German chariot-wheels. It is a work for the sober-sensed Englishman. But Englishmen are so lazy!' (*CR* 37 (1923), 35). In a letter of 8 February 1917 to Wentworth Thompson he went further: 'If University Professors are not to add to knowledge, who on earth is to do it? It irritates me to find every advance in my field + Burnet's the work of a German. Because Germans are (most of them) such wooden-headed, unsympathetic, unimaginative duffers. An Englishman can do far better work than a German – in Latin and Greek at any rate. But – our Scottish professors! They seem satisfied to remain at the level of knowledge ("a little higher" than the angels they coach for the MA degree), the level of knowledge which enabled them to win a professorship. Their ample leisure they dribble away in their petty bickerings about details of statutes or university regulations' (University Library, St Andrews, Ms 41306).

25. Housman financed the five volumes of his *Manilius* (1903-30) and *Juvenal* (1905); Lindsay, along with M.R. James and J. Cunningham, funded the six volumes of *Palaeographia Latina* (1922-9). All of these projects were financial losses.

26. An obvious counterexample on Lindsay's part, his 1887 school edition of Plautus' *Captiui* (rev. 1923), was effectively erased from his scholarly contribution by his full-scale *editio maior* of 1900.

27. For attribution of this quality to Housman see, among others, Gow 1936a, 31, 35; to Lindsay see Rose 1937, 487, 500, 502. For Lindsay's outlook, compare his tender obituary of Franz Skutsch at *CR* 26 (1912), 238.

28. Lindsay spent part of the post-graduation year of 1881-2 examining for Glasgow University; Housman taught in the sixth form at Bromsgrove but also returned to Oxford to study for the Pass degree.

29. Naiditch 1995, 76 n. 1, observes that both were elected to the Oxford Union Society on the same day but notes that there is no evidence that the two men met there.

30. I wonder whether the decision by Lindsay to paste cuttings of the Hoppé photograph of Housman in his late years (cut from obituaries) onto the endpaper and title-page respectively of his copies of Housman's Lucan (University Library, St Andrews, PA6478.A2F26) and Juvenal (University Library, St Andrews, PA6446.A2F05) reflects a desire to put a face to the name after his death.

31. Perhaps it is indicative that, in a generally laudatory review of Lindsay's *Latin Language*, R.S. Conway laments Lindsay's lack of familiarity with recent Cambridge scholarship at *CR* 9 (1895), 404.

32. See Reeve's chapter (esp. n. 47); Housman preferred to work from the (often untrustworthy) reports of others rather than collate himself. Lindsay leapt into the field from an early age, in 1884-6 collating for Friedlaender manuscripts of Martial in London (cf. n. 20), Oxford, Edinburgh, Paris and Leiden, and in 1890 (for OUP) the Escurial ms of Nonius.

33. These two letters were first published 30 years ago by P. Godman, who discovered them among Lindsay's correspondence at St Andrews (Godman 1978), but they have since been re-edited by Burnett.

34. Of course the two scholars would have been well aware since the late 1880s of each other's interests and modes of approach. As to Housman's potentially fierce reviews, Lindsay was probably long in agreement with Ellis, who wrote to him in an undated letter (from the summer of 1894?): 'I very greatly object to the tone which Housman took against Schulze, in the Classical Review: I do not see that anything is gained by swearing at a man (and his publisher!) because his view of the relation of MSS to each other does not agree with one's own. That attack seemed to me insufferable, although I am on friendly terms with H." (University Library, St Andrews, Ms 36326.114).

35. Preserved at St John's College, Housman Cabinet 2.

36. For instances of 'You lie', 'liar', 'damned liar' and 'ugh' in Housman's extant copies of Lindsay's books see Naiditch 2005, 175, 176, 178-9, 181.

37. Most damningly, alongside the opening sentence of Lindsay's Conclusion (142-50) – 'We have seen how the Revival of the Plautine Drama a generation or more after the poet's death caused a parting of the ways of text-tradition' – Housman added three simple words: 'We have not'.

38. *JPh* 30 (1907), 265 = *CP* 738-9.

39. The postcard can be found with other scraps of paper before the beginning of the third book of Manilius in Jacob's 1846 Berlin edition (Trinity College, Cambridge, adv.c.20.39).

40. It is perhaps fortunate that Lindsay wrote 'No reply needed' at the top of the postcard, as Housman's response would have presumably not shown equal optimism in W.R. Hardie's metrical researches (see my other chapter).

41. *CR* 19 (1905), 462-5; Housman's Juvenal is discussed at 464-5.

42. Duff reviewed Lindsay's Martial OCT (1903) at *CR* 17 (1903), 220-3. Although his reception was mostly favourable, he showed scepticism about Lindsay's excessive conservatism.

43. A mix of praise and criticism can likewise be seen in his remarks upon Housman's work on Juvenal at *Year's Work* (1906), 114.

44. Compare also Housman's mocking the pervasiveness of schemes of *Textgeschichte* at *CR* 22 (1908), 89 = *CP* 772.

45. Lindsay later defined this term himself as 'the classification of the MSS. and the history of the tradition of the text' (*CR* 32 (1917), 57).

46. *CR* 35 (1921), 29.

47. *CR* 51 (1937), 50. Jocelyn 1996, 99 n. 41, plausibly suggested that C.J. Fordyce may have penned the notice.

48. *Oxford Magazine* (7 June 1918), 314. Housman's own copy of this work (Trinity College, Cambridge, adv.c.20.59) contains very many polemical marginalia against the excessively scientific methodology of Clark and includes a cutting of Lindsay's review (unmarked).

49. The quotation is presumably from Housman's second article entitled 'Horatiana' (published in 1888), in which he emends *Carm.* 3.5.37-8 to ... *unde uitam sumere iustius, / pacemque bello miscuit* and then states, '[i]t is scarcely an exaggeration to say that "iustius" and "inscius" are the same thing: to illustrate the error would be mere waste of time' (*CP* 101). Although this piece was written many years before Lindsay's *Introduction to Textual Emendation*, perhaps he saw sufficient grounds to mock Housman's curt refusal to illustrate palaeographical errors? Nevertheless, Housman certainly provided copious evidence for common scribal corruptions in his later works.

50. Cf. also Lindsay's Martialian aside '*quid pote simplicius?*' when quoting Housman's statement at *CR* 32 (1918), 123.

51. For instance, Lindsay knew what he was doing when he began an article as follows: 'When Leo proclaimed to a too credulous world his startling theory of the history of Plautus' text, I had an inkling that the same arguments could be used about Terence as he used about Plautus, but was kept silent by the lack of information on Terence's MSS.' (*CQ* 19 (1925), 28). In a discussion of *Überlieferungsgeschichte*, Lindsay clearly records that he does have an 'inkling'; other than here, Lindsay only employed the word in print when citing Housman's aforementioned quotation (both referenced in the prec. n.).

52. It is worth comparing the far wider breadth of different corruptions treated in Havet 1911.

53. Similarly, one would expect talk of emendation in 'On the text of the Truculentus of Plautus' (*AJPh* 17 (1896), 438-44) but one rather finds a discussion purely of palaeography and the putative script of the archetype.

54. A French translation by J.-P. Waltzing appeared soon after (Paris, 1898). The utility of Lindsay's book was acknowledged by Postgate, who, in a mixed review, makes the observation that 'some even of those who write as experts upon subjects of textual criticism and palaeography might read it with profit' (*CR* 11 (1897), 408). Perhaps Housman was a figure in Postgate's mind.

55. The same limitation can be seen in the three surveys that Lindsay provided under the title 'Latin textual criticism and palaeography' for *The Year's Work in Classical Studies* 1906-8, where his analysis lies firmly on the history of manuscripts and palaeography. See *Year's Work* 1906 (109-17), 1907 (101-7), 1908 (119-22); the authorship of the surveys thereafter shifts to A.C. Clark.

56. This viewpoint can be illustrated by several passages from Lindsay's works but the most striking are: *Year's Work* 1908 (122); *CQ* 3 (1909), 133; *CR* 26 (1912), 131; *CR* 31 (1917), 57.

57. Review of Schenkl's *Zur Kritik und Ueberlieferungsgeschichte des Grattius und anderer lateinischer Dichter* (Leipzig, 1898) (*CR* 13 (1899), 410). Cf. *CR* 28 (1914), 209-10, a passage which ends: 'Yet the flow [of textual suggestions] never ceases. What a waste of time it seems to write them! And how unsatisfying to read them! Sauce, much sauce, is needed for the meagre fare.'

58. Recorded in his Notebook X, p.160. Compare the well-known comment from his 1921 address to the Classical Association: 'Palaeography is one of the

things with which a textual critic needs to acquaint himself, but grammar is another, and equally indispensable, and no amount either of grammar or of palaeography will teach a man one scrap of textual criticism' (*CP* 1058).

59. In his generally negative review of Lindsay's *Captiui* of Plautus (Oxford, 1887), F. Haverfield criticised Lindsay's discussion of textual variants as '[t]he least satisfactory part of the notes' (*CR* 2 (1888), 178). We should however cite Lindsay's words from the one-page preface to the book: 'This little book does not claim to be a critical edition of the *Captivi*. Textual emendation does not come within its scope.' Cf. Lindsay's review of Palmer's edition of Plautus' *Amphitruo* (London, 1891) at *CR* 6 (1892), 25.

60. Autobiography, 493.

61. An apparent anomaly in Lindsay's publications is 'Notes on the Lydia' (*CR* 32 (1918), 62-3), which shows an unusual interest in emendation.

62. Lindsay 1923, 53. Lindsay at this point retorts 'No: the transmission of texts was not so capricious as Mr. Feet-on-the-hob's 'emendations' nor so ignorant as his justification of them.'

63. Lindsay 1896, v, wrote of 'the rules of the game'.

64. This viewpoint can occasionally expose naivety. To return to the same short essay quoted above, Lindsay states (1923, 54): 'Emendation cannot be dispensed with. But the difficulty of emending a Carolingian MS. is slight; it is the Renaissance texts, altered by the caprice of emendators, which, in the absence of earlier MS. evidence, offer the hardest problem.' On this view, the emendation of Lucretius and Manilius, to select but two, is an easy task. Lindsay will find himself rather alone in this opinion.

65. *CR* 36 (1922), 132. In his obituary of the scholar he wrote that his death 'inflicts a quite irreparable loss on the *twin studies* of Latin Palaeography and Latin Textual Criticism' (*CR* 21 (1907), 188) (my emphasis).

66. 'Notes on the text of Martial', *CR* 17 (1903), 48-52, at 49.

67. J.D. Duff, *CR* 17 (1903), 221.

68. Lindsay's excessive faith in his Plautine recension led E.A. Sonnenschein, in his admittedly over-critical review of Lindsay's *OCT* (1904-5), to ask '[o]f what classical author can it be said that the consensus of all the MSS. minus the "inevitable" errors represents the *vera manus* of the writer?' (*CR* 19 (1905), 312).

69. *Year's Work* (1906), 109.

70. A point made by Kenney 1989, 624.

71. In a passing remark at *Year's Work* 1906, 112, he observes: 'Perhaps I have clung too closely, like a limpet, to the rock of tradition; but the course of Plautine textual criticism since Ritschl's time has shown that a reading shared by our two families of MSS. generally turns out in the end to be correct.' For earlier expression of a similar view see *JPh* 26 (1899), 279 and Plautus *OCT* (1904-5), I [vii].

72. Review of Salonius' *Vitae Patrum* (Lund, 1920), *CR* 35 (1921), 112. Cf. 'How any editor of Plautus can become one of the slash-cut-and-carve critics I cannot understand. The fair garden-beds of Plautus are scored all over with the hoof-prints of the reckless emender' (*CQ* 12 (1918), 140).

73. *CR* 35 (1921), 29-30.

74. *CR* 31.2 (1917), 57, *CR* 33 (1919), 26.

75. Lindsay added an interesting note to the apparatus of Housman's Juvenal at 4.128 (University Library, St Andrews, PA6446.A2F05), which shows his dissatisfaction with the latter's nit-picking as the basis for emendation. In supporting his change of *in* to *per* in the transmitted text of 127-

8 *peregrina est belua* [= *rhombus*]: *cernis / erectas in terga sudes?* Housman wrote 'dorsuales pinnae, quas *sudium* nomine significari apparet, *in terga* erigi non possunt, cum sint in tergo; laterales autem in rhombo perparuae sunt neque ullam habent cum sudibus similitudinem'. Lindsay has added: 'enim meminerimus Veientonem caecum fuisse. Iam in laevom conversus, ubi sibi dextra iacebat belua, quomodo sciret utrum rhombus magnas sudes in terga haberet annon? re vera nescire possumus utrum Iuvenalis "in" an "per" ipse scripserit. Quid enim ibi est illa "ratio et res ipsa" Bentlei?'

76. The term arises from an expression of Ingram Bywater: 'Those who care for MSS. *per se* are usually dull dogs' (Jackson 1917, 88).

77. Elsewhere Lindsay records his preference of *Lydia* 4-6 to *Last Poems* (*AJP* 44 (1923), 53-4).

78. *CR* 19 (1925), 36.

79. *CQ* 20 (1926), 103.

80. 'Varus and Varius', *CQ* 10 (1916), 206-21.

81. 'The *Thyestes* of Varius', *CQ* 11 (1917), 42-9 = *CP* 941-9.

82. Varius' *Thyestes CQ* 16 (1922), 180.

83. Housman acknowledged this point publicly, and probably privately, although did not regard it as a matter of great import. In an addendum to 11.148 in *Juvenal*[2], liv: 'Mr Lindsay asserts in Class. Rev. 1905 p. 465 that "nothing is commoner than the miscopying of *quisquam* as *quis*." Scribes will miscopy anything anyhow, and Mr Lindsay, whose acquaintance with MSS is much greater than mine, has probably come across some examples of this miscopying; but it is so far from common that I cannot remember a single one.'

84. 'Draucus and Martial XI 8 1', *CR* 44 (1930), 114-16 = *CP* 1166-7. For another reference to Lindsay's conservatism with regard to the text of Martial, cf. 'neque enim codicum lectionibus, ut editoribus [= Lindsaio et Heraeo] placeant, necesse ut ullum intellectum habere credantur' (*Hermes* 66 (1931), 411 = *CP* 1182).

85. We can also compare Lindsay's calling Housman the 'archpriest of the emendator-sect' at *CQ* 20 (1926), 102.

86. Housman's interest in glossaries was low. His only article in the field ('On Vat. Lat. 3221', *JPh* 20 (1891), 49-52 = *CP* 227-30) was a series of emendations, often ingenious, designed to tweak a number of the suggestions offered by H. Nettleship on the same Vatican manuscript (*JPh* 19 (1891), 113-28, 184-92, 290-5, *JPh* 20 (1892), 183-4, 185-90), a witness to the so-called 'Abolita' glossary. When Lindsay came to edit this text, however, he only mentioned one emendation from Housman's hand (*GL* 3 (1926), 91-183: *destillatum* for *destinatum* at *IN* 121). One wonders whether Lindsay could have had Housman's article (written when he was 31) in mind when he wrote: 'Occasionally a young scholar who intends to spend his life in the pleasant sport of conjectural emendation tries his prentice hand on glosses, but with comical results. Knowledge is necessary for successful emendation. In all cases, knowledge of "Ueberlieferungsgeschichte" and the practice of medieval scribes' (*CQ* 12 (1918), 58).

87. Kay 1985, 83.

88. A few words should be said on comparative philology, a subject in which Lindsay achieved international success but for which Housman, having mocked it as an undergraduate, never showed evident respect. Lindsay's own interests moved away from the field after his *magnum opus* of the 1890s but a formidable knowledge of the histories of Latin, Greek and other significant Indo-European languages infused his later work. In his obituary of Friedrich Leo, Lindsay

made the observation that '[i]f Leo's work on Plautus had a weak side, the cause lay in his want of sympathy with Comparative Philology' (*CR* 28 (1914), 31). Lindsay would presumably have said the same of Housman.

89. *CQ* 21 (1927), 191 n. 2

90. Bowra 1966, 253.

91. Perhaps this partial *volte face* was influenced by Housman's words of praise for his Martial two years earlier (see below).

92. Application to the Electors to the Corpus Professorship of Latin from Eduard Fraenkel (s.l., [1934]), 7.

93. Housman did however record Lindsay's name often when citing (as he regularly did) Lindsay's edition of Nonius (and later of Festus and Isidore).

94. 'Corrections and explanations of Martial', *JPh* 30 (1907), 229-65 at 241 = *CP* 720.

95. *JPh* 31 (1910), 236-66, at 252 = *CP* 829.

96. In the apparatus of his Martial *OCT* ad loc.

97. *CQ* 11 (1917), 38-41, at 41.

98. *CQ* 12 (1918), 29-37, at 33 = *CP* 954 (cf. *CP* 957); for fuller citation of this passage see Reeve's chapter.

99. *CQ* 13 (1919), 151 n. 1 = *CP* 998 n. 1.

100. Direct criticism of Lindsay's method of conjecture survives only in manuscript: Housman privately wrote 'Mr Lindsay's are the sort of conjectures which might be made by a good and industrious schoolboy if you stood over him with a stick and told him that he must conjecture something' (Notebook Y, 16); 'Mr Lindsay speaks of conjectural emendation as a sport [n. 86 above], and I had already inferred from his own conjectures that he took that view of it' (Notebook X, 156); '[t]hat idle fumbling with letters which is what Mr [Lindsay] mistakes by textual emendation' (ibid., 164).

101. *PCA* 18 (1922), 67 = *CP* 1058.

102. The copy survives at Merton College, Oxford (27.B.5), along with a letter of 1958 from Basil Blackwell, who chose to retain the copy and, contrary to Housman's wishes, not to erase any marginalia.

103. Rev. of W. Heraeus, *M. Valerii Martialis Epigrammaton libri* (Leipzig, 1925), *CR* 39 (1925), 199-203, at 199 = *CP* 1099; for the citation see Reeve's chapter.

104. I follow Leach (see his chapter) in identifying this book with the edition of Plautus' *Captiui* not his *Early Latin Verse*.

105. Housman's copy survives at St John's College, Housman Cabinet 1.

106. Two marginal notes are particularly instructive in relation to what has been discussed hitherto. First is Housman's response to Lindsay's statement (ad 288) that 'a scribe would not change a familiar to an unfamiliar form': 'ignoramus'; the second is the objection to Lindsay's note on 882 Heg. *iam diu*-Erg. ναὶ τὰν Πραινέστην. Heg. *uenit?* Erg. ναὶ τὰν Σιγνέαν: 'What does it [i.e. *iam diu*] mean? You oppose a conjecture [i.e. *tam diu*], and fancy you are defending the text.' Housman's comment on Lindsay's defence of the paradosis at 578: 'You utter ass! Read the passage' is evidence only of his frustration with Lindsay's methodology.

107. At *CQ* 21 (1927), 3 = *CP* 1116 he mocks Lindsay's credulity in metrical anomalies; for citation of this passage see my other chapter, n. 64.

108. In a postcard of 26 July 1917 (University Library, St Andrews, Ms 41364) he confessed to D'Arcy Wentworth Thompson: '[i]n metre (except Plautine) I am not well posted.'

109. An uncharacteristically negative statement from his hand was reported by Sir Kenneth Dover (1994, 40) written by Lindsay on the flyleaf to Fraenkel's

Iktus und Akzent (Fraenkel 1928): 'Where in the world, except in Germany, would three hundred pages of this rubbish find a publisher?'

110. It does seem striking that, in 1919, Lindsay thought Gilbert Murray the best man to ask about hiatus in Greek trimeters. Murray's response is basic, ending with the apology '[m]y books are packed up or perhaps I could have given a more precise answer'. Lindsay has fairly written at the top of the page '[n]ot a very satisfactory answer. Write again in October unless you have found the right answer meanwhile' (University Library, St Andrews, Ms 36326.359).

111. *CQ* 7 (1913), 1-11, at 11.

112. *Oxford Magazine* (7 June 1918), 314.

113. 'The primary ms. of Probus *inst. art.*', *AJP* 48.3 (1927), 231-4, at 231.

114. *CR* 51 (1937), 50.

115. A firm judgment of Lindsay's contribution to Latin scholarship remains to be made. Respectively understatement and exaggeration can be seen in the two following remarks: '[Lindsay was] one of Scotland's greatest Latinists' (Briggs 1987, 362); 'Lindsay ... was one of the greatest, perhaps *the* greatest, Latin scholars ever born in these British Isles' (Lapidge 1996, ix). I also find it hard to believe, as is stated by Lapidge 1991, 23, that Lindsay had 'an unrivalled knowledge of Latin'. It cannot be doubted that Lindsay's knowledge of the history of the Latin language was among the best of British during his lifetime but in terms of the knowledge and understanding of the language as a grammatical and syntactical tool employed over several centuries, Housman was manifestly his superior.

116. Timpanaro (1985, 97-8) was, I believe, therefore right to state: 'Non si tratta di contrapporre Lindsay a Housman: la genialità di Housman, Lindsay certo non l'ebbe. Si tratta di rivalutare una figura di studioso che fu pur sempre tra i maggiori latinisti dell'età tra la fine dell'Ottocento e i primi decenni del nostro secolo, e non ricalcò le orme altrui, ma lavorò quasi sempre in campi fin allora insufficientemente esplorati.'

11

Housman and A.S. Hunt

L. Lehnus

The new documents

That A.E. Housman and A.S. Hunt (1871-1934) had been corresponding was already apparent from Hunt's prefaces to volumes XV and XVII of the Oxyrhynchus series, both mentioning Housman (along with Gilbert Murray, in the second instance) with thanks.[1] Six letters, four annotated sheets, and one postcard addressed by Housman to Hunt have now resurfaced from among Hunt's uncatalogued papers that had been bequeathed by his widow Lucy Hunt to the Ashmolean Museum Library, now Sackler Library, Oxford.[2]

All but one of these new documents come from a period shortly before or immediately after publication of P.Oxy. vol. XVII, which appeared around Christmas 1927. Indeed, that Hunt had applied to Housman in time for obtaining advice on Callimachus' *Aetia Prologue*, P.Oxy. XVII 2079 (1927), was already known to us from a couple of notes that he had sent to A.C. Pearson in October 1926.[3] Now, only letter 1 among those published below deals with a subject other than Callimachus, that is Pindar's *Paeans* P.Oxy. V 841.[4]

On the *Paeans* of Pindar Housman had already published as early as 1908;[5] letter 1 thus largely predates all other pieces, and vouches for direct contact between Housman and Hunt since the very beginning of the century.[6] More we do not know about the externalities of their scholarly intercourse; though c. 1922 the two must have been further corresponding on P.Oxy. XV 1790, 1793, 1794 and 1796.[7] On A.S. Hunt suffice it here to record that by 1908 he had already become one of the two best known British papyrologists. Together with B.P. Grenfell (also of Queen's College, Oxford) Hunt had excavated at Oxyrhynchus in Middle Egypt from winter 1896/97 to early 1907. In six campaigns a huge amount of papyri had been discovered, and volume I of the Oxyrhynchus Papyri series was already published by 1898. By May 1908 Grenfell had fallen sick, and it was only natural that Housman would correspond with Hunt, incidentally the more philologically gifted (for Grenfell's skill lay chiefly in history) of the Oxford Dioscuri.

A few of the letters that follow had been sighted by me in 1995, gathered into special pockets inside the binding of Oxyrhynchus volumes VII and XVII from the personal library of A.S. Hunt; more have come out on a second inspection in 2001 from a box containing scattered papers by Grenfell and Hunt now in the Papyrology Study Room, Sackler Library. Among this second set of papers were a couple of notes on Callimachus *fr.* 1.11-12 Pf. which I happen to have made use of already, a few years ago, in a study of mine on the relevant Scholion Londinense.[8]

Here are the letters, with just essential comments appended:

1.   University College, London
                                                                        6 May 1908
Dear Mr Hunt,

   There is nothing to identify the Τμᾶρες with the Τμάριοι or Τόμουροι. The fragment in Ox. pap. II p. 59 leaves their locality indeterminate.[9] When Diels proposes Τμᾶρες for Τάλαρες in Strabo p. 434 he apparently overlooks the fact that the name occurs twice and will want altering twice.[10] But, if he is right, then the identity is disproved; for Strabo is speaking of a tribe which had its abode in Pindus in Thessaly. He says they came from Τόμαρος: perhaps they did, perhaps he merely thought they ought to; just as lexicographers down to this very hour connect <u>Ionium mare</u> with <u>Ionia</u>. But even if Τμᾶρες and Τόμαρος were really akin it would not follow that the α of Τόμαρος could be long, any more than πλᾱ̄θω would justify πελᾱ̄θω, or θρᾱ̄ξαι ταρᾱ̄ξαι.[11]

   Here are a few marginalia on your last volume, some of which may perhaps be useful.

p. 18. Why, in II ep.[12] l. 13, do you make the 1st syllable of ἰηίε long on its first occurrence and short on its second?[13]

p. 20. The scansion of VI ep.[14] l. 3 does not correspond with the text of verse 106 (πατρωΐοις).[15]

p. 22. The 1st syllable of IX should be *u*.[16]

pp. 32, 33. The arrangement of the fragment does not match.

p. 46. verse 117 schol.: the α[...]ων which you supply as ἄ[λλ]ων ought, one would think, to be Δ[ελφ]ῶν: can the doubtful α be a δ?[17]

p. 61. frag. 49]σ φρασ[σ: why the additional σ?"

p. 83. The last sentence of the note on 28-9 belongs to 27.

p. 96. verse 74: who says that Panthous was a priest at Delphi?[18]

p. 107. IX verse 7: ἱπποσόα is Bergk's, not Blass's.[19]
   "   " 9: εἰς is Bergk's.

You do not call due attention to Blass's remarkable achievement in discovering in 1869 the antistrophic structure of the fragment, now thoroughly proved by the papyrus. (As I have made it one of my missions in life to go about restoring <u>suum cuique</u>, I don't feel precluded from doing so even when <u>suum</u> happens to be <u>meum</u>; so I will say that on p. 314, No. 464, you ascribe to Ludwich and Kroll a number of corrections which I made five months before them in Class. Rev. 1903 pp. 385-6.)[20]

I am yours sincerely
A. E. Housman.

2.

Trinity College
Cambridge
16 Nov. 1925

Dear Hunt,

In the second piece I think there should be a full stop at ὁδούς, so that the construction is βασκαίνει πύργον ἐ[γειρόμεν]ον (hymn. II 64) καὶ (βασκαίνει) εὖτε etc.; and then

μερμνοῦ
$\begin{cases} μὲν \\ μοι \end{cases}$
πτερύγεσσι[ν ὑπ᾽ αἰγυπι]οῦ τε νέοιο,

εἴ κοτ᾽ ἐπὶ ξ[είν]ην λαὸν ἔποικον ἄ[γοις].

'may the omens of hawk and vulture conduct you on your way, if ever you lead colonists to a foreign country'.[21] I suppose these are birds of good omen, mentioned in contrast to the ἅρπασος and ἐρωδιός, as Horace mentions the <u>oscinem coruum</u> in carm. III 27. μοι might be defended as ethic dative, 'I pray', but μέν seems better.

Before making any suggestion about the other piece I should like to have the distich or sentence immediately following Ἐγκελάδῳ.[22]

A. E. Housman.

3.

Trinity College
Cambridge
23 Nov. 1925

Dear Hunt,

The first passage is a great puzzle, chiefly on account of the two ἵνα's in the fifth verse;[23] but γῆρας... ἐμοὶ βάρος ὅσσον ἔπεστι / τριγλώχιν ὀλοῷ νῆσος ἐπ᾽ Ἐγκελάδῳ is clearly an allusion to Eur. Herc. 637-40 ἁ νεότας μοι φίλον αἰεί· τὸ δὲ γῆρας ἄχθος βαρύτερον Αἴτνας σκοπέλων ἐπὶ κρατὶ κεῖται. I don't think it is safe to assume that the next verse began οὐ νέμεσις, which would not follow well upon a wish. \The beginning of the pentameter apparently also differed in aet. and ep./[24] In the fifth verse I think ην must be ἦν, μέν being added to the relative as in Hom. Il. I 234: δρόσον ἀείδειν

219

is very artificial, but resembles Pers. scaz. 14 <u>cantare nectar</u> and Call. pap. Ox. \1011,/ 225 δάφνην ἀείδει (as I explain it).[25]

In the second piece, if ὑπ᾽ does not suit, perhaps πτερύγεσσι μετ᾽ would, as he does use μετά c. dat. for 'with'. The second bird might be ἰκτίνου, if αἰγυπιοῦ would not do; or it might be perhaps πτερύγεσσιν ὁμοῦ πέρκου τε.[26]

Yours sincerely
A. E. Housman.

4.

Trinity College
Cambridge
10 Oct. 1926

Dear Hunt,

Many thanks for the proofs, and especially for taking the trouble to copy out the British Museum fragment for me.[27]

The approach of term will curtail my leisure, so I send at once what I have got straight at present.

As to your note on 33-6, 'Heracl.' generally means Heraclidae.

Yours sincerely
A. E. Housman.

5. [sheet]   10 Oct. 1926

2079

9 sq.[28]   ἀλλὰ καθέλκει

[δρῦν πολὺ] τὴν μακρὴν ὄμπνια Θεσμοφόρος.

Corn is much better than acorns, though they grow on a tall tree. καθέλκει is 'outweighs', like καθταβρίθειν in Theocr. XVII 95 and <u>deducere</u> in Gratt. 299 <u>leuis</u> (acc. plur.) <u>deducet pondere fratres</u>, a passage usually misunderstood.[29]

11 sq.[30]

[τοῖν δὲ] δ[υ]οῖν, Μίμνερμος ὅτι γλυκύς, [ἄμμε τὸ μεῖον]

[βιβλίον] ἡ μεγάλη δ᾽ οὐκ ἐδίδαξε γυνή.

We have learnt the sweetness of Mimnermus from the slighter of his two volumes, not from the portly Nanno.[31] That he wrote two is stated by Porphyrion at Hor. epist. II 2 101. ἄμμε, though not properly Ionic, is in Theogn. 1273, and Callimachus has ἄμμιν.[32] βιβλίον is seven letters instead of six, but two of them are iotas.

A. E. H.

6. [sheet: 2 pages]   Trin. Coll. Camb.
     12 Oct. 1926

2079

13-16.[33]   In verses 14 and 15 the numbers of letters missing is not the same on slips 19 and 20. I have taken the former as correct.

[φρὴν μὲ]ν ἐπὶ Θρήικασ ἀπ' Αἰγύπτοιο [γέγηθεν],
   [φρούδασ] Πυγμαίων ἠλεμά[τη γ]ερά[νουσ,
[σήμασιν ο]ἷσ αἱ [τάγ]μα [μαθεῖν Εὔβ]οιον ἐπ' ἄνδρα
[ἤγαγον· ἀδονίδεσ δ' εἰσὶν ἀοιδότεραι.
Or ὦρσαν ἀηδονίδεσ

The light-witted Pygmies are glad when the cranes have packed off from the Nile to the Strymon, the cranes, from whom Palamedes learnt how to arrange his characters. In other words, the crane is formidable in warfare and famous in the history of civilisation; but the nightingale has a better voice.[34]

From the figures traced on the sky by the cranes in their migration Palamedes learnt either the letters of the alphabet or their arrangement, for there were two accounts.

Of many passages which in different ways are more or less apposite these three seem to me the most so.

Philostr. heroic. X 2-3[35] ἐν ἐκκλησίᾳ δέ ποτε τῶν Ἀχαιῶν ὄντων γέρανοι μὲν ἔτυχον πετόμεναι τὸν εἰωθότα αὐταῖσ τρόπον. ὁ δὲ Ὀδυσσεὺσ ἐσ τὸν Παλαμήδην βλέψασ 'αἱ γέρανοι' ἔφη 'μαρτύρονται τοὺσ Ἀχαιοὺσ ὅτι αὐταὶ γράμματα εὖρον, οὐχὶ σύ. καὶ ὁ Παλαμήδησ 'ἐγὼ γράμματα οὐχ εὖρον' εἶπεν 'ἀλλ' ὑπ' αὐτῶν εὑρέθην. πάλαι γὰρ ταῦτα ἐν Μουσῶν οἴκῳ κείμενα ἐδεῖτο ἀνδρὸσ τοιούτου, θεοὶ δὲ τὰ τοιαῦτα δι' ἀνδρῶν σοφῶν ἀναφαίνουσι, γέρανοι μὲν οὖν οὐ μεταποιοῦνται γραμμάτων, ἀλλὰ τάξιν ἐπαινοῦσαι πέτονται, πορεύονται γὰρ ἐσ Λιβύην ξυναψοῦσαι πόλεμον σμικροῖσ ἀνθρώποισ· σὺ δ' οὐδὲν ἂν περὶ τάξεωσ εἴποισ, ἀτακτεῖσ γὰρ τὰσ μάχασ.'

Mart. XIII 75 GRVES.
   turbabis uersus nec littera tota uolabit
   unam perdideris si Palamedis auem.

Claud. bell. Gild. 474-8
   pendula ceu paruis moturae bella colonis
   ingenti clangore grues aestiua relinquunt
   Thracia, cum tepido permutant Strymona Nilo:
   ordinibus uariis per nubila texitur ales
   littera pennarumque notis conscribitur aer.

ἀλεμάτω in Theocr. 15 4 is corrupted to ἀδεμάτω, ἀδειμάντου, ἀδαμάντου.[36]

Hesych. Εὐβοεύσ· ὁ Παλαμήδησ. The adjective Εὔβοιοσ is cited only from Stat. silu. V 3 137.[37] It is one of those which are formed without increase from substantives whose terminations have an adjectival look, Μελίβοιοσ from Μελίβοια in Lucretius and Virgil, Steph. Byz. ed. Mein. pp. 151 sq.[38] Ἀχελῷοσ ποταμόσ... τὸ ἐθνικὸν Ἀχελῷοσ ὁμοφώνωσ.
οἶσ possessive, as ὅν hymn. III 103.
ἐπ᾽ ἄνδρα ἤγαγον tmesis for ἐπήγαγον ἄνδρα: C.Q. 1910 p. 115.[39]

For ἀοιδότεραι see anth. Pal. X 195 5 sq. ἐν γὰρ ἀμούσοισ / καὶ κόρυδοσ κύκνου φθέγξετ᾽ ἀοιδότερον.[40] It may have been a recollection of Callimachus which made Lucretius substitute gruum for the κολοιῶν of his model anth. Pal. VII 713 7[41] in IV 181 sq. paruus ut est cycni melior canor, ille gruum quam / clamor in aetheriis dispersus nubibus Austri.

A. E. Housman

7. [sheet] Trin. Coll. Camb.
14 Oct. 1926

2079

7-9[42]

φῦλον ἄ[ιδρι
μοῦνον ἐόν] τήκειν ἧπαρ ἐπιστάμενον,

ἤν, { ἔγνωκ᾽ / ἔξοιδ᾽ } ἄ]ρ᾽ ἐ[ὼν] ὀλιγόστιχοσ·

It is the ἧπαρ of the Τελχῖνεσ themselves that wastes away: you quote anth. Pal. XI 193 ὁ φθόνοσ... τήκει... φθονερῶν... κραδίην, and Aglauros in Ouid. met. II 807 sq., infected by Envy, lenta ... miserrima tabe / liquitur. The ancients often say that one does things when one only suffers them, as Hom. Od. XIX 263 sq. μηδ᾽ ἔτι θυμὸν / τῆκε, Callim. pap. Oxy. 1011 10 θυμὸν ἀμύξειν.[43]
ἔρρε is rendered unsuitable by the discovery of ἔλλετε below,[44] and no verb is needed in the verse. The colon in the papyrus is correctly used to lock up the vocative and its retinue. εὖ ποιῶ in 9 does not lead up to ἀλλά. ἐόν = ὑμέτερον, which itself would be less good, as μοῦνον is needed.

11. I wonder if the name of Mimnermus' other book was μέλισσαι.[45]

17 sq.[46] αὖθι δὲ τέχνη[ι

<κρίνετε>, μὴ σχοίνῳ Περσίδι τὴν] σοφίην.

In Plutarch μὴ and σχοίνῳ are in contact, and the verb must be plural imperative between ἔλλετε and διφᾶτε.[47] αὖθι, straightway, as an immediate result of these instructive remarks; hymn. III 46.

39 sq. In this distich he compared himself to the dying swan, singing its loudest when its flying days are over.[48]

A. E. Housman

8. [sheet]   Trin. Coll. Camb.
                                                    15 Oct. 1926

2079

33-6 I now think that in the relative clause ἀείδω is intransitive, ἥν the object of ἔδων, and πρώκιον εἶδαρ in apposition.[49]

ἵνα... ἵνα, as it seems to be used here, has a curiously close parallel in the Latin qua ... qua = et ... et. That construction often, like this, lays the stress on the first member of the comparison, 'A as well as B': Plaut. mil. 1113 consectare qua maris qua feminas, 'males as well as females', trin. 1044 rapere properant qua sacrum qua publicum.

In 35 we want the verb governing γῆρας and δρόσον and the subject of that verb, and the B. M. scholia may be of some help. ὤφελον shows that the verb expressed a hopeless wish and was past indicative,[50] and τὰ καύ[ματα] would be a suitable sort of subject, for dew is dispersed by the heat of day. The sense then was probably 'if only the sun drank up old age as he does the dew!'; but I will not guess at the words.

There should be a full stop at the end of 32.

In this passage he may be remembering that the τέττιξ, to which he compares himself, was once Tithonus.

I think I have now come to the end of what I have to say, until I hear about the name of Mimnermus' book. If it were μέλισσαι, 11 sq. should perhaps be τὸ μικρὸν / θηρίον (Theocr. XIX 5 sq. τυτθὸν / θηρίον ἐντὶ μέλισσα).[51]

A. E. Housman

9. [postcard]   Trin. Coll. Camb.
                                                    18 Oct. 1926

I did not cast any doubt on your decipherment of δ in line 14. On the contrary, I assumed that it was right, and therefore cited Theocr. 15. 4.[52]

A. E. H.

10.

Trinity College
Cambridge
25 Dec. 1927

Dear Hunt,

Many thanks: I have the volume, and if I had two copies I do not know what I should do with them, I am so straitened for room.

You and Mair between you have cleared up 2079 33-5.[53] Since Ammonius took αὖθι as μετὰ ταῦτα, it follows that he took ἵνα in a temporal sense. The temporal clause must have a verb, and this must be got from the second ἵνα: ἵνα γῆρασ ἱμᾷ δρόσον, 'when age draws off the dew of my poetical inspiration.'

I am writing some notes on vol. XVII and sending them to a journal in a few days.[54] Shall I add this, or would you rather publish your new matter yourself?

I see that in 2079 9 you print ἔξοι]δ', as if a δ were in the papyrus; but it is not on the opposite page. Unless it can be made out, I prefer ἔγνω]κ' as a verb Callimachus uses.

Yours sincerely
A. E. Housman.

11.

Trinity College
Cambridge
29 Dec. 1927

Dear Hunt,

I think that you and Lobel are right. πάντωσ will go with εἴην and mean 'in every respect': the τέττιξ not only feeds on dew \and sings/ but has got rid of old age, having been Tithonus in its former existence; μέν will gain significance; the change from subjunctive to optative is justified because he actually does sing, while getting rid of old age is far from actual; and the order of words at the beginning of 35 is not too bad for Callimachus. So you shall publish yourself and let me drop out.

Yours sincerely
A. E. Housman.

What we have learnt

It is difficult to say whether the new material will add to the intriguing discussion on the degree of Housman's knowledge of Greek.[55] Needless to say, nobody would take at face value his contention that he was making no more than 'a manful pretence of knowing the language', as he wrote to Pearson. Indeed, dazzling intuitions such as αἰγυπιοῦ at Call. *fr.* 43/50.66, δρῦν at the beginning of *fr.* 1.10,[56] ἀηδονίδεσ soon to be confirmed by papyrus[57] at *fr.* 1.16, and μοῦνον ἐὸν at fr. 1.8,[58] do feature here, along with information that is novel to us.

It now appears, just to mention a couple of cases, that the restoration of vv. 39-40 of the *Aetia Prologue* that is familiar to Callimachus readers from Pfeiffer's apparatus did not belong to Housman but to Hunt; though at the same time, that the old poet 'compared himself to the dying swan, singing its loudest when its flying days are over' (letter 7) remains secured to Housman as his lasting contribution to the interpretation of that tangled passage. And it is vintage Housman when we now read how quick he was in understanding the peculiar construction of 33 δρόσον ἀείδειν through comparison with Persius *Chol.* 14 *cantare nectar* (letter 3).

Housman had published copiously on Bacchylides in 1898,[59] and was about to write on Pindar's *Paeans*. That Hunt started collaboration with him by applying to his experience in the field of Greek lyric poetry is easily understood (letter 1). But what turns out to be by far the largest portion of their exchange happened to deal with Greco-Roman learned poetry. Here Horace, Ovid, Persius, Statius and Martial line up with Theocritus and the Greek Anthology in helping explaining Callimachus. Definitely Hunt, who for vol. XVII of the Oxyrhynchus series (Hesiod, Sappho, tragedy, and Hellenistic poetry) had enrolled the help of Lobel and Gilbert Murray, along with that of Housman, need not have been puzzled on who was the best Greek scholar of contemporary England. He had the best and the aptest ones at his disposal – all of them, no need to choose.[60]

Notes

1. Cf. A.S. Hunt, 'Preface', in B.P. Grenfell and A.S. Hunt (edd.), *The Oxyrhynchus Papyri XV* (London, 1922), and 'Preface', in A.S. Hunt (ed.), *The Oxyrhynchus Papyri XVII* (London, 1927).

2. For information on the Hunt 'Nachlass' see Lehnus 2007, 247-55.

3. Alfred Chilton Pearson (1861-1935) was Housman's *collega proximus* as Regius Professor of Greek in Cambridge. Housman trusted him: 'one who unites the characters of an acute grammarian, a vigilant critic, and an honest man' (*CP* 1093).

4. Pindar *frr.* 52a-52l Maehler.

5. Cf. A.E. Housman, 'On the paeans of Pindar', *CR* 22 (1908), 8-12 = *CP* 763-9.

6. P.Oxy. III 464 ('astrological epigrams', now Anubion fr. 15 Obbink) had already attracted Housman's attention since 1903, cf. A.E. Housman, 'Oxyrhynchus Papyri, Vol. III No. 464', *CR* 17 (1903), 385-6 = *CP* 598-601.

7. Above, n. 1.

8. Cf. Lehnus 2006, 133-47. Let it be recorded here that Housman's annotated set of P.Oxy. I-XVII is preserved at Waseda University, Tokyo (Special Collections AK 4386, cf. Naiditch 2002, 65).

9. P.Oxy. 221 (= P.Lond.Lit. 178) col. iii 3 = Ammon. ad Hom. *Il.* 21.111.

10. Strab. 9.5.11 and 12, p. 434C. Cf. H. Diels, 'Ein Phrynichoscitat', *RhM* 56 (1901), 30-1.

11. On the *Tmarioi/Tomouroi* question see most recently Filoni 2008, 34-6.

12. *Pae.* 2 epode (p. 18).

13. Pind. *fr.* 52b.35 Maehler.

14. *Pae.* 6 epode (p. 20).

15. The symbol of a short was dropped (Pind. *fr.* 52f.109 Maehler).

16. *Pae.* 9 strophe (p. 22).

17. Δ[ελφ]ῶν Schol. Pind. *Pae.* 6.118b (p. 36* Radt, 304 Rutherford) thus belongs contemporarily to Housman, Ernst Diehl, and Wilamowitz.

18. Cf. Schol. T Hom. *Il.* 12.211. Hunt had only mentioned Verg. *A.* 2.319ff.

19. Bergk *PLG²* (1853) had indeed restored Pind. *fr.* 52k.7 ἱπποσόα, but the whole ἱπποσόα θοάς, as quoted by Hunt, remains Blass's, cf. Blass 1869, 387.

20. Cf. B.P. Grenfell and A.S. Hunt (edd.), *The Oxyrhynchus Papyri V* (London, 1908), 314 ('Appendix I'); for Housman's article see n. 6 above. Naiditch reminds me of *Juvenal²*, xlv: 'My notes of 1905 assigned to their authors the conjectures *eo de* in this verse [III 205] ...; and this was "editorum in usum".'

21. P.Oxy. 2080.65-9 = Call. *fr.* 43.63-7 Pf., 50.63-7 Massimilla; Housman does not seem to cast any doubt on Hunt's ἐπὶ ξ[είν]ην. Hunt would renew his thanks to Housman for P.Oxy. 2079-80 at *The Oxyrhynchus Papyri XVII* (as n. 1), 47.

22. P.Oxy. 2079.36 = Call. *fr.* 1.36 Pf./Massimilla. It appears from the following letter that '[t]he first passage' corresponds to lines 29-36 of the papyrus.

23. P.Oxy. 2079.33 = Call. *fr.* 1.33 Pf./Massimilla.

24. Respectively μὴ λοξῷ and the corrupted ἄχρι βίου in *fr.* 1.38 Pf./Massimilla and *epigr.* 21.6 Wil.

25. *Fr.* 194.27 Pf. Housman fully anticipates Kambylis 1965, 86-7 n. 55.

26. All this passage is marked with sceptical jottings in pencil by Hunt.

27. P.Lond.Lit. 181 (so-called Scholia Londinensia to the Aetia Prologue), cf. Lehnus (as n. 8 above).

28. P.Oxy. 2079.9-10 = Call. *fr.* 1.9-10 Pf./Massimilla.

29. Cf. Housman, 'Notes on Grattius', *CQ* 28 (1934), 129 = *CP* 1225-6. On καθέλκει 'outweighs' see Gargiulo 1992, 123-8.

30. P.Oxy. 2079.11-12 = Call. *fr.* 1.11-12 Pf./Massimilla.

31. In fact, Nanno must have been νάννος, as Karl Kalbfleisch observed on 17 February 1928, cf. Lehnus (as n. 8 above), 143. See also letter to Pearson of 15 October 1926.

32. Dian. 186, Del. 171.

33. P.Oxy. 2079.13-16 = Call. *fr.* 1.13-16 Pf./Massimilla.

34. Allusion to Palamedes does not seem to have appealed to anybody else besides Hunt.

35. Philostr. *Her.* 33.10-11, p. 42,7 De Lannoy.

36. ἀλεμάτω was Scaliger's. Papyrus l. 14 seemed to have ηδεμά... (ἡδομένη Pf.).

37. *Euboea* M (*Eubois* Heinsius, *Euboica* Phillimore).

38. Now Steph. Byz. α 567 Billerbeck.

39. Cf. Housman, 'On the Aetia of Callimachus', *CQ* 4 (1910), 151 = *CP* 802.

40. Dioscorid. *AP* 11.195.5-6.

41. Antip. Sid. *AP* 7.713.7.

42. P.Oxy. 2079.7-9 = Call. *fr.* 1.7-9 Pf./Massimilla.

43. Call. *fr.* 75.10 Pf.

44. At v.17.

45. P.Oxy. 2079.11 = Call. *fr.* 1.11 Pf./Massimilla, cf. Porphyr. in Hor. *Ep.* 2.2.101 *Mimnermus duos libros luculent<is uers>ibus scripsit* (quoted by Housman in the letter to Pearson).

46. P.Oxy. 2079.17-18 = Call. *fr.* 1.17-18 Pf./Massimilla.

47. V.19.

48. P.Oxy. 2079.39-40 = Call. *fr.* 1.39-40 Pf./Massimilla. Giving Housman a ὡς κύκνο]ς ἐ[πεὶ] πτερὸν οὐκέτι κινεῖν / [οἶδε, πέλει φων]ῇ τ[ῇ]μος ἐνεργότατος, Pfeiffer's apparatus is misleading: Housman's was the idea, as we now know, but the whole restoration was Hunt's. Cf. *The Oxyrhynchus Papyri XVII* (as n. 1 above), 55. ως κυκνο[σ ε[πει] ?? and φωνη]ι τ[η]μος are actually jotted by Hunt in pencil.

49. On the syntax here cf. Luppino 1958, 345-9.

50. Schol. Lond. Call. *fr.* 1.33-5 Pf./Massimilla.

51. See also letter of same day to Pearson.

52. Above, n. 36.

53. Cf. A.W. Mair (ed.), *Callimachus and Lycophron* (London, 1921 [1922]), 338.

54. Actually, he gave up, so we have to be content with what Hunt recorded and what we have here. See end of letter **11**.

55. History of the query in P.G. Naiditch, 'Housman's knowledge of Greek', *LCM* 13 (1988), 142-4, reprinted with changes and additions at Naiditch 1995, 64-7. See also Diggle 2007, 145-69.

56. Cf. W. Wimmel, 'Philetas im Aitienprolog des Kallimachos', *Hermes* 86 (1958), 346-53.

57. And immediately declared 'poss(ible)' by Hunt in pencil.

58. D'Alessio's ap. G. Massimilla, Callimaco, *Aitia: libri primo e secondo* (Pisa, 1996), 60 οἷον (same sense) is possibly to be preferred.

59. Cf. Housman, 'Notes on Bacchylides', *CR* 12 (1898), 68-74 = *CP* 442-54; Bacchylides Ode XVII', *CR* 12 (1898), 134-40 = *CP* 455-64; 'Critical Notes on Bacchylides', *CR* 12 (1898), 216-18: = *CP* 465-9; and see Diggle 2007, 162-3.

60. I am grateful to the editors for asking me to write this paper, to Dirk Obbink (Oxyrhynchus Project, Sackler Library, Oxford) and to the Society of Authors (on behalf of the Estate of A.E. Housman) for allowing me to publish the Housman letters now in the Papyrology Rooms at the Sackler Library. Permission for studying the Housman/Hunt Callimachus material there and for freely quoting from it had already been granted to me by Graham Piddock. Many a useful remark was communicated to me by David Butterfield and Paul Naiditch.

12

Classical Scholarship in Housman's Correspondence

J.H.C. Leach

The publication of a selection of A.E. Housman's letters in 1971, edited by Henry Maas, was both welcome and frustrating: for, as the editor said (xi), he had published 'about half' (actually, rather more than half) of the 1,500 or so letters which he had then traced. Thus it was even more welcome when, in 2007, Archie Burnett edited, in two substantial volumes, no fewer than 2,237 letters – certainly a very high percentage of those letters which still exist: for who knows how many have been lost or thrown away with the passing of the years? It is known, for example (1.359)[1] that the widow of Arthur Platt, one of Housman's closest friends, disposed of Housman's letters to her husband, as being too 'Rabelaisian',[2] and this is a grievous loss. And whereas volume 2, of 539 pages, covers little more than the final nine years of Housman's life, volume I, of 643 pages, takes us up to 1926, when Housman was already 67. Burnett's substantial achievement has been extensively noticed in reviews of widely, even grotesquely, varying relevance and quality; it was left to David Butterfield, in by far the most authoritative review to have appeared (2008e), to point out that what classical scholars learn from the collection is 'less exciting than one might expect ... there is disappointingly little of great interest'. But the field is not quite barren.

We shall not find any overarching scheme within the letters, since the majority of them are replies to correspondents or, in two notable cases, to reviews. Very rarely are conjectures proposed, and then only for intended publication, though here again it will be appropriate to look in detail at a few of them. Nor is the Housman of the letters the Housman of the prefaces or the poetry. The language, always precise, is only rarely wounding – though when wounding is intended, as we shall see, it is calculated to draw blood; in general, he was politer in correspondence than when considering in a paper for a learned journal the work of that same scholar. He always remains true to himself, and that self can be very prickly when he believes that he is being misrepresented or that what is *his* due has been given elsewhere.

Housman held no academic post until 1892 – if his brief period of

teaching a decade earlier at his old school Bromsgrove is excluded –
when he was already 33 years old, although he was of course by then a
noted contributor of papers to the learned journals, and had become a
member of, and speaker at, the Cambridge Philological Society from
1889.[3] Something of his tone when writing on an academic subject
around this period may be gathered from a letter to his friend A.W.
Pollard (1.66-8) of 25 October 1890: '[J.H.] Frere's translation from the
Alcestis is very charming although a good deal of it is out of his own
head. [Prof. Lewis] Campbell apparently does me the honour to admire
everything I write ... though I wish that both he and [E.D.A.] Morshead
would not add so many beauties of their own to those of their author.'
The author in question is Sophocles; and we shall see in due course that
Campbell's admiration had its limits. Housman himself had also made
translations for Pollard from Aeschylus, Sophocles and Euripides.[4]

Letters from this relatively early period are not many, and discussion
of one of them will be deferred until later. In October 1891, the gist of a
short and somewhat grudging letter to Robinson Ellis (1.71), in reply to
two notably helpful letters from him, is to correct an error in his report
of a manuscript: Housman's contemptuous opinion of Ellis is too well
known to need repetition. In defiance of chronology, it is worth
mentioning a much later and less austere letter of April 1919 to J.S.
Phillimore (1.405) – of whose edition of Propertius (1901, 1907[2])
Housman held no high opinion (2.265)[5] – about Mart. 12.59.8:
'*pediculosi* got into the text in the 16th century and stuck there more
than 300 years, the creature being notoriously hard to dislodge': the
correct reading is *periculosi* – though *pediculosi* is given in Lewis and
Short ad loc., and will adhere there, unless that work is ever revised.
Incidentally, a noticeable feature, doubtless deliberate, of his few letters
to the much younger H.W. Garrod – also an editor of Manilius – is its
formality of address ('Dear Sir' or 'Mr'), at a time when the simple
surname was Housman's normal practice.

It is thus that he invariably addresses H.E. Butler, his successor as
Professor of Latin at UCL, in correspondence which touches on matters
classical from time to time: thus Prop. 4.1.124 appears twice to have
perplexed Butler (2.164, 193) in 1930. The line, in S.J. Heyworth's OCT
(2007), reads *et lacus aestiuis intepet Vmber aquis*. Housman had
conjectured *non tepet* after L. Müller's *iam tepet* and Butler, in his
edition with E.A. Barber of 1933, read *agris* for *aquis*.[6] In the first of
those letters, Housman makes a pretty point: 'As what happens when *es*
follows a vowel is aphaeresis rather than elision, it would be logical for
the vowel to retain its quantity;[7] and a long vowel does so in anth. Lat.
Ries. 462 28 impius hoc *telo es*, *hoc* potes esse pius. The poem is a very
correct piece of verse, of the 1st cent. after Christ at the latest I should
say, and possibly Seneca's.' However, the relatively cordial tone of the
(relatively frequent) correspondence is not matched in Housman's

severe reviews of H.E. Butler's first edition of 1905,[8] and its revision with Barber in 1933.[9]

Naiditch not unjustly writes (1988, 170) '[i]n comparison [sc. with Greek scholars] Housman's relations with British Latinists were far more formal and restrained': he cites (169) Housman's friendships with Platt, Henry Jackson, 'perhaps Walter Ashburner [who was, however, mainly a Jurisprudent], and, latterly, Andrew Gow'. In support of Naiditch, one might adduce the fact that the Letters do not, as it happens, include even one to Housman's near coeval and contemporary as Corpus Professor of Latin at Oxford, A.C. Clark, although Housman admits to having 'molest[ed]' him – doubtless for information on given manuscripts – in a letter to F.W. Hall of 1930 (2.173).

The quality of Housman's scholarship is of course seen in the most spectacular manner in the corrections which he made to a wide range of texts. But there is much more to it than that, as is apparent not only in the introductions and commentaries in his editions of Manilius, Juvenal and Lucan, as well as in his many contributions to classical journals, but in the way in which he replied to queries, demonstrating his mastery of an extraordinary breadth of reading allied to an enviably retentive memory. Thus, when the first volume of Housman's Manilius was published in 1903, he sent a copy to his coeval and friend J.W. Mackail. That was in late June; Mackail's duties with the education department of the Privy Council – which by 1903 had become the Board of Education – can hardly have been unduly demanding, since the queries which he sent to Housman, and to which the latter replied (1.151-3) before the end of July, implied a rapid and careful study of the work (a fact acknowledged in Housman's reply). Just two instances call for attention here. First, it is clear that Mackail had questioned Housman's emendation at line 88:

> et uagus in caecum penetrauit nauita pontum
> fecit et ignotis *linter* commercia terris,   (1.87-8)

where the mss read variously *itiner*, *inter*, or *iter in*. Housman's reply first seems to deal with a point to which we no longer have access, though it is possible that Mackail had conjectured the univerbation *intercommercia*, a *uox nihili*: Housman states that he knows of no Latin word where *inter* is followed by a preposition and goes on to remark, '[t]he first ship might naturally be supposed to be a *linter*, a hollowed trunk' (cf. the definition at *CGL* II 125,17, cited by Housman in the Addenda to vol. I at *Man.* V, 120: '*linter* εἶδος μονοξύλου πλοίου πρωτοκατασκεύαστον'). The proposed wording is lengthily defended in the note *ad loc.* on palaeographical grounds and because of 'horum locorum similitudo'. But it is not compelling: the sentence has an adequate subject in *nauita*, and the standard reading *iter in* is perfectly acceptable – as Housman, again ad loc., admits. In his *editio minor* of 1932 *linter* is relegated to the apparatus criticus, as it is in G.P. Goold's Teubner (1985); it does not even earn a mention in the same editor's Loeb edition (1977a); of classical scholars, perhaps only H.W. Garrod[10] and J.S. Phillimore[11] have accepted it. (One is reminded of a distinctly similar proposed palaeographical change in Martial 14.217.2 (*CP* 738-9), where Housman wished to change the *decipit et* of the mss to *accipiter*:[12] neat and perfectly relevant, but not accepted by Shackleton Bailey 1993.)

The second case, at line 825, is both more interesting and more difficult:

> in breue uiuit opus, *coeptus*que incendia fine
> subsistunt pariterque cadunt fulgentque cometae.   (1.825-6)

coeptus is Housman's correction of the mss' *coepta* or *coepto*. Mackail had clearly suggested that *coepta* (or possibly some other – but irrecoverable – participle) was an ablative but Housman disposes of that idea, and since he does not repeat the actual word proposed by Mackail, it cannot have seemed at all plausible to him: but his doubts are understandable. In Housman's note ad loc. improbable proposals by Scaliger, Pingraeus (A.G. Pingré, whose 'correction' is unmetrical) and Bechert are summarily dealt with; and Bentley's typically bold *citraque incendia limen* receives only 'Bentleius translatione minime apta'. The sense is indeed clear enough: Goold 1977a accepts the conjecture and renders 'the fires last no longer than the moment of their beginning'. Housman's note could hardly be clearer: he writes 'coeptus fine subsistunt, ultra inceptionem non progrediuntur', leaving *incendia* to be understood. *Coeptus* as a fourth-declension noun is rare but is found at e.g. Stat. *Theb.* 12.644 – and wins the acceptance of Madvig at Cic. *Fin.* 4.41 and Dyck (*inter alios*) at Cic. *Cat.* 1.6: thus the way to extract sense from the lines is to take *coeptus* as a genitive, i.e. *incendia sub fine coeptus sistunt*. Housman's *editio minor* retains the correction (and the Addenda to the Book in *Man.* V do little more here than offer a jibe at Breiter's Latinity and, by extension, the *TLL*).[13] One rather admires Mackail, who had departed from his fellowship at Balliol some nine years earlier, for his assiduity and (occasional) acuity; and where so many critics of distinction have paused and stumbled, it is perhaps with a degree of ruefulness that one accepts that nothing better than Housman's correction has been found or is likely to be found.

Publication in 1912 of Book 2 of Manilius, when Housman again sent a presentation copy to Mackail, elicited another letter from him, to which Housman replied on 22 May (1.291-3), mainly dealing with points of Latinity. One item deserves to be given in full: '891. *que* is not attached to words ending in *c* by poets earlier than the 4th century

(Madvig Cic. de fin. V 40, Haupt opusc. III pp. 508-10): the exception, Ouid. fast. IV 848, is one of those which prove rules. *huice* is not used in the classical period at all.' Just so: and it is typical of Housman that he does not quote the line from Ovid, which runs *'sic'que 'meos muros transeat hostis' ait*. Platnauer (1951, 93), perhaps misses the point when he records 'sicque' (so printed) as one of several cases where Ovid's 'ear did not rebel against sounds which seem cacophonous to modern taste'. But the pause implied by the inverted commas after *sic* reduces any cacophony; the ever-ingenious Ovid knew what he was doing; and cf. *Tr.* 4.2.51-2 *'io'que ... canet* for similar use of the device).

Publication of Housman's third volume in 1916 drew a letter from Mackail to which Housman replied only briefly (1.361), defending his adoption of Bentley's *curret* at 361 against the *currit* of the mss, 'not for equality but for sense, as in 333' (where the future *ducentur* is also a conjecture). Both conjectures appear in the *editio minor* and are accepted by Goold in both his editions. Mackail appears not to have written to Housman when the fourth volume appeared in 1920, but Housman replied to his letter of 'approbation ... congratulation and condolence' when the fifth volume was published in 1930, by which year Mackail had himself passed his seventieth birthday, although he lived until 1945.

Gilbert Murray's tenure of the Regius Professorship of Greek at Oxford from 1908 to 1936 was almost coterminous with Housman's tenure of the Latin Chair at Cambridge. The letters to Murray (which include intermittent attempts at persuading Murray to accompany him to a music-hall)[14] are often written in a more light-hearted manner than is customary with him. Yet one wonders how comfortable the two, both alumni (and Honorary Fellows, elected at the same time in 1911) of St John's College, Oxford, but very different characters, were with one another.[15] It is certainly a pity that no letter from Murray to Housman survives. But we may gather one of the reasons why Housman preferred to concentrate on Latin when we read (1.168) of his telling Murray in 1904 that 'Attic tragedy has been studied so long and so minutely by such great men that all the corrections which consist in iteration of syllables, or separation of letters or the like, must almost necessarily have been made already.' (Professor E.R. Dodds was some five decades later known to have held a similarly pessimistic opinion about the prospect of successfully emending the tragedians,[16] though the view is certainly not universally shared.) Perhaps more familiarly and tellingly, though, A.S.F. Gow (1936a, 15) reports Housman as having said that he 'found [he] could not attain to excellence in both [sc. Latin and Greek]'. In the same letter of 1904, Housman goes on to praise Verrall's conjecture at Hor. *S.* 1.9.39 of *(i)sta re* for the transmitted *stare*, calling Lachmann to his aid: and it is indeed attractive, though it has found little favour. Other letters to Murray are few and inconsequential, although we glimpse a familiar aspect of Housman when he congratulates Murray in 1908 upon his election to the Regius Chair (1.226-7): 'since you are a much better scholar than the one [= Jowett] and a much better man of letters than the other [= Jebb], the public will be a gainer without knowing it, and good judges (by which I mean myself) will be less at variance with the public': hardly words to delight the recipient.

A much more frequent correspondent was J.D. Duff (of whose edition of Juvenal (1898) Housman approved).[17] In 1905 (1.180), Housman mildly chides Duff for not accepting his own (Duff's) correction of Mart. 9.3.14 in his edition of the poet for Postgate's *Corpus Poetarum Latinorum* (1905²), i.e. *quo* for *quod* (which Shackleton Bailey accepts). He adds, 'I suppose I shall be driven to edit Martial myself': that of course did not happen, but a long paper of exceptional quality appeared in 1907 (*CP* 711-39), followed up by a short note (*CP* 770) and preceded by a paper of 1901 (*CP* 536-8) which includes his certain restoration of the last line of *Spect.* 24 (XXI in Housman's paper): *haec tantum res est facta* παρ' ἱστορίαν.

Most of Housman's correspondence with Duff was in connection with the latter's Loeb translation of the *Punica* of Silius Italicus (1934). This work was dedicated to Housman and W.T. Vesey (a fellow of Gonville and Caius) and bore a note of gratitude to them in the Foreword. Silius was by no means a poet to whom Housman had paid much attention in print, though his extant copies of Bauer's Silius and the text in Walker's *Corpus Poetarum Latinorum* (London, 1875) have been closely worked through, and contain emendations throughout: the *Classical Papers* can show just one note, on *Pun.* 13.800, included in a paper on Ovid (*CP* 906). His numerous replies to Duff are as authoritative as ever – and invariably accepted. However, in only a few of them are textual matters discussed. At *Pun.* 1.373 Duff seems to have supported *certatim*, which has manuscript authority (but is the *lectio difficilior*), for the favoured *certantum*, also transmitted. The passage reads:

> surgebat cumulo certantum prorutus agger,
> obstabatque iacens uallum, ni protinus instent
> hinc atque hinc acies media pugnare ruina.   (1.373-5)

Duff accepts Housman's assertion (2.315) that '*certatim* with *prorutus* would be foolishly irrelevant ... it must mean each part of the debris tried to rise higher than the rest', and obelises *cumulo certantum* as seeming 'to be corrupt'. Possibly so, though the conceit in a Silver Latin author is not impossible: and *certatim* need mean little more than 'strenuously', as at Verg. *A.* 5.778 (*certatim socii feriunt mare, et aequora uerrunt*), where the idea of competition would be ludicrous. In the latest edition of Silius (Delz 1987), *certatim* is preferred. Again, at the puzzling lines[18] *Pun.* 1.70-1, Housman (2.342) writes to Duff: 'I have got in my margin *laudem puero patrius furor ausus*', where Bauer, in his Teubner (1890), had preferred a *variorum* version: *addiderat tantam* [sc. *rabiem* from the preceding line] *puero patris heu furor altus*.

Duff prints Housman's suggestion (on which he does not enlarge), but the hexameter close of two disyllables combined with the absence of diaeresis after the fourth foot is deeply unappealing, and indeed unique in Silius (it is perhaps mitigated in Bauer's case by his *heu*); in a line such as *Pun.* 1.60 (*sanguinis humani flagrat sitis. his super, aeui*) the rhythm is altogether superior, with diaeresis and sense pause after the dactylic fourth foot (i.e. the bucolic diaeresis), while *his super* functions as a metrical unit. Since Housman was perfectly well aware of all this, it is perhaps not surprising that he never expanded on his marginal jotting; perhaps just one of 'the mere guesses which we all jot down in our margins simply to help us take up the thread of thought tomorrow where we drop it today' (quoted at Gow 1936a, 23, but without reference (= *CP* 46)). As it happens, the 'jotting' printed by Duff was by no means Housman's only attempt to rectify the line, and one such had the metrically perfect *puero patriis furor ossibus ortus*, with its attractive echo of Vergil (*A.* 4.625, *exoriare aliquis nostris ex ossibus ultor*). However, Delz does no better, offering *laudem puero patrius furor. ortus* [sc. *Hamilcar*], a reading not without problems on grounds of poetical practice, since there is usually a valid and particular reason for such a strong pause at that place in the hexameter, as at (say) Verg. *A.* 5.633 or 12.526.[19]

At *Pun.* 14.391 Housman commends (2.368) J.H. Withof's reading: *intraret fluctus solis quasi pulsa lacertis*; this is perhaps unremarkable, were it not for the fact that the proposal is made in *Kritische Anmerkungen über Horaz und andere Römische Schriftsteller* (Dusseldorf, 1791-1802). Housman's good opinion of Duff receives confirmation from his letter to his brother Laurence (1.595) of 18 August 1925, in which he writes that, if he should die while on holiday in France, Duff should be asked to finish the Lucan, and see it through the press.

Inevitably, in almost all cases, we see only one side of the correspondence. Not so, however, when Housman replies (2.267-8) to Hugh Stewart's long and meticulous review (*CR* 45 (1931), 183-9) of *Man.* V. It would be too much to suggest that a note of petulance occasionally creeps into Housman's response, but when he writes, '[y]ou say that no parallel is adduced for *ora frontis*. That phrase is not in my text [sc. at 450-1]', and one turns to the edition to read '*facit ora seuerae / frontis is ac uultus componit pondere mentis*', it does seem rather hard on Stewart. Even more haughty is his comment on 114: Stewart had not favoured Housman's *uincunt* for *uictum*, to which Housman retorts that he would listen to Scaliger or Bentley telling him that *uincunt* was no improvement, but 'when one of you gentlemen says it ... he ought to be more modest'. Elsewhere, he accepts eighteen of Stewart's corrections, 'some of which I had already made, together with a larger number which you do not mention'. At least he expresses gratitude for Stewart's noting the error *totamque* at 385, and the *editio minor* duly reads *totamue*. Finally, Housman's *uix una trium* at 461 – essentially an 'anagrammatic' conjecture based on the transposition of letters, one of Housman's favourite (particularly in his earlier work) and often successful techniques – is described by Stewart as 'bordering on the grotesque', survives into the *editio minor*. It vanishes without trace, however, in Goold's revised Loeb edition (1997), where *uix una trium* has become (influenced by Watt 1994) Bentley's *uiui bustum* (cf. Lucr. 5.993). This instance is noteworthy for two reasons, first because it is one of his three conjectures in Manilius which he 'judge[d] to be quite certain' (*Man.* V, xxxiv)[20] and secondly because Goold follows Housman far more often than not (see Goold 1977a, viii-ix). With some grace, however, Housman prefaces his letter to Stewart by paying a tribute 'not only of gratitude but of admiration and almost of awe' for his 'care, patience and altruism'.

Housman's interest and distinction in Greek was notable (even if it hardly seemed so to Jebb, a fact emphasised by Naiditch (1988, 178), who says of Jebb's treatment of Housman's work on Sophocles, '[h]e acted as if [Housman's articles] had not been published'). When the beautifully written papyrus of Bacchylides was first edited by Kenyon in 1897, it aroused what can only be called a 'feeding frenzy' among scholars. Of course, Housman was among them, working, it seems, largely in collaboration with his friend at University College, Arthur Platt, the Professor of Greek since 1894.[21] James Diggle (2007, 162) lists the numbers of his supplements or corrections (made independently or jointly) that have been accepted or reported: to his (maximum) fifteen, I add only that Campbell's Loeb (1992) cites sixteen. This hardly matters, and here it is only a totally neglected conjecture that nonetheless illustrates Housman's methods, which calls for attention. Housman wrote to the weekly journal the *Athenaeum* in December 1897 offering a number of supplements, including, at 17.88, κατουρον (without an accent, though the accented form appears in the margin of his copy of Kenyon's edition). What he had in mind became clear only in his papers on Bacchylides of 1898 (*CP* 455-69). What is happening in this passsage? Minos, sailing to Crete with youths and maidens on board, laid hands on Eriboea, who called on Theseus for help. Following a challenge from Minos, Theseus leapt into the sea. Housman argues that Minos now ordered the ship, which was running before the wind (κάτουρον), to halt (ἴσχειν), but 'fate ordained another course (ὁδόν)' and sent the ship on its way. Jebb (1905) objected to Housman's κάτουρον, saying that it could not be made to mean the same as τὴν κατ' οὖρον πλέουσαν (true enough in a prose writer); ἴσχειν meant 'direct' (the ship before the wind, κατ' οὖρον), and ὁδόν, says Jebb, means 'issue', although we are in a context of journeying on a sea voyage. To be sure, ὁδός can be used figuratively ('course of action/life'), as at Pindar *O.* 8.13, πολλαὶ ὁδοὶ εὐπραγίας and elsewhere, but, as Housman saw, when it appears *tout court* as here, that is not its natural or expected meaning; and a lyric poet is unlikely to write (he might have added) like Xenophon.

Although Housman's interpretation has been universally rejected, it shows his willingness to approach a text in an entirely logical way. Maehler (2004) translates ὁδόν as the 'path (of events)', Campbell (1992) as simply 'course': have they faced the difficulty? Did Jebb? Because, in effect, they all have the ship sailing along, taking a *different* ὁδός – and then continuing to sail along.

One may feel that Jebb would have been in any event unlikely to respond favourably to a view from Housman so markedly divergent from his own. The two scholars had already clashed over Bacchylides, with Jebb responding to Housman's provocation in a manner both unworthy and, in the main, incorrect (cf. Naiditch 1988, 180-5, for a frankly entertaining account, with a characteristic wealth of detail), though it is only fair to add that in his edition Jebb accepts (according to Naiditch) 'nearly a score' of Housman's proposals, and makes reference to 28 more). At this time Housman was Professor of Latin at UCL but his suggestions in Bacchylides mean that he can be counted, along with Kenyon, Jebb, Blass, and Wilamowitz, as one of the main contributors to the establishment of the text. Incidentally, it is certain (Naiditch 1988, 180) that Jebb was given a considerable 'head start' by Kenyon, who showed him the proofs of his book. Housman was later to make important contributions to the papyrus texts of Pindar, Callimachus and (to a markedly lesser extent) Menander, where he found himself anticipated by Leo and Wilamowitz.

Housman once referred to those 'minute and pedantic studies' (1.586) in which he was fitted to excel, and matters of orthography and related topics recur frequently in the correspondence. In 1934 he sent a long Latin letter in response to the youthful Otto Skutsch (2.425-7) concerning the Latinisation of Greek names, notably as to whether, say, Achilles in Latin fell into the third or fifth declension (with particular reference to Prop. 2.9.13), and at what times (and for what reasons) changes occurred. In the same year he tells A.B. Ramsay (2.418) that *bellum* and *uellum* are merely correct and incorrect spellings of the same word, and that *b* and *u* are interchanged in inscriptions of the second century A.D. (Ramsay had been enquiring about Lucr. 4.968 at the prompting of a letter from his past pupil at Eton, N.H. Romanes, but the same problem arises at 5.1245 and 1289, and elsewhere); he might well have added as a further example of the pronunciation error his own necessary correction of *repleuit* to *replebit* at Man. 1.799. The draft of a long and detailed letter of 1928 to the youthful Ulrich Knoche (2.90-2) in response to an article that Knoche (1928) had sent him, among much else, sternly admonishes the recipient that '*tantum* is not "hinter das dadurch hervorgehobene Wort"' (literally, 'after the word stressed by it') at seven listed places in Juvenal, that *hi* rather than *qui* is the more difficult reading ('die schwierigere Lesart') at 2.45, and that a confusion ('Verwechslung') of *e* and *F* would be more probable in uncial script; in this instance he adds that Lachmann had been in error at Lucr. 1.830, where he had written 'ex quo intelligi potest quonam scripturae genere exaratum fuerit exemplar archetypon', i.e. 'litteris capitalibus'.[22] And we see the typical Housman when he says: 'You report me as saying the opposite of what I said. I said that both *Antigones* and *Melanippes* belonged to *personam* (at Iuu. VIII.229). Buecheler saw that Antigone could not be joined to Thyestes and separated from Melanippe, but he did not see that *personam* could be taken ἀπὸ κοινοῦ. Here I add that you do not report me accurately (on pp. 354 and 355). *Seu* may very well be true; but in what you say about palaeographische Wahrscheinlichkeit[23] you forget that your reading is not *antigonesen* but *antigonessen*; and your reference to XI.28 is altogether irrelevant.'

Three letters to Friedrich Vollmer (1.226, 231, 235) of 1908 and 1909 are courteously worded and are of sufficient interest to send one for purpose of comparison with his review (*CP* 88-9) in 1908 of Vollmer's edition of Horace (1907). Censure there, to be sure, is not lacking; but he also has this to say: 'Energy and industry [Vollmer] never lacked, and these virtues, now that he employs them on the work of thinking, have made him a considerable scholar, though hardly yet a critic and certainly not a metrist ... As to criticism, freedom of judgment is half the battle, and Mr Vollmer has now outgrown the prejudices of the vulgar and released himself from the dogmas of a sect.' (Despite the *de haut en bas* tone of this, Vollmer, it should be said, was only eight years younger than Housman.) The courtesy of the letters, be it added, is not matched by the tone and content of Housman's fairly frequent and severe criticisms of Vollmer's work appearing throughout the *Classical Papers*: 585 (on the *Ciris*) is only one notable example.

In his Latin letter to Eduard Fraenkel of 1925 (1.627-8), following his long and highly favourable review of Housman's Lucan, there is much more carping than gratitude: 'reprehensionum ... ne unam quidem iustam esse agnosco, nisi quod recte interpungis IX 491.'[24] (One may feel that Housman's meticulous devotion to giving the correct ascription of suggested emendations – even to his own disadvantage, as at *CP* 465, where he gives up 'ownership' of four conjectures in Bacchylides – just as he repeatedly makes reference to places where emendations have been later confirmed by the discovery or collation of manuscripts (see the list in Naiditch 1988, 179) is cut from the same cloth.)

And if he is less than gracious to Fraenkel, one can hardly say he is much more so in writing – complaining, rather – to Professor D.S. Robertson, his Cambridge colleague in the Regius Chair of Greek, in 1931 (2.260-1) about the 'additional work' which he was being called on to carry out in Plautus: worth noting because 'the students will require so much preliminary matter ... about rival theories of Ueberlieferungsgeschichte', i.e. the history of textual transmission, notoriously one of Housman's favourite objects of scorn, and famously described by him in his *Lucan* (xiii), as 'a longer and nobler name than fudge'. The letter continues with a snipe at W.M. Lindsay's work on Plautine metre,[25] (concerning which Fraenkel himself was markedly less severe),[26] referring primarily to the matter of 'Iambenkürzung', nowadays perhaps more familiar as the *lex breuis breuians*.

Here it should be noted, as is indeed well known, that Housman's interest in metre was no less keen and no less informed than in matters of orthography, although the subject comes up only occasionally in the correspondence and then only when he is the object of an enquiry. Thus in 1916 he writes to A.S.F. Gow (1.355-6) about the ending *–it* in the perfect ('originally long in the 4th as in the other conjugations, and remains so in Plautus; but by Virgil's time it had become short in the regular verbs'): he refers to Lachmann (1850) on Lucr. 3.1042, adding that the 'only material addition that I find in my margin is Stat. Theb. XII 396, *te cupiit unam*', i.e. with lengthening of the *-it* of *cupiit*. This might hardly seem worth mentioning, were it not for Housman's continuation: 'which may seem to show natural length, as Statius does not elsewhere allow artificial lengthening except at the caesura in the 3rd foot'. (The line in question runs, *te cupiit unam noctesque diesque locutus*; the inferior mss read *cupiens*.) Platnauer (1951, 59-61) has relevant detail on vowel lengthening, and, as is useful for his purpose, points out that Housman had shown (*CQ* 21 (1927), 2-12 = *CP* 1114-26) that five places in the elegists which showed a lengthened naturally short *-a* at the main caesura all needed correction; the article in question, 'Prosody and Method [I]', discusses much but the lengthening of *-it* is not relevant to his discussion.

Housman responded with exemplary completeness to the intermittent enquiries concerning astronomical or astrological matters which he received from correspondents: some fifteen appear in the Letters, including a reply of considerable length and detail to Dr Frank R. Robbins (2.409-12) on the Michigan Astrological Papyrus. We know also that he assisted the editors of Liddell and Scott on these matters (2.228, n. 1), while he himself put what can hardly have been an easy question to Dr P.H Cowell of the Nautical Almanac Office (1.543-4) concerning the zodiacal situation of the planets on 'XVI kal. Febr. A.U.C. 705', or 28 November 50 BC in the reformed calendar; Cowell's replies to Housman's various queries allow him to have fun at the expense of Lucan's ignorance (cf. 1926, 325-7). Again, in a letter of 1899 to P.G.L. Webb (1.116), his knowledge of astronomy allows him incidentally to correct *binos* (twice a year) to *bimos* (once every two years) in Germanicus' *Prognostica*: the point at issue is the orbit of Mars round the sun. The answer to a numismatic question raised with G.F. Hill (1.144) allows Housman to posit that Libra was the natal star of Tiberius (*Man.* I, lxx-lxxi; in a footnote on the latter page he recommends 'chronologers and numismatists to study astrology before they write about it', adding three unfortunate examples).[27] Nor did he disdain writing, in 1924, to *The Times* (when that newspaper still concerned itself about such matters) to show (1.571-2) that a quotation could not be from Livy, but was in fact from Sulpicius Severus, as could be observed (from a photograph in vol. XXXII of the *Memoires de l'Institut National de France* (*Academie des Inscriptions*) of 1884) in a ninth-century manuscript held at Quedlinburg. Housman is rarely so at a loss as to seek help; but faced with a new papyrus of Callimachus in 1926, he writes twice to A.C. Pearson on a point of Greek: but his tentative supplements did not appear in the relevant volume of *The Oxyrhynchus Papyri* (XVII, 1927).[28] This is perhaps the only place, other than those mentioned above, where Housman actively sought help in the surviving correspondence: for what the cause was of his 'molesting' Clark is regrettably unknown.

There was another side, all too familiar, to Housman. He still held no academic post when he wrote two letters in March 1891 to the editor of the *Academy* (1.69-71), concerning a fragment of a lost play of Euripides, the *Antiope*, identified in the Flinders Petrie papyri. In one case, where W.G. Rutherford, in a less than fortunate phrase, proposed a supplement[29] which 'would restore' an iambic trimeter (l. 89 Diggle) to Euripides, Housman, unable to resist a gibe, wrote that it was a senarius 'which Euripides, I think, would restore to Dr. Rutherford' (although Housman uses the term 'senarius', that word is more commonly applicable to Latin). However, the line (as given in Page 1941, I 68) is indeed sadly defective: σὺ μὲν [......]υτο πνεῦμα πολεμίων λαβών, and the somewhat revised text in Diggle 1998, l 89, offers little by way of advance, while (as it happens) just possibly helping Rutherford: σὺ μὲν....το....μ. πολεμίων λαβών.

Housman goes on to criticise Lewis Campbell (Professor of Greek at the University of St Andrews) for allowing a trimeter obviously defective in both metre and grammar to slip through, and here again the victim had made himself a target by writing (*CR* 5 (1891), 125) 'when the guesses have been heaped together, and it is known where they will jump, it will be time to cease from guessing and to begin the sober work of criticism'. Accordingly, Housman wrote that he would perform a 'menial office [sc. of correcting the line], at the risk of incurring Prof. Campbell's censure for premature sobriety'. Campbell imprudently returned to the fray, by arguing that a correction might be 'too much a matter of course to be worth mentioning', and received a blast from Housman on the subject of inaccurate accentuation, who went on: 'The further fragments of Prof. Campbell's Antiope (a drama which I much admire and hope to see completed) ... have been slightly corrupted by the scribes': a few trivial corrections ensue. Under the circumstances, one can only admire Campbell's magnanimity in supporting Housman's application for a Professorship at UCL in the following year. To close this story, Naiditch (1988, 212-13) quotes two disobliging comments by Campbell on Housman dating from the previous year, and suggests (237) that these had 'irked' Housman. As Campbell had written in one of his comments, '[h]ere Mr. Housman again acts the jackal to Dr. Verrall' (*CR* 4 (1890), 301), Naiditch's supposition seems far from unlikely.

After these disobliging words, it is only proper to quote from Housman's commendation of Eduard Fraenkel in 1934 to the Electors to the Corpus Professorship of Latin at Oxford (2.448): 'Dr. Fraenkel is a Latinist of European repute, who won celebrity in 1922 by his *Plautinisches im Plautus*, a work of notable industry, grasp, and originality, which revealed him as a writer of high qualifications both in scholarship and in literature and has exerted a powerful influence on the subsequent course of Plautine study.' Housman had hoped that Fraenkel would succeed him at Cambridge, and what he wrote then about Fraenkel has stood the test of time.[30]

Perhaps, however disappointingly, it will be accepted that Housman's correspondence yields rather little about the scholar that is new. The sword, too, is for the most part kept in the scabbard (so that it is somewhat unexpected when he refers, in a letter to Vollmer mentioned above (1.226), to 'the disorderly and untrustworthy production of Ellis': the reference is to Ellis' edition, which had just appeared, of the *appendix Vergiliana*; not that – as previously stated – Housman was any kinder about Vollmer's work on the *Ciris*). Again, it is a feature of this substantial body of correspondence that, although Housman is found relatively frequently to be answering, with exemplary care, questions from his interlocutors, he himself initiates correspondence only rarely: letters to the *Athenaeum* propounding suggestions in Callimachus are in a different category, for he was seeking priority of attribution. To be sure, there is the implication, as already noted, that he wrote to Clark at Oxford more than once, and since he uses the word 'molested', the implication is that he was seeking information: but nothing survives. He does, as we have also noted, from time to time apply to specialists for expert advice in areas where he could not claim expert knowledge, and that too does not surprise, for he mistrusted those who laid claim to polymathy; as he observed elsewhere, '[Friedrich] Wolf, like all pretenders to encyclopaedic knowledge, had a

241

dash of the impostor about him.'[31] If one may, however tentatively, draw a conclusion, it is that Housman was a scholar so confident in his own abilities that he felt no need to rely upon others, a conclusion which his publications wholeheartedly support. It is perhaps a corollary of this that he scarcely ever, in these two volumes, commends an emendation from a correspondent: Duff's correction (mentioned above) of Mart. 9.9.14 is an exception, and he approved (2.377) of a suggestion in Plato (*Rep.* 369d) by R.W. Chapman, the Secretary to the Delegates of OUP.

One reviewer of these admirably edited volumes (*HSJ* 33 (2007), 104-9) wrote of Housman's 'mordant frustration with his lot', his denial that 'he is a scholar of the first rank', who is living 'for work he confesses is of little or no merit' (presumably here confusing the quality of the poetry of Manilius with that of the work of his editor). These statements are as close to the opposite of the truth as makes no matter. For these volumes confirm, time and time again, as do the justly acclaimed editions of his chosen poets, that he was indeed both supremely suited for, and deeply engaged with his task, and that – as he confidently believed – the quality of his scholarship will long endure. For Housman accuracy was notoriously a duty, not a virtue, and we can see that in his letters, as in his editions and his contributions to classical journals, he constantly sought the truth. If that truth might prove unpalatable to the recipient, so be it.

Notes

1. Bare numerical references are to Burnett 2007 by volume and page.
2. See Maas 1971, 144.
3. Naiditch 1988, 76.
4. Published in Pollard 1890, 15, 85-7, 109-11, and most conveniently found in Burnett 1997, 165-8.
5. One need merely cite the couplet that Housman has added to the title-page of his copy: '*quae, Philomore, fui carmen iuuenile Properti / Cynthia, nunc crimen sum iuuenile tuum*' (cited also in Heyworth's chapter).
6. Butler had retained the paradosis in his previous edition of, and commentary on, Propertius (1905).
7. The reference is almost certainly to 2.21.7 and whether *te* could be omitted (it is retained by Heyworth).
8. *CP* 630-6.
9. *CP* 1234-8.
10. Garrod 1912, 209.
11. Phillimore 1925, 2.
12. It is evident from marginalia in his copy of Friedlaender's edition (Leipzig, 1886, preserved at St John's College, Oxford) and Lindsay's 1903 OCT (preserved at Merton College, Oxford) that his first proposal was to read *deiecit*, which he subsequently rejected for *accipiter*.
13. Compare the remarks of Courtney in his chapter.
14. Cf., e.g., 1.221.

15. The chapter by Malcolm Davies in Stray 2007, 167-78, provides more detail.

16. In conversation with the present writer.

17. *Juvenal*, xxix.

18. In Duff 1934 they read (from a variety of manuscript and editorial choices): *hanc rabiem in fines Italum Saturniaque arua / addiderat laudem puero patrius furor orsus.*

19. If the line is not to be obelised, David Butterfield attractively suggests *addiderant tantam puero patris usque furores*, which provides good sense and restores metrical propriety: the corruption would have arisen from mistaken contraction of *patris usq;* to *patrius*, with *-q[ue]* added at verse end (leading in turn by misdivision to the transmitted nonsense *furor escus / oscus*).

20. For further discussion see Courtney's chapter.

21. For further discussion of this episode see Stray's chapter.

22. Misprinted in Burnett.

23. Misprinted in Burnett.

24. The letter is cited in full in Oakley's chapter.

25. Burnett's note here implies that Housman was referring to Lindsay's *Early Latin Verse* (Oxford, 1922), but the large metrical introduction to the same scholar's edition of Plautus' *Captiui* (London, 1900) is, in the context, more likely. For Housman's notes in this volume, see Butterfield on Housman and Lindsay, n. 106.

26. Based upon remarks at one of Fraenkel's seminars upon Plautus attended by the present writer. Fraenkel favoured Lindsay's Introduction to *Captiui* (see previous note) over the same author's *Early Latin Verse*, in which, however, Lindsay had written (viii-ix) less than courteously (and quite possibly unfairly, cf. Naiditch 1995, 78-9) about Fraenkel's greatly admired Leo.

27. Housman later changed his mind: see his n. ad Man. 4.548-52; cf. Shackleton Bailey 1997, 397-8, n. 3.

28. For further evidence about Housman's involvement with the editing of *The Oxyrhynchus Papyri* see Lehnus' chapter.

29. σὺ μὲν χερῶν τὸ πνεῦμ' ἐκ πολεμίων λαβών.

30. For further discussion of the relationship between Housman and Fraenkel see Oakley's chapter.

31. *Man.* I, xvi n. 1.

Part III

HOUSMAN'S LEGACY

13

Lessons Learned from a Master

G. Luck

I was introduced to the scholarship of A.E. Housman by Shackleton Bailey about fifty years ago, first through his *Propertiana* (1957), which I read with enthusiasm right after their publication and later, after I had met Shackleton personally, in our conversations during long walks in England and Switzerland, when I began to realise who Housman was and what he meant to my friend in whom I saw the heir of a great legacy. These were eye-opening experiences. Before reading *Propertiana*, I had tried to avoid textual criticism, but now I became very interested.

At the time (1955-8) I was at Harvard, working on Ovid's *Tristia*, a text whose manuscript tradition, as Housman himself pointed out, was not very good and whose editors had not done all one could desire (also Housman's complaint). Later, when I prepared my own edition of the *Tristia* (1967-77), I was fortunate to have the generous help of E.J. Kenney.[1]

Today, we can extract many of Housman's contributions to scholarship from the *Classical Papers*, edited by J. Diggle and F.R.D. Goodyear.[2] Frank was another friend whose approval and encouragement meant a great deal to me, and it is very sad that we lost him so early. In addition to those three volumes, one can consult Housman's editions, his letters[3] and the books written about him. On the whole, a fairly clear and coherent image emerges, though he was obviously not a man without contradictions.

In this acknowledgment of my own debt to him, I will first try to put down a few more general ideas and then show to what extent I have followed him, not only as a critic and editor, but also as a maker of conjectures. One has to separate these two aspects, I think. There are competent editors who never make a conjecture, perhaps because they feel that none is necessary in their texts, or else because they have no confidence in their own ability to remove errors. If they are aware of any problems, they indicate them by *cruces desperationis* or a note in the apparatus and leave it to others to come up with a solution. Others are apt to suspect many corruptions in their text, and they trust their own gift in removing them *ope ingenii*. The best editors, scholars like

247

Housman himself, make their reputation by identifying corruptions (those recognised before and those spotted for the first time) and offering plausible solutions.

It may be worthwhile, at the beginning, to ask a question: Who were the critics Housman respected and admired? That is bound to tell us something right away. Here we find the names we might expect: Bentley and Markland, but also Scaliger (for Manilius) and Beroaldus (for Propertius, no doubt) and Marullus (for Lucretius, I suppose). There are also a few less familiar names, such as Withof, Horkel, Palmer and Rossberg (the last had anticipated some of Housman's conjectures in Propertius). He praises the merits of each of those scholars; but he can be critical even of Bentley, when he says, e.g. that Bentley 'treats the MSS. much as if they were fellows of Trinity'.[4]

In his article on Housman in the *Encyclopaedia Britannica* (rev. 14th ed.), John Sparrow says something important: 'As a scholar [he] invites comparison with Richard Bentley for learning, ingenuity and controversial vigour. He led the attack on superstitious fidelity to the "best manuscript" and "palaeographical probability" and brought to the defence of common sense in scholarship an armoury of sarcastic wit which helped to make him the most widely feared of contemporary scholars.'

This, to me, is a fair assessment in a nutshell. Housman's common-sense was more or less what Bentley described as *ratio et res ipsa*, and his sarcastic wit makes him so readable even where he may be wrong or, perhaps, not quite fair. Human nature being what it is, one enjoys even today some of his devastating reviews which could be described in terms I once heard in the editorial offices of *Gnomon* in Mainz as 'ein rituelles Schlachtfest auf drei Seiten'. The fact is that he was simply incapable of being boring or tedious.

Housman insisted on the need for finding as many readings as possible, including all the conjectures that can be attributed to a scholar. Often we cannot be sure whether a reading found in a Renaissance ms (sometimes as a correction or a marginal note, but often in the text) is not, in fact, someone's conjecture. If it is wrong, we call it an 'interpolation'; if it seems right, we put into the text, although it is doubtful whether it came via a direct line from the archetype.

To give an example, consider Prop. 2.14a.25-6:

> magna ego dona tua figam, Cytherea, columna,
>   taleque sub nostro munere carmen erit

The main paradosis offers *nomine* for *munere*, although it is clear that *munus* repeats *dona* and that Propertius' name stands in the distich *under* the votive offering. Scaliger's emendation appears already in one of the lost 'recentiores', the *Cuiacianus*, where he seems to have found it.

More than once Housman complained about the lack of straight progress in textual criticism. By this he probably meant that there were better textual critics three or four hundred years ago than in his time. I do not think he meant that modern editions of the classics are not as good as those of the past. The opposite is true, I think: on the whole the modern editions in the OCT, Teubner, Loeb and Budé series are better now than, say, fifty years ago. Thinking of Ovid's *Amatoria*, there has been very little progress from Heinsius to Merkel, but there has been great progress from Merkel to Kenney and Ramírez de Verger. Progress in scholarship does not always move in a straight line, but the simple fact that every new editor is in a position to look at new readings and new interpretations, some of which will inevitably be useful, shows that it is possible. The next editor, of course, may throw everything that is useful out of the window, but at least there is an accessible record of it for others.

In his very valuable survey of Latin philology in Great Britain in the nineteenth century, E.J. Kenney assesses Housman's achievements fairly.[5] He cites L.P. Wilkinson's examination of the fate of Housman's conjectures in Propertius and Horace[6] and says (625): 'Of 246 emendations proposed by him in the text of Propertius E.A. Barber in his extremely judicious Oxford edition [1953, 1960²] accepted 6, mentioned 65, and ignored 175.'

These proportions have changed dramatically in the latest Oxford edition by S.J. Heyworth (2007a), and it seems worthwhile to study briefly what happened. But we should keep in mind: (i) that Barber's access to Housman's published comments was not as convenient as it is today, thanks to Diggle and Goodyear; (ii) that Heyworth was able to use a number of Housman's ideas that were not published before.

Moreover, to measure Housman's influence, we may have to be more specific and ask, for instance, whether the modern editor recognised the textual problem that Housman detected, even if he (she) did not accept his solution. It often happens that a problem was recognised before Housman, e.g. by Scaliger or Heinsius, and that since then several emendations have been proposed from which the editor chooses the one that seems most plausible.

The fact that the editor does not adopt Housman's own solution does not mean that he ignores his diagnosis of a problem. When I became interested in Naugerius' work as editor of Ovid,[7] I realised how often this outstanding critic saw a problem that he could not solve *ope codicum* or *ope ingenii,* given the limited material available and the time limits imposed on him. But two hundred years later, new witnesses became available or someone like Heinsius had a brilliant idea, and the problem was solved. To that extent, there *is* progress in editing.

A brief assessment of Heyworth's edition may be helpful. I have also compared his text with those of P. Fedeli (1994), S. Viarre (2005a) and G. Giardina (2005).

Adding up the results, it appears that Heyworth has accepted 47 of Housman's conjectures (including transpositions, etc.); he has mentioned 91 of his solutions, without accepting them but recognising a textual problem; he has mentioned about 30 of Housman's suggestions, thus acknowledging textual problems. Many cases he has discussed in his *Cynthia* (2007b), e.g. 1.4.24, 7.23-4, 2.25.41-7, 3.10.17-18, 11.70, 4.1.124, 8.3. It becomes clear at once that Heyworth has accepted many more of Housman's ideas than Barber and that he acknowledges him more often. Still using Wilkinson's figures, it seems that Heyworth decided that only about 115 of Housman's suggestions were not worth continued consideration by readers (see Heyworth 2007a, lii for a brief statement of his policy). But there are also the new conjectures not counted by Wilkinson: 9 are adopted in the new OCT, 11 others cited. Even if such statistics may not be very meaningful, they certainly show a new appreciation of Housman as a textual critic, and in this respect Heyworth goes much farther than the other recent editors of Propertius.

Let us look at the Budé edition of Viarre (2005a): in evaluating Housman's ideas, she sometimes seems to look for safety in numbers, and tends to trust him mainly where he follows someone else, for instance Burman, or where he is followed by someone else, notably Goold.[8] Unlike Heyworth (2007a), she mentions Housman in her apparatus only when she adopts one of his ideas. I have counted about 29 cases, fewer than Heyworth's total. She agrees with Heyworth in 20 cases, with Housman (against Heyworth) in about 10. One cannot help noticing the sequence of (almost) round numbers: 30 − 20 − 10. Perhaps Pythagoras was right, and everything − even the degrees of probability of textual conjectures in Latin poets − can be expressed in mathematical terms.

Finally, let us look at Giancarlo Giardina's edition (2005). Giardina is definitely not a conservative critic, and he accepts many conjectures, some older ones (quite a few good ideas that have been ignored or forgotten) and a great many of his own, but in comparison to Heyworth, he does not follow Housman very often. He accepts a few transpositions, a few deletions proposed by Housman, but only two of his textual changes, in 2.34a.8 and 4.3.10.

My own edition (with a German translation) of Propertius[9] owes a great deal to Housman. Since it was not meant to be a critical edition in its own right, I did not go into his work on the manuscript tradition. But this part of his research is largely superseded today by J.L. Butrica (1984) and S.J. Heyworth (2007a) who, in the Preface to his edition, mentions Housman six times, twice as the author of conjectures (List 28), twice as a conjectural critic (lx), once as editor of Juvenal and Lucan (lxv), and once as an investigator of corruption (l, n. 26).

It seems to me that the potential of the main mss has been almost exhausted and that more is to be gained from a careful study of the more recent editions and especially from Smyth's critical thesaurus (1970). In fact, the large number of good readings found in the 'recentiores' and the many emendations made by scholars both famous and forgotten, shows how little we can trust the paradosis.

There is a striking analogy in the textual history of Catullus, as shown by J.M. Trappes-Lomax in his remarkable *Catullus: A Textual Reappraisal*.[10] Here, too, the older mss are, on the whole, so unreliable that we depend, to a large extent, on the *emendatio ope ingenii* as practised already by the Italian humanists.

In my text, I accepted a fairly large number of conjectures, including over 30 by Housman. Today, I would probably print even more. A few of Housman's transpositions appealed to me, but, like Simone Viarre, I do not believe that we can plausibly transpose lines from one poem (unless it is adjacent) or from one book to another, as he did. I also found Housman's elucidations of passages, scattered in his commentaries and in the *Classical Papers*, very helpful.

To illustrate the character of some of the work made after Housman but based on his ideas, I have picked two passages:

(a) Prop. 2.6.41-2 = 7.1-2. In *AJP* 100 (1979), 77-8, I argued that the last distichon of 2.6 in the mss and in previous editions should really be the first of 2.7. At the time, I did not know that L. Havet had had the same idea long before me, but he did. If Havet and I are right, 2.6 ends with:

> 39 nam [sed *Heyworth*] nihil inuitae tristis custodia prodest:
> quam peccare pudet, Cynthia, tuta sat est.

and 2.7 begins with 2.6.41-2:

> nos uxor numquam, numquam diducet [*recc.*, *Lachmann* : me ducet
> Ω] amica:
> semper amica mihi, semper et uxor eris.

I noted that the emphatic address to Cynthia in the last couplet of an elegy has parallels, and that other names in the vocative often appear at this place. Lachmann's reading (following some recc.) is supported by 2.7.3 *diducere amantes*; 25.9 *at me ab amore tuo diducet* [recc. : *deducet* Ω] *nulla senectus*; Sen. Mai. *Contr.* 9.3.3.

Simone Viarre (2005a) also separates the two poems in this way but she attributes the idea to L. Havet (1916) and G.P. Goold (1990, 1999²). Goold mentioned me, but not Havet. I have now been able to get hold of Havet's pamphlet. There he deals (39-43) with the elegies 6 and 7 of Book 2. He divides them into three pieces: 6.1-22, 23-40, 41-7.20. He also recognises the significance of the repeated vocatives *Cynthia* in 6.40, 7.1 and 7.20. Clearly, Propertius likes to end a poem with a direct address. Havet's division of 2.6 into two parts seems artificial to me;

there is no break between verses 22 and 23. Still, Havet deserves credit for an idea which occurred to me sixty years after the publication of his book. I still think that he was right in placing 2.6.41-2 at the beginning of the following poem and that the dividing line between the two elegies was misplaced at one point in the textual tradition, but I see that Fedeli (1994), Giardina (2005) and Heyworth (2007a) dismiss the idea. Giardina notes that Scaliger transposed verses 41-2 after 2.7.20, and Heyworth places the distich after 2.7.6, following an unpublished suggestion by Sandbach. Fedeli observes in addition that Struve and Jachmann wanted to delete the lines and that Hetzel transposed them after 2.7.12. Housman himself (*CP* 31) approved of this, though he attributed the transposition to Baehrens.

It would be difficult to show that 2.6.41-2 would make a better opening couplet than 2.7.1-2. I can only point out the obvious connection between *diducet* (recc., Lachmann) in 2.6.41 and *diducere* (codd.) in 2.7.3. Moreover, the lines 41-2 make excellent sense in the whole context of 2.7. It is clear that the new law, as originally issued by Augustus but then withdrawn, would have separated Propertius from Cynthia by forcing him to marry someone else and have children. It might be easier to show that 2.6.39-40 make a better ending than the following couplet. The poet likes to end a poem with *nam*-clause or a similar causal particle; cf., e.g., 2.13.58, 22a.41, 30.40; for *quare* cf., e.g., 2.16.55, 24a.9; for *cum* cf., e.g., 2.8.39-40, 25.47.

To sum up, Housman, following Scaliger and Baehrens (or Hetzel) felt that verses 41-2 had lost their original place, and Sandbach agreed with him. They all disagreed about the original position of the couplet in 2.7. To leave it where it is but consider it as the first couplet of the following poem virtually involves no change at all – in an early copy the poems were probably not separated by a space or a clear dividing line – and still seems the most economical solution.

The uncertainty in the division of the elegies can be illustrated by this very poem: almost all known mss begin a new elegy with 2.7.13. It was Volscus, perhaps following the '*antiquus codex*' known to Perreius and Puccius, who established the unity.

(b) 3.5.17-22:

Lydus Dulichio non distat Croesus ab Iro:
    optima mors, carpta quae uenit acta die.
me iuuat in prima coluisse Helicona iuuenta,
    Musarumque choris implicuise manus.   20
me iuuat et multo mentem uincire Lyaeo,
    et caput in uerna simper habere rosa.

This is the text I printed in 1996. Today, I would still print *carpta* (Baehrens) for *parca* (N L P alii) in v. 18. As far as I can see, Housman never dealt with this passage, but I have a feeling that he would have approved of the conjecture. First, he had a fairly high opinion of Baehrens' conjectures, and second, one of his general comments (*CP* 928 (1916)) could be applied to this particular instance: 'The rules of criticism are a very inadequate outfit for the practice of emendation, which is mainly an affair of natural aptitude and partly even of mere luck ... but problems will now and then present themselves which the rules of criticism, with no aid from genius or fortune, are competent to solve.' Third, as Stephen Heyworth kindly tells me, 'Housman favoured *carpta* to the extent that he noted the Horatian parallel in the margin of Baehrens.'[11]

Heyworth, following Goold (1966, 81), also accepts *carpta*, but changes *acta* to *ante* with Helm. Viarre (2005a), following Fedeli (1994), accepts Lachmann's *Parcae*. She translates 'c'est la meilleure mort qui vient au jour que la Parque a fixé' and refers, like Fedeli, to Verg. *A.* 12.150 *Parcarum ... dies et uis inimica propinquat*, but this implies a violent death, while Propertius has in mind the things that he enjoys most in life. Giardina (2005) introduces two changes of his own, reading *optima mors propero quae uenit acta gradu* and translating 'la morte migliore è quella che arriva spinta da un rapido passo', which could only mean that Propertius is in a hurry to die whereas, in fact, he wants to live long enough to study science and philosophy (23-47, concluding with *exitus hic uitae superet* [recc. : - *est* Ω] *mihi*).

One need not assume that *carpta ... die* is a direct allusion to Hor. *Carm.* 1.11.7-8 *dum loquimur, fugerit inuida / aetas. carpe diem, quam minimum credula postero*, although there is enough evidence that Propertius, by the time he wrote the elegies of Book 3, had read the first three Books of Horace's *Carmina*. There is also a difference: Horace is thinking of a single day which may very well be one's last, while Propertius has in mind life as a whole (see *OLD* s.v. *dies* §9 for the singular used collectively).

If *carpta* is right, we should probably also read *iuuet* in 19, as proposed by Bürger, and in 21, as preserved by N F L and other witnesses. Here I agree with Fedeli, though his comparison of 25 *libeat* and 2.13.11 *me iuuet in gremio doctae legisse puellae* is not compelling. As I see it, the poet is not quite ready to change his way of life; he seems to say 'let me still enjoy worshipping Helicon, ... let me enjoy tying up my mind with plenty of wine ...'. I would change my text accordingly today and also consider Burman's *a* (for *in*) *prima ... iuuenta*. Goold, Heyworth and Viarre all read *iuuat ... iuuat*, while Giardina prints *iuuat ... iuuet*. In Heyworth's opinion (*per litt.*) 'the whole run of thought demands that Propertius is living the life of love in 3.5, but can (for the moment) see the attraction of a future in natural philosophy'.

*

It should be said that Housman's influence is not limited to the conjectures of his that were accepted by later critics, but is evident also in the many interpretations of the transmitted text that he offers. He is very often right in defending the paradosis against fashionable tamperings. If genius is the ability to take infinite care to go to the bottom of a problem, Housman certainly had it. Many times he returns to a problem he dealt with before and adds new light. In sum, there are very few difficult passages in Propertius that he did not scrutinise at least once with his common sense, his vast learning and his devastating wit.

Years ago, reading a biography of J.P. Mahaffy,[12] I found two passages that could be applied to Housman. Mahaffy (1839-1919), not quite forgotten today, was an influential Hellenist in his own time and the tutor of Oscar Wilde at Trinity College, Dublin; they travelled together to Italy and Greece. The first passage (171) records a piece of advice given by C.G. Cobet, the prolific Dutch emendator of texts, to Mahaffy: 'The real combination for a scholar is English good sense with French taste, and if he wants to be respected by the Germans he must lash them well.' The second (172), written by Mahaffy himself (in his edition of Euripides' Hippolytus), seems even more pertinent: 'There is no chance [of an editor's] pleasing everybody. If he is conservative, he is called by that school safe – by his opponents dull ... If he is sceptical, he is called brilliant by one side – rash and reckless by the other. If he pursues an eclectic course, possibly he will incur the censure of both. But on the whole, the conservatives are most numerous, and perhaps the most intolerant' (J.P. Mahaffy and J.B. Bury, *The Hippolytus of Euripides* (London, 1881), ix-x).[13]

Notes

1. See Luck 2006.
2. Housman 1972, a very valuable collection. I also found Carter 1962 useful and said so in *Gnomon* 34 (1962), 299-300.
3. The most recent and comprehensive collection is Burnett 2007.
4. Preface to *Man.* I, cited by Carter 1962, 29.
5. Kenney 1989.
6. Wilkinson 1974, 33.
7. See my articles in *Ex. Class.* 6 (2002), 1-40 and 9 (2005), 155-224.
8. She compares Goold's two editions (1990 and 1999) in Viarre 2005b.
9. Luck 1996, a revised version of the 1964 edition.
10. Trappes-Lomax 2007; see my forthcoming review in *MH* 2009.
11. For a fuller discussion of Housman's Propertian marginalia see Heyworth's chapter.
12. Stanford and MacDowell 1971.
13. I am very grateful to David Butterfield and Stephen Heyworth for a number of critical comments that helped me improve this paper.

14

'For we are also his offspring'[1]

E.J. Kenney

There sits on my desk a framed postcard reproduction of Francis Dodd's drawing of Housman in the National Portrait Gallery. When I had it in my rooms in College, my admirable bedmaker, who dusted it faithfully every day, asked if it was my father. I had to disillusion her, but in a sense she was right, for I am one of a number of English classical scholars who can say of him, 'we are also his offspring'.[2]

In the preface to his edition of Manilius Housman referred to a scholar whom he admired, Johannes Schrader, as *Heinsius dimidiatus*, 'half a Heinsius'.[3] Precisely what fraction of a Housman I might represent I leave to the charity of my friends; but some part of me, for better or for worse, is undoubtedly Housman.

He is not one of my favourite poets, perhaps because I first read him rather late in life. Had I encountered him in my teens it might have been a different story, but excellent as was the teaching of English at Christ's Hospital, not neglecting the moderns, I cannot remember ever hearing Housman mentioned. But the fact that he was a poet is central to his scholarship: 'in [his] invectives against the follies and perversities of his fellow-scholars it is not difficult to hear the voice of the Shropshire lad turned critic ... he knew well, and said in print, that just literary perception, congenial intimacy with one's author, and familiarity with the speech of poets were a necessary part of a critic's equipment.'[4]

Housman's combination of talents might seem to have marked him out *ab initio* for Cambridge rather than Oxford. Here what Skutsch has described as his 'fastidious sense of accuracy, the revolt against the vague and high-sounding'[5] would at the outset have found a congenial home. Here scholarship at that date (whatever he might have thought it means now) meant, in his own words, 'scholarship with no nonsense about it'.[6] As to poetry, there can never have been any argument: it is Cambridge that has been the nest of singing birds. In scholarship there is scope for argument. In an idle half-hour I made lists *à la* G.H. Hardy of all-time cricket teams of classical scholars to represent the two ancient Universities.[7] Though in Cambridge Housman affected to regard himself as an exile, '[in] a more serious mood ... he said that

255

Oxford left little mark upon him except in the matter of friendships formed there'.[8] I nevertheless in a spirit of generosity put him on the Oxford side, but I still think Cambridge would then have had the best of it. Be all that as it may, when in 1911 Housman did finally come to Cambridge, and to Trinity, it was a delayed home-coming: 'in Cambridge Housman found ... such happiness as he was capable of'.[9]

Housman once wrote of another scholar whom he respected, Herbert Richards, words that might have served for his own epitaph: 'There are too few severe and thorough scholars of his sort.'[10] Severity and thoroughness we can never have too much of in scholarship, and in other matters too. But severity and thoroughness to what end? It has often been remarked as strange, and many would say deplorable, that Housman, a poet and connoisseur of poetry, widely and deeply read in some of the best literature of the world, should have spent so much of his life editing and explaining a poet for whom he did not pretend to feel anything but contempt. For professional scholars concerned with the usage of Latin poets his great edition of Manilius is an indispensable reference book, but his choice of author removed his most valuable and characteristic contribution to scholarship outside the horizon of many who might otherwise have profited from it. Manilius, it seems to me, was clearly a substitute for the 'great and congenial poet' – the words are Gow's, but applied by him to Propertius[11] – that Housman ought to have edited: Lucretius. That way, however, given his peculiar temperament, was closed off for him: for Lucretius had already been taken in hand by the English scholar whom, after Bentley and Porson, Housman most admired, whom he called 'the foremost English Latinist of the century' and to whom he applied the words that I have already used of Housman himself, 'for we are also his offspring'[12]: H.A.J. Munro.

Most of us, as Lucretius sardonically observed, want to escape ourselves, to be somebody else (3.1068-9). Somebody once told me that even Eduard Fraenkel would have liked to be W.M. Lindsay. I do not know what authority he had for this suggestion, but I think I know what he meant. Munro, I think, is what Housman wanted to be. There is no more striking demonstration of his indebtedness than the prefaces to vols I and V of the Manilius, with their magisterial surveys of the efforts of his predecessors. His pulverisation of the hapless van Wageningen over five closely-printed pages[13] was clearly written with Munro's more temperately expressed but no less devastating exposure of van Wageningen's countryman Havercamp in mind.[14] Where Munro had written of 'scissors and paste', Housman wrote of 'thefts' and 'open falsehood', and it was this sort of language that alienated many scholars at home and abroad and delayed the recognition of his work that in effect began with Fraenkel's review of his edition of Lucan in 1926.[15]

Nothing, I think, does Housman more honour than his admiration for the great scholars of the past. He ended his Inaugural lecture with a powerful plea for due veneration of the dead: 'to study the greatest of the scholars of the past is to enjoy intercourse with superior minds'.[16] 'The principle,' comments Gow, 'is not set out expressly elsewhere in his writings, but it is readily recognisable in his flashes of anger with those who had light-heartedly brushed aside the proposals made by eminent scholars of a former age.'[17] That Housman should have been brushed aside in his turn would not, I think, have greatly surprised him. In 1929 he published a devastating review of Henri Bornecque's edition of the *Heroides*, but his verdict that 'A recension of Ovid by this scholar can have no importance'[18] did not deter Bornecque from going on to publish equally bad editions of the *Amores*, the *Ars Amatoria* and the *Remedia Amoris* in the same series; nor did it send a warning signal to the Commission technique of the Association Guillaume Budé, under whose aegis there has subsequently appeared a series of editions of other works by Ovid by scholars who had not troubled to acquaint themselves with what Housman might have taught them.[19]

This lesson of receptivity to what the past has to offer is a fundamental one. Not that it was new, as Housman would have been the first to point out. Bentley, the scholar whom he admired above all others, said of the ancients 'as I despaired of raising myself up to their standard upon fair ground, I thought the only chance I had of looking over their heads was to get upon their shoulders';[20] and he was echoing what had been said long before by Bernard of Chartres, that the men of today are dwarfs standing on the shoulders of giants. It is this wholesome inculcation of proportion and humility – however little I may have managed to translate it into practice – that has been for me one of the chief rewards of studying Housman's work.

*

At the beginning of her account of her brother's boyhood Katharine Symons refers to 'the exact path he took'.[21] It is a good phrase. Exactitude was the key-note of his entire life, as it was of his scholarship. Whether on literature, architecture, or scenery his opinions were precise, firmly held, and securely based. Perhaps the most familiar, and the best documented of his extra-professional interests was his love and knowledge of food and drink, copiously illustrated in the record of his friendship with his publisher Grant Richards.[22] He was a frequent and sometimes sharply critical contributor to the Trinity High Table Kitchen Suggestions Book; in the years between 1911 and 1934 can be found some twenty remarks or complaints by him. The most striking thing about these observations, taken by and large, is their ordinariness. Most of his pleas are for the recognition of straightforward excellence of things in their several kinds: for English vegetables in their seasons – leeks, salsify, cabbage, potatoes, turnips, spring onions; for the proper preparation of English fruits in their season – young gooseberries, rhubarb, raspberries; and for the simple treatment of food, where simplicity is appropriate. Above all there is an insistence on basics, on getting things right. 'With boiled mutton we ought always to have turnips as well as carrots, there should be plenty of both, and the turnips should be mashed.' 'Irish stew should have more potato and more onion than it had tonight.' 'Green-gooseberry pie, so long as the gooseberries are really young, should always be cold.' 'The "sauce aux huîtres" which we had last night with the cod was not oyster sauce but Hollandaise into which an oyster or two had been dropped, combining no better than the Duke of Clarence with the Malmsey.' 'When there is no R in the month it may be necessary to have egg-sauce with cod, but the evil day should not be anticipated, as it was yesterday. [This does not apply to the salt cod on Ash Wednesdays and Good Fridays, for which egg-sauce is quite proper].' In plain cooking, as in scholarship, accuracy for Housman was a duty, not a virtue.

Writers of Housman have often fastened on some words that he wrote about another scholar whom he admired, Arthur Platt: 'A scholar who means to build himself a monument must spend much of his life in acquiring knowledge which for its own sake is not worth having and in reading books which do not in themselves deserve to be read.'[23] That was obviously to Housman's own address. To many if not most people it must seem a repulsive thought, but the underlying idea, imaged in the metaphor of the monument, is instantly recognisable to any classicist and consistent with Housman's philosophy. He has recorded that he became a deist at thirteen and an atheist at twenty-one.[24] The word 'monument' immediately recalls the last Ode of Horace's third Book and the concluding lines of Ovid's *Metamorphoses*: the pagan idea of personal survival in and through a man's work. So long as classical scholarship is seriously pursued, Housman's work will be remembered; but it is perhaps probable that his poetry will outlive his scholarship, even though one may grant that '[i]n the hierarchy of scholars his name must, on any estimate, stand higher than in that of poets'.[25] I can only say that it is Housman the scholar that has meant most to me.

First Elevens

Cambridge	Oxford
Badham, C.	Beazley, J.D. (vice-capt.)
Bentley, R. (capt.)	Bywater, I.
Dawes, R.	Conington, J.
Dobree, P.P.	Elmsley, P.
Gruter, J.	Gaisford, T.
Headlam, W.G.	Housman, A.E.

Jebb, R.C.	Jones, W. (capt.)
Markland, J.	Murray, G.
Munro, H.A.J. (vice-capt.)	Nettleship, H.
Porson, R.	Ross, W.D.
Sandys, J.E.	Rutherford, W.G.
Mayor, J.E.B.	Ellis, R.
(scorer and twelfth man)	(scorer and twelfth man)

The selection was not deeply pondered and could no doubt have been improved. When Professor James Diggle chanced to see the list in the *Housman Society Journal* some years later he commented: 'The Cambridge team is not only strong in itself but can call up powerful reserves: Blomfield C., Monk J.H., Wakefield G., Pearson J. What the Oxford team lacks in strength it makes up for in youthfulness. It can also call up able reserves, and I fancy I should put some of them in the first team: Musgrave S., Tyrwhitt T., Jowett B. [in which case I think Housman would have walked out], Heath B., Toup J.' It would be invidious to add his lists (this was in 1981) of contemporary teams.

Notes

1. An adapted and expanded version of a speech proposing the toast of 'The Immortal Memory of A.E. Housman', delivered on the occasion of the Housman Society dinner held in Cambridge in Trinity College in 1976; and as such an expression of personal homage rather than an attempt at a balanced appraisal. For essays in that kind see Kenney 1973a, 127-9, 149-50 = 1995, 164-7, 194-5; 1975b, 5-7; 1989, 621-30.

2. See n. 12.

3. *Man.* I, xx.

4. Gow 1936a, 34.

5. Skutsch 1960, 2.

6. Housman 1969, 25. He was in fact alluding (in 1911) to a distinction between Oxford and Cambridge scholarship which 'cannot be said to exist at present', and certainly does not exist now; but it was Munro as what he saw as representative of that type of scholarship that he no doubt had in mind.

7. See ad fin.

8. Gow 1936a, 5.

9. Gow 1936a, 54.

10. To Grant Richards, 11 February 1916 (Burnett 1.355).

11. Gow 1936a, 13.

12. Housman 1969, 20-1.

13. *Man.* I, xxvii-xxxii.

14. Munro 1886, 17-19.

15. Fraenkel 1926.

16. Housman 1969, 44.

17. Gow 1936a, 36.

18. *CP* 1161 (1929).

19. Most flagrantly evident in an edition of the *Ibis* compiled in evident ignorance of, or indifference towards, the fact that Housman had previously edited it (Kenney 1964, 268).

20. Cumberland 1806, 14-15.
21. Symons 1936, 7.
22. Richards 1941, 38-43, 115-18, 223-63 passim.
23. Housman 1927, x.
24. To Katharine Symons, 10 November 1935 (Burnett 2.504).
25. Gow 1936b, 54.

15

Housman's Cap and Pen

J. Diggle

Why, in 1962, the modest library of Rochdale Grammar School should have possessed a copy of Gow's memoir of Housman, I do not know. I do know that, from the moment I read it, I had one ambition: to wear Housman's mantle. That schoolboy ambition I gave up long ago. I am content to have achieved something slighter, and unlooked for: the opportunity to wear his cap.

But first a little more about Gow, to whom I shall at last pay public thanks for a generous and lapidary *mot* which I have silently treasured for nearly forty years. I met him only once, not long before he died, and here is what happened.

When Cambridge University Press agreed to publish *The Classical Papers*, Frank Goodyear and I and the Press faced a dilemma: whether or not we should inform Gow of our plans. On the advice of a senior officer of the Press, Peter Burbidge, who was an old acquaintance of Gow, we decided not to do so, since we expected that he would object, and we did not wish to act in defiance of an expressed objection, even though the objection could have no legal force. Instead, Burbidge arranged that he and I should formally present a copy of the work to Gow on publication, in the hope of placating him after the event. So, a time having been arranged, we visited him in his rooms in Trinity. After pausing to admire his collection of French impressionist paintings on the walls of his outer room, we found him in his sitting room, muffled up, in a bathchair. Burbidge handed him the three volumes. He turned the pages slowly, and at length looked up and said 'Within the limits of my disapproval I congratulate you.'[1]

*

And so to the cap. When Housman died, an admirer of his poetry, Mr H.P. Dixon,[2] wrote to a Porter at Trinity College, Mr A. Jex, to ask if he could secure for him some memento of Housman. Mr Jex bought from Housman's bedmaker a cap, for two shillings and sixpence, then sold it to Mr Dixon. Mr Dixon preserved it in wrappings of newspaper until his death in 1973, when his widow offered it for sale to the British Museum, which directed her to the Victoria and Albert Museum, which directed her to what it must have imagined to be Housman's undergraduate College. Thus misdirected, she applied to the Librarian of St John's College not in Oxford but in Cambridge, and he (the late Guy Lee) directed her to me.

Mrs Dixon sent me the cap. And with the cap she sent a pen. 'I suddenly remembered that Percy (my husband) always wrote poems with the pen that Housman had used. So I looked in my husband's pen box at once, and there it was; not with the original nib, of course, but I recalled that my husband always made a replacement similar to the original nib which would, in time, I suppose, have corroded. I remembered too that Mr Jex had told him that Professor Housman always preferred to use this simple wooden pen.' The pen is a stem of wood, 5 inches long, with a metal ink-stained nib. The stem is inscribed in inked capitals (presumably by Mr Dixon) 'HOUSMAN PEN T.C.C.'.

Mrs Dixon also gave me a letter which Mr Jex had written to her husband. 'Please accept my very best thanks for the very great kindness for what you sent me, for the small service that I rendered you, and it is very satisfying to me to know that you appreciated having the "cap" so much. I might also add the thanks of both my wife, and daughter (8), as they have both had a new pair of shoes each, which if it had not been for your generosity they may have had to have waited some time for.' And Mrs Dixon wrote: 'I know, as sure as I sit here, that my dear husband knows all about this; and that he is delighted. About Housman's reaction I cannot be as sure; sardonic, yes; but pleased, too, I think. No man is without a little innocent vanity. Both might smile that a little girl benefited with a new pair of shoes nearly forty years ago and that now an elderly woman's telephone bill can be paid – out of a cap and a pen.'

In August 1935 Housman banged his head hard on getting into a taxi in Lyon, and he had the wound sewn up and bandaged at a hospital. He described this in a letter to his sister Katharine Symons on 28 August.[3] Three weeks later, after his return home, he told her how he had bought a cap to conceal the wound: 'My head has healed very well, but as it was partly shaved at the hospital I shall have to wear a skull-cap for some time. I have discovered that skull-caps are unknown in France, and I have got myself what is called a calotte, a taller affair.'[4] He wrote in similar terms to Lady Frazer: 'There seem to be no skull-caps in France, so I got a *calotte* for indoor wear: this seems to be becoming, and made my companion say that I might be taken for a great scholar.'[5] That same autumn, he was seen wearing 'a cap of black velvet that covered most of his head – which made him look like some old Venetian doge'.[6] The black velvet is brightly embroidered with multicoloured silk threads in a floral pattern, and there is a rich tassel of similar threads.[7]

A final word to Mrs Dixon: 'It is pleasant for me to know that the cap has given delight. Had I not found you, and had it been discovered after my death, it would probably have ended up in a jumble sale or as a child's toy – as there is no one now to appreciate its associations.'

So I wear the cap, sometimes. The pen I have never used.

Notes

1. For a more formal statement of events surrounding the publication of *The Classical Papers* see my memoir of Goodyear in *PBA* 74 (1988), 364-5.

2. Horace Percy Dixon (1898-1973), music critic (diploma in journalism, UCL, 1921), journalist and author of *Poems* (Oxford, 1940) and the lyrics to *Three Songs* (Oxford, 1941; music set by Harry Gill). The reviewers of both of these publications commented on their Housmannian nature.

3. Burnett 2.490-1.

4. Burnett 2.492.

5. Burnett 2.494. In the meantime, he mentioned the accident (but not the cap) in a letter to Percy Withers (Burnett 2.493).

6. Anderson de Navarro 1936, 265. Her reminiscences of Housman appear to have gone unnoticed by his biographers. I am indebted to David Butterfield for bringing them to my notice.

7. Both the cap and pen can be seen on the front cover of this book's dustjacket.

Bibliography

Ackerman, R. (1987) *J.G. Frazer: His Life and Works* (Cambridge).

Alton, A.H. (1916) review of Owen 1915, *CR* 30, 229-32.

Anderson, W.B. (1927) 'Housman's Lucan', *CR* 41, 26-33.

Anderson de Navarro, M. (1936) *A Few More Memories* (London).

André, J. (ed.) (1963) *Ovide: Contre Ibis* (Paris).

Axelson, B. (1939) *ΔΡΑΓΜΑ Martino P. Nilsson ... dedicatum* (Lund).

—— (1987) *Kleine Schriften* (Stockholm).

Bajoni, M.G. (1999) bibliography of Manilius 1950-99, *Lustrum* 41, 105-93.

Barber, E.A. (1953) *Sexti Properti Carmina* (Oxford; 1960²).

Bauer, L. (1890) *Silius* (Leipzig).

Barrett, W.S. (1956) 'Dactylo-epitrites in Bacchylides', *Hermes* 84, 248-53.

—— (1964) *Euripides: Hippolytus* (Oxford).

—— (2007) *Greek Lyric, Tragedy and Textual Criticism: Collected Papers* (Oxford).

Birt, T. (1913) *Kritik und Hermeneutik* (Berlin).

Bischoff, B. (1998) *Katalog der festländischen Handschriften des neunten Jahrhunderts (mit Ausnahme der wisigotischen)* Teil 1 (Wiesbaden).

Blass, F. (1869) 'Pindaros Hyporchem auf die Sonnenfinsternis', *JKPh* 99, 387-90.

Boeckh, A. (1811-22) *Pindari Opera quae supersunt* (2 vols, Leipzig).

Bömer, F. (1969-86) *P. Ovidius Naso, Metamorphosen* (Heidelberg).

Bornmann, F. (ed.) (1988) *Giorgio Pasquali e la filologia classica del Novecento* (Florence).

Bowersock, G. (1990) 'The Pontificate of Augustus', in K. Raaflaub and M. Toher (edd.), *Between Republic and Empire* (Berkeley and Los Angeles), 380-94.

Bowra, C.M. (1966) *Memories 1898-1939* (London).

Bresslau, H. (1921) 'Geschichte der Monumenta Germaniae historica', *Neues Archiv* 42.

Briggs , W.W. Jr (1983) 'Housman and polar errors', *AJP* 104, 268-77.

—— (1987) *The Letters of Basil Lanneau Gildersleeve* (Baltimore).

—— and Calder, W.M. III (edd.) (1990) *Classical Scholarship: A Biographical Encyclopedia* (New York and London).

Brink, C.O. (1986) *English Classical Scholarship: Historical Reflections on Bentley, Porson and Housman* (Cambridge and New York).

Bühler, W. (1959) 'Maniliana', *Hermes* 87, 475-94.

Burman, P. (ed.) (1727) *P. Ovidii Nasonis opera omnia* (4 vols, Amsterdam).

Burnett, A. (ed.) (1997) *The Poems of A.E. Housman* (Oxford).

Burnett, A.P. (1985) *The Art of Bacchylides* (Cambridge, MA).

Butler, H.E. (1905) *Sexti Properti Omnia Opera* (Oxford).

Butrica, J.L. (1984) *The Manuscript Tradition of Propertius* (*Phoenix* suppl. 17) (Toronto).

Butterfield, D.J. (2008a) 'Lucretiana quaedam', *Phil.* 152, 111-27.

—— (2008b) 'Ten Lucretian emendations', *Latomus* 67, 634-42.

—— (2008c) 'The poetic treatment of *atque* in poets from Catullus to Juvenal', *Mnem.* 61, 386-413.

—— (2008d) 'Sigmatic Ecthlipsis in Lucretius', *Hermes* 136, 188-205.

—— (2008e) review of Burnett 2007, *BMCR* 2007.08.40.

Buurma, R.S. (2005) 'The anonymous system: anonymity and corporate authority in nineteenth-century British literary culture' (PhD, University of Pennsylvania).

Calder, W.M. III, Dubischar, M.C., Hose, M. and Vogt-Spira, G. (edd.) (2000) *Wilamowitz in Greifswald* (*Spudasmata* 81) (Hildesheim).

Campbell, D.A. (1992) *Greek Lyric*, vol. IV: *Bacchylides, Corinna and Others* (London).

Carter, J. (1962) *A.E. Housman: Selected Prose* (Cambridge).

Chiesa, P., Fagnoni, A.M., Guglielmetti, R. and Maggioni, P. (edd.) (2008) *Scritti di filologia mediolatina* (Florence).

Chiesa, P. and Castaldi, P. (edd.) (2004) *La trasmissione dei testi latini del Medioevo 1* (Florence).

Clackson, J. (1990) *Inscriptions from the Chapel of Trinity College, Cambridge* (Cambridge).

Clark, A.C. (1913/14) 'Robinson Ellis 1834-1913', *PBA* 6, 517-24.

—— (1918) *The Descent of Manuscripts* (Oxford).

Cole, M. (1949) *Growing Up into Revolution* (London).

Coleman, K.M. (2006) *Martial: liber spectaculorum* (Oxford).

Courtney, E. (1980) *A Commentary on the Satires of Juvenal* (London).

—— (2005) 'Four suggestions on Manilius', *SIFC* 4th s., vol. 3, 117-19.

Cumberland, R. (1806) *Memoirs of Richard Cumberland* (London).

Dale, A.M. (1968) *The Lyric Metres of Greek Drama*² (Cambridge).

Delz, J. (ed.) (1987) *Sili Italici Punica* (Stuttgart).

Diggle, J. (1994) *Euripidea: Collected Essays* (Oxford).

—— (1998) *Tragicorum Graecorum Fragmenta Selecta* (Oxford).

—— (2007) 'Housman's Greek', in P.J. Finglass, C. Collard and N.J. Richardson (edd.), *Hesperos: Studies in Ancient Greek Poetry Presented to M.L. West on His Seventieth Birthday* (Oxford), 145-69.

Dover, K.J. (1994) *Marginal Comment* (London).

Duff, J.D. (1898) *Fourteen Satires of Juvenal* (Cambridge).

—— (1928) *Lucan: The Civil War* (Cambridge, MA).

—— (1934) *Silius Italicus: Punica* (2 vols, London).

Easterling, P.E. (1999) 'The speaking page: reading Sophocles with Jebb', in Stray 1999, 25-46.

Ellis, R. (1877) 'On the *Ibis* of Ovid', *JPh* 7, 244-55.

—— (ed.) (1881) *P. Ovidii Nasonis Ibis* (Oxford).

—— (1885) 'New suggestions on the *Ibis*', *JPh* 14, 93-106.

—— (1896) 'New remarks on the *Ibis* of Ovid', *JPh* 24, 178-87.

—— (ed.) (1904) *Catulli Carmina* (Oxford).

Endt, J. (ed.) (1909) *Adnotationes super Lucanum* (Leipzig).

Enk, P.J. (1959) review of La Penna 1957, *Mnem.* 12, 366-9.

Fantham, R.E. (1992) *Lucan: de bello civili Book II* (Cambridge).

Fedeli, P. (1994) *Sexti Properti elegiarum libri IV* (Stuttgart and Leipzig).

Ferrari, M. and Navoni, N. (edd.) (2007) *Nuove ricerche su codici in scrittura latina dell'Ambrosiana* (Milan).

Fiesoli, G. (2000) *La Genesi del Lachmannismo* (Florence).

Filoni, A. (2008) *Il Peana di Pindaro per Dodona (frr. 57-60 M.)* (Milan).

Bibliography

Fraenkel, E. (1924) 'Lucan als Mittler des antiken Pathos', *Vorträge der Bibliothek Warburg* 4.229-57 [= Fraenkel 1964, II 233-66].

—— (1926) review of Housman's *Lucanus*, *Gnomon* 2, 497-532 [= Fraenkel 1964, II 267-308].

—— (1928) *Iktus und Akzent im lateinischen Sprechvers* (Berlin).

—— (1932) 'Kolon und Satz I', *NGG* 197-213 [= Fraenkel 1964, I 73-92].

—— (1933) 'Kolon und Satz II', *NGG* 319-54 [= Fraenkel 1964, II 93-130].

—— (1948) review of E.K. Rand et al. (edd.), *Servianorum in Vergilii carmina commentariorum editionis Harvardianae* vol. II, *JRS* 38, 131-43 [= Fraenkel 1964, II 339-68].

—— (1949) continuation of Fraenkel 1948, *JRS* 39, 145-54 [= Fraenkel 1964, II 368-90].

—— (1950) *Aeschylus* Agamemnon (Oxford).

—— (1957) *Horace* (Oxford).

—— (1962) *Beobachtungen zu Aristophanes* (Rome).

—— (1963) *Zu den* Phoenissen *des Euripides* (*SBAW*, Heft 1) (Munich).

—— (1964) *Kleine Beiträge zur klassischen Philologie* (2 vols, Rome).

—— (1965) *Noch einmal Kolon und Satz* (*SBAW* Heft 2) (Munich).

—— (2007) *Plautine elements in Plautus* (tr. T. Drevikovsky and F. Muecke from *Plautinisches im Plautus* and *Elementi Plautini in Plauto*) (Oxford).

Gaertner, J.F. (2005) *Ovid*, Epistulae ex Ponto, *Book 1* (Oxford).

Gargiulo, T. (1992) 'L'immagine della bilancia in Callimaco, fr. 1, 9-10 Pfeiffer', *QUCC* 71, 123-8.

Garrod, H.W. (1912) *Oxford Book of Latin Verse* (Oxford).

—— (1913) review of *Man.* II, *CR* 27, 135-7.

—— (1917) review of *Man.* III, *CR* 31, 107-8.

Ghidetti, E. and Pagnini, A. (edd.) (2005) *Sebastiano Timpanaro e la cultura del secondo Novecento* (Rome).

Giardina, G. (2005) *Properzio: Elegie* (Rome).

Gibbins, J.R. (2007) *John Grote, Cambridge University and the Development of Victorian Thought* (Exeter).

Godman, P. (1978) 'Two unpublished letters of Housman', *PCPhS* 204, 41-2.

Goold, G.P. (1959) 'Adversaria Maniliana', *Phoenix* 13, 93-112; repr. in Holden and Birch 2000, 134-53.

—— (1965) '*Amatoria Critica*', *HSCPh* 69, 1-107

—— (1966) '*Noctes Propertianae*', *HSCPh* 71, 59-106

—— (1977a) *Manilius: Astronomica* (Cambridge, MA and London).

—— (1977b) *Ovid: Heroides Amores* (Cambridge, MA and London).

—— (1979) *Ovid: The Art of Love, and Other Poems* (Cambridge, MA and London).

—— (1985) *Manilius: Astronomica* (Leipzig; 1998²).

—— (1990) *Propertius* (Cambridge, MA and London; 1999²).

Gotoff, H.C. (1971) *The Transmission of the Text of Lucan in the Ninth Century* (Cambridge, MA).

Gow, A.S.F (1936a) *A.E. Housman, A Sketch, Together with a List of his Writings and Indexes to his Classical Papers* (Cambridge).

—— (1936b) 'A.E. Housman', *Cam. Rev.* 57 (8 May 1936), 365-9; repr. as 'Cambridge', in K.E. Symons et al., *Alfred Edward Housman* (Bromsgrove, 1936), 51-5.

Graves, R.P. (1979) *A.E. Housman, the Scholar-Poet* (London).

Håkanson, L. (1979) 'Problems of textual criticism and interpretation in Lucan's "de bello civili"', *PCPhS* 205, 26-51.

Halporn, J.W. (1984) 'The editing of patristic texts', *REAug* 30, 107-26.

Harrison, S.J. (2002) 'A.E. Housman's Latin elegy to Moses Jackson', *TAPA* 132, 209-13.

Havet, L. (1911) *Manuel de critique verbale appliqué aux textes latins* (Paris).

—— (1916) *Notes critiques sur Properce (Bibliothèque de l'Ecole des Hautes Etudes,* Fasc. 220) (Paris).

Headlam, W.G. (1891) *On Editing Aeschylus: A Criticism* (London).

Heitland, W.E. (1901) 'Prof Housman, Bentley, Lucan', *CR* 15, 78-80.

Henderson, J.G.W. (1998) *Juvenal's Mayor: The Professor who lived on 2d a Day* (Cambridge).

Heyworth, S.J. (2007a) *Sexti Properti elegi* (Oxford).

—— (2007b) *Cynthia: A Companion to the Text of Propertius* (Oxford).

Hofmann, H. (ed.) (1990) *Latin Studies in Groningen 1877-1977* (Groningen).

Holden, A.W. and Birch, J.R. (edd.) (2000) *A.E. Housman, A Reassessment* (Basingstoke and London).

Hollis, A.S. (2007) *Fragments of Roman Poetry, c. 60 B.C.-A.D. 20* (Oxford).

Hopkins, C. (2005) *Trinity: 450 Years of an Oxford College Community* (Oxford).

Horsfall, N.M. (ed.) (1988) *Vir bonus discendi peritus: Essays in Honour of Otto Skutsch (BICS* Suppl. 51) (London).

—— (1990) 'Eduard Fraenkel', in Briggs and Calder 1990, 61-7.

Hosius, C. (1913) M. *Annaei Lucani belli civilis libri decem*[3] (Leipzig).

—— (1933) review of Housman 1932, *PhW* 53, 1189-90.

Housman, A.E. (1883) '*Ibis* 539', *JPh* 12, 167.

—— (1893) 'The manuscripts of Propertius [III]', *JPh* 22, 84-128.

—— (ed.) (1894) *P. Ovidi Nasonis Ibis,* in J.P. Postgate (ed.), *Corpus Poetarum Latinorum* (2 vols, London) I 590-5.

—— (1901) 'The new fragment of Juvenal [II]', *CR* 15, 263-6 [= *CP* 539-43].

—— (1903) review of Owen 1902, *CR* 17, 389-94 [= *CP* 602-10].

—— (1904) 'Owen's Persius and Juvenal: a caveat', *CR* 18, 227-8 [= *CP* 617-18].

—— (1905) review of Ellis 1904, *CR* 19, 121-3 [= *CP* 623-7].

—— (1915a) 'Ovid, *Ibis* 512 and *Tristia* III 6 8', *CQ* 9, 31-8 [= *CP* 905-12].

—— (1915b) 'Juvenal and two of his editors', *JPh* 34, 40-6 [= *CP* 964-8].

—— (1915c) review of Owen 1915, *Cam. Rev.* 37, 60 [= *CP* 903-4].

—— (1917) 'Transpositions in the *Ibis* of Ovid', *JPh* 34, 222-38 [= *CP* 969-81].

—— (1920) 'The *Ibis* of Ovid', *JPh* 35, 287-318 [= *CP* 1018-42].

—— (1921) review of Rostagni 1920, *CR* 35, 67-8 [=*CP* 1049-51].

—— (1927) Preface, in A. Platt, *Nine Essays* (Cambridge).

—— (1969) J. Carter (ed.), *The Confines of Criticism: The Cambridge Inaugural, 1911* (Cambridge).

—— (1972) J. Diggle and F.R.D. Goodyear (edd.), *The Classical Papers of A.E. Housman* (3 vols, Cambridge).

Housman, L. (1936) *A.E.H.* (London); repr. as *My Brother, A.E. Housman* (New York, 1938; Port Washington, 1969[2]).

Hübner, W. (1984) 'Manilius als Astrologe und Dichter', *ANRW* 32.1, 126-320.

—— (1987) review of Goold 1985, *Gnomon* 59, 21-32.

Hunt, J.M. (1994) 'A.E. Housman: *imitator imitandus*', *LCM* 19, 98-107.

Jackson, W.W. (1917) *Ingram Bywater: The Memoir of an Oxford Scholar 1840-1914* (Oxford).

Jebb, C. (1907) *The Life and Letters of Sir Richard Claverhouse Jebb* (Cambridge).

Jebb, R.C. (1905) *Bacchylides: The Poems and Fragments* (Cambridge).

Jenkyns, R. (ed.) (1992) *The Legacy of Rome: A New Appraisal* (Oxford).

Bibliography

Jocelyn, H.D. (1988) *Philology and Education: A Review Discussion of C.O. Brink's* English Classical Scholarship (Liverpool Classical Papers 1) (Liverpool).
—— (1992) 'Three Letters from W.M. Lindsay to E.K. Rand', *Sileno* 18, 87-100.
—— (1996) 'W.M. Lindsay's Oxford Career', in id. (ed.), *Aspects of Nineteenth-Century British Classical Scholarship* (*Liverpool Classical Papers* 5) (Liverpool), 99-135.
Johnstone, J. (ed.) (1828) *The Works of Samuel Parr* (8 vols, London).
Kambylis, A. (1965) *Die Dichterweihe und ihre Symbolik* (Heidelberg).
Kay, N.M. (1985) *Martial Book XI* (London).
Kelly, T. (1981) *For Advancement of Learning* (Liverpool).
Kenney, E.J. (1959) review of La Penna 1957, *CR* 9, 38-41.
—— (1974) *The Classical Text* (Berkeley).
—— (1982) 'Ovid', in id. (ed.), *The Cambridge History of Classical Literature*, vol. II: *Latin Literature* (Cambridge), 420-57.
—— (1989) 'Great Britain: Latin philology', in G. Arrighetti et al. (edd.), *La filologia greca e latina nel secolo XX. Atti del Congresso Internazionale, Roma, 17-21 Settembre 1984* (3 vols, Pisa), II 619-49.
Kenyon, F.G. (ed.) (1891) *Aristotelous Athenaion Politeia* (London).
—— (1897) *The Poems of Bacchylides* (London).
Knoche, U. (1928) 'Ein Iuvenalkodex des 11. Jahrhunderts in Beneventanischer Schrift und seine Einordung in die Handschriftliche Überlieferung', *Hermes* 63, 342-63.
Knox, P. (1995) *Ovid: Heroides, Select Epistles* (Cambridge).
La Penna, A. (ed.) (1957) *P. Ovidi Nasonis Ibis* (Florence).
Lachmann, K. (1876) *Kleinere Schriften* (2 vols, Berlin).
Lapidge, M. (1991) 'Textual Criticism and the Literature of Anglo-Saxon England', *Bulletin of the John Rylands Library* 73, 17-45; repr. in D. Scragg (ed.), *Textual and Material Culture in Anglo-Saxon England* (Cambridge, 2003), 107-36.
—— (1993) 'Medieval Latin philology in the British Isles', in E. Follieri et al. (edd.), *La filologia medievale e umanistica Greca e Latina nel secolo XX*, I (Rome), 153-88.
Lenz, F.W. (ed.) (1937) *P. Ovidii Nasonis Ibis* (Turin).
Lehnus, L. (2006) 'Prima e dopo αἱ κατὰ λεπτόν', in G. Bastianini and A. Casanova (edd.), *Callimaco: cent'anni di papiri* (Florence), 133-47.
—— (2007) 'Editing the new finds: glimpses from the correspondence of A.S. Hunt', in A.K. Bowman, R.A. Coles, N. Gonis, D. Obbink and P.J. Parsons (edd.), *Oxyrhynchus: A City and its Texts* (London), 247-55.
Lindsay, W.M. (1896) *An Introduction to Latin Textual Emendation* (London).
—— (1897) *A Handbook of Latin Inscriptions* (Boston and London).
—— (1907) obituary of Ludwig Traube, *CR* 21 (1907), 188-9.
—— (1923) 'Collectanea Varia VI: transmission of texts', *Pal. Lat.* 2, 53-5.
—— (1996) M. Lapidge (ed.), *Studies in Early Mediaeval Latin Glossaries* (Aldershot).
Lloyd-Jones, H. (1971) 'Eduard Fraenkel', *Gnomon* 43. 634-40 [= Lloyd-Jones 1982, 251-60].
—— (1982) *Blood for the Ghosts: Classical Influences in the Nineteenth and Twentieth Centuries* (London).
Löfstedt, E. (1928-33) *Syntactica* (2 vols, Lund).
Luck, G. (1967-77) *P. Ovidius Naso: Tristia* (2 vols, Heidelberg).
—— (1996) *Properz, Tibull: Liebeselegien* (Zurich).

—— (2006) 'Remembering Shackleton Bailey', *Ex. Class.* 10, 3-17.

Luppino, A. (1958) 'Esegesi catulliana e callimachea', *RFIC* 86, 337-45.

Maas, H. (1971) *The Letters of A.E. Housman* (London).

Maas, P. (1914-21) *Die neuen Responsionsfreiheiten bei Bakchylides und Pindar* (2 vols, Berlin).

—— (1927) *Griechische Metrik* (Leipzig).

Mack, S. (1988) *Ovid* (New Haven and London).

Maehler, H. (2004) *Bacchylides: A Selection* (Cambridge).

Mayer, R.G. (1979) 'Pharsalica damna', *Mnem.* 32, 338-59.

Meier, C. (1997) 'Organisation of knowledge and encyclopaedic *ordo*: functions and purposes of a universal literary genre', in P. Binkley (ed.), *Pre-Modern Encyclopaedic Texts: Proceedings of the Second COMERS Congress, Groningen, 1-4 July 1996* (Leiden), 103-26.

Merkel, K.R. (ed.) (1837) *P. Ovidii Nasonis Tristium libri quinque et Ibis* (Berlin).

—— (ed.) (1884) *P. Ovidius Naso* (3 vols, Leipzig).

Miller, J.F. et al. (edd.) (2002) *Vertis in Vsum: Studies in Honour of Edward Courtney* (Munich).

Mommsen, T. (1899) 'Schlussbericht über die Herausgabe der Auctores antiquissimi', *Neues Archiv* 24, 287-90.

Morgan, J.D. (1990) 'The death of Cinna the poet', *CQ* 40, 558-9.

Most, G.W. (1997) 'One hundred years of fractiousness: disciplining polemics in nineteenth-century German classical scholarship', *TAPA* 127, 349-61.

Mozley, J.H. (ed.) (1947) *Ovid: The Art of Love, and Other Poems* (Cambridge, MA and London).

Mueller, L. (1861) *De re metrica poetarum Latinorum praeter Plautum et Terentium* (Leipzig; 1894[2]).

Müller, K. (1961) *Petroni Arbitri Satyricon* (Munich).

Munder, H.M. (1954) *Publii Papinii Statii Thebaidos liber secundus* (Groningen).

Munk Olsen, B. (1982-9) *L'étude des auteurs classiques latins aux XIe et XIIe siècles* (3 vols, Paris).

Murray, G. (1913) 'Professor Robinson Ellis', *CR* 27, 286-7.

Naiditch, P.G. (1988) *A.E. Housman at University College, London: The Election of 1892* (Leiden and New York).

—— (1989) 'A.E. Housman and W.M. Lindsay: two notes', *LCM* 14.2/3, 29-31.

—— (1995) *Problems in the Life and Writings of A.E. Housman* (Berkeley Hills).

—— (1996) '"The slashing style which all know and few applaud": the invective of A.E. Housman', in H.D. Jocelyn (ed.), *Aspects of Nineteenth-Century British Classical Scholarship* (*Liverpool Classical Papers* 5) (Liverpool), 52-69.

—— (1998) 'Bibliography and the history of classical scholarship', *Classical Views* 42, 645-62.

—— (2002) 'The extant portion of the library of A.E. Housman. I: Greek', *HSJ* 28, 53-69.

—— (2003) 'The extant portion of the library of A.E. Housman. II: Latin literature', *HSJ* 29, 110-51.

—— (2005) *Additional Problems in the Life and Writings of A.E. Housman* (Los Angeles).

—— (2006) 'Memoir of J.D. Duff', *Quaderni di Storia* 64, 340-90.

Neil, R.A. (1893) 'Editions of the Herodas papyrus, *CR* 7, 314-18.

Bibliography

Nisbet, R.G.M. (1969) review of Ricks 1968, *Essays in Criticism* 19, 132-9.
—— (1978) 'Notes on the text of Catullus', *PCPhS* 204 (1978), 92-115.
—— (1989) 'On Housman's Juvenal', *ICS* 14, 285-302.
—— (1991) 'How textual conjectures are made', *MD* 26, 65-91.
—— (1995) S.J. Harrison (ed.), *Collected Papers on Latin Literature* (Oxford).
—— and Russell, D.A. (2007) 'The study of classical literature at Oxford 1936-1988', in C.A. Stray (ed.), *Oxford Classics: Teaching and Learning 1800-2000* (London), 219-36.
Nowell-Smith, S. (1967) *Letters to Macmillan* (London).
Oakley, S.P. (1997-2005) *A Commentary on Livy, Books VI-X* (Oxford).
Owen, S.G. (1902) *A. Persi Flacci et D. Iuni Iuuenalis Saturae* (Oxford).
—— (1904) 'Owen's Persius and Juvenal. A rejoinder', *CR* 18, 125-31.
—— (1914) 'Notes on Ovid's *Ibis, Ex Ponto Libri*, and *Halieutica*', *CQ* 8, 254-71.
—— (ed.) (1915) *P. Ovidi Nasonis Tristium Libri quinque, Ibis, Ex Ponto Libri quattuor, Halieutica, Fragmenta* (Oxford).
—— (1926) 'John Percival Postgate 1853-1926', *PBA* 12, 337-47.
Page, D.L. (1941) *Greek Literary Papyri* (2 vols, London).
Page, N. (1983) *A.E. Housman, a Critical Biography* (London).
Palmer, A. (1883) *Q. Horati Flacci Sermones. The Satires of Horace* (London).
—— (1898) *P. Ovidii Nasonis Heroides with the Greek Translation of Planudes* (Oxford).
Pasquali, G. (1934) *Storia della tradizione e critica del testo* (Florence; 1952²).
Phillimore, J.S. (1901) *Sexti Properti Carmina* (Oxford).
—— (1925) *Silver Latin Book* (Glasgow).
Platnauer, M. (1951) *Latin Elegiac Verse* (Cambridge).
Pollard, A.W. (ed.) (1890) *Odes from the Greek Dramatists* (London).
Postgate, J. (2001) *Lethal Lozenges and Tainted Tea* (Studley).
Postgate, J. and Postgate, M. (1994) *A Stomach for Dissent: The Life of Raymond Postgate 1896-1971* (Keele).
Postgate, J.P. (1894) *On Certain Manuscripts of Propertius* (TCPhS 4.1).
—— (1920) 'On some quantities in Phaedrus', *Hermathena* 42, 52-63.
—— (1922) *Translation and Translations* (Cambridge).
Postgate, R. (1958) 'Portrait of a classical scholar', *The Listener* 60 (11 Sep.), 378-9.
Quinn, V. and Prest Q. (edd.) (1987) *Dear Miss Nightingale: A Selection of Benjamin Jowett's Letters to Florence Nightingale 1860-1893* (Oxford).
Radke, A.E. (ed.) (1998) *Candide Iudex: Beiträge zur Augusteischen Dichtung. Festschrift für Walter Wimmel zum 75. Geburtstag* (Stuttgart).
Reeve, M.D. (1973) 'Notes on Ovid's Heroides', *CQ* 23, 324-38.
—— (1980a) 'The Italian tradition of Lucretius', *IMU* 23, 27-48.
—— (1980b) 'Some astronomical manuscripts' *CQ* 30, 508-22.
—— (1991) 'Acidalius on Manilius', *CQ* 41, 226-39.
—— (2004) *Vegetius: Epitoma rei militaris* (Oxford).
—— (2005) 'The Italian tradition of Lucretius revisited', *Aevum* 79, 115-64.
Reynolds, L.D. (ed.) (1983) *Texts and Transmission* (Oxford).
Richards, G. (1941) *Housman 1897-1936* (Oxford).
Richmond, J. (2002) 'Manuscript traditions and the transmission of Ovid's works', in B. Weiden Boyd (ed.), *Brill's Companion to Ovid* (Leiden), 443-83.
Ricks, C. (ed.) (1968) *A.E. Housman: A Collection of Critical Essays* (Englewood Cliffs, NJ).
—— (ed.) (1988) *A.E. Housman: Collected Poems and Selected Prose* (London).
Rose, H.J. (1937) 'W.M. Lindsay 1858-1937' *PBA* 23, 487-512.

—— (1938) 'Wallace Martin Lindsay', *JAW* 262, 15-27.
Rostagni, A. (1920) *Ibis: storia di un poemetto Greco* (Florence).
—— (1922) 'Per la critica dell'*Ibis* (Risposta al Signor A.E. Housman)', *RFIC* 50, 76-80.
Sandys, J.E. (ed.) (1893) *Aristotelous Athenaion Politeia* (London).
Schenkl, K. (1883) review of Ellis 1881, *Zeitschrift für die österreichischen Gymnasien* 34, 259-71.
Schmidt, P.L. (1988) 'Lachmann's method: on the history of a misunderstanding', in A.C. Dionisotti, A. Grafton and J. Kraye (edd.), *The Uses of Greek and Latin* (London), 227-36.
—— (1995) 'Rezeptionsgeschichte und Überlieferungsgeschichte der klassischen lateinischen Literatur', in C. Leonardi and B. Munk Olsen (edd.), *The Classical Tradition in the Middle Ages and the Renaissance* (Spoleto), 3-21.
Shackleton Bailey, D. R. (1957) *Propertiana* (Cambridge).
—— (1959) 'A.E. Housman as a classical scholar', *The Listener* 61, 795-6.
—— (1973) review of Housman 1972, *Cam. Rev.* 94, 189-90.
—— (1979) 'The Loeb Manilius', *CPh* 74, 158-69.
—— (1981) 'Notes on the younger Pliny', *PCPhS* 297, 50-7.
—— (1982) *Profile of Horace* (London).
—— (1987) 'Lucan revisited', *PCPhS* 213, 74-91.
—— (ed.) (1988) *M. Annaei Lucani de bello civili libri X* (Stuttgart; 1997²).
—— (1990) M. *Valerii Martialis Epigrammata* (Stuttgart).
—— (1993) *Martial: Epigrams* (3 vols, Cambridge, MA and London).
—— (1997) *Selected Classical Papers* (Ann Arbor, MI).
—— (2003) 'With Jackson's help', *TAPA* 133, 193-4.
Shuckburgh, E.S. (1910) *P. Ovidii Nasonis Heroidum Epistulae XIII*⁴ (London).
Skutsch, O. (1960) *Alfred Edward Housman 1859-1936* (London).
—— (1985) *The Annals of Q. Ennius* (Oxford).
Smyth, W.R. (1970) *Thesaurus Criticus ad Sexti Propertii textum* (*Mnem.* suppl. 12) (Leiden).
Stanford, W.B. and McDowell, R.B. (1971) *Mahaffy: A Biography of an Anglo-Irishman* (London).
Stray, C.A. (1990) review of Naiditch 1988, *CPh* 85, 244-8.
—— (1992) *The Living Word: W.H.D. Rouse and the Crisis of Classics in Victorian England* (Bristol).
—— (1997) ' "Thucydides or Grote?" Classical disputes and disputed classics in 19th century Cambridge', *TAPA* 127, 363-71.
—— (1998) *Classics Transformed: Schools, Universities, and Society in England 1830-1960* (Oxford).
—— (ed.) (1999) *Classics in 19th-century Cambridge* (*PCPhS* suppl. 24).
—— (ed.) (2003) *The Classical Association: The First Century 1903-2003* (Oxford).
—— (ed.) (2005) *The Owl of Minerva: The Cambridge Praelections of 1906* (Cambridge).
—— (2007) 'Jebb's Sophocles: an edition and its maker', in id. (ed.), *Classical Books* (London), 75-96.
—— (2010) *Sophocles' Jebb: A Life in Letters* (London).
Sullivan, J.P. (1962) 'The Leading Classic of his generation', *Arion* 1, 105-18 = Ricks 1968, 146-62.
Symons, K.E. (1936) 'Boyhood', in id. et al., *Alfred Edward Housman* (Bromsgrove), 1-30.
Thomas, R.F. (2008) 'David Roy Shackleton Bailey 1917-2005', *PBA* 153, 3-21.

Bibliography

Timpanaro, S. (1985) *La genesi del metodo del Lachmann*[3] (Padua).

Todd, R.B. (ed.) (2004) *Dictionary of British Classicists* (3 vols, Bristol).

Trapp, J.B. (ed.) (1983) *Manuscripts in the Fifty Years after the Invention of Printing* (London).

Trappes-Lomax, J.M. (2007) *Catullus: A Textual Reappraisal* (Swansea).

Traube, L. (1909-20) *Vorlesungen und Abhandlungen* (3 vols, Munich).

Treloar, G. (1998) *Lightfoot the Historian: The Nature and Role of History in the Life and Thought of J.B. Lightfoot (1828-1889) as Churchman and Scholar* (Tübingen).

Trevor-Roper, H. (1974) 'Apologia transfugae', *Didaskalos* 4, 393-412.

Turner, E.G. (1968) *Greek Papyri: An Introduction* (Oxford).

Tyrrell, R.Y. (1909) *Essays on Greek Literature* (London).

Usener, H. (1869) *M. Annaei Lucani commenta Bernensia* (Leipzig).

van de Loo, T. (ed.) (2006) *Conradi de Mure Fabularius. Corpus Christianorum. Continuatio Mediaeualis*, vol. 210 (Turnhout).

Verrall, A.W. (1892) *'On Editing Aeschylus': A Reply* (London).

Viarre, S. (2005a) *Properce: Élégies* (Paris).

—— (2005b) 'Quelques réflexions sur les tendances actuelles de l'édition de Properce: à propos des éditions de G.P. Goold (Loeb) 1990 et 1999', *Caesarodunum XXXVI-XXXVII bis* (Clermont-Ferrand), 492-9.

Vollmer, F. (1907) *Q. Horatii Flacci Carmina* (Leipzig).

Watson, L.C. (1991) *Arae: The Curse Poetry of Antiquity* (Leeds).

Watt, W.S. (1994) 'Maniliana', *CQ* 44, 451-7.

West, M.L. (1980) *Greek Metre* (Oxford).

West, S. (2008) 'Eduard Fraenkel recalled', in C.A. Stray (ed.) *Oxford Classics: Teaching and Learning 1800-2000* (London), 203-18.

Whitaker, G. (2007) '"Brevique adnotatione critica ...": a preliminary history of the Oxford Classical Texts', in C.A. Stray (ed.), *Classical Books* (London), 113-34.

Wilkinson, L. P. (1955) *Ovid Recalled* (Cambridge).

—— (1974) 'A.E.H., scholar and poet', *HSJ* 1, 32-46.

Williams, G.D. (1996) *The Curse of Exile: A Study of Ovid's Ibis.* (PCPhS Suppl. 19) (Cambridge).

Williams, G.W. (1970) 'Eduard Fraenkel', *PBA* 56, 415-42.

Willis, J. (1972) *Latin Textual Criticism* (Illinois Studies in Language and Literature 61) (Urbana, IL).

Wilson, E. (1938) *The Triple Thinkers* (London).

Winstedt, E.O. (1899) 'A Bodleian MS. of Ovid's *Ibis*', *CR* 13, 395-6.

Wiseman, T.P. (1974) *Cinna the Poet and Other Roman Essays* (Leicester).

Withers, P. (1940) *A Buried Life: Personal Recollections of A.E. Housman* (London).

Zetzel, J.E.G. (1981) *Latin Textual Criticism in Antiquity* (Salem, NH).

Index Locorum

General Index

Abbott, E.A., 193
Academy, 156, 157, 169n.20
Agar, T.L., 134n.34
Alington, C.A., 183
Allen, E., 175, 186n.5
Allen, T.W., 175
Anderson, W.B., 80
Archer-Hind, R., 165
Arnold, M., 163, 172nn.54-5
Ashburner, W., 113n.43, 198, 231
Athenaeum, 156, 157, 168nn.8&9, 236
Avancius, H., 148n.2
Axelson, B., 50

Bacchylides, early discussions of, 120-2, 155-63, 166, 168-71, 173, 236-7, 238
Badham, C., 258
Baehrens, E., 12, 17-18, 31, 139, 143, 146, 148n.3, 178, 252, 253
Bailey, C., 123, 134n.33
Barber, E.A., 27 n.22, 84, 230-1, 249, 250
Barnes, J., 189n.61
Bauer, L., 234, 235
Beazley, J.D., 258
Bechert, M., 31, 232
Bekker, I., 146
Bentley, R., 13, 18, 40, 49, 61, 65, 66, 75, 76, 88, 92nn.42&57, 101, 123, 131, 180, 181, 193, 232, 235, 236, 248, 257, 258
Bergk, T., 218
Bernard of Chartres, 257
Beroaldus, P., 248
Billanovich, G., 149n.26
Birt, T., 127, 137n.64
Bischoff, B., 151n.62
Blackwell, B., 67, 215n.102
Blakeway, A.A., 85
Blass, F., 120, 121, 159, 218, 237
Blomfield, C.J., 259

Boeckh, A., 161, 171n.39
Bornecque, H., 257
Bower, E., 50
Bowra, C.M., 84, 204
Breiter, T., 29, 30, 32, 180
Brink, C.O., vi, 102
Browning, R., 160, 163, 170n.31, 172n.55
Brugmann, K., 193
Buecheler, F., 46, 50, 56, 61, 150n.45, 198
Burbridge, P., 261
Burman, P., 253
Burton, E., 135n.42
Butcher, S.H., 160-3, 166
Butler, H.E., 16, 27 n.22, 230-1
Butrica, J.L., 250
Bywater, I., 214n.76, 258

Cambridge Review, 169n.18
Cambridge University Press, 165, 187n.21
Campbell, L., 230, 240-1
Campbell, T., 8
Chapman, R.W., 132n.5
Christ, W. von, 131nn.3-4
Clark, A.C., 148, 151n.54, 203, 208n.6, 212n.55, 231, 241
Classical Association, 182, 186n.1, 196
Classical Quarterly, 182
Classical Review, 155, 156, 165, 166, 168n.9, 169n.15, 172-3n.64, 173n.66, 177, 182, 188n.39
Cobet, C.G., 254
Cockerell, S.C., 169n.19, 178-9
Collins, S.T., 61
Conington, J., 258
Conway, R.S., 211n.31
Cook, A.B., 167, 173n.77
Cornhill Magazine, 168
Corpus Professorship of Latin, 1934 election to, 83-5

www.ingramcontent.com/pod-product-compliance
Lightning Source LLC
Chambersburg PA
CBHW071453110726
47908CB00003B/600